THE SEARCH FOR A NEW ALPHABET

THE SEARCH FOR A NEW ALPHABET

LITERARY STUDIES IN A CHANGING WORLD

IN HONOR OF DOUWE FOKKEMA

Edited by

HARALD HENDRIX
JOOST KLOEK
SOPHIE LEVIE
WILL VAN PEER

JOHN BENJAMINS PUBLISHING COMPANY
AMSTERDAM/PHILADELPHIA

∞™ The paper used in this publication meets the minimum requirements of American National Standard for Information Sciences — Permanence of Paper for Printed Library Materials, ANSI Z39.48-1984.

Library of Congress Cataloging-in-Publication Data

The search for a new alphabet : literary studies in a changing world : in honor of Douwe Fokkema / edited by Harald Hendrix ... [et al.].
   p.   cm.
  1. Fokkema, Douwe Wessel, 1931- . 2. Literature--History and criticism--Theory, etc. 3. Canon (Literature) 4. Hermeneutics. 5. Cultural relativism. I. Hendrix, Harald. II. Fokkema, Douwe Wessel, 1931-
PN441.S395   1996
809--dc20   96-14855
ISBN 90 272 2156 1 (Eur.) / 1-55619-510-9 (US) (alk. paper)   CIP

© Copyright 1996 - John Benjamins B.V.
No part of this book may be reproduced in any form, by print, photoprint, microfilm, or any other means, without written permission from the publisher.

John Benjamins Publishing Co. • P.O.Box 75577 • 1070 AN Amsterdam • The Netherlands
John Benjamins North America • P.O.Box 27519 • Philadelphia PA 19118-0519 • USA

Table of Contents

Preface   xi

Els Andringa
    The Art of Being Anti-Conventional: The Case of the Prose Poem   1

Hans Bertens
    From Over-Confidence to Clear and Present Danger: Comparative Literature and Intellectual Fashion   7

Jean Bessière
    Literature, Cultural Relativism and the Efficacy of Cognitive Minimalism   13

Lisa Block de Behar
    Hermeneutics as a Quest for Literary Conjunctions and Conjectures   19

Jan den Boeft
    Ancient Lyric Poetry and Modern Theory   25

Jeroen Bons
    Fact and Fiction: Isocrates on Truth and the Rules for the Encomium   30

Frank Brandsma
    Dialogue and Direct Discourse   34

Wim Bronzwaer
    To Purify the Language   39

Tania Franco Carvalhal
    Towards the Study of the Canon in Brazilian Literature: Machado de Assis and Jean-Ferdinand Denis   44

Han-liang Chang
    Semiotics and Liberal Arts Education   49

Yves Chevrel
    On the Need for New Comparative Literature Handbooks   53

Ampie Coetzee
    To Join Instruction with Delight: On Literary Studies and Literary
    History   57

Amiya Dev
    Globalization and Literary Value   62

Katinka Dijkstra
    Cultural Values in a Multicultural Perspective   67

Lubomír Doležel
    Polyfunctional or Monofunctional Language?   73

Nils Erik Enkvist
    Canons in Linguistic, Stylistic and Literary Competence   78

Gerald Gillespie
    Historical Referentiality as a Condition of Literary History 83

Frank de Glas
    The Parnassus of the Twenty-First Century Turns into a K2   89

Jaap Goedegebuure
    Daughter of Theology   94

Rik van Gorp
    Literary Genres and Intercultural (Mis)Understanding   99

Ina Gräbe
    Brutalization of Cultural and Universal Values in
    Marlene van Niekerk's *Triomf*: Relativity of Cultural Relativism
    or Redefinition of Universal Validity?   105

Elrud Ibsch
    The Conventions of Interpretation   111

Halina Janaszek-Ivaničková
    Post-Totalitarian Culture in a Postmodern Labyrinth:
    From the Perspective of Poland   118

Table of Contents

Eva Kushner
    Theory, Theories, Theorizing and Cultural Relativism   124

José Lambert
    Literary Theory and the Dynamics of the Media Age:
    Static versus Dynamic Models   129

Margreet de Lange
    Censorship and Literature in a Democratic South Africa   135

Geert Lernhout
    Against Interpretation: Hermeneutics and Empirical Studies   140

Paisley Livingston
    Justifying the Canon   145

Earl Miner
    Canons and Comparatists   151

Jozien Moerbeek
    Canons in Context   156

Hans Mooij
    Interpretation and Explanation   162

Ulla Musarra-Schroeder
    Influence versus Intertextuality   167

John Neubauer
    The Structure of Literary Revolutions   172

Ziva Ben-Porat
    Cultural Relativism and Models for Literary Studies   177

Ann Rigney
    Where Invention and Representation Meet   182

Frans Ruiter
    Should We Have Insured Ourselves Against Nietzsche?   187

Roseann Runte
    Northrop Frye and the Problem of Cultural Values:
    The Case of Canada   192

Siegfried Schmidt
    Empirical Studies of Literature—What Else?   198

Rien Segers
    Cultural and Literary Identity: Disease or Medicine?
    A Dialogue with Douwe Fokkema   202

Maria Alzira Seixo
    Literary Studies, Media and Low Culture: Some Minor Clues
    for a Major Topic   208

Dan Shen
    Traveling Theory: A Twisting Movement   213

Horst Steinmetz
    Uniqueness and Contingency   219

Hans van Stralen
    An Ambiguous Story: Sartre's *Dépaysement* between
    Modernist and Existentialist Conventions   223

Leon Strydom
    Genology: In Search of Adequacy   228

Susan Suleiman
    Diary as Narrative: Theory and Practice   234

Milhály Szegedy-Maszák
    Universalism and Cultural Relativism   239

Joachim von der Thüsen
    Flaubert and the Transformation of Idyll   245

Steven Tötösy de Zepetnek
    Political Satire in Hungarian Exile Literature:
    Systemic Considerations   250

Horst Turk
    Between *Prise de Position* and *Habit-Taking:* The Contribution
    of Operative Semantics to the Semiotics of Culture   256

Mario Valdés
    Hermeneutics *and* Empirical Studies   261

Table of Contents

Hennie P. van Coller
 Yardstick or Straight Jacket? Notes on the Process
 of Canonization — 267

Raymond Vervliet
 The Ambiguity of Canon Issues in Modernism:
 A Praxiological Approach — 272

Reinhold Viehoff
 Once upon a Time there Was a Researcher ... A "Historical"
 Approach to the State of Art of German Literary Studies at the
 End of the Second Millenium — 278

Joris Vlasselaers
 Literature in the Mass Media: The Challenge of Changing
 Enunciative and Receptive Modalities — 284

Wang Ning
 Cultural Relativism and the Future of Comparative Literature:
 An Oriental Perspective — 290

Jean Weisgerber
 Should Literary Studies Be Unreadable? — 296

Lies Wesseling
 Holier Than Thou: Literature, Science and the Empirical Turn — 301

Sytze Wiersma
 Something New From the Old Alphabet: A Match for Giono,
 Borges and Calvino? — 306

Yuan Heh-Hsiang
 From Cultural Relativism to Cultural Respect — 311

Yue Daiyun
 Western Literary Theory in China 1985—1995 — 316

Rolf Zwaan
 How Empirical is the Empirical Study of Literature? — 321

Preface

The present volume appears on the occasion of Douwe Fokkema's 65th birthday, and his retirement from Utrecht University.

For almost thirty years, from 1968 onwards, Douwe Fokkema has served the Department of Literary Studies, first as junior member, later as professor. During that period he published numerous books and scholarly articles, gave innumerable lectures and conference papers, and fulfilled an impressive number of duties in academic and scientific organizations both nationally and internationally. To enumerate all these would no doubt conflict with his modesty. Let it suffice therefore to recall that from 1985 to 1988 Douwe was President of the International Comparative Literature Association (ICLA), of which he still is Honorary President.

When we, his most immediate colleagues decided to prepare a *Festschrift* for Douwe Fokkema it became clear immediately that it would be virtually impossible to provide room in it for all those colleagues who would like to contribute. In order nevertheless to keep their number as large as possible, but also to produce a somewhat more spirited volume, we chose not to request solid pieces of academic research, but rather stimulating short contributions of approximately 2000 words each. "We would like to request you to submit a provocative thesis or to take a controversial stand on some matter central to present-day debates in literary studies, comparative literature, or literary theory." Thus ran the official invitation to contribute to the volume, which was sent out to all members of the Department, former and current Ph.D. students, his fellow Professors of Literary Studies in the Netherlands, and a number of foreign colleagues with whom Douwe enjoyed a working relationship over the years. The response to our invitation has been overwhelming.

In order to prevent too great a fragmentation, we also requested the authors to address one of the following topics: canon formation, conventions, cultural relativism, hermeneutics versus empirical studies, and the problem of values. Without any doubt these are themes that are very much central to current discussions in our discipline; to each of them, Douwe Fokkema has contributed significantly; we would like to recall, in this respect, publications such as *Cultureel relativisme en vergelijkende literatuurwetenschap* (Amsterdam 1971), *Literary History, Modernism, and Postmodernism* (Amsterdam 1984), and (together with his wife, Elrub Ibsch) *Theories of Literature in the Twentieth Century* (London / New York 1995^2) and *Literatuurwetenschap en Cultuuroverdracht* (Muiderberg 1992).

The contributors responded most candidly and in a wide variety of ways to our request; also our enticement to be provocative met with very diverse responses. Taken together the contributions provide a variegated picture of a discipline in a changing world. Literary Studies today certainly looks very different from what it was when Douwe Fokkema started his academic career, and it looks certain that the discipline will continue to change over the decades to come. It is continually involved, so to speak, in "The Search for a New Alphabet." Given Douwe's unremitting efforts to move non-Western literatures into the center of our discipline, and in view of his knowledge and interest concerning Chinese culture, we believe it appropriate to borrow that phrase as the title of this book, from one of Lu Xun's essays, *Kuan-yü hsin-wen-tzû* (Hanyu pinyin *Guanyu xinwenzi*).

While preparing the volume, we have been helped especially by Aart Balk, who we would like to thank for his meticulous copy-editing. Sixty-one colleagues and four editors together remind us of Douwe's 65th birthday: on that occasion we all testify to the feelings of collegiality, respect, and friendship that we will continue to cherish toward him.

Harald Hendrix
Joost Kloek
Sophie Levie
Will van Peer

The Art of Being Anti-Conventional

The Case of the Prose Poem

Els Andringa
Utrecht University

A question that has fascinated literary theory since Russian Formalism is why and how literary conventions change over time. Several theories on innovative impulses and mechanisms have been developed and illustrated. Fokkema and Ibsch (1992: 98) refer to three explanatory approaches. The first, which the authors call *epistemological*, claims that a changing and developing society continuously requires new modes of representing, interpreting and reflecting the perception of 'reality.' The second approach is *anthropological* in nature and concentrates on the impulse to (re)establish or distinguish cultural identity by modernizing outworn conventions. The third — *Formalist* — theory focusses on the dynamics of the old and the new and explains changes psychologically from satiation with established forms and the desire to 'reset' perception by means of disorganizing literary and linguistic norms. The first theory relates literary change to the perception of the outside world, the second to the concept of cultural consciousness, and the third explains it from impulses within the literary system itself. The second and third have in common that they regard the force of regeneration as a set of reactions to existing conventions and established norms.

This short article cannot fully examine the validity and explanatory power of the three approaches and the ways they are related to or distinct from each other. I will rather show that they sometimes at least offer complementary interpretations of change. My example is the development of a non-canonical, but still effective genre sometimes called the *Prose Poem*.

Conventions and conventionalized forms play a role on different levels of literary communication. Globally speaking, there are basic communicative conventions like principles of coherence and "Sinnkonstanz" (Hörmann 1976: ch. 7), and more specifically narrative and literary practices such as modes and schemata of narrating, genre conventions, and linguistic or stylistic norms. Impulses for change and innovation differ in force and radicality. They are 'positive' when artists try to intensify or surpass conventionalized principles in order to bring them to a higher level of perfection; they are 'negative' when attempts are made to revolt against existing norms by destroying or replacing them. Reactions may also differ in quantity: they may concern one single convention, for example, the place of the volta in a sonnet. However, in times of important historical development, like, for example, the transition from Romanticism to Realism or from Realism to Modernism, whole systems of conventions have been subverted.

In spite of millenia of change, there are remarkable constants as well. The basic literary forms, epic, dramatic, and lyric, have persisted, while main genres like the novel, novelistic narrative, parable and legend, and even a highly specific form as the sonnet, have continued to exist for ages. Although they have been reshaped over and again, their characteristics vary greatly, and many sub-genres have developed (D'haen 1989), such canonical forms still constitute the foundation of literary production. Apparently, the forces of change and revolution are counterbalanced by basic communicative restrictions and tendencies towards literary representation. In this context, it is significant that attempts to invent completely new forms or to radically break away from existing constraints have resulted in 'genres' which remain at the periphery of literary production and seem to continue the status of an 'experiment.' The Prose Poem is a prime example of such a perpetuous experimental form.

Some descriptions of the Prose Poem trace it back to lyrical epics from Antiquity onwards and even include the poetic style in novels by Woolf, Joyce, and Faulkner. However, more precise reconstructions of its origin, focusing on its briefness and other formal features, locate its roots in the pre-Romantic and early Romantic eras (Füger 1976). At that time, the desire to go beyond the limits of experience and the longing for infinity and universality were expressed by crossing the borders between the domains of art and literature. Different genres were mixed, the constraints of conventional narrative structure in prose were abandoned, and experiments were carried out to give up meter and rhyme in poetry. The struggle to liberate oneself from traditional forms was reflected, for instance, in a sample of short poetical, sometimes contemplative, sometimes fantastic, dreamlike, loosely structured prose sketches that are hard to define in terms of genre. Examples are Macpherson's pseudo-translations of "Ossian" (1765), Geßner's *Idyllen* (1772), Blake's *Poetical Sketches* (1783), Novalis' *Hymnen an die Nacht* (ca. 1799), and somewhat later, E.T.A. Hoffmann's *Phantasiestücke* (ca. 1814). At the 'fin de siècle,' some ideas of Romanticism were continued or extended under a perhaps more pronounced tendency of pulling away from existing norms on all levels of literature: thematically, morally and formally. Baudelaire, inspired by Bertrand's *Gaspard de la nuit* (1842), dreamt of "le miracle d'une prose poétique, musicale sans rythme et sans rime, assez souple et assez heurtée pour s'adapter aux mouvements lyriques de l'âme, aux ondulations de la rêverie, aux soubresauts de la conscience" (Baudelaire 1972: 24). This famous sentence explains or motivates Baudelaire's creations, which were published under the title *Spleen de Paris. Petits Poèmes en Prose* in 1861. Baudelaire's *Spleen* soon regained international recognition and became a source of inspiration to, among others, Ivan Turgeniev (*Prose Poems*, 1882), Peter Altenberg (*Studien*, from ca. 1896) and the English 'yellow nineties.'

A whole spectrum of developments converges in this new 'genre.' These developments seem to originate from different sources and impulses. We will follow three of them, trying to successively connect them to one of the types of explanations.

First, a range of features can be observed that indicate a radical departure from formal conventions in traditional poetry. French poets challenged all kinds of poetic regularities in search of new forms. Baudelaire's Prose Poems have given up verse, rhyme, stanzas; however, they have also preserved or rather cultivated other features traditionally linked to poetry: symbolic condensation, prosodic, syntactic and semantic parallelisms, images and melodic elements (see for a characterization of Baudelaire's Prose Poems: Bernard 1959). During the same period, Rimbaud tried out different kinds of 'deviations' from traditional poetry, in rhyme and meter, in punctuation, and in visual presentation (see Macklin 1990), finally arriving at complete de-versification in his *Illuminations* (from ca. 1886).

Abandoning traditional poetic constraints was not the only innovative trend. The prosaic components of the paradoxical 'genre' constitute an analogous attack on communicative and narrative conventions. There was a tendency to eliminate principles of coherence and continuity, such as formal settings and endings (Sonnenfeld 1983), narrative progression, and the determination of time and place. The forms became fragmentary, sometimes discontinuous, intermingling dreamlike fantasy, reflection, impressions of the senses, snatches of story and dialogue. Baudelaire's Prose Poems sometimes exhibit a resistance to conventional coherence, and Mallarmé even did without syntactic and semantic constraints in his *Divagations* (1897), setting the example for later poets like, for example, Saint John Perse, Char and Ponge. However, prose poetry is not at all form*less*. On the contrary, conventional coherence was more or less replaced by symbolic reference, allusion, contrast, metonomy, repetition and parallelism.

Second: The developments sketched above can be interpreted in the light of Formalist theory, explaining changes from impulses towards 'de-familiarization' within the system of poetic and narrative conventions. However, there are still other developmental features. Most striking, for example, is the tendency to modify, parody or invert conventional short prose genres that used to represent moral or didactic principles: legends, parables, fairy tales, biblical texts, prayers and sermons (see for the question of "pre-texts": Riffaterre 1983). Prose Poems often re-use those genre-forms by converting them to mocking or ironic 'anti-tales.' The transformation of the 'positive' forms simultaneously indicates that the old forms are worn out and, at the content level, refers to the decay of traditional moral values and beliefs. It implicitly expresses social criticism of hypocrisy and rigidity. In this way, the poets change the traditional didactic and moral function of the old forms. Blake was among the first to parody stories from the Old Testament by modelling some of his sketches after them. Apart from Baudelaire's *Spleen*, other examples can be found among Wilde's *Poems in Prose* (1894), Dowson's *Decorations in Prose* (1899) and Turgeniev's *Prose Poems*. Some pieces of parabolic short prose by Kafka and Brecht, although definitely not presented as Prose Poems by the authors themselves, are to be mentioned in this context as well (Fülleborn 1976).

Although such changes of genre conventions can also be explained by the Formalist theory as a development within the literary system, and possibly even by the 'epistemological' approach, the critical transformation of the traditional didactic forms could perhaps be better interpreted as an attempt to assign them a new cultural function. The poets make their readers aware of the cultural tradition of didactic narration and, simultaneously, they try to innovate it. As Fokkema and Ibsch are not particularly clear about the 'cultural' explanation of change, this might serve as an example.

Third: Doubtlessly there were also extrinsic forces enhancing the development of the Prose Poem. A thematic thread in some collections of Prose Poems is modern city life as observed by the 'flaneur' from the cafés, streets and parks (Nienhaus 1986). Early pieces are E.A. Poe's *The Man of the Crowd* (1842) and Stifter's *Wien und die Wiener* (ca. 1844). The most obvious examples are, again, Baudelaire's *Spleen* and Altenberg's *Studien*. It is as if, in these works, city life is refracted in a whole spectrum of sensations and impressions. While realistic novels and novellas presented a more or less coherent model of 'reality,' symbolically reflected in well ordered patterns of space, this space seems to fall apart in the Prose Poems. The fragmentation of genres and the dissolution of conventional narrative boundaries seem to be repeated in the depicted multiplicity of city life. Formal appearance and thematic content both mirror a loss of unity and an increasing complexity of perception of life at the turn of the century. It is here that we could apply the 'epistemological' explanation of literary change: modern life produces continuous shifts of attention, different emotional tones, different sensory experiences, various levels of perception and interpretation. It is this 'polyphony' in perception which is expressed in the Prose Poem, not only in the composition of individual texts, but also in the arrangement of volumes like *Spleen* and Altenberg's collections.

As we may conclude from this highly condensed and simplified sketch of its development, the Prose Poem is a product of many different impulses towards innovation. As Murphy (1992) argues in her excellent book, it is a model for literary anarchy and revolt against convention. Remarkably, it has never crystallized into a canonical form, but defines itself by perpetual innovation as a "genre of evolutionary change" (Koschmal 1993). A manifestation of its instability is the fact that its names in titles and subtitles differ constantly: *Poèmes nocturnes* (Baudelaire 1957), *Decorations in verse and prose* (Dowson 1899), *Pages* (Mallarmé 1897), *Studien* (Altenberg 1896), *Improvisations* (W.C. Williams 1918), *Prosicles* (Huxley 1919), *Proêmes* (Ponge 1965), *Maulwürfe* (Eich 1967), *Aufzeichnungen* (Kaschnitz 1973). In its changing quality the Prose Poem has been indicating innovation for over a century, moulding Romantic ideals, Symbolist resistance to tradition, Modernist polyphonic perception, and dramatic social and political experience in more recent work of, for example, Char, Solzhenitsyn, and Kunert.

References

Baudelaire, Ch. 1972 [1869]. *Le spleen de Paris. Petits poèmes en prose.* Yves Florenne (ed). Paris: Librairie Générale Française.
Bernard, S. 1959. *Le poème en prose de Baudelaire jusqu'à nos jours.* Paris: Nizet.
Caws, M.A., and H.B. Riffaterre (eds). 1983. *The Prose Poem in France: Theory and Practice.* New York: Columbia University Press.
D'haen, Th. 1989. "Genre Conventions in Postmodern Fiction." In Th. D'haen, R. Grübel, and H. Lethen (eds), *Convention and Innovation in Literature.* Amsterdam / Philadelphia: Benjamins, 405-420.
Fokkema, D.W., and E. Ibsch. 1992. *Literatuurwetenschap en Cultuuroverdracht.* Muiderberg: Coutinho.
Füger, W. 1973. *Das englische Prosagedicht. Grundlagen — Vorgeschichte — Hauptphasen.* Heidelberg: Carl Winter Universitätsverlag.
Fülleborn, U. (Hrsg). 1976. *Deutsche Prosagedichte des 20. Jahrhunderts.* München: Wilhelm Fink Verlag.
Hörmann, H. 1976. *Meinen und Verstehen. Grundzüge einer psychologischen Semantik.* Frankfurt am Main: Suhrkamp.
Koschmal, W. 1993. "Das Prosagedicht als Gattung des evolutionären Wechsels. Ein Beitrag zur slavischen Komparatistik." In R. Grübel (Hrsg), *Russische Literatur an der Wende vom 19. zum 20. Jahrhundert.* Amsterdam / Atlanta: Rodopi, 143-161.
Macklin, G.M. 1990. "Aspects of the Rimbaldian Prose Poem: Pattern and Disorder in the 'Illuminations.'" *Orbis Litterarum* 45(3): 248-272.
Murphy, M.S. 1992. *A Tradition of Subversion: The Prose Poem in English from Wilde to Ashbery.* Amherst: University of Massachusetts Press.
Nienhaus, S. 1986. *Das Prosagedicht im Wien der Jahrhundertwende: Altenberg, Hofmannsthal, Polgar.* Berlin: De Gruyter.
Riffaterre, M. 1983. "On the Prose Poem's Formal Features." Caws and Riffaterre 117-132.
Sonnenfeld, A. 1983. "L'Adieu suprême and Ultimate Composure: The Boundaries of the Prose Poem." Caws and Riffaterre 198-211.

From Over-Confidence to Clear and Present Danger

Comparative Literature and Intellectual Fashion

Hans Bertens
Utrecht University

With hindsight, the 1950s and early 1960s seem a time of innocence, a decade in which the Western world, after the unimaginable atrocities of the Second World War, with astonishing rapidity refound its faith in man. In countless war movies the evils of Nazism were exorcised by turning them into the mad and ultimately self-destructive policies of a small group of wholly amoral criminals, who for their genocidal crimes relied primarily on other fairly small groups within the German war machine, notably the SS and the Gestapo. The ordinary German soldier — and, by extension, citizen — was largely exonerated while German generals, such as for instance Erwin Rommel (affectionately nicknamed 'The Desert Fox'), could even be admired for the operations of the Wehrmacht units they had commanded. Except for hardcore Nazis and the gangsters who served in the SS and the Gestapo, the average German once again was not really different from the average Frenchman, Englishman, or American. That this new brotherhood of man was deeply Eurocentric is illustrated by those movies of the period that present the war in the Pacific Theater. There the attitude towards the Japanese is implacable, and the respect for enemy commanders and enemy courage that hovers in the background of filmic representations of, say, the Battle of the Bulge, is totally lacking. The Oriental enemy is cruel, irrational, hysterical — in short, uncivilized.

Still, in the immediate postwar years and through the 1950s the emphasis was on what mankind had in common rather than on what kept it divided. As a result we got the United Nations (1945) and the Universal Declaration of the Rights of Man (1948). This spirit of an underlying, essential sameness suffered a setback with the onset of the Cold War but it survived on a more modest scale in for instance the North Atlantic Treaty Organization (1949) or the beginnings of the European Economic Community (now superseded by the European Union) in supranational policies regarding the steel and mining industries. Although both NATO and the beginnings of the European Economic Community confirmed the Eurocentric, North Atlantic character of this vision of unity that the Cold War had already revealed, it was still implicitly offered to all of mankind, even to those whose leaders unfortunately refused to see the light. Moreover, what unified mankind was not its propensity to evil, as John Calvin from Geneva had so sincerely believed, but its innate desire to do the civilized thing based on its inherently rational disposition.

This faith in man informs countless expressions of 1950s popular culture. Evil is almost never seen as a tell-tale sign of difference, as arising, for instance, out of circumstances of social, psychological, or racial inequality. It is rarely traced to structural causes. It is, all of a sudden, simply there, as the evil of the Nazis in the war movies of the time, or the wholly unexpected invasion from outer space that we see in such movie classics of the period as Don Siegel's *Invasion of the Body Snatchers* (1956). On the contrary, in the popular culture of the 1950s and early 1960s even animals, far from representing the forces of violence and destruction (as in, for instance, Steven Spielberg's *Jaws* of 1975), are definitely man-like in their attempts to help and care for us. Which untold crimes or disasters would have taken place if not for Lassie, the collie, or Flipper, the dolphin? And how boring life would have been but for Mr Ed, the talking horse? (Interestingly, although I am not sure what it means, Mr Ed is unthinkable in color.) What perhaps best represents this 1950s spirit of universal brotherhood is the famous, and highly significantly titled, photo exhibit *The Family of Man*. Showing 503 pictures that had been selected from a staggering four million (the organizers had, among other things, worked their way through the entire photo files of *Life* magazine), *The Family of Man* drew what at the time was a record of 275,000 visitors to New York's Museum of Modern Art in the first four months of 1955. After its wholly unexpected success in New York, the exhibit toured Western Europe to similar acclaim and finally, in the summer of 1959, was seen by an astonishing number of 2.7 million Russians when it was shown in Moscow. *The Family of*

Man seemed at first sight to emphasize the diversity of the cultures that man had created over time. However, as its title already indicates, what the exhibition really sought to establish was the interconnectedness of all of mankind, man's essential unity, even if political differences temporarily hid that unity from sight. Korea, the fall of Dien Bien Phu, the Suez crisis, the crushing of the Hungarian uprising — all such disquieting historical events were ultimately nothing but the result of willful blindness to that fact.

The optimism reflected in *The Family of Man* and in the various political institutions that owed their life to views similar to those that informed the exhibit now seems unreal. But we can only appreciate its intentions if we see it in its proper historical context. We are dealing with a wholesale effort on the part of Western culture to overcome, through a deliberate act of faith, the social Darwinism that was seen as having been most radically embodied by Nazism and that was held accountable for its genocidal policies. Where social Darwinism had preached difference and natural antagonism between social groups and cultures, resulting in endless and often vicious struggle, the immediate postwar period, trying to ban Nazism from the world's consciousness, stressed sameness and global solidarity.

Apart from all other things, the effort of the founding fathers, and the occasional founding mother, of Comparative Literature to get their field off the ground as a distinct discipline must be seen against this backdrop of a sometimes declared, but mostly undeclared, faith in man's essential sameness, that is, in a deep kinship underlying all of man's cultures and imaginative efforts. It may be true, as Emily Apter has recently reminded us in her contribution to Charles Bernheimer's *Comparative Literature in the Age of Multiculturalism*, that "[t]he discipline of comparative literature...is unthinkable without the historical circumstance of exile" (Apter 1995: 86), but that only reinforces the point: comparative literature was, apart from all other things, a deliberate effort to overcome exile, to establish transnational ground where national ground was lacking. As François Jost put it: "The comparatist's effort and reward is to perceive the literary world in its fundamental unity" (Bernheimer: 7). That this attitude lasted well into the 1970s is illustrated by the so-called "Greene report," commissioned by the American Comparative Literature Association in 1975, which speaks of the "new vision of *global* literature" that it sees emerging, a vision "embracing all the verbal creativity during the history of our planet" (Bernheimer: 30). Although the report shows an incipient awareness of the Eurocentrism that up till that point had pervaded such encompassing visions, it does not question the new vision's feasibility. Its tacit assumption is that, even if those of European stock will have to take more of a backseat than they have ever done, the basis of comparative literature as a discipline — the belief that crosscultural and translinguistic comparisons are possible and meaningful — has remained intact.

However, twenty years later we can no longer take that assumption for granted. It is not necessary to spell out once again what the prophets of difference — Foucault, Derrida, Lyotard, and others — have since the mid-sixties repeatedly told us. It is clear that especially in the last fifteen years the idea of sameness has met with increasing suspicion. It has not only become associated with a principle of reduction that is encountering increased intellectual resistance, but it has, paradoxically, also become associated with one of the very evils it sought to combat: totalitarian repression (see the various contributions in Cornwell 1995). Whether such a charge is founded is unfortunately at this moment not really to the point. In the struggle between the nominalists and the universalists, the latter are in clear and present danger. What is worse is that the universalists' plight is compounded by a social, as opposed to intellectual, trend towards the nominal, a trend in which difference is vastly preferred over sameness. In the US, Afro-American literature has increasingly become the territory of Afro-American critics, and is often taught exclusively in Afro-American literature courses. The last twenty years have witnessed similar developments with respect to Native American literature, Chicano literature, gay and lesbian literature, and even with respect to literature written by women. This new multicultural awareness that has sprung up all over the West is emphatically multicultural rather than inter- or crosscultural. Its segregationism is deeply anti-comparatist on both social and theoretical grounds. Where comparatism assumes an underlying common identity for all human beings, multiculturalism assumes irreconcilable differences, an assumption that puts an awkward spoke in the comparatist wheel.

There is, moreover, the matter of language. In her contribution to *Comparative Literature in an Age of Multiculturalism*, Mary Louise Pratt berates her fellow Americans for their "blind commitment to monolingualism" and their "tendency to cede the terrain of 'globalization' to English" (Bernheimer: 62). Astonishingly, she offers as an example of a successful and recent comparatist effort a meeting of scholars from various Southeast Asian cultures at which everything was read and taught in English. Surely the "deep intercultural understanding" and the "genuinely global consciousness" she sees as important aims for a revamped comparative literature must similarly be thought of as wholly dominated by the English language. The implicit message is that English is the superhighway of future efforts at comparativism — a superhighway fed by major interstates such as French, German, Spanish, Russian and Japanese, by county roads such as Dutch and Tamil, and by dirt tracks such as Basque, Irish, and Maori.

It is hard to see how such an Anglophone global consciousness can avoid being severely reductive just like it is, more in general, hard to see how comparatist efforts can avoid being reductive. The charges leveled at comparative literature are, at least in part, undeniable. But while the sort of pressure in the direction of sameness that characterized the 1950s must absolutely be rejected, we should, on the other hand, not be oversensitive to a little reductiveness. After all, even the multiculturalists share much more than they want to see, let alone admit, with each other. What is more, they share it with most non-multiculturalists too. Their manifestoes invariably refer, no matter how obliquely, to the Enlightenment: what they are after can always be redefined as freedom, equality, and brother/sisterhood. What they emphatically do not want is the sort of fundamentalist difference preached by the ayatollah Khomeiny and his followers (even if their rhetoric sometimes reminds us of that unfortunate example). As a matter of fact, multiculturalism owes its existence to Enlightenment principles, even if, paradoxically, the freedom and self-determination that multiculturalism implies had to be wrested from the official guardians of those principles. There is no denying that in the second half of the twentieth century a global horizon has emerged and that those who cling to an older dispensation — the defenders of apartheid, those who practise ethnic cleansing, and those who lay *fatwahs* upon erring writers — have become a small minority, at least in theory. We may think this is a reason for rejoicing, for mourning the passing of an older order, or for both, but in any case it is there. There is hope, then, for comparatists. Even if this does not help us in dealing with past, pre-Enlightenment difference, it certainly helps us to deal with differences we face today. And let us by all means preserve them. Difference is what we thrive on, even if too much of it makes our job impossible. There is no point in comparing if the differences are unbridgeable. But there is also no point in comparing if there is no difference at all. A genuine global consciousness is surely the very last thing we want and need.

References

Apter, Emily. 1995. "Comparative Exile: Competing Margins in the History of Comparative Literature." In Charles Bernheimer (ed), *Comparative Literature in the Age of Multiculturalism*. Baltimore and London: Johns Hopkins University Press, 86-96.

Cornwell, John (ed). 1995. *Nature's Imagination: The Frontiers of Science*. (Intro. Freeman Dyson.) New York: Oxford University Press.

Literature, Cultural Relativism and the Efficacy of Cognitive Minimalism

Jean Bessière
Sorbonne Nouvelle, Paris

The assumptions and practices of making literary comparisons, whatever the means and ends attached to them, are governed by the duality between exact relativism and exact universalism. The concept of literature and its correlatives, the notions of transhistorical and transcultural identities, allow one to handle this duality and link up relativism and universalism. Such reference to the concept of literature does not preclude specific anthropological or intercultural discussions of the relativism/universalism duality.

The debate on the use of the concept of literature to resolve the relativism/universalism duality, is therefore still ongoing. That use permits the concept of literature to be defined at once as both a maximal and a minimal concept. As a maximal concept, literature is a hypothesis which can account for all the objects to which it refers. As a minimal concept, literature is a hypothesis designed to account for literary objects and objects qualified as literary, according to their mutual differences. Because it presents such a duality, the concept of literature appears to be untenable, yet it is also indispensable. It cannot be dispensed with, first of all, because discourses expose themselves as literary by various markings and variations of stress on these marks, and, secondly, because discourses are qualified as literary according to various criteria, some of which may be contradictory. These markings and criteria depend upon cultural data and conventions; they also confirm the interaction between universalism and relativism, since they ultimately refer to the concept of literature.

This hypothesis — the concept of literature — may be re-expressed as a paradox borrowed from Gilles Deleuze, who contrasts sameness and difference and raises the question of the articulation of thought: "With the same, one is able to think straight with all one's might, without having a ghost of a thought; don't we have, on the contrary, with the different, the highest level of thinking, but which cannot be thought?" (Deleuze 1981: 292). In terms of literature, this can be read as follows: With the concept of literature, the concept of the identity of literature, one is able to think straight and with all one's might, without having a ghost of a thought about literature; on the contrary, with the different, do we not have, in a literary object, always specific and unique, the highest of thinking about literature, but which cannot be thought?

This formulation underscores that any thinking about literature, committed to either universalism or relativism, is a *de facto* cognitive commitment. Such commitment is caught in a duality which is not thought. During this century, diverse literary formalisms, sundry linguistic and semiotic studies of literature, various conventionalisms and the notion of general or universal writing have all tried to account for the interplay between the one and the many, from which the concept of literature cannot be dissociated. These formalisms, linguistic and semiotic methods, and the notion of general writing share the drawback of squeezing the concept of literature into frameworks and epistemological references which do not *ab initio* refer specifically to literature. On the contrary, the various conventionalisms should be considered interesting because they draw topologies of cultural and literary conventions, and hypothesize that shared readings of these topologies and conventions are possible. This assumption may be specified as follows. Various topologies and conventions may be understood and read as modes of symbolization, ways to fit symbols to their uses and ends. The operation of these topologies and conventions may be studied with various methods and procedures because they deal with conventional systems, as well as references, situations and aims, associated with them. Defining progress towards understanding these conventional systems is like defining the ability to improve and extend the analysis of these modes of symbolization and the ways symbols are fitted to uses and ends. Such understanding also means the intelligibility of the cognitive process, as defined in two ways: the cognitive process involved in arranging and practising these conventions, and that involved in the comparatist's approach to conventionalism.

Reconsidered from a conventionalist point of view, the concept of literature should be questioned less for the hypothesis it implies or the relativism/universalism duality than for its *relevance*. The concept of literature cannot be dissociated from literary issues — the distinguishing features of discourses presented as literary and the criteria by which discourses are recognized as literary or from the beliefs, opinions and knowledge both kinds of discourse convey. Rejecting both exact universalism and relativism leads one to question the relevance of the concept of literature which is inseparable from cognitive minimalism. Cognitive minimalism may be defined as that act of understanding which implies a limited number of conventions, representations and inferences in a given cognitive environment

Consequently, one can characterize the concept of literature as follows. In various contexts depending on culture and the moment in time, it refers to the hypothesis that the discourses presented or recognized as literary have *similarities* with respect to their *relevance*. Such identities and similarities relate to the definition of literature, as well as the beliefs, knowledge, and questions these discourses harbor, and the concretization of literature they represent, or the recognition of literature they cause to exist.

Relevance may be defined as that feature of a statement a subject can interpret, in a given context, according to references to and similarities with his own representations. For literature, this entails the individual's representation of other literature, and the beliefs, opinions and conventions conveyed by that literature. Relevance so defined is inseparable from the principle of communication implicit in any literary discourse or discourse deemed as literary. Although the concept of literature is transhistorical, it requires less that one make note of identities and differences than one identify a discourse as literary, whether that is done through formal features or the reader's decision or the establishment of similarities between a discourse identified as literary and the means used to identify it as such, namely, the idea one has of literature and its changeable representations. This idea of literature conveys its own relevance since the definition and interpretation of the concept of literature proceed from a similarity between one definition of literature and another. To affirm that literature is transhistorical, one must be capable of recognizing salient features in both a discourse, literary or recognized as literary, and another representation of literature. Identifying literature on the basis of its formal features is an extreme case in which there is maximum similariy between literary discourses and representations of literature.

Since such maximum identification of literature is not continuous in history, and cannot prescribe a series of formal features to serve as the criteria for representing literature, the hypothesis that literature has some transcultural and transhistorical identity calls for a kind of 'deliteralization' of the concept of literature. This concept cannot be interpreted in a 'literal' manner, however precise the representation of literature linked to this concept may be. Literature can be represented and thought of only with respect to the criteria of a particular community. Because these criteria are shared in society, they make it possible to recognize the similarities through which literature is identified, and they become a means to justify literature.

Stressing that the concept of literature so defined and considered in its transhistorical, transcultural features, and specifically historical and cultural features, makes comparisons possible and points to its relevance, similarity, representation, and 'deliteralization,' and amounts to specifying that literary comparisons may be made in two ways: by formal comparison and by comparing the representations of literature, implicit in the literary works and the 'doxa.'

The concept of literature in fact entails transference. Transhistorical and transcultural transference is underdetermined by criteria referring to relevance and representation of literature, which rely on literary contexts, particularly those of the subject making comparisons among literary discourses. Under such conditions, comparison is tantamount to reinterpretation of a literary discourse or of a discourse recognized as literary, according to the terms and conventions of some other literary discourse. Comparison calls for the perception and description of these discourses with regard to their relevance, similarity and representation. Such transference may influence the concept of literature as well as the literary field to which the concept is transferred. When a comparison deals with historical and cultural data, this transference presupposes that there are connections in the similarities and representations making this endeavor possible.

The concept of literature hence appears to be a relativist concept, although it is usually associated with assumptions about continuity and transhistoricity in literature. Relativism presupposes a specification of the literary discourse, for the literary discourse gives rise to expectations which are then exploited. That presupposition in turn flows from a recognition of the principle of communication, governing literary and any other discourse. The presupposition requires that literature, which is always a matter of innovation, and the assertion of differences due to historical and cultural diversity, be defined as a discourse people can share. It also requires sharing those representations of literature that allow for the identification and recognition of literature. An individual can recognize literature as such if he or she observes that what it is at some point in time, and has a mental representation of literature. This representation is inseparable from the cognitive environment that individual shares with others in the community of listeners, readers and critics as well. This representation indicates that the concept of literature is linked less to the duality mentioned at the beginning of this essay, than to a specific discursive intentionality, i.e, the intentionality inspired by the realization that the interplay between relevance, representation, and similarity, is a part of discursive communication and that the 'literalness' of discursive communication constitutes an exception. Without such intentionality and knowledge, the issue of the relevance of common and literary discourses would not exist. Representations of literature in various communities with respect to given criteria or similarities are ways these communities respond to the fact that they realize that discursive 'literalness' is an exception.

The assertion at the outset that the concept of literature entails minimal cognitivism anticipated the notions it leads to here. The representation of literature is, finally, only that of the discursive practice a community recognizes as being able of offsetting the lack of 'literalness' in a discourse, and which is deemed to be relevant. The relevance requires this representation and solution to be congruous with the cognitive norms of the community. Noting the transhistoricity and continuity of literature is a way to highlight the character and function of representations of literature. Literature and its representations figure in a community as a means to deal with the interplay of 'literalness' and a lack of 'literalness' in discourses, enabling community members to establish shared references to this lack of 'literalness' of discourses, using representations of their cognitive environment. These representations and references imply cognitive minimalism, which means that literature and its representations interact within restricted cognitive associations with the constant aim of achieving relevance. This aim prevents literary works and the representations of literature from drawing too many inferences.

The task of Comparative Literature should be to compare representations of literature and kinds of relevance associated with them, and, from a cognitive perspective, to point to similarities in conventions and representations, which make one able to practise literary comparisons and to think about literature.

Reference

Deleuze, Gilles. 1981. *Différence et répétition*. Paris: Presses Universitaires de France.

Hermeneutics as a Quest for Literary Conjunctions and Conjectures

Lisa Block de Behar
Universidad De La República, Montevideo

> *El que lee mis palabras está inventándolas.*
> Jorge Luis Borges, "La dicha"

At the end of last century, the negative statement "There is nothing but interpretations" could have been surprising. It was uttered as a challenge against confidence in truth and in the possibilities of knowledge. After a century during which different authors have spoken about "the scarce reality of reality" (Breton 1934), or underscored its fabulation: "Once upon a time there was reality" (Aragon 1926), reality is still invoked, albeit with reservations. It is mentioned with reticence, condescending to an accomplice-like skepticism, as if reality was but *topoi koinoi*, the *common place* or a necessary 'argument' but, mainly, an unavoidable reference, and as such it appears written between inverted commas or uttered together with a gesture which imitates the impossibility of avoiding, even in oral discourse, typographical conventions, those iconic, ironic passwords which allow for an allusion authorized by writing. Thus is admitted the verbal nature of a *revoked reality*, a trodden repetition, less than a quote or a metalinguistic mention, reducing referential stratification and involving it in the interiority of discourse: a logical *va-et-vient* between a quest for reality and a substitutive verbality; it does not suspend repetition but it annuls the extradiscursive reference.

This extradiscursive shortcoming, recognized as a feature of the literary text, capable of hinting at an inaccessible beyond, finds now, more than ever before, its *monstruous* counterpart in the culture of the media. The image no longer discovers — contrary to what classical aesthetics defended — a world behind the world (Levinas 1975: 23), an exterior, anterior world, one which transcends discourse. The images of the planet demonstrate a domestic figure, measured in inches, enclosed inside four walls, framed by their four sides, multiplied in excess and at the same time reduced to a plane which revokes the here and now of individual experience through a universal technological construction. The extremes of maximum reach and of minimum extension coincide in those daily, still disturbing, square black holes, where microcosms from different universes collapse: everything disappears inside that regular geometry which Malevitch's black square may have anticipated.

Paradoxically, little is left of everything and within this abundant precariousness oppositions have collapsed, confronted by systems which, after receiving the greatest acclaim, seem to be more forceful than in force, more rigid than rigorous. Confrontations have been shuffled, some due to conciliation, most of them due to indolence.

For more than a decade now, facing the progressive decadence of systems and doctrines, of disbelief in the basic principles of absolute knowledge, there is a prevalent, albeit faint, reflection, self-denominated "pensiero debole," and the very thinkers who think in this way (Vattimo and Rovatti 1983) try to install, instead of a philosophy based on a single, definitive, normative premise, the preponderance of *hermeneutics*, the practice of a rising discipline which deals with interpretations.

Massive intermediation has certainly favored the habit of providing interpretations, but this appreciation had begun long before. Douwe Fokkema, opposing the points of view of Symbolist poets to those of the Modernists, remarked that the latter "advanced their intellectual conjectures in an attempt to impose a hypothetical order and a provisional meaning on the world of their personal experience." Those Modernist conjectures evolve into later conjunctions: fiction and nonfiction, invention and reality, literature and philosophy, "the facing opposition between 'high' literature and 'popular literature', literature and the other arts, as one of the major characteristics of Postmodernism" (Fokkema 1984).

Dedicated originally to the study of religious texts, hermeneutics, which consisted in an authorized — sometimes authoritarian — reading, tended to become secularized in favor of "a logic of individual discourse" (Schleiermacher 1987). So was it presented by Friedrich Schleiermacher and it continues to be so to this day — by a line attentive to practices of reading oriented by Heidegger, Gadamer, Jauß, and those who apply (or do not apply) the theories of reception aesthetics. A more recent instance of the same line, although it adopts the flexibility of theories of different filiation, has contributed to making interpretation what it perhaps was in the beginning: a form of *re-creation*, a sort of short-term creation, an ephemeral interpretation followed by another interpretation which, without revoking it, continues it. Like the dynamics of unlimited semiosis with which it has been compared for some time, interpretation does not stop in front of a definitive or permanent meaning, but it remains a constant displacement, an infinite recoil which could either be assimilated by the myths of eternal return or by a deconstructive drift (Eco 1990: 326), which ignores both the existence of a determined sense and that of an extratextual statute: "Il n'y a pas de vrai sens d'un texte" (Paul Valéry) to "il n'y a pas de hors-texte" (Jacques Derrida), sense and reference seem to resolve among texts, without disappearing. When Fokkema introduces "The challenge of semiotics," he does not rule out that this malleability in permanence be attributed to the predominantly symbolic relationship between signified and signifier which appears at once resistant and flexible (Fokkema and Ibsch 1984: 199).

Taking into account the antecedents of interpretation, not restricted in ancient times to the sacred space, bearing in mind that "The institution of interpretation has not greatly varied since the Greeks" (Riffaterre 1994), and considering the discussions which created an epistemology of literary interpretation, it is impossible not to mention Ion, Plato's (or Socrates', but mainly Homer's) rhapsodist. Rather than as a reference to the subject of inspiration, which it certainly illustrates, this dialogue can also be read as the origin of a reflection on interpretation which stands, at least, in a *double sense*, rescuing dualities later recovered by contemporary thought: on the one hand, interpretation as critical activity, analysis, study, an exercise in knowledge or in the rational understanding of a text by the reader who, within his historic context *com-prehends* it; on the other, interpretation as recreation, aesthetic activity, vision and beauty together: the activity which, making a text real, introduces it into an actuality which also *appropriates* it. This *appropriation* is twofold, since it is property — it makes the text its own — and adaptation — it conforms it to its own purposes. This distinction neither coincides nor impugns the function differentiation required by Fokkema and Ibsch, from the very beginning, between the theoretician and the literary critic (1984: 13). Rather it attempts to subscribe to that "dynamic linguistic construction" which, for J. Tynianov, literature is (as quoted by both authors), to the exhaustion of literary mechanisms, as in Chinese Third Century poetic treatises, remarking that the poet resorts to newly coined or to long forgotten words (18).

According to Ion, no-one knows Homer like Ion. Likewise, the scholar, the researcher, the professor, the critic, all strive to know an author in depth, they interpret his work, they give his figuration their *own meaning*. They undertake an intellectual meditation, their specific mediation: "we are bound to conclude that — as in the case of interpretation — their justification depends on both the literary historical source material and a particular frame of reference, interest or hypothesis" (Fokkema and Ibsch 1987). But, like Ion, they contribute on another, less intellectual plane, to the realization of another intermediation which, without ruling out the first one, consists in recreating Homer, in giving Homer his voice: the rhapsodist interprets, the actor interprets, the musician, animating the text, is certain, if nothing else, of a certain interpretation.

The duality of the interpretation carried out by Ion lies at the core of knowledge, on that double possibility which is part of the cultural imagery where reflection can be an intellectual meditation but also an image reflected on a more or less undulated surface, and speculation is an abstract quest of reason. One must bear in mind the visual, spectacular origin of *theoria* — albeit attenuated by intellectual excesses. Before it became the rigorous and systematic formulation of a piece of knowledge it was contemplation, watching a ceremony or a theatrical representation.

For Plato, for Socrates, interpretation allows for this double meaning of which Ion would be an emblem. In this dialogue, one of Plato's most enigmatic (Hartmann 1994), it is admitted that art uses recipes, learned techniques; however, it insists on the fact that Ion is privileged by a form of *enthusiasm* thanks to the god who infuses with his divinity those who possess him.

Rather than examining the history of the different theories of *interpretation*, it might be more interesting to consider it as the capacity to formulate *hypotheses*, as a complementary part of a quest which does not stick to the strictly methodological steps in order to gain access to the forms of knowledge, but as raptures which are alien to the rational workings of theory, although they do not discard it. In talking about *hypotheses*, I refer to the logical operations which, starting from methods of induction and deduction, Charles S. Peirce called *abduction*. (Although the notion is associated with his doctrine of signs and diffusion, Plato and Aristotle had already used it to name a method of mathematical demonstration.) This would be another possibility of reducing, through time, the distance between the aesthetics of reception and semiotics, a distance which according to Fokkema is not insurmountable, since the problems of both schools are comparable and sometimes even similar (Fokkema and Ibsch 1987: 322).

For Peirce, *abduction* is the cognitive capacity of adventuring conjectures, the audacity of proposing hypotheses which are not based on any previous knowledge but on flashing associations which illuminate the mind like lightning. It is a well-known fact that the term abduction also means kidnapping, which is not too far removed from the enthusiasm of the rhapsodist. Hypotheses underlie the text and literary interpretation uses this "singular guessing instinct" on which reading depends and the result of which reading is a resource of knowledge, but above all of imagination (Peirce 1931-58: 7.218).

"In principle, all interpretations are admissible and can be defended, but we do not agree that just any argument is capable of justifying an interpretation. It is only when the reader's frame of reference, his interest or — to be more exact — his decoding system is known and accepted as a given fact that we can judge his observations on particular texts" (Fokkema and Ibsch 1987: 332). For several reasons — some of them theoretical, other more biographical or circumstantial, like some theoretical reasons are deep down — I am interested in formulating a hypothesis here. Therefore, in spite of the tautological construction, it would not be that redundant to propose *the hypothesis that interpretation is a hypothesis*, a conjecture, a supposition which turns on itself, a logical figure but also a play of imagination. Someone said that in this age in which *positions* become increasingly less drastic, in which *oppositions* are nonchalantly defended, it would seem that it is possible to find in *suppositions* the valid personal approach to this scarce reality, to approach a truth increasingly less convincing, less conditioned to the rigidity of methods, Structuralist, Marxist, psychoanalytical, and other more or less dogmatic methods between which those schools alternated.

Both hypotheses and suppositions reveal an underlying operation. To suppose means to interpret, a form of comprehending, understanding — even I don't believe the word "understand" to be associated with standing underneath — as the anagrammatic strategy consisting in a revision, a sort of *sub-version*, a secret text woven below words. Paragram or hypogram in Saussurean terms (or *les mots sous les mots*, Starobinski 1971), it is a moveable transposition of words which responds to the unpredictable combinatory of any *lector-elector-selector*, a reader who enjoys in each reading the freedom of an option which revises and defines meaning.

Through interpretation different spaces and times are not opposed; they converge and coincide in the "common place" of reading. The prefix *inter-* which introduces the word interpretation exhibits the condition of something that lies in between, in the middle, between two media: one is the medium that precedes the work, the medium of the author; the other is the medium to which the work gains access, the medium of the reader. Between two media, as if between two reigns: one of fiction, the other of reality; between two spaces: one interior, unlimited, where imagination roams, the other exterior, determined by the force of things. Interpretation puts them at stake, in a play which restitutes a primordial unity.

References

Aragon, Louis. 1926. *Le paysan de Paris*. Paris.
Breton, André. 1934. *Introduction au discours sur le peu de réalité*. Paris.
Eco, Umberto. 1990. *I limiti della interpretazione*. Milan.
Fokkema, Douwe. 1984. "Approaching Postmodernism." Workshop on Postmodernism, Utrecht, 21-22 September 1984. (I thank Joris Vlasselaers for his kind response in sending the original version of this paper to me years ago.)
Fokkema, Douwe W., and Elrud Ibsch. 1984. *Teoría de la literatura del siglo XX*. Madrid. (Spanish edition.)
——. 1987. *Modernist Conjectures: A Mainstream in European Literature, 1910-1940*. London: C. Hurt and Co.
Hartmann, Pierre. 1994. "La leçon herméneutique. Goethe lecteur de Platon." *Poetique 99*.
Levinas, Emmanuel. 1975. *Sur Blanchot*. Paris.
Peirce, Charles S. 1931-58. *Collected Papers*. 8 vols. Charles Hartshorne, Paul Weiss, and Arthur W. Burks (eds). Cambridge, MA: Harvard University Press.
Riffaterre, Michael. 1994. "Intertextuality versus Hypertextuality." *NLH* 25: 778-79.
Schleiermacher, Friederich D.E. 1987. *Herméneutique. Pour une logique du discours individuel*. Paris.
Starobinski, J. 1971. *Les mots sous les mots*. Paris.
Vattimo, Gianni, and Aldo Rovatti. 1983. *Il pensiero debole*. Milan.

Ancient Lyric Poetry and Modern Theory

Jan den Boeft
Utrecht University

Horace's *Ars Poetica* proves that in its author's time serious poetry had definitely acquired a respected place in Roman society. Two centuries separate the sophisticated and confident poem from poetry's modest beginning, when the pioneer Livius Andronicus, a Greek by birth, was allowed to form a guild of actors and *scribae*, 'men who were writing.' Actors were not socially esteemed by the elite, and there is every reason to assume the same about the poets, *poetae*, as they styled themselves with a Greek loan-word. For all their conservatism, however, the Romans were never loath to accept other peoples' inventions and customs, when these could be adapted to the Roman way of life. That opened the door at least to drama and epic. Quite early men like the African dramatist Terentius and the Calabrian epic poet Ennius even introduced some literary reflections in their works. Such reflections obviously remained on the poets' agenda, but only in the course of the first century BC programmatic poetics began to develop, first among the *poetae novi*, among whom Catullus was the *primus inter pares*, and then with the love-elegists. None of these poets, however, testifies to the sustained interest which is typical of Horace, who in his early career devoted no less than three of his eighteen satires to a discussion of the genre he had chosen and, one may say, to literary questions of a more general nature. Later he wrote three substantial essays about the art and function of poetry and its representatives. These essays were addressed to important members of the elite, one even to the emperor himself, which may illustrate the statement at the beginning of this contribution.

The longest of the three pieces deals with the specifically artistic demands made on the poet. Quite soon it was called *Ars Poetica*, which tallies well with its continuous emphasis on all aspects of professional technique. It is an instructive and delightful piece of work, which provides the erudite reader with literary pleasure through the author's clever use of the refined hexametric style which he had developed in his *sermones* (satires) and *epistulae*. The typically Horatian satiric vein is clearly palpable and, as always in Horace, form and substance are in full harmony, also in the sense that the subject, viz. professional poetic skill, is treated in a poem which itself shows all the necessary characteristics of such skill. Its instructiveness does not merely consist in the poet's own experience but also in his considerable knowledge of Hellenistic literary theory. This is already mentioned by an ancient commentator of the *Ars Poetica* and has been decisively proved by modern scholarship. Of course, this knowledge is not presented in the systematic order of a textbook but elegantly interwoven with the 'conversational' structure of the text.

Yet, for all such admirable sides of what was to become an influential text, there is also occasion for disappointment. It is unfortunately impossible to establish the precise date of publication — the evidence available simply does not allow this — but in any case it postdates books 1-3 of the poet's *carmina*, a collection of lyric poems, published in 23 BC. These *carmina* are without doubt the poet's prime achievement, indeed a "memorial more lasting than bronze," as he says in the concluding poem 3.30. The least a modern reader would have expected is an explicit treatment of the specific features and rules of lyric poetry. Such an expectation is, however, defeated, since the only poetic genera which receive ample attention are drama and epic, neither of which belongs to Horace's own poetic domain.

The most likely reason of this curious state of affairs is the powerful authority of the tradition. Hellenistic literary theory, treading in Aristotle's footsteps, had also focussed on drama and epic. All systematic reflection on lyric poetry is lacking. Whereas in his *carmina* he showed himself to be well-informed on the lyric poetry of the various phases of Greek literature, as a literary critic Horace keeps to the track beaten by his Hellenistic predecessors. Dealing with a somewhat different subject, George Kennedy expressed his disappointment, maybe even his disgust, in this phrase: "Careful comparison of the subtle literary techniques of Horace in his *Odes* with the warmed-over rhetoric of his verse treatise, *The Art of Poetry*, well illustrates the gulf between practice and theory." Although this judgment seems a shade too harsh, it is not entirely unfair. In this field theory was conspicuous by its absence and Horace was obviously unable to fill the gap. This is the more remarkable in that here and there in the *carmina* there are traces of poetical reflection. Indeed, in a unique poem (3.25) Horace tries to convey in language the process of lyric inspiration. It is an impressive experiment, for which the poet makes use of a comparison with the extatic Maenads of the Dionysiac cult. As far as I know, this is the nearest any ancient text comes to tackling the tantalizing problem what lyric poetry is about. Of course, one can adduce enough passages in which the Muses are called upon to provide inspiration or in which the divine origin of the inspired poet is preached, but these remain, so to speak, on the outside, concerning the poet's status rather than the essence of his poetry. This is deplorable.

Admittedly, no literary theory can ever exhaustively analyze or define the actual practice, but on the other hand the theoretical literary reflections which are *en vogue* in a given historical period at least shed some light on that practice, and there often is some sort of reciprocity between theory and practice. The part played by systematic rhetoric in forensic oratory and also in other types of prose — and even in poetry — is a point in case.

Be this as it may, there is another side to every coin. The Classical philologist who is looking for methods or models to get some grip on ancient lyric poetry is simply and salutarily forced to leave his customary workshop in order to search the modern markets of literary concepts. However, this will not prove to be an easy undertaking in which *l'embarras du choix* is the only drawback. For instance, alphabetical surveys of literary terms and concepts tend to use phrases like 'personal feelings' or 'subjective experience' or even 'spontaneous expression' in their descriptions. It would seem that such an approach is not particularly fruitful, since such characteristics do not exclusively belong to lyric poetry.

What one is looking for in the first place is the specific 'elements' which such poems are composed from, or rather, to use Walter Killy's phrase, "die von alters her ein Gedicht begründet haben." In his instructive study *Elemente der Lyrik* (1972), Killy deals with a number of these elements, illustrating his argument with examples provided by poetry from Antiquity onwards. In the very first chapter, entitled "Natur," one finds a striking observation which can be regarded as hitting the very center of much lyric poetry. Killy quotes a hymn on the rising sun sung by a primitive tribe, in which the sun's arrival is described in human forms. It is a non-intellectual interpretation of an impressive phenomenon of nature: "Die reale Beobachtung geht in poetischer Anschauung auf." Evidently, in such a specimen of lyric poetry the outside world is not done away with but perceived in an entirely different way. A sunrise can be described in a colorful or emotionally moving way in an epic digression or a passage of a novel, it can be used as a metaphor or in an allegorical sense, it can figure at the start of an episode to herald a new development, and so on, but in these cases, even if 'poetical' terminology is employed, the text will never step outside the boundaries of normal perception. Surely, the divergent lyric perception will be further enhanced by typically poetic means, some of which are dealt with by Horace and his predecessors too, but as such they are also fully at home in other literary and even non-literary texts.

Precisely this state of affairs, viz. the fact that in lyric poetry the text often testifies to a different human perception, is analyzed by Käte Hamburger from another viewpoint in chapter 4 of her *Die Logik der Dichtung* (1973; in English *The Logic of Literature*). Her referential framework is "the relation of literary genres to the statement system of language" and her aim is defining the lyric I as a statement-subject, the statements of which differ entirely from those of the objectively oriented pragmatic statement-subjects. At the end of her complicated and learned argument she concludes that the statements of the lyric I "are not directed toward the object-pole, but instead draw the object into the sphere of subjective experience, thereby transforming it." In spite of the intricate character of this hypothesis, it certainly is enlightening in that it does not intend to find the specific features of lyric poetry merely in the treasury of poetic technique.

There is, however, a curious corollary involved. Religious poetry, such as psalms and hymns, is banished from the domain of lyric poetry, because the first person of the texts in question is a *pragmatic* statement-subject, even in the case of the individual use of such a text by a faithful person as the expression of his feelings and convictions. An exception is made for the original poet in whose work the context of official religious worship is absent. This way of reasoning strikes one as being somewhat strained. Why does a lyric poem necessarily lose its specific character when it is read or sung by those who want to identify themselves with the 'statement-subject' and to make the same 'statements'? All forms of Greek choral lyric would be excluded and the same can be said about the great hymns composed by bishop Ambrose in late fourth century Milan. His most famous hymn may be taken as an example.

Like Killy's tribal hymn, *Aeterne rerum conditor* is concerned with early morning, viz. *gallicinium*, the cock's crowing, which calls forth the first glimmer of daylight. Its arrival is described in terms of salvation from the powers of darkness. Later on in the hymn this is parallelled by the cock's crowing that did away with Peter's denial of the Lord and his subsequent salvation. It is impossible to present an analysis of the hymn here, but its 'statement' certainly can be better understood with the help of Killy's observations or Hamburger's more thorough theory. Yet Ambrose wrote this hymn for his congregation and there is every reason to assume its success, when his opponents' claim that he mesmerized his flock by his *carmina* is taken into consideration.

There is no ancient literary theory which could shed a penetrating light on the typical character of Ambrose's lyric creations. As in other fields of Greek and Roman literature, modern conceptions can be quite beneficial, but they need some adaptation. In Ambrose's case late Antique tendencies to view phenomena in the everyday world as signs of an otherworldly reality should be taken into account. As a result one will be able to understand even better that "reale Beobachtung" can take the shape of "poetische Anschauung" and that in the statements of the lyric I 'objective' reality is being 'transformed.'

References

Hamburger, Käte. 1973. *Die Logik der Dichtung*. 2nd ed. Bloomington.
Killy, Walter. 1972. *Elemente der Lyrik*. 2nd ed. München.

Fact and Fiction

Isocrates on Truth and the Rules for the Encomium

Jeroen A.E. Bons
Utrecht University

To praise a tyrant by writing an encomium on him is a questionable endeavor to start with, and to do so incorrectly, i.e., violating the conventions of genre, is even worse. Precisely the last point seems to have prompted the Athenian rhetorician and teacher Isocrates (436-338 BC) to compose such an encomium himself. Its subject is the tyrant Busiris, on whom his rival teacher of rhetoric Polycrates of Samos had also recently published an encomium. Considering that Isocrates expressly states that his works are all intended to be morally useful and relevant to both private persons and society as a whole, to treat a subject like this may seem inappropriate to him. Indeed he considers the subject unworthy, but it is Polycrates' faulty attempt at producing a discourse of praise which requires correction.

Busiris is the name of a legendary king of Egypt, who because of his savagery and cruelty became the epitome of tyranny in the bad sense of the word and was described as such throughout all Antiquity. At the time of Isocrates his bad reputation was already firmly established. For this very reason Busiris was sometimes chosen by teachers of rhetoric as a subject for discourse: by defending or even praising Busiris one could exhibit one's skill and virtuosity. The paradoxical theme would surely draw attention and the discourse might thus bring its author pupils (and fees).

Isocrates' "Busiris" is conceived as a lesson by example. The introduction (1-9) is followed by a specimen of laudatory discourse, which conforms to the traditional structure of the genre. Moreover, consistent with the educational purpose of the discourse these sections already contain some rules on how to write an encomium. First, the subject should be serious, by which Isocrates means it should be morally and didactically useful; secondly, there is amplification which in a given situation can overrule truthfulness; and thirdly the discourse must be consistent.

In the third section of the "Busiris" (30-43) Isocrates switches from the exemplary to the theoretical mode. He now provides in general terms two more principles of what is considered valid eulogy, and these are treated as mutually related: credibility and truth (*alètheia*). Polycrates' description of Busiris' extravagancies like changing the course of the Nile and cannibalism cannot be believed, says Isocrates, because Polycrates offers no proof. An encomium is credible only if what is said can plausibly be expected in that context. And Isocrates adds another point: even if he says more about Busiris than is historically correct (which in itself would be justified on the basis of amplification), he will avoid criticism because he is using arguments one expects him to use in writing a discourse of praise:

> Even if both of us say what is false (*pseudè*), I, at any rate, have only used such arguments as writers of eulogies must use; you, on the other hand, have used such as is appropriate to revilers. (32)

This is clearly a prescription: an encomium may contain arguments that are false or untrue, as long as they are appropriate to the genre. The criterion of truth (*alètheia*) and falsehood or, maybe more correctly in this context, fiction (*pseudos*) is part of the conventions of encomium.

Next, the assessment of the question whether Busiris is in fact the *auctor intellectualis* of all the praiseworthy exploits which Isocrates attributes to him, provides further clarification of this criterion. Isocrates says:

> If it clearly were somebody else who had done the deeds which I attributed to him, I acknowledge to be exceedingly audacious in trying to change men's views about matters of which all the world has knowledge. But as it is, since the question is open to general judgment and one must form an opinion on it, whom would one, investigating from what is probable, consider to have a better claim to the authorship of the institutions of Egypt? (34)

The fact that one cannot be sure about this issue means that it is open to general judgment, which in turn implies that one can at most have an opinion (*doxa*) on the subject. To form an opinion is to reason on the basis of probability, or, in Isocrates' phrase, "to investigate from what is probable." (*ek tôn eikotôn skopeisthai*) In this case, says Isocrates, one should decide the issue in favor of Busiris because of his ancestry, the argument being that the expectation on the basis of the concept of *noblesse oblige* appears to be confirmed in most cases.

In this instance Isocrates reveals an attitude towards the past one might characterize as scientific, which means to say that he shows himself to be rational and critical in his assessment of historical data. This especially emerges from the technical use of *skopeisthai* ('investigate'), a verb which refers to the process of cognition based on observation. Furthermore, words like *logismos* ('reasoning'), *epideixai* ('to prove'), and *exetasis* ('scrutiny'), used by Isocrates in contexts similar to this one, point in the same direction. This scientific attitude, in which he proves himself an heir to the rationalistic approaches to myth and history as advocated by philosophers of nature and the Sophists, reveals itself in a number of instances in other works, for instance, in the *Helen* (45-47). There he argues that in order to make an intelligent qualification of Paris' choice for Aphrodite in the famous beauty contest, one should not apply one's own criteria of right and wrong, but acknowledge the authoritative views of contemporaries and the gods.

Another element of the truth-criterion is historical correctness. According to Polycrates it was Heracles who killed Busiris, but Isocrates challenges this opinion by using an argument from chronology. A simple calculation on the basis of the data provided by the chroniclers shows that Busiris and Heracles cannot possibly have been contemporaries.

Thus it seems that the criterion of truth can be applied in two ways. This quality can, on the one hand, be attributed to what one knows to be true, on the other to what one considers to be true. In the context of the encomium more can be subsumed under the category of truth than what is true in the strict sense. As we have seen, the generic principle of amplification can cause the author to go beyond the boundaries of factual truth, provided his statements and arguments remain credible, which in turn depends on their possibility and probability. It is interesting to note that the triad of requirements for poetic representations, viz. that they be probable, possible, and credible, drawn from Aristotle's *Poetics* (1451 a 28; 39; b 16, etc.) looks very similar to the criteria advocated by Isocrates. Here, as in some other instances, Aristotle might very well have used the results of literary theory as it was taught by the Sophists and their successors, of whom Isocrates is the most important representative.

That rhetoricians did employ the notion of truth in a broad sense, especially regarding the persuasiveness of discourse, clearly emerges from Plato's *Phaedrus* (259 e 7ff.). While discussing "the nature of good and bad speaking and writing," Socrates remarks that good discourse presupposes a knowledge of truth in the speaker's mind. To this Phaedrus reacts:

> As to that, dear Socrates, what I have heard is that the intending orator is under no necessity of understanding what is truly just, but only of what is likely to be thought just by the body of men who are to give judgment; nor need he know what is truly good or noble, but what will be thought so, since it is on the latter, not the former, that persuasion depends.

Both what is true and what seems to be true can be conducive to persuasion, and both categories are therefore relevant to the rhetorician. Needless to say, Plato has Socrates disapprove of the second category.

That the formation of a set of rules for the encomium was indeed an issue at the time, and that the question of truth was part of the problem, is indicated by a passage in Plato's *Symposium* (198 d 1 ff.). As it is his turn to speak in the competition of eulogies on Eros, Socrates has some general remarks on the genre before delivering the specimen of his own. First, he says to have agreed to speak without knowing about the rules by which to eulogize: "I had not the least idea how this or any other eulogy should be conducted." Then he raises the question of truth: he thought that one was supposed to tell the truth, being the known facts, and to select from this the most suited material. Then he says:

> But the truth, it seems, is the last thing the successful eulogist cares about; on the contrary, what he does is simply to run through all the attributes of power and virtue, however irrelevant they may be, and the whole thing may be a pack of lies, for all it seems to matter.

Clearly the passage contains a good measure of Socratic irony, but it can still serve as an indication for the fact that eulogy and its rules was debated by rhetoricians, and that the inclusion of both truth and fiction was an issue.

Isocrates' view can be summarized as follows. In an encomium both the actual truth and seeming truth or fiction have their proper place. The latter case requires that the demands of credibility are met. What matters most for the composition of a successful encomium is that its author abides by the rules or generic conventions and provides his audience with what they can believe.

References

Isocrates. 1968. *The Works of Isocrates*. Loeb Classical Library. Vol. III. Trans. Larue Van Hook. Cambridge, MA / London: Harvard University Press.
Plato. 1989. *The Collected Dialogues of Plato*. Edith Hamilton and Huntington Cairns (eds). Princeton: Princeton University Press.

Dialogue and Direct Discourse

Frank Brandsma
Utrecht University

In the age of DWF, three research institutes have arisen in Utrecht University's Faculty of Arts. Douwe Fokkema himself saw the Research Institute for History and Culture (Dutch acronym: OGC, which stands for Onderzoekinstituut voor Geschiedenis en Cultuur) through its first five years as its scientific and managing director. At the same time the linguistic Research Institute for Language and Speech (OTS) came into being, while in recent years the Center for Language and Communication (CLC), slightly different in name and nature from the other institutes, was set up to accommodate research in the field of communication studies. Even though all these acronyms are not exactly helpful in the Search for a New Alphabet, I introduce them in order to give you a little footing in the local university world Douwe helped change.

Based as they were on the existing work and research plans of the scholars present, the new institutes established connections between related work and also set out new lines for research under an overall theme. In the OGC, for instance, this theme is 'cultural participation.' It provides a frame for a number of research groups, like that of the medievalists who work on orality and literacy in a fruitful collaboration of historians, art historians, musicologists and medievalists from the different languages, and comparative literature. As guidelines, themes like 'orality and literacy' and 'cultural participation' have proven their worth by generating interdisciplinary (or multi-disciplinary) research that resulted in new insights, laid down in many a book and article.

While 'bonding' the scholars of a research group and institute together, however, the three institutes and groups of scholars seem to have become more separate than is desirable in a faculty where academics from all three groups are together responsible for the educational programs of, for instance, Dutch or English Language and Literature. In the Dutch system a (assistant-) professor has both educational and research tasks. It goes without saying that the cooperation in teaching does not benefit from the separation in research. And at the moment there is a tendency to divide the faculty even further by organizing the research in specific fields — like Medieval Studies and Literary Studies — on a nationwide scale in so-called Research Schools, which are to cooperate with the local research institutes. This new development may have positive effects for the (organization of) research, but it may also increase the formation of idiosyncratic little groups in the faculty. A division — and even conflict — of loyalties looms, where the combination of teaching and research within one person could be an inspiration for both sides of the job. In my view, the faculty and the departments need more cohesion on the research level, a cohesion the research institutes might provide through collaboration instead of separation.

A first step in this direction, a first bridge across the widening gaps, might be the establishment of a research theme common to — but by no means dominant in — all three institutes. Apart from the obvious fact that they all deal with language, there is a common denominator in the OTS and CLC that might be more deeply investigated in the OGC: speech. In the linguistic OTS the phonetic, phonological, syntactic and semantic aspects of speech are studied, whereas the structures and conventions of, for instance, interviews and other conversations are investigated in the CLC. Research from the OGC side might provide a historical dimension to these topics and also generate new topics like the developments in the presentation of direct discourse in literary texts throughout the ages and its relation to the aural reception of texts, the reflexivity of language (its metalinguistic aspects) in poetry, and the differences between the aural and visual reception of a text: listening versus reading. The texts and documents usually studied by the OGC scholars may provide (historical) data and may even show authors experimenting with the various aspects of reported speech, as, for instance, Jane Austen does in *Emma* (1816). On the other hand, the OTS and CLC methods and insights may prove valuable in the OGC field as well. I will give an example, a problem I have come across in my field, Medieval romance.

As a stylistic device, reported speech is an interesting aspect of a Medieval text, which — as we assume for the romances of Chrétien de Troyes, for instance — were read aloud to an audience. Did the performer let the listeners *hear* that s/he was quoting a character? Did the author indicate the direct discourse in his text in a special way (our modern system of inverted commas being absent in the Medieval manuscripts)? Do the manuscripts take over the authorial indications or do they provide and/or add their own, in the form of, for instance, initials or paragraph signs? The questions are manifold, and very interesting in view of topics like listening-reading and orality-literacy, but answers are hard to find. The manuscripts are the only trustworthy evidence available and even they date only rarely from the time of the creation of the text.

A new approach to direct discourse in Medieval literature was introduced by a Parisian professor of historical linguistics, Bernard Cerquiglini. In his book *La parole médiévale: Discours, syntaxe, texte* he compared the presentation of spoken words in the verse and prose versions of Robert de Boron's *Joseph d'Arimathie* (ca. 1200) and, even more important, showed how a quantitative analysis of the texts might yield new information about the narrative techniques and structures used by Old French poets and about the differences between verse and prose texts. For Middle Dutch literature, Evert van den Berg has shown that the statistical analysis of grammatical patterns may provide a 'hard' basis for the determination of the date and geographical origin of a text.

When, working along these lines of linguistic and statistical analysis, I studied samples of direct discourse in Old French and Middle Dutch Arthurian romances in verse and prose, two regular patterns emerged, one dominant in prose, the other in verse texts. Without going into details, one might say that the patterns differ in the position and distribution of the components of reported speech (like the speaker, the 'verb of speaking,' the addressee, the actual speech, etc.). Whereas the verse texts tend to introduce a speech in an explicit way, giving the speaker and the verb of speaking before the actual speech, the prose texts very often begin with the first one or two words the character speaks, then the speaker and verb of speaking appear, which are followed by the rest of the character's words. It is the difference between

> A: He said: 'Of course, later in the evening I'll tell you all about it.'

and

> B: 'Of course,' he said, 'later in the evening I'll tell you all about it.'

that is at stake here. It may seem trivial in modern eyes, used as we are to inverted commas and colons, but if you ignore these modern conventions and read the examples without looking at the punctuation, it seems evident that A is less difficult to read aloud than B, since in A the beginning of the actual speech is easily recognized, whereas in B the exact beginning of the second part of the speech may be hard to see at a glance: does 'later in the evening' belong to the narrator's or to the character's words? Opacity of this kind is a severe handicap for someone reading a text aloud.

It would, of course, be premature to project the implications of this modern English example on the Medieval Dutch and French texts, especially since none of the samples shows only units of the verse (cf. A) or prose pattern (B). Units of direct discourse of both patterns occur in all texts, but one pattern predominates in each sample. There even is a prose text (the 'Charrette'-section of the prose *Lancelot*) which shows a remarkable shift from the prose to the verse pattern in a section which turns out to have been added later by a scribe. This indicates that the analytical method enables us to distinguish between different writers. The fact that the patterns changes so drastically, within the same text, performance or reading-session, is even more significant, since this shift would be inconceivable if only one of the two patterns were apt for reading aloud. Given this shift and given the fact that units of both patterns occur in each text, it seems best to be very careful with regard to the alluring assumption that the two patterns represent different modes of performance and reception. Yet the patterns remain and call for an explanation that goes beyond the assumption of stylistic preferences of the authors.

Reported speech-research in the OTS/CLC fields may provide new openings here. The linguistic specialists have presented their work in books like John Lucy's *Reflexive language: Reported speech and metapragmatics* and Florian Coulmas' *Direct and indirect speech*. They show how other languages use, for instance, special prefixes to indicate reported speech. This may have a parallel in the prose pattern, since the words found in the first part of the speech are quite often typical for that position: they might serve as markers, indicating 'here begins direct discourse!' In Old French prose texts words like 'certes' (comparable to 'Of course' in examples A and B), 'or' ('now' and 'si' ('and') often indicate the beginning of direct discourse. Although these words do not occur exclusively in that context, they still are important signals for the reader to be aware of a change in the narrative, which may turn out to be the beginning of a new episode, a change in perspective, a change from report to reported speech or — within a dialogue — a change of speaker. Thus there is method to the prose pattern as well. Once grasped, as the Medieval performer and his audience undoubtedly did and as we may do due to the linguistic parallel, this prose system may have assisted the reader as well as the more straightforward presentation in the verse pattern. In other words, the Medieval equivalents of B may, within the context of the manuscript, have been just as easy to read aloud as those of A.

There are other interesting linguistic perspectives on direct discourse — like Maya Hickmann's study of the way children learn to distinguish and represent reported speech — in the books edited by Lucy and Coulmas, but I will leave it at this one example. In my view, it corroborates Coulmas's statement: "reported speech is one of those phenomena whose proper treatment necessarily transcends departmental boundaries" (1). Within the local Utrecht research context, the word 'departmental' could be replaced by 'institutional,' since only collaboration between the three research institutes may truly result in new, transcendental, insights in the intriguing phenomenon of direct discourse. This is just a suggestion for a combined effort in a field, which I would gladly give for other 'transcendental' themes. Yet I hope it demonstrates the usefulness and importance of studying and discussing similar issues, if only to keep the Utrecht research institutes and their participants on speaking terms.

References

Cerquiglini, Bernard. 1981. *La parole médiévale. Discours, syntaxe, texte.* Paris.
Coulmas, Florian, (ed). 1986. *Direct and Indirect Speech.* Berlin.
Lucy, John, (ed). 1993. *Reflexive Language: Reported Speech and Metapragmatics.* Cambridge.

To Purify the Language

Wim Bronzwaer
Catholic University of Nijmegen

There is no better way to pay homage to a respected colleague than to quote him. But in doing so there is always the risk that he will find himself misquoted, for anyone whose career as an academic writer on general and comparative literature has been so fruitful, so varied and so prolonged as Douwe Fokkema's, might well consider each quote as from the wrong source or from the wrong period in his development. My quote certainly runs this risk: it will probably not seem very typical of Fokkema's work nor very central to this major concerns. Yet, what a man has written, he has written.

In the *Yearbook of Comparative and General Literature* of 1977 Douwe Fokkema wrote: "Let me summarize: the main social significance of the poetic function of literature is its renewing and purifying effect on the use of language" (8). The statement is, of course, carefully argued in the article, entitled "The Social Significance of Literature as Art." Fokkema envisages other social (in our days, he would have written 'ethical' perhaps) functions for literature as well. But the notion of purification of the language is clearly his main point, for he repeats it a number of times, sometimes using different wordings. The precise wording of the quote is nevertheless relevant, for it will, by dint of an obvious verbal echo, evoke the famous line from Mallarmé's sonnet "Le tombeau d'Edgar Poe":

... donner un sens plus pur aux mots de la tribu

which T.S. Eliot transcribed in "Little Gidding," the fourth of the *Four Quartets*:

... to purify the dialect of the tribe.

There might, at first sight, seem to exist a surprising agreement between the literary scholar and the two poets on that perennial question of what poetry can do, what its use and its justification might be, in short, of its social function. In fact, the juxtaposition of the three short texts reveals not an agreement but a profound disparity, one that, it seems to me, is essential to anyone who raises the perennial question. For the answer that Fokkema provides, illustrates precisely its own shortcoming: it is couched in the language of the tribe — a language, that is, unpurified.

Of course I am not trying to detect an untruth in Fokkema's statement. His views on the social significance of literature can easily be appreciated as an intelligent and, in 1977, a timely attempt to correct certain one-sided ideas, then current, of the Russian Formalists and Roman Jakobson in particular as spokesmen for an 'art for art's sake' ideology. As such, the article voiced ideas that will have been welcomed by many a reader. What intrigues me, is that both Mallarmé and Eliot, with considerable differences between them, are saying something that precludes the possibility of any such statement as Fokkema's — in fact, of any scholarly or theoretical pronouncement at all that seeks to define, or even to describe, any aspect of literature such as it is conceived by the two poets. What is at stake is the problem of the distinction that we wish to maintain between object-language and meta-language, and on this problem Fokkema's views have been very consistent and very explicitly stated. But there is more to be said, once we have been overtaken — perhaps unwillingly — by the intertextual shadows of Mallarmé and Eliot.

The article from which the quote derives was written in a period when the scholarly pursuit of literary knowledge was under strong pressure to justify itself in terms of 'social significance' or 'relevance to society,' relevance, that is, to the ideology of the welfare state. In such a climate, prevailing in the Netherlands but not only there, anyone who wanted a job in literature or wished to raise funds for literary research projects, did well to stress the social significance of what he had in mind. Any manifestation of an art for art's sake ideology was clearly suspect and it is interesting to see how Fokkema's article, in such a context, adopts the strategy of silencing the enemy by embracing him. For Russian Formalism *could* indeed be mistaken for a manifestation of the art for art's sake ideology and indeed sometimes was so — especially by the Marxists of course. But it could also be marshalled to the opposing camp — and that is what Fokkema did in the 1977 article. I do not wish in any sense to suggest that in so doing he 'misinterpreted' the theories of the Russian Formalists. But he employed them in a strategy that was different from their own —

different, because the historical and social conditions in which his strategy was called for, were not those under which the Formalist theories were developed.

If the term can be used at all without leading us too far astray, *purification* was an epistemological concept for the Formalists, denoting a set of procedures that could enable us "to see the stone as stone," in Shklovsky's famous phrase. His epistemology was, unexpectedly, Thomistic and, less surprisingly, essentialistic. Shklovsky's essentialism goes underground in Jakobson's theory, as Fokkema notes; there, stress is laid on the dichotomy between the signifier and the signified object. And so Jakobson is brought in line with Machiavelli, Hobbes and Orwell, with the long tradition of authors who have opened our eyes to the possibility that language can be impurely used, especially for political purposes. And so the programme of poetry — the purification of language — becomes, basically, a political or ideological programme. It is the task of poetry to make or keep us aware of the fact that what *is said* is not what *is*, which is what the politicians are always trying to make us believe.

There is, then, an ideological urge behind Fokkema's wish to call the Russian Formalists to arms in a battle fought against art for art's sake. We can certainly find political urges at work in the Formalists' writings, which were not only avantgardist but also, in a non-Marxist sense, revolutionary. But from Shklovsky to Fokkema, from the concept of "deautomatization" to that of "purification," is a larger step than the reader of the 1977 article might think. And here I should wish to return to the 'intertexts' by Mallarmé and Eliot that Fokkema's phrase evokes — even if he did not purposely wish to evoke them. In Mallarmé's sonnet, the notion of purification is, by common consent, taken to refer to what in the French poet's early poetology culminates in the notion of "une langue immaculée," and ultimately in the notion of "le Livre du rien" — a book that could only *conceivably* be written and only under the strict condition that the dichotomy between signifier and signified object would have become absolute. There is, incidentally, an obscure link between the sonnet and post-Koranic theological literature, a link that runs via Mallarmé's translation of Edgar Allan Poe's poem "Israfel" (1831). Poe found the angel Israfel, epithetized "Lord of the Trumpet," not in the Koran, as Mallarmé thought, but in the "Preliminary Discourse" that George Sale prefixed to his translation of the Koran in 1734. In the sonnet, Israfel (whose name might well be a corruption of the Hebrew *serafim*) is evoked in lines 3 and 4, as many commentators think — and indeed, if the angel mentioned there is not Israfel, who is he? For in the *Apocalypse*, to which we are referred by line 5, it is clearly Michael who defeats the Dragon, and he does so by military, not by musical means.

In Poe's poem, Israfel's music silences the music of the spheres. Symbolically, he stands for the power of art to transcend even the *harmonia mundi*. There are a few cues, in Poe's poem as well as in Mallarmé's sonnet, that compel us to believe that this is so precisely because Israfel sings "a mortal melody" (Islamic lore presents him as blowing his trumpet at the last judgment). On the other hand, Mallarmé describes Poe as a poet in whose voice "la Mort triomphait." The 'purified' voices of Israfel and of Poe are emphatically *not* voices singing in eternity, or exempt from death. Mallarmé's 'purity' is not a religious or even a metaphysical concept — it is a poetological one.

More importantly, it is certainly not a concept that could possibly be fitted into a theory of communication. Fokkema's 'purification' *can*, as he makes very clear when he writes: "I see a major contribution of poetry, and of literature in general, to social life in its function of purifying and renewing language as a means of communication." The last phrase, "language as a means of communication" can, of course, be taken in its neutral sense as a 'sign' out of the metalanguage of communication-theory. But if we replace it into the sociohistorical context in which it was used and reconstruct the ideological load it had in 1977, it becomes an example of "une langue maculée," of unpurified language. Language as a means of communication was precisely what Mallarmé wished to transcend.

Intertextuality can be a tricky game, it would seem. Everything that can be said about Mallarmé's notion of the pure poetic language goes absolutely against the grain of Fokkema's argument — and yet he also uses the word 'purify.' Should we leave it at that and simply conclude that Fokkema did not have Mallarmé's line in mind when he wrote his article? Nor Eliot, in whose passage from *Little Gidding* where Mallarmé's line is transcribed the argument is quite clearly that language, even if it is purified according to Mallarmé's recipe, fails to take us into that realm where "you must move in measure, like a dancer," the Plotinian realm where souls communicate with God and with each other *without* language?

Or should we accept the view of the Deconstructionists that no writer can ever be entirely in control of what he writes because he inevitably has to use words that have been used before, and differently? Douwe Fokkema has, in his published writings, firmly resisted Deconstruction so far (nor do I expect that he will ever succumb). Perhaps the little case I have presented demonstrates that it is precisely in studying *how* words differ from the ways in which they have been used before, that knowledge and insight can be extended, not by claiming that any user of language can lay down rights to a language that is completely under control, perfectly unambiguous, utterly metalingual and wholly transparent. For, to quote *Little Gidding* once again, if "last year's words belong to last year's language," that does not make them meaningless.

Towards the Study of the Canon in Brazilian Literature: Machado de Assis and Jean-Ferdinand Denis

Tania Franco Carvalhal
Universidade Federal do Rio Grande do Sul, Porte Alegre

There are neither religious, nor political reasons for establishing a canon. There are, however, pedagogical, literary, historical, and aesthetic arguments for designing a canon or more than one canon.

Douwe Fokkema, "The Canon as an Instrument for Problem Solving."
Sensus Communis, 1986: 251.

In an anthology of 1873, entitled "Literatura Brasileira: Instinto de Nacionalidade," Machado de Assis gives us an excellent synthesis of the Brazilian literature at the time. Bearing in mind the most well-known writers in whom he recognizes the general desire to create a more independent literature, De Assis states that their works were stamped by the search for the "local color," of the uniqueness that would express American nature in its most distinctive features. According to him, the desire to express the "national," with the aim of distinguishing Brazilian literature from the Portuguese, was understandable in a newly formed literature, but it could also limit and impoverish its scope. This limitation on the themes, imposed by national elements, ruled over writers as well as public, for the preference was present in the very reception of the literary works: the applause, according to De Assis, was given to works that explored the local color, that placed in the scene the first inhabitants of the country, the Indians, in short, that insisted on everything that was "national." In this context, De Assis attracts our attention to the danger of a critical stance ruled by the same intention. Centered, many times, on nationalist requirements, it discarded the writer's talent and the qualities of the text to evaluate it according to criteria which were more ideological than aesthetic. He is sympathetic towards a "doctrinaire" critique whose analysis "corrects or kindles invention," a critique that is able to shape, in broad terms, the individual and collective taste. This critique would be the source of a more vigorous Brazilian literature which he considered to be on a stage of development towards a great destiny.

In the first part of his study, De Assis establishes fundamental notions for understanding our literature at the time of its consolidation, and we recognize in his writing a clear insight and a sharp perception of literary problems. On the one hand, he requires from the writer the expression of a certain "private feeling," an "instinct of nationality," that are a witness of his belonging to a specific nation and to a specific time, despite the diversity of themes he deals with; on the other hand De Assis believes in the existence of a "common background" of all literatures, to which writers contribute in interaction among themselves. As he says: "neither the old nor the modern had all."

De Assis's conception of literature as a network in which every contribution has a visible place, has held its relevance up until today. In addition, he had already developed a concept of literature as a set formed by writers, the works and the public, a totality which depended, for its constitution, on the active role of criticism.

In his essay, we also detect a concern not to fix a canon for Brazilian literature, for while he handles several genres (the novel, poetry and drama) he overlooks almost all the writers' names. Even if in the domain of poetry and drama some names are mentioned, in relation to the novel, however, he discusses aspects of the genre. Could the silence with regard to fiction writers indicate the genre's literary poverty? Absolutely not. In the introduction, De Assis makes a reference to the predominance of this genre over the other forms of literary expression by listing some famous Brazilian fiction writers: José de Alencar, Bernardo Guimarães, Joaquim Manuel de Macedo, Escragnolle Taunay, and Franklin Távora. However, as he emphasizes, in all of them he reads the same tendency to inscribe the "local color," above all in the study of manners and customs. Often, De Assis defines the novel as the genre "that gathers the study of human passions in poetry's delicate and unique touch" and complains about the absence of observation and analysis of Brasil. In his considerations, it is not difficult to perceive the intention to criticize the excessive nationalist strokes of the nineteenth-century Brazilian novels and to suggest other possibilities for contemporary writers such as the urban novel, in the fashion he himself had set out to develop. In a sense, he was denouncing the risks the genre was subjected to.

We recognize, then, in De Assis's writings a concept of nationalism that tends to the universal. The American writer is, in his point of view, part of a wholeness in which his work is integrated. These ideas are materialized when he chooses the example set by Shakespeare, a writer who rehearsed all themes by getting a little inspiration in every place without limiting himself to the expression of the "local." By writing in this way, De Assis thinks that Shakespeare was not "less" British but rather a universal genius. Finally, one needs to add that De Assis, a great novelist himself, uses his essay to comment on the genre by exposing his own ideas about it.

In the perspective that guides our comments, this essay by De Assis is not only a "piece of news" on Brazilian literature or even the privileged space for developing ideas about the writer as a literary critic, but must also be taken as a reply to the notions established by Jean-Ferdinand Denis (1798-1890) in one of our first historiographic works, the *Résumé de l'Histoire Littéraire du Portugal suivi du Résumé de l'Histoire Littéraire du Brésil* (1826). No doubt, De Assis establishes a productive intertextual dialogue with the ideas of Denis, in which there is a radical change of orientation for reasons not only historical but also literary and aesthetic. This dialogue can be an example of the two divergent ways in which both writers developed notions that are helpful in the formation of the Brazilian literary canon, even today, for didactic purposes.

Denis was one of the three historians who dealt with Brazilian literature in the nineteenth century. The first was Friedrich Bouterwek in 1805 and, after him, J.C.L. Simonde de Sismondi in 1813. But Denis is the first to consider Brazilian literature in its own terms, distinct from Portuguese literature. To read Denis today means to identify a frame of thinking that struggled for an independent Brazilian literature, pregnant of the *teinte locale* (the terms, used by De Assis and largely used in Brazilian criticism, were Denis'). First, he wanted to make the nation's independence, in 1822, coincide with its literary independence. He says: "L'Amérique doit être libre dans sa poésie comme dans son gouvernement" (1826: 516).

For De Assis, on the contrary, the literary independence should not necessarily correspond to the political one, as according to him, "that independence [...] cannot be achieved overnight but slowly, to be long-lived; it won't be the task of one or two generations; many will work hard till the task is achieved."

According to Denis, each nation should found its own literature based on its own past; to imitate its own writers without paying homage to foreign nations. The basis, for him, was to stimulate national consciousness in every nation of the world. Each nation had to find its distinctiveness. Hence, his conviction that each literature should have a well-defined *teinte locale* and that it should highlight its specificities. This argument forms the basis of the value criteria he subscribes to in his work, as well as the choice of elements he praises in each writer he studies. When he analyzes, for example, the epic poem *Caramurú* by Santa Rita Durão, he writes: "J'ai cru devoir donner une analyse de l'ouvrage de Durão parce que, malgré ses imperfections, il est *national*, et qu'il indique assez bien le but vers lequel doit se diriger la poésie américaine" (1826: 553).

Back to the essay by De Assis; we can see that he recognizes Durão and Basilio da Gama as precursors of Brazilian poetry as they searched for the elements of a new poetry that came to define the first features of our literary profile. However, these observations give him the chance to state that Tomás Antonio Gonzaga, the poet who followed closely the model of the Classical Arcady even though he breathed the atmosphere of the country, was overlooked by the critics. They did not forgive him for having used foreign models. This attitude De Assis regards as a mistake.

On his part, Denis underestimated the poets who, like Gonzaga, followed the Arcadian models. In Claudio Manuel da Costa, Denis condemned the Italian influence by judging him, "trop européen dans ses images." For Denis, da Costa "dédaigne la belle nature qui l'entoure et manque d'originalité, car ses églogues semblent soumises aux formes poétiques imposées par les siècles précédents, comme si l'habitant des campagnes du Nouveau Monde devait rencontrer les mêmes images que celles qui nous sont offertes" (1826: 573).

As De Assis rightly pointed out, Denis' critical orientation prevented him from evaluating correctly the poetry of da Costa, whom the Brazilian critic, Sérgio Buarque de Holanda in *Capítulos da Literatura Colonial* (1991), praises for its originality, in terms of the contextual difference of the poet in relation to the works of the Italian Metastasio, his inspiring source.

The contribution of Denis was essential for the constitution of our Romantic nationalism. This literary nationalism, a result of historical circumstances and of Romantic trends, served well in the first phase of the Brazilian literature, though in some cases, as shown by Antonio Candido in the chapter "Pré-romantismo franco-brasileiro" of his work *Formação da Literatura*

Brasileira: Momentos Decisivos (1959), the celebration of the *teinte locale*, required by Denis, became sometimes an obstacle for the development of the creative imagination of the new poets.

The ideas put forward by Denis had a lot of influence on Brazilian literature as they set a sort of guideline for the emerging literature. Denis delineates the paths to be followed. Thus, the tendency to express the specificity of the local, that De Assis refutes in his essay, was, no doubt, stimulated by Denis' thoughts. This same tendency was responsible for the constitution of the literary canon as the expression of national identity at the beginning of Brazilian literature.

Almost at the end of the century, De Assis answered the questions posed by Denis half a century before. What De Assis affirms is that the requirement of the *teinte locale*, acceptable and useful at the moment Denis had defined it, did not hold the same interest later and could be substituted by the notion (or requirement) of the *instinct of nationality* as he defines it in his essay. With no intention of establishing a literary canon but as propaedeutic as Denis, De Assis wants to change the prevailing orientation and suggest other possibilities for Brazilian literature, such as the development of the urban and psychological novel, possibilities that he himself pursued and that remain, today, signs of his modernity.

References

Assis, Machado de. 1957. "Literatura Brasileira. Instinto de Nacionalidade." In W.M. Jackson (ed), *Crítica Literária*. Rio de Janeiro.
Candido, Antonio. 1959. *Formação da Literatura Brasileira*. 2 vols. São Paulo: Martins.
Denis, Jean-Ferdinand. 1826. *Résumé de l'Histoire Littéraire du Portugal suivi du Résumé de l'Histoire Littéraire du Brésil*. Paris: Lecoint et Durey, Libraires.
Holanda, Sergio Buarque de. 1991. *Capítulos de Literatura Colonial*. São Paulo: Brasiliense. (Organized by Antonio Candido.)

Semiotics and Liberal Arts Education

Han-liang Chang
National Taiwan University

The Polish sinologist Janusz Chmielewski once pointed out that Chinese philosophy is persuasive rather than demonstrative (1962). The distinction made here evokes a time-honored debate between rhetoric and logic in the West which can be traced back to Plato and Aristotle but has received renewed critical attention, especially by American neo-pragmatists, over the last two decades. One is reminded, among other things, of the distinction between two critical models of demonstration and persuasion which Stanley Fish makes in the tradition of the Sophists. As Fish rephrases it, whereas demonstration is the procedure of logic and scientific enquiry, "in which interpretations are either confirmed or disconfirmed by facts that are independently specified," persuasion is based on and constitutes facts that are always already interpreted (1980: 365).

The debate has been otherwise interpreted as that between the two traditionally hostile disciplines of philosophy and rhetoric. This opposition gets a linguistic turn in Paul de Man's celebrated essay "Semiology and Rhetoric" where the author casts new light on the issue by situating it in Medieval liberal arts education system (1979) and by introducing the role of the as-yet-nonexistent discipline of semiotics. According to De Man, among the three language-focussed disciplines that constitute the trivium, logic is closer than grammar and rhetoric to the quadrivium that accounts for the Medieval scholar's knowledge of the world. He does not bother to dwell on the tension between logic and rhetoric, but moves to discuss the discrepancy between grammar and rhetoric, grammar and logic, which French semiologists such as Todorov and Genette have failed to notice, as revealed by their conflation of the trivium in such titles as *Grammar of the Decameron* and *Figures III*.

De Man seems to be suggesting a new spectrum of relationships among the seven arts, based on their truth-claims or their transitivity to the world under investigation, and that rhetoric, with the signified truth bracketed, standing at one extreme of the spectrum, is less 'transitive' than any other discipline. Notwithstanding the seven arts' intransitivity, it is not my intention in this short paper in honor of Douwe Fokkema to challenge De Man. On the contrary, I believe De Man's attempt at reconstructing semiology in the trivium has opened up a line of enquiry into the possibility of semiotics in relation to the six arts required of a Confucian scholar in ancient China.

As is well-known now, the liberal education of seven arts, though traceable to Classical Antiquity, was formulated in the late Roman period and the early Middle Ages, in particular by Martianus (fl. 410-39) in his *De nuptiis Mercurii et Philologiae* and Boethius (ca. 480-524) in his *De Topicis Differentiis*, and it is essentially the latter's organization that was to be followed throughout the Middle Ages. As if anticipating De Man, Boethius makes the distinction between trivium and quadrivium already on the basis of the former's linguistic instrumentality as *organika* and the latter's coverage of areas of knowledge. A question can be raised here: Does the trivium's instrumentality serve the purpose of the quadrivium? Or: Is there transitivity between the two, i.e., three paths leading to four paths? The answer seems to be negative. If one examines the quadrivium, one finds all the four Pythagorean mathematical sciences — arithmetic, geometry, astronomy, and music — have their own distinct representational system which is non-verbally symbolic, nor does it need re-articulation in a metalanguage. Not only is there an unbridgeable gap between the trivium and the quadrivium, but also there is another gap between the quadrivium as abstract speculations and the absolute knowledge in the incorporeal world to which they aspire. In the enclosed logocentric system, the signifier of the quadrivium points towards the ultimate signified that is the harmonious order of divine creation. What is needed is a general semiotic rather than the language-focussed semiology, based perhaps on the technologized digital 'language,' which can bridge the linguistic and numerical systems of trivium and quadrivium.

It is no accident that Charles Sanders Peirce formulates his general semiotic in terms of the trivium. First, he explicitly equates semiotic with logic (Peirce 2.227); but in his characteristically cryptic argument for triads, semiotic contains three branches: pure grammar, logic proper, and pure rhetoric because every sign (representamen) is connected with three things — ground, object, and interpretant. Logic as semiotic (or the other way around, semiotic as logic) subsumes the trivium, including logic itself. Or perhaps one should say: *logic* as theory of signs covers the trivium, including logic proper, which is not *logic* proper. This word-play is not so trivial as it first appears if seen in the light of the fortune of rhetoric in twelfth- and thirteenth-century scholasticism, where dialectic dominates the trivium, and rhetoric is even reduced to a branch of logic (Camargo 1983: 107-108). At this point we could surmise the Peircian semiotic's possible linkage with the trivium, the author's indebtedness to scholasticism being a commonplace. From this, one can infer that the general semiotic Peirce proposes is derived from the language-focussed trivium, but it can be expanded to deal with other representations, such as the mathematical quadrivium as long as its members fulfill the conditions of ground, object, and interpretant. In fact, it is quite possible to recode the quadrivium in terms of the tripartite icon, index, and symbol.

If an analogy may be drawn with Classical and Medieval training of the trivium in the West, where rhetoric mediates and subverts grammar and logic amongst the three sciences of language, one would see that the rhetoric popularized by Chuang Tzu and even Mencius has enfeebled the organum of dialectic promoted by Kung-sun Lung and the Moists. Such sociolinguistic reflexions might give rise to a narrative about why the logical school which modern Chinese 'pragmatists' like Hu Shih endorse has never really thrived in China.

In the absence of grammar in ancient China, rhetoric and logic remain the two discursive procedures which might have given rise to semiotics in the loose sense. This disciplinary approach which has appropriated the trivium is not entirely ungrounded. In ancient China, following the tradition of the nobility, a Confucian (ju) is supposed to master six arts, li (ritual), yüèh (music), shè (archery), yü (charioteering), shu (writing), and shù (number). The first four belong to the general category of ritualistics, while the remaining two refer to more elementary training of writing and computing. If the six arts are compared with their Western counterparts, then *shu* falls into the category of trivium, *shù* and *yüèh* into the quadrivium. What about the remaining more practical arts? In the late Middle Ages, the seven arts have been expanded; or one could say some of the practical arts in Greece have been reinstituted. William of Conches, for one, re-maps scholastic knowledge. It includes eloquence (the trivium) and wisdom, the latter including the theoretical quadrivium and the practical ethics, economics, and politics (McInerny 1983: 270).

It makes no sense trying to draw, if possible at all, a correspondence between the two educational systems, but clearly there is a parallel between the trivium and the lower status of *shu*, where language plays a major role, and that between *shù* and arithmetic which serves as the foundation of the quadrivium. The role played by *shu* and *shù* is in fact ancillary to that of the ritualistic disciplines in that with their system-specific autonomy writing and number are more removed from the world of social praxis.

Chinese philosophers in the fourth century BC could not have been aware of their Greek contemporaries, nor possibly anticipated neo-rhetoriticians like Fish and De Man. However, it is the writings of the latter which have occasioned my preliminary enquiry into the Chinese concepts of sign — a topic which needs more elaboration than is allowed here.

References

Camargo, Martin. 1983. "Rhetoric." Wagner 96-124.
Chmielewski, Janusz. 1962. "Notes on Early Chinese Logic." *Rocznik Orientalislyczny* 26(1): 7-22.
De Man, Paul. 1979. *Allegories of Reading: Figural Language in Rousseau, Nietzsche, Rilke, and Proust*. New Haven: Yale University Press.
Fish, Stanley. 1980. *Is There a Text in This Class? The Authority of Interpretive Communities*. Cambridge, MA: Harvard University Press.
McInerny, Ralph. 1983. "Beyond the Liberal Arts." Wagner 248-72.
Peirce, Charles S. 1935. In Charles Hartshorne, Paul Weiss, and Arthur W. Burks (eds), *The Collected Papers of Charles Sanders Peirce*. 8 vols. Cambridge, MA: Harvard University Press, 1935-1966.
Wagner, David L. (ed). 1983. *The Seven Liberal Arts in the Middle Ages*. Bloomington: Indiana University Press.

On the Need for New Comparative Literature Handbooks

Yves Chevrel
Université de Paris-Sorbonne

Comparative Literature (henceforth CL) claims to be an institutional discipline just like others, taught in universities, producing theses and scientific books and articles. On the other hand, CL scholars often lament the lack of recognition by academic authorities: cutting off money, closing programs and, more recently, merging CL into something rather vague: cultural studies. Many literary disciplines are suffering the same fate, especially in periods of recession, but it seems that CL does suffer more than other (well or better?) established disciplines. More than practical problems, the cause could be the primary reason mentioned above, a lack of recognition. But why are comparatists unable to be, or to feel, recognized as such?

Every discipline must have its aims, methods, rules — and handbooks; it must be able to define itself. If we turn first to the very beginning of the statutes of the International Comparative Literature Association, we read the following: "The ICLA seeks to foster the study of literature from an international point of view"; we have an aim ("the study of literature") and — what exactly should it be called ("from an international point of view") — a method? Or a rule? A perspective? Or a location (of the student)?

'Literature' is a very large concept, which may embrace, theoretically, every collection of lines and pages ever written by someone on earth (not to speak of oral literature). It is usually, however, reduced to creative works whose artistic qualities have been recognized by institutions like schools and universities. And it is possible to propose a kind of world literary anthology: the use of 'great books' is well-known, and is not to be despised; to offer new objects to people who were not aware of their existence may be considered as progress. Étiemble even calculated that in a man's life one could read a little more than 18600 literary works: "une misère," he concluded. But, no matter how many books comparatists may read in their life, they do not hesitate to write histories of world literature which make it easier for their readers to select information, and the ICLA is editing a *Comparative History of Literatures in European Languages*: is it not already a good answer to possible detractors and a good way of demonstrating that CL does exist by producing *comparative histories* of literature(s), even though ontological and methodological problems are not all solved (for instance: literature or literatures)? Such problems normally belong to handbooks.

We also have CL handbooks (henceforth CLH): in the last two decades (from approximately 1977 on) we had even to face an increasing number of *manuels, précis, Einführungen, compendios*, etc. in the field. Their main purpose is, or must be, not to offer new objects, even if they also do so, but to suggest new position(s) in the study of literature(s): they attempt to displace the readers from their habits, from their national point of view. It is therefore necessary to know where those readers place themselves. Who is the intended reader of a CLH?

Such a reader may be a future CL student, what the French call 'grand public cultivé' or Germans 'philologisch gebildetes Publikum,' not to speak — but why not? — of the colleagues who will be eager to discover whether their names and their works are mentioned, discussed, or at least included in footnotes and bibliography. Is it possible to define a 'common reader' of a CLH? Students as well as the 'grand public' have been educated, in most cases, in their cultural environment, including training in one language and one literature. If we overview the list of CLH published in the last two decades, we find unsurprisingly that: (1) most of them have been written originally in English, French and German (it seems that there are but a few exceptions — compared to the number of human languages — and we can mention recent original CLH in Chinese, Hungarian, Italian, Japanese, Polish, Portuguese, Slovak, Spanish, and probably in some other languages), and (2) some of these CLH have been translated in other languages. This fact refers to the growth and expansion of the discipline since the first CLH (Posnett 1886): France, the USA and Germany are the countries which developed CL as an academic discipline. The situation is still to be taken into consideration, because of the moot points it may reveal.

Those points are at least of four kinds:

1. CLH tend to be rooted in a rather narrow tradition, which can be defined by what is sometimes called the 'triple stream,' i.e., the stream formed by the literatures written in English, French and German. The point of view is then international only in so far as it is considered that these literatures (with adjunction of some others!) are the base of a normative appreciation of literary studies.
2. Even inside the narrow literary corpus as it has been defined, there are some imbalances in the instances which are put forward to illustrate methodological considerations. It would be interesting to study — and to compare! — the translations of CLH originally written in the three 'basic' languages into other languages (including 'reciprocal' translations inside the 'basic' group): which transformations do those translations and, in many cases, adaptations reveal? Intended readers are not alike in Asian, African or South-American countries, and even inside the literatures of the 'triple stream' a German student does not have in mind the same references as an American or a French one does.
3. Besides methodological considerations, authors of CLH generally attempt to offer also 'new' material, i.e., material they supposed unknown to a large part of their readers. But is not this new material predetermined by the structures (genres, literary system, etc.) existing in the literatures known to the authors (and their intended readers)?
4. A major problem seems to be excluded, or scarcely dealt with: what is exactly 'comparing'? The naive question, often quoted and felt as 'provocative' by comparatists: 'which literatures do you compare?' is not that ridiculous.

Those difficulties, among others, are not easy to solve; maybe they are unavoidable, if not insuperable. There are some proposals that could be considered.

1. Many CLH are now written not by a single author, but by teams. A solution would be to constitute international teams, i.e., groups of scholars belonging to different cultures and eager to collaborate (not only to juxtapose ideas). It may demand much from contributors and editor(s) but is surely worthwhile. But what we need first, in my opinion, are new CLH written by scholars rooted in their literatures, especially in non-European

literatures, and trying to suggest comparative ways of exploring them. We already have some, especially from India, which are written in English; comparatists who do not read Asian languages ought to be interested in discovering what their Chinese, Japanese, or Korean colleagues consider as comparative literature — and perhaps also as literature. European CLH have been translated into Chinese and Japanese, but we lack translations of CLH coming from non-European countries.

2. We also need more reflections on the process of comparing. There are at least two (opposite) ways of dealing with this question. Either we assume that comparing is a usual behavior in all scientific ventures (many disciplines have 'comparative' in their wording: anatomy, linguistics, philology, etc.), or we assume that the process itself must be explored as far as the study of literature is concerned and is specific to CL. "Comparative literature is not literary comparison" — well, but what exactly is "comparing"?

3. The CLH that were accessible to me are concerned exclusively with research problems (there are but a very few exceptions). Is it not high time to make use of pedagogical situations and experiences which have been observed? What do we teach? How do we teach it? How do we introduce European Romanticism to French and to German students, aesthetics and reception theory to Japanese and to European graduates? How do we help CL students to become comparatists of the next generation? Which are the exercises that we use, the first steps of research works that we suggest?

Comparatists, however many languages they may master and how many literatures they may refer to, are never in a position to take "le point de vue de Sirius." They are always more or less deeply rooted in their own cultural and literary traditions. They often see themselves as 'border crossers' and are always eager to proceed farther; new CLH should help them to mark precise territories.

To Join Instruction with Delight

On Literary Studies and Literary History

Ampie Coetzee
University of the Western Cape

What if the author is dead? What happens to literary study, to the division of genre? What happens to literary history, an author's oeuvre; to periodization by author and genre?

These Poststructural questions do not differ much from the following: what if most of the voices in a country have not yet been heard, if its literature has only partially been written — as in the recently decolonized South Africa?

There are two ways of reading the canonized, anthologized literary text. One: to read it as discourse in its own right, autonomous, intransitive; language affirming its own existence, addressing itself to itself, writing itself, speaking about itself, primarily also negatively mimetic. The poem being the meaning of the poem. The other: to read it as part of the social apparatus organizing existence in society. It then becomes dispersed, a statement within a dialogue, or part of the creation of a construct. In this kind of reading the marginalized, 'literary' text also becomes a voice within a discourse.

Literary analysis, commentary and literary history cooperate in systematizing the most important documents in the literary culture of a nation. By analyzing every document, its structure and hidden truth is revealed. Only momentarily, however, for within decades other commentators will again analyze the same texts, seeking different literary truths — assuming that the text has never really revealed its secrets.

In most of the old and established countries of Europe where democracies have been attained after the Second World War, where life has become ordered, it is satisfying to be able to say: this is our language, this is our economy, these are our religions, this is our knowledge, this is our culture. It is there that the Library neatly retains and records Literature and everything written about it.

But the situation regarding culture and literature needs serious rethinking in a country like South Africa. New constructs are being created, physically as well as mentally: new boundaries and new names (eventually also for the country, perhaps). Newly liberated cultural organizers are seriously discussing a 'national culture.' The neglected manifestations of the oppressed cultures in the past should now be recognized and encouraged — perhaps even at the detriment of the Eurocentrism which came through colonial inheritance! Literary historians are discoursing on a 'South African Literature,' affirming that there are now eleven literatures to be developed — in the newly officialized languages of the country. A situation which is, of course — irrevocably? — problematized by the fact that two of these literatures — in Afrikaans and English — have been privileged in the past because of historical and political factors.

The concept 'one literature, one nation' can, of course, be written off as pandering to the political construct of 'one-nationness' at the moment being created in South Africa. But if the divisions by which the apartheid of the past had ruled with its misery and suffering can be exorcized through creating a unity of the people then the question should also be asked whether some kind of cultural and literary unity within diversity could be constructed. 'Unity within diversity' is a cliché. But how does the literary historian and literary theoretician stand outside the enterprise of one-ness being created at the moment? By saying that literature is autonomous, is elevated above concerns such as 'unity' or 'the people'? Or by saying: if there are eleven literatures, historicize and describe them separately? Or by attempting to read literature in another way: to accept that the destinies of the people in this country have been intertwined since the arrival of the Westerners and the intrusion and appropriation of the country by their texts?

In my research I have been investigating the possibility of using — misusing — literature as an integral part in the narration of the nation, in the narrating and constructing of a country as we experience it today. But then the autonomy of Literature becomes reduced to becoming part of an analysis of society and power.

Of course, the two ways of reading literature are not new. The Roman poet Horace made his well-known division into the 'dulce et utile,' in his *Ars Poetica*:

aut prodesse volunt aut delectare poetae (333)

and:

omne tulit punctum qui miscuit utile dulci (343)

(Freely translated: "A poet should either instruct or please" and "he who mixes instruction with delight is important.")

These two functions of literature — broadly to be interpreted as the aesthetic and the use-value — can be read within the rules of discursive formations: literature as autonomous, as text within its own right creating its own particular discourse ("to [...] shine in the brightness of its being," Foucault 1985: 300), as opposed to literature as statement within other discourses in society. Reading literature as autonomous would attempt reading it outside of the mimetic, as transgressive, where language is act. But language is also referential, and even the non-mimetic in literature will have historical relationships with a society and a culture. The question to be considered is whether a compromise can be made between the study of literature as autonomous text, and the insertion of the literary text into the history of the dialogues of power.

Then one has also to consider the relationship between history and literary history. In the last paragraph of the first chapter of *Discipline and Punish* Michel Foucault writes:

> I would like to write the history of this prison, with all the political investments of the body that it gathers together in its closed architecture. Why? Simply because I am interested in the past? No, if one means by that writing a history of the past in terms of the present. Yes, if one means writing the history of the present. (31)

History is then not to be seen as consecutive teleological development. There is no real beginning, only a series of disruptions and events which can be identified within the present within definite discursive formations made by the regular dispersion of statements. Genealogy is the descent of practices as a series of events and history is the questioning of our existence, an investigation into the events that have constituted us as subjects today, focusing as a diagnosis on "the moment of arising" (Rabinow 1994: 203).

By making use of the concept of the discursive formation within literary history — where the literary text is seen as part of the society and history in which it is produced — one could be enabled to identify the different dialogical formations within a society. When these discourses have been identified it becomes necessary to determine in what way they are written into, or have been written by, the literatures of a country.

In an investigation of this nature, where the text identified as 'literary' — whether it is 'good' or 'bad' literature does not matter — the literariness of the text as statement (its particular discourse as literature) is still of the utmost importance. Discursive formations are not themes. Photography is a comparable example: the theme of a photograph cannot be executed without light, shade, lens-opening, angle, etc. A theme in textual discourse such as land-appropriation and the redistribution of land (which is part of the history of the present in South Africa) will be found in legal texts, land redistribution bills, statements of politicians — but also in the farm novel. The upsurge of the farm novel — especially among Afrikaans writers today — contributes toward such a discourse on land; but as a literary — not legal, political or other — statement within that discourse.

Identifiable discursive formations within the present South African literary scene, from which a totalizing narrative of a nation could be written can be constructed from the regular dispersion of recurring statements.

Without specifying the details of statement and formation the following discourses can be identified as present, but simultaneously historical, unities. Travel, where the travel journal/novel of today bears many similar statements to those in the first texts of Western colonization. Landscape, which can be a statement within a travel text, but also widens out to become discourse on its own as an attempt at inscribing a country and its people. Missionary discourse, which is not only the creation of subjects in the past through missionary enterprise, but also the impetus to the 'emergence' of most of the literatures in the autochtonous African languages (the Bible and John Bunyan's *Pilgrim's Progress* especially). The 'other': from the descriptions, representations, constructs of the aborigine in the first travel texts to the other in especially Afrikaans and English literature today; but also the voice of the other within these literatures (as 'Black' English and Afrikaans writers). Discipline and punish: the South African penal system during the decades of apartheid — begun at the beginning of colonialism with the first prisoner, Autshumao, at the time of Jan van Riebeeck in the second half of the seventeenth century — being the discontinuity creating a large body of literature. Land and appropriation. Industrialization and the dispersion and uprooting of people, migration, cultural divisions. The accumulation of wealth. Labour and the master-slave relationship. The diary and its mapping of the relationship between the individual and society or country; particularly womens' diaries with the intercourse between madam and maid, the role of the colonized woman (still today). Gender. The body and sexuality. The discourse on language, where the following statement can be made: will the writing and the translation of literatures into the language of power, English, not cause 'South African Literature' to be in English? And does it really matter? Does the language in which a literature is produced really matter? Then, ultimately, the text: travel journal as map, but eventually text for a country, signifier without a signified. Although one ends with the Postmodern, self-reflexive text, the discourse on text and meaning in terms of mimesis and the creation of constructs is not necessarily a modern phenomenon, as the writers of the first *roteiros* for sailors finding their way to India, searching for signs to guide their route, eventually only had the text as signifier. The text has been a symbol of European intrusion into Africa, creating Africa, creating discourse — and still creating the discourses of today.

If one can then bridge the gap between literature as autonomous discourse and literature as statement within various discourses the different literatures in South Africa may be 'unified' within a narrative of a nation — although that narrative will not be teleological and in terms of a 'historical development.'

Ultimately, of course, this means relegating Literature to the margin for the sake of participating in the major discourses of a country. Literary studies, then, will be not for the sake of Literature, neither for literature as sociology, nor literature as the 'reflection' of social reality; but as co-construct of discourse, as peripheral vision, as 'instruction' — as knowledge. But peripheral, as all knowledge is.

References

Foucault, Michel. 1977. *Discipline and Punish: The Birth of the Prison*. London: Penguin Books.
— . 1985. *The Order of Things: An Archaeology of the Human Sciences*. London: Tavistock Publications.
Horati Flacci, Q. 1957. *Opera*. E.C. Wickam (ed). London: Oxford University Press.
Rabinow, Paul. 1994. "Modern and Counter-modern: Ethos and Epoch in Heidegger and Foucault." In Gary Cutting (ed), *The Cambridge Companion to Foucault*. Cambridge: Cambridge University Press.

Globalization and Literary Value

Amiya Dev
University of Calcutta

Marshall McLuhan must have been prophetic, though his 'global village' had few takers in the thick of the cold war. Today information technology has so advanced that McLuhanesque or not, a globalization has set in. And it does not take much to see that this globalization is different from the earlier forms of internationalism. In fact it seems to be doing away with the familiar notions of self, other, difference and situs — to be here in the new orientation is to be everywhere. Its literary antecedents may be traced to Goethe, though I would still argue that "Weltliteratur" was a bourgeois progressive concept. Of course the piece of Chinese fiction that had led him to that historic pronouncement, or the classical Indian play that had flashed to him to be a unique combination of the earthly and heavenly, or the great Persian Hafeez whose poetry had inspired his *West-Östlicher Divan* was a gift of the Enlightenment not untouched of the latter's self-righteous attitude to the other, though not perhaps entirely moulded by it, for else the so-called Orientalists would all prove out to have been Joseph K's 'courtroom' audience, court officials in disguise humoring him into blasphemy. Anyway, if not Goethean "Welt-" then is this globalization Schillerian "Universal-," old wine in a new bottle?

Yet "Universalpoesie" was a more immediate product of the Enlightenment and has possibly a more chequered track record — at least it is the hegemony hidden within "Universalpoesie" that came to be the target of cultural relativism in the wake of field anthropology. And no one would deny that literary value is now largely anti-universalist, though there is a continuous bid for power on the part of some languages over the others. In interliterary relations we have become wary of the notion of influence not simply because of its relative amorphousness as a poetic category but because of the high-low differentiation that it often presupposes.

Reception, on the other hand, has been the order of the day, for that does not undermine the so-called low against the so-called high, no matter how 'high'-strung the international book trade may be. A British or North American English Language publisher's Africa may be a matter of the platter, yet faraway reception may winnow away the silver husk and get to the golden grain.

Now the question is, is this reception going to wither away in the new order and turn into a simultaneous appropriation everywhere as also perhaps into a matter of pure aesthetic? In other words, are cultural specificities on which interliterary reception is in part based going to be liquidated rendering all cultures similar, or is reception going to be altogether dissociated from culture and made a laboratory affair? The former would mean a denial of history and the latter a coercion, for cultures build up from below and over time, and literary consumers are not simple electronic counters, no matter how sophisticated, to record signals emitted by literary texts. Besides, texts too are not semiotic constructs of single signification set out in all directions. A swan is still a non-migratory water bird to me in India, a symbol at one level of ideal unruffledness, unlike "le cygne" à la Mallarmé. Can it be overnight shed of its specificity, Indian or Mallarméan? And again, what semiosis will it attain to answer the same simultaneous reception everywhere, a water bird of a certain size, shape, color and habit, without reference to the climate?

I once read Umberto Eco on the semiotics of the blue jeans and immediately recognized that he was not speaking of my culture, for there the blue jeans first came, not as a symbol of social rebellion but of status and fashion, their prices ranging beyond the ordinary social rebel's reach. I am not saying that there has not been any shift in this semiosis; there has been, for cultures are never static ponds to breed the same fish forever. But there might have been some built-in globalization in the blue jeans industry that fed on an ever wider market. I know that I am laboring the obvious, but I am only trying to decode the newly raised globalization slogan.

Since I am sitting at the wrong end of the table in the world economic order today I would like to ask: in what way is it different? Does it mean a new world order, or is it only a new name for the old one? Pardon me, reader, if I happen to be speaking from my end of the table. If it were possible I would have tried to speak from somewhere above the table, but situs is as yet integral to speech. Cultural relativism has taught us to value diversities and surely diversities include those of situs too. The so-called 'universal' situs of the yesteryear has proved out to be a sleight of rhetoric.

I have said elsewhere how as a student I had the temerity to raise an issue with a redoubtable Classical scholar after his lecture on Homer by referring to the Mahābhārata and how he simply said that the Mahābhārata was a different matter altogether because it was so vast, so unmanageably vast. I recognize today that he was true to his situs no less than I was to mine. I also remember how at another time I exasperated a European scholar in search of a universal dictionary of literary terms by saying that his universal primarily meant Aristotle to Wolfgang Iser with a bit here and there from Arabic and Persian, Chinese and Japanese, and possibly classical Indian. Instead I proposed to him a dictionary of dictionaries gathered from various poetic-aesthetic traditions. I recognize now his difficulty, for he too had his situs, maybe without knowing it, which explained his universalist zeal.

At a colloquium three years ago in Germany a Bangladeshi student retorted sharply to an English Tagore translator's judgment in the name of a universal poetic by saying, "universal, whose universal?" The translator was addressing an international audience, but his situs was perhaps at work in delimiting that. This is not to question the value of his intercultural function as a translator, but that alone does not give a 'universal' authenticity to his judgment. We translate *into* not just translate *from*. And it is on this dialectic of 'from' and 'into,' of siti, that internationalism can thrive. Is globalization about to thwart that principle of internationalism?

Yet languages are many and howsoever may we try there is no immediate possibility of one world language. Esperanto is obviously a kind of underground, a movement that thrives on its smallness. But perhaps we should make a distinction between 'one world language' and 'a world language,' for there are languages, a few at least, that have a world-wide circulation. Besides, information technology presupposes a world language, unless of course we are veering towards either IPA communication or communication by display of objects à la Academician of Lagado through whom Swift made fun of all communication utopia. And if pure communication of either sort becomes the order of the day then we may come to sending messages next-door through national and international networks proving true that humorous story in my language where a newcomer to the city looking for the famous 'Round Pond' though standing by its very side and not recognizing it because of its square shape, the name 'Round' being a matter of tradition, is directed to the same place by a fun poking passerby by means of going round (a pun was intended in that) the length and breadth of the whole city.

Anyway, it could be that the world-wide circulation which a few languages are claiming is tantamount to globalization, in the sense that a text produced in any of them is immediately available everywhere. Maybe the text is simultaneously manufactured in many countries to minimize transmission, and with a computer worldnet in operation the quality of printing could be the same everywhere by a simple transmission of files. Besides multinationals being involved in quality control in the paper industry the imprint in country X may not look different from that in country Y.

But what is true of a world language may not be true of a language that does not have a world-wide circulation (my own, for instance). It is spoken in a part of India and in Bangladesh and in a small way in places both near and far where there is a community on sojourn or settled. It too may take a global proportion in the sense of simultaneous production and consumption of literary works; but surely this simultaneity is lilliputian against a veritable world language's Brobdingnag. And what happens in the case of languages that have a single location alone — are they not going to be altogether left out of globalization? I would not like to venture any speculation, but that may mean extinction.

This sounds quite dystopian; yet what would globalization be as a utopian proposition? Speculation may admit a kind of consortium where the members are not bound by allied interests alone but a common, 'global' concern, a kind of European Community galore bereft of its problematics. That would turn literary value as well into a consortium of literary tenets. If we take the analogy from Esperanto, the only world language in existence now, then it is likely that the global literary tenets will contain elements from various systems, taken not necessarily arbitrarily but perhaps by association. Of course the question will still remain, who does the choosing and what is the politics of this choice?

It would be presumptuous for me to comment on Esperanto which I do not know, but I can always speculate on the mechanics of literary value to be on a global scale. Looking at the world today and recognizing the relative, possibly willy nilly, ubiquity of the Aristotelian and post-Aristotelian poetic-aesthetic, it may not be too difficult a prolepsis. And yet the economic globalization is not probably going to be the hegemony of a few nations but of a synod of multinational companies run by master computers and irrespective of national origins. Are the global literary tenets going to be computer-determined common denominators of tenets belonging to participating systems? I am sure the issue is clumsily put and the emerging texts are rather confusing, but the distinction I am trying to make between internationalism and globalization is too serious to ignore. We often speak of a crisis in comparative literature. Is this a new crisis? How are we going to define our job now?

Yet cultures are resilient. They were not one day created, one made into many, they have grown up from roots. Even when they have been transplanted, they have begun by striking roots in the new place. No matter how unusual American English may sound in Britain, British English sounds equally outlandish in America. It may so happen that globalization will affect cultural differences only up to a point, beneath which they will retain their individuality. Rather than cultures going global, only their surface may do so — the result will be a limited sameness everywhere. Let me use an analogy from Indian history. Prakrits were the languages that were spoken in various parts of the North, but Sanskrit was the *lingua indica*, the language in which the elite would converse across the country. In fact the two words, 'Prakrta' and 'Samskrta,' contained this semiosis, one actual and the other purified. And this distinction was in part reflected in the Sanskrit theatre where the lower caste and women spoke Prakrit and the upper caste Sanskrit. If globalization only affects the 'Sanskritized' part of a culture its 'Prakritized' part will remain unchanged. It is there then, in the 'Prakritized' part of cultures, that we may be called to address our attention as comparatists.

Comparative literature in the globalized world may not stay above ground to do lip service to world literature in the wrong sense of the term. It may go underground to serve world literature in the true sense, that is, to gauge subterranean interliterariness. It may ordinarily seem that globalization will bring us happy days. But if we reckon right we have a tough time ahead. We will be touched by a lot of fanfare, but deep down the same streams will continue to flow. Our task will be to stay unperturbed by the fanfare above and dive under to reach the real streams. And since information is only a technology we can ride it instead of letting it ride us. Globalization can only be a new world hegemony, not a new world order. As comparatists committed to holding up cultural identities and assessing cultural interrelations we will be called to subvert that hegemony, of course in our own way of letters of which no hegemony can ever dispossess us.

Cultural Values in a Multicultural Perspective

Katinka Dijkstra
Florida State University

Cultural values — they bring about unity where there used to be variance division and strife

cultural values — they're something to cling to to take refuge behind.

Marjolein Dietzel

A couple of years ago, an American professor was staying at our home. Before starting to eat dinner, my husband took off his watch and put it next to his plate. Noticing this, the professor asked: "Is it a European custom to put your watch next to your plate before you have dinner?" First, we considered this remark to be funny, because taking off the watch was motivated by the fact that it was uncomfortable. Then, we realized that we as members of the European Union do not have a concept of a European culture. Apparently, the American professor, who travels through Europe each year, thought there was such a concept. In addition, he assumed this concept was different from American culture because otherwise he would not have asked his question.

Being Dutch but having resided in the United States for some time now, I have become more aware of my European side because Americans perceive me as European in the first place. The reason for their perception is presumably that those who have never been to the Netherlands do not have a concept of this country beyond tulips and windmills. At the same time, my impression of American culture has changed dramatically. Stereotypes existing among Europeans regarding Americans have vanished, such as the idea that most Americans are loud, ill-mannered, and overly self-confident. As to the American culture, it seems to comprise more different cultures the longer I live here.

This personal example illustrates a general phenomenon: the proximity of a culture has an effect on one's perception of it. Therefore, cultures should be brought closer to each other by studying them in a multicultural context. This thesis will guide my line of thought in this paper in which I address the following questions: Is there such a thing as the American culture? How can we study cultures?

Is there such a thing as American culture?

The literary scholar E. D. Hirsch states in his bestseller *Cultural Literacy: What every American needs to know* (1988) that human communities are founded upon specific shared information. Americans are different from Germans because each group possesses specifically different cultural knowledge (xv). Sharing a substantial amount of cultural knowledge is the key for effective and successful communication. In a pluralistic society as the United States, this implies a fundamental choice of perspective: the choice for the many, the integration of the diversity, instead of the one (96). Therefore, Hirsch proposes to teach mainstream cultural knowledge in schools and colleges because it is accessible to everyone who attends school.

However, there is a another side to this perspective. Minority cultures would challenge the conception that education is equally accessible to everyone. Additionally, they might not be interested in focusing on being educated in 'mainstream' cultural knowledge because they consider it to be dominated by white cultures and their cultural values. Involuntary minorities, people initially brought into the United States through slavery, conquest, or colonization (cf. Ogbu 1991) were incorporated into the American society against their will and withheld from education until after the Civil War. Some of these cultures try to establish their own cultural identity rather than melting into a general one.

The different perspectives have to do with the proximity of culture. For people being brought up and educated in one culture, their need for establishing its values and identity might suppress the urge to incorporate or show an interest in other cultures. The more members of a culture feel challenged, the stronger their need for establishing its identity. Despite efforts to integrate different cultures, the fact these days is that the pluralistic composition of

American society cannot be ignored or easily melted into a stew that is tasteful to everyone. What can be done, however, is to study American culture in its multicultural context and thereby acknowledge the social value of these different cultures.

I share the viewpoint of Fokkema and Ibsch (1992) that as scholars we can analyze and explain the cultural system but that we become members of the cultural system when we try to change it. However, a better understanding of the composition, values, and identities of different cultures will contribute to mutual understanding and perhaps to better communication between members of different cultures. In this way, the study of culture might give way to future changes.

The relevance of analyzing American culture in its multicultural context and in a broader perspective is that this approach might prove to be useful for the study of European culture. Despite the historical, social, geographical and linguistic differences in the establishment of American and European cultures, the opening up of the boundaries in the European countries and the flow of immigrants in those countries will result in a greater cultural resemblance of the two continents. Even though most Europeans have a better concept of their national cultures than a European one, gradually, as mobility for travel and work increases, such a concept might start to grow in the near future.

How can we study culture?

My first thesis is that the study of culture should be based upon observable cultural features, such as life style features and the social characteristics of its members. In my view, general theories of culture are often a burden for (empirical) research. In the first place, these theories are too static too follow changes in society. Few theories on culture have taken pluriformity, ethnicity, and demographic changes into account. These dimensions in culture are crucial for a complete understanding of what culture and cultural values entail. In the second place, theories of culture generally are too abstract to give way to testable hypotheses on culture. How are we supposed to apply a notion as 'cultural capital' used by the sociologist Bourdieu? In the third place, explanations for participation in culture might hold true for some cultures and not for others. The "public motive" (cf. Fokkema and Ibsch 1992), i.e., the motive to distinguish oneself from others in order to gain status, for instance through participation in (elitist) cultural events, might pertain to the 'high society' visiting the Opera in Vienna but be irrelevant for cultures that try to survive economic problems. Therefore, in my proposal for the study of culture I will concentrate on observable cultural features from different cultures.

Pluriformity in cultures means that a number of cultures exist alongside each other in one society. These cultures can be:

— ethnically based such as the ones by African-Americans or Native-Americans;
— gender and/or politics based, such as feminist, or conservative culture;
— geographical, such as North and South (not only recognizable as different cultures in the United States, but also in Belgium, the Netherlands, Germany, and Italy, to name only a few);
— professional, such as artists and business people;
— age-related, such as teenagers, or senior citizens.

In most cases, people belong to several cultures because of their gender, race, and age. However, it depends on the relative importance of one of these features for members of a culture to become active participants in it.

Life styles are observable cultural expressions that are characteristic for a culture. For instance, youth culture is characterized by dress codes and specific musical preferences. For other cultures, such as Muslim cultures, the way of clothing is the result of religious beliefs in which the female body has to be covered. Studies by Bourdieu and Ganzeboom have shown how life styles represent different cultures. Participation in relatively inaccessible cultural events is representative for highly educated, culturally competent, progressive cultures (cultural elite); a chic, conservative way of living represents financially secure cultures (economic elite).

Life styles and social characteristics of members in a culture illustrate who belong to it and how they behave. They are founded upon specific shared information. My second thesis is that the study of culture should focus not only on the kind of knowledge that is shared among members of a culture but connect this knowledge to the situations in which they are acquired and practised. In my opinion, E.D. Hirsch's proposal to become culturally literate through learning a vocabulary that is used by the cultural elite ignores the fact that cultural literacy depends on the culture people are part of and on the situations in which it is acquired.

School is the most obvious situation in which literacy is acquired and practised. Here, children learn how to read and write. Generally, cultural values are being taught through literature, history, and geography classes. Another situation in which cultural literacy is acquired, is home. Many studies have stressed the importance of parental stimulation for the acquisition of cultural knowledge. For instance, children who have been stimulated to read at a young age, continue to do so when they are adults. A third situation that contributes to the acquisition of cultural literacy, is the peer group. Similar interests among peers and a positive attitude towards learning stimulate the growth of knowledge.

If we specify the situations in which cultural literacy is acquired for different cultures, we might be able to explain some of the differences in cultural literacy among these groups. In the US, voluntary minorities do better at becoming literate than involuntary minorities because the various situations in which literacy is acquired coincide. Generally, the collective orientation of voluntary minorities, including family and friends, is to get a good education in order to be successful in life. Success in school and business in the Asian culture is a common example of how school, parents and peers can affect a student's performance positively when they all have the same goal. However, for involuntary minorities in the US, the story is different. Studies have shown that from an African-American perspective peer pressure discourages individual school success. It is considered to be 'not cool,' and 'white' to perform well in school. Those who wish to succeed academically, are subject to peer criticism and isolation (cf. Ogbu 1991). An explanation for this phenomenon could be: values of a culture, in this case African-American youth culture, do not support literacy even though the situation at home or at school do just that.

In general, cultural values are the unifying factor in a culture. That is why the problem of cultural illiteracy becomes such a difficult one in cultures where there are opposing attitudes towards literacy. It challenges the unity of a culture and the knowledge its members share. Therefore, the analysis of cultural values should focus on their unifying elements. Some ways of analysis could be: interviewing members of a culture about their values and analyzing the contents of published materials belonging to that culture. The cultural values of religious cultures, for instance, are founded upon (interpretations of) a book, such as the Bible, Torah, or Koran. Interviews with members of a culture could reveal how their cultural values relate to each other. The more overlap there is, the closer their relations could be. My third thesis is that the unity of a culture depends on the extent to which its members share the same cultural values.

Now, more than ever, in our pluriform and rapidly changing society, we should deal with the issue of cultural values and put it in a global perspective. It is the merit of Douwe Fokkema that as one of the few theorists he has taken current changes in society into account (cf. Fokkema and Ibsch 1992). He has clearly illustrated the dilemma Europeans are faced with these days: do they feel European in the first place or do they feel they first belong to a national culture? Whatever the decision, it will have major consequences for cultural life. 'Choosing' the European side will broaden the view on other cultures. A 'European cultural literacy' shared among people who feel European might arise. However, the consequence may be that people will feel less involved in national or regional cultures, which might lead to a disintegration of these cultures and loss of cultural values and traditions.

As I see it, the choice is not one between two cultures but one for the — unavoidable — development towards a more global perspective in a multicultural environment. As long as we are aware of the fact that the proximity of a culture affects people's perception of it, we could improve communication between cultures by keeping an open mind for them. Perhaps, and only then, Europeans will be considered to be a unity one day, and Americans will be considered to be modest and sophisticated by every European.

References

Fokkema, Douwe W., and Elrud Ibsch. 1992. *Literatuurwetenschap en Cultuuroverdracht*. Muiderberg: Coutinho.
Hirsch, E. D. Jr. 1988. *Cultural Literacy: What Every American Needs to Know*. New York: Vintage Books.
Ogbu, John U. 1991. "Minority Status and Literacy in a Comparative Perspective." In Stephen R. Graubard (ed), *Literacy: An Overview by 14 Experts*. New York: The Noonday Press.

Polyfunctional or Monofunctional Language?

Lubomír Doležel
University of Toronto

All cognitive activities, including the study of literature, depend critically on language. For this reason, a philosophy of language, whether explicitly formulated or implicit in the researcher's beliefs, is central to any epistemology. The recognition of the fundamental role of language in human cognition is a feature of twentieth-century intellectual culture and is shared by its two most prominent trends, Structuralism and Poststructuralism. However, Structuralism and Poststructuralism diverge radically in their views on the nature of language, its semiotic capacity and its functioning. This contrast is known to us primarily from the controversy over referentiality — whether the linguistic signs do or do not relate to a world. Yet, in my opinion, the issue of referentiality is part and parcel of a more general problem in the philosophy of language — whether language is polyfunctional or monofunctional.

The idea of language as a polyfunctional semiotic medium is derived from its participation in human private and social acting. To live means first and foremost to act, to do something, either as an individual, or as a member of a social group. The relationship between individual and social acting can be contemplated from both positions: in models of social acting we theorize how the individual's actions and interactions — in cooperation or in conflict — contribute to more or less organized social acting; in models of individual acting we take account of supra-individual, social factors or restrictions imposed on acting persons. The dialectic of individual and social acting is a challenge to all human and social sciences. Their theories differ primarily in how they balance individual and social acting, whether they emphasize the one or the other term of the dialectic.

The link of language communication with human acting has been recognized at least since Plato. In the twentieth century, Karl Bühler, Charles Morris, J.L. Austin and many other philosophers, semioticians and linguists have shown that verbal communication is inextricably tied to non-verbal acting and interacting. Austin made us aware that speech acts can be equivalent in their effect to non-verbal actions: they bring about changes in the world. A felicitous performative speech act turns a private into a general, a provincial teacher into a prime minister, a committed bachelor into a husband, a single woman into a wife.

It can easily be observed that both individual and social acting are highly diversified, pursuing many different goals or purposes. Humans are involved in economic and political activities, they make and enforce laws, they engage in mathematics, science and philosophy, they create films and TV programmes, they stage theatrical performances, they write poems, novels and dramas, they act as parents, children, lovers, friends and so on. From the viewpoint of communication, individual and social acting appear as a network of channels which imposes different conditions on communication, requires different communication strategies. In adapting to these conditions, language has developed a multitude of functions. The argument for the polyfunctionality of language is simple: if there is a fundamental difference between, say, science and poetry, then there must be a fundamental difference between scientific and poetic language. If poetic language needs, indeed, thrives on constructiveness (or self-referentiality), maximal deautomatization and lack of truth-valuation, scientific language needs just the opposite — conventional reference, stabilized terms and truth-valuation. Arguing for a plurality of language functions does not imply the rejection of a unifying linguistic system, of the force of language norms and of the communal (social) character of a national language. Language without *langue* is an inoperative fiction.

Poststructuralist philosophy of language does not accept the polyfunctionality of language; language is seen as monofunctional. But to understand the Poststructuralist position properly and in all its consequences, we have to recognize that it does not assign to language a universal, neutral function, but a specific, i.e., poetic function. More precisely, in Poststructuralist philosophy, language for all channels of communication is assumed to have properties which the polyfunctional conception reserves for poetic language.

In the philosophy of Nelson Goodman, it is the constructional character of poetic language that is extended to all language use: "There are words without worlds, but no worlds without words." It is tempting to ask where the "words without worlds" exist, but that question is not relevant in this context. What is relevant is that in Goodman's and cognate philosophies of language, language is denied the reference function — pointing to an independently existing world — and is restricted to the poetic (poietic) function — constructing, creating language-dependent worlds. The influential philosopher Jacques Derrida ascribes to language the poetic properties of self-referentiality and permanent deautomatization. Being trapped in the infinite regress of *différance*, all discourse becomes "generalized poetic discourse." In such a discourse, it is impossible to fix reference and define truth-conditions.

Just as the pitiable American politician could not walk and chew gum at the same time, so Goodman, Derrida and Co. cannot imagine that in certain domains of use language is constructive, world-producing, but in others it is referential, world-describing. It is radically counterintuitive to claim that we never speak or write about the world, that we never describe what happened, what we saw, what we are trying to understand. On the other hand, it would be absurd to claim that language cannot lie, cannot posit counterfactuals, or, to put it in general terms, cannot construct alternate, possible worlds. The existence of two basic language functions, one referential (descriptive), the other constructive (creative), is a feature of language, which makes it flexible to serve the needs of diverse human activities.

In the Poststructuralist's world all communicative activities have to be conducted in a language which is essentially poetic. We are expected to believe that humankind is unique among communicating species in that its fundamental semiotic medium is a language without reference, a language which does not allow us to ask what is true and what is false, who is innocent and who is guilty. It is difficult to see how a modern society could function and survive with such a language.

At first sight, the Poststructuralist transformation of all language into poetic language might look like a triumph of poetry. But, in the final account, this privileging of poetic language turns against poetry. If Hegel or Freud or Einstein 'are to be read' in the same way as Mallarmé or Kafka, then literature (Dichtung) loses its *raison d'être*. Blurring the distinction between poetic and non-poetic discourse means not only that we have to accept a claim that

Einstein's papers on relativity theory are poetry, but also a claim that Joyce's *Ulysses* is a treatise in physics.

At this point, we gain a new perspective on the contrast between Structuralism and Poststructuralism. The contrast is not in the philosophy of language itself, but in the way the opposite philosophies are construed and how they face human praxis. Structuralism was a stage in the tradition of *empirical* theorizing. Its theory of language functions was an attempt to explain the evident diversity of communication in human praxis. It is legitimate to ask of an empirical theory of communication, whether it is compatible with the sociology of social systems, with the psychology of intention and motivation, with praxeological research, or with mathematical communication theory. In contrast, Poststructuralism is a stage in *speculative* theorizing; its philosophy of language is derived from general ontological assumptions of idealistic philosophy and/or radical epistemological skepticism. Speculative theorizing is scholastic in that it proceeds on a purely verbal level. The speculative philosopher is able to construe any statement, especially if his language is allowed to be figurative, ambiguous, indeterminate. "The world is a human construct," "history is a text," "communication is impossible," such and similar slogans (as well as their opposites!) can be produced *en masse*, if they do not have to be confronted with human praxis. In speculative theorizing, philosophical 'explanation' supersedes human praxis.

Because of its speculative character, the Poststructuralist philosophy of language can be and has been linked to German aesthetic idealism, especially to its claim that all language in action is poetic. It is instructive to note that this claim was ignored outside the community of idealistic philosophers and poetry enthusiasts; economic, cognitive, legal and all other practical human activities continued using their non-poetic languages. The neo-Romanticism of Poststructuralism is faced with the same challenge: will its conception of language remain restricted to the community of idealistic philosophers and poetry enthusiasts, or will it force contemporary science, economy, law, philosophy, historiography, etc. to abandon their specific languages and use poetic language instead?

To conclude: Poststructuralism is not so much a development or replacement of Structuralism, but rather a switch to a different level, to a different mode of theorizing. Structuralism and Postructuralism replay the persistent opposition between speculative thinking and empirical theory that has characterized the history of epistemology since Plato and Aristotle. No wonder that in those fields where Postructuralism prevailed, we observe a pause in empirical research and theory testing. But that does not mean that the principles of empirical research and testing of theories by human praxis have been abandoned. The two modes of epistemology have been present in the pre-Structuralist, Structuralist and Poststructuralist eras and will remain with us in the coming post-Poststructuralist time. What superficially appears as a change of epistemological paradigms is, on closer inspection, just a shift in the power of persuasion and influence.

Canons in Linguistic, Stylistic and Literary Competence

Nils Erik Enkvist
Societas Scientiarum Fennica, Helsinki

To be understood, and even appreciated, a piece of discourse need not be well formed in the schoolmaster's sense. In impromptu speech — in several respects the most fundamental mode of linguistic communication — all of us mess up our syntax with false starts, anacolutha, hesitations, corrections, insertions, slips of the tongue, spoonerisms and other 'performance errors.' Actually we should beware of calling them 'errors.' Obviously languages are structured to tolerate such latitudes of expression. If speech had to be as faultless as a bank account ought to be, speaking would be risky and the world, for better or for worse, a quieter place than it is. Also, 'deviant' language can be an important source of literary effect.

Fortunately, our conversation partners usually anticipate what we say, or, rather, what they think we ought to have said. One reason why they can do so is that they are used to language in context. They have stored a set of usages relating them to a range of specific situations. They project past experience into present expectations, often to an extent where they do not even notice possible oddities and shortcomings in sentence structure. The various redundancies built into language at various levels also help us to interpret impromptu speech. Altogether, in oral communication, fluency is often more important than syntactic correctness, and fluency is partly the result of skilful use of hesitation and correction devices, and indeed of 'aberrant' syntax in the form of false starts, repetitions, anacolutha and the like. We should not lament 'performance errors.' We should rather congratulate ourselves for having at our disposal libertarian devices that ease the stresses of impromptu communication, and conversation partners experienced enough to divine what we mean. And we should rejoice in the potential interest of 'deviant' language, in poetry and in advertising, for instance.

So, the interpretability of a piece of discourse cannot be defined in terms of syntactic well-formedness alone. A more realistic approach is to say that a piece of discourse is interpretable to those who can, under prevailing circumstances, surround it with a scenario in which it makes sense (Enkvist 1990). And this in turn is a process which must be based on experience of language in a range of situations, and thus on canons in the wide sense of the term.

All linguistic competence beyond a basic smattering of tourist phrases must contain a component reckoning with the fact that, in different situations, people speak and write differently. Knowing a language in fact involves competence in a large number of sublanguages. Of language varieties or lects, styles and registers are the ones that correlate with situational contexts (Enkvist 1973). Learning a language involves responding to, and, with time, reproducing characteristics of specific situation-bound styles. When we hear an utterance we must be capable of judging whether it would be likely to occur in a sermon or on the barrack square. And when we speak or write, we should adjust our language to the situation including relations between sender and receptor. We should not behave like Gladstone, who irritated Queen Victoria by addressing her like a public meeting. We must not swear in church, as the saying goes, however natural swearing might be to us in certain other environments.

However, nobody is born with a command of the range of situationally conditioned language varieties that characterize the linguistic competence of an adult. We begin by gurgling at our parents, we go on to nursery language, we gradually learn to avoid taboos and, in some enviable cultures, to be polite to our elders. And in school and university we learn to appreciate and to use a number of other registers: those of a widening range of classroom subjects, of sports, of bawdy, of insults, of courting and love-making, of formal lecturing and of informal seminars. Widening one's experience of situationally conditioned styles and registers is a lifelong business. There is, of course, a difference between a native speaker and a foreign-language learner in that the latter usually operates fewer styles and may gain his experience through a graded and staged process: an adult starting on a foreign language does not usually begin from nursery language and pre-school children's idioms. But in principle, natives and foreign learners learn styles and registers in the same way, namely by associating certain types of language with certain ranges of situations, and vice versa. And this is where canons come in. In a wide linguistic sense, a canon is definable as a body of text or discourse which satisfies a definite set of linguistic and social criteria. Prominent among these criteria is a successful linkage between a specific sublanguage and a specific range of situations. This in turn leads those who define canons to look for parameters of situational contexts, of which a number have been proposed by students of language, style, and literature.

In its literary sense, a 'canon' suggests a body of text which is regarded as culturally precious and therefore worth preserving and teaching. There are groups, Bible scholars for instance, who use 'canon' more narrowly in ways of their own. In traditional canons of literature, cultural value has often, though far from always, involved aesthetic excellence. So-called 'minor writers' have been included in many canons because they often mirror their *Zeitgeist* more faithfully than their less time-bound superiors. And traditional canons of American literature differ from British ones in including writers such as Cotton Mather and Jonathan Edwards, not because England was devoid of sermonizers but because they reflect the development of American thought and institutions. Even within the same national canon, writers have their ups and downs: John Donne's canonical stature is a case in point.

We should, however, note that in the general linguistic sense, a literary canon is just one of the types of textual corpora which have been stored and ordered into a matrix so that they can be used as a frame for placing new texts. What makes literary canons in principle different from the style-and-register canons of other modes and genres of language is the choices of criteria for inclusion. The decisive contextual parameters in the definition of literary canons are cultural values, seen in terms of time, place, author and other features of textual provenance, as well as the effect and appreciation of the text.

Once we admit that literary canons are one of the kinds of corpora providing a frame for a diagnosis of discourse, an aggressive denial of the existence of a canon in literature becomes nonsensical, or at least misleading. All bodies of text which satisfy certain definite criteria are in fact potential canons, and canons can form a hierarchy of major canons and subcanons. There can be canons of black literature or of gay drama just as well as there have been canons of Elizabethan plays or of nineteenth-century novels or of the Great Writers and Great Books.

In this view, then, all criticism involves a comparison of a text with a canon or elements thereof, either one the critic has experienced and carries with him in his memory, or one which he is actively creating by manipulating canons from his memory, for comparison with the text. Presumably most critics operate with a synthesis of creation and memory when they compare a text with what it might have been.

If I am right, we should not waste time in discussing whether canons exist and are necessary. Whatever we think and do, they are with us because they have been built into language. What we should discuss are the premises and criteria speaking for the conscious or subconscious compilation, use, and propagation of one specific canon rather than another.

A canon can change, grow or shrink with the body of textual experience we include in it. Where the choice of canons takes place deliberately and with explicit criteria — as in the teaching of languages and literatures — both canons and their selection for teaching may change, and indeed cannot help changing, with revaluations of the criteria on which they are based. But dissatisfaction with 'the canon' (meaning the currently dominant, and often conservative, set of norms) can only mean rejection of some old canon or canons, rather than an abolition of all canons.

Perhaps I should be more explicit on a point in favor of canons which has already been hinted at above. Let me repeat that all impressions of the quality of discourse, not least literary discourse, are based on tacit or explicit comparison. Such impressions are inevitable parts of basic discourse comprehension: we always evaluate whatever discourse we hear or read. Now if we are to pinpoint the characteristics of literary innovations, we must be familiar with the classical canon to see what is noteworthy in the moderns. And the other way round: we constantly revaluate classics against the background of what happened since their day.

Those opposing canons are aware of a notorious classroom risk, namely the allocation of excellence by authority and tradition rather than by a response of one's own. The conservative weight of an establishment appears in many ways, one of which is the use of established anthologies, textbooks and reading lists. But if our students are to feel in their bones why Shakespeare, for instance, should still rank as a great author, they should have considerable experience of other writers, pre-Shakespearean, Elizabethan, post-Shakespearean, and contemporary. In other words: they need a canon. Those students who cherish a recent, perhaps relatively little-known and tradition-breaking writer, also need some sort of tacit or explicit canon with parameters from language, literature, society and life, if they are to understand and argue their own preferences. So much the better if they can relate their gut feelings to something objectively describable in an actual corpus of text (cf. Enkvist 1995).

References

Enkvist, Nils Erik. 1973. *Linguistic Stylistics*. The Hague: Mouton.
— .1990. "On the Interpretability of Texts in General and of Literary Texts in Particular." In Roger Sell (ed), *Literary Pragmatics*. London and New York: Routledge, 1-25.
— .1995. "The Epistemic Gap in Linguistic Stylistics." In Werner Winter (ed), *On Languages and Language*. Presidential Addresses of the 1991 Meeting of the Societas Linguistica Europaea. Trends in Linguistics. Studies and Monographs 78. Berlin and New York: Mouton de Gruyter, 109-126.

Historical Referentiality as a Condition of Literary History

Gerald Gillespie
Stanford University

The following observations are a long footnote pendant to Douwe Fokkema's survey of "Questions épistémologiques" in 1989. His essay is unsurpassed as a meticulous argument that we can work toward a clearer definition of "scientific rules" for analyzing literary expression in the context of onflowing semiotic systems. Although Fokkema feels quite positive about elaborating certain kinds of empirical research amenable to control, he is relatively less sanguine about dealing with "le domaine de l'histoire littéraire où la possibilité de la vérification empirique est limitée ou même inexistante" (329). I would suggest that literary history should not be wholly written off as impervious in epistemological terms, on the grounds Aldo Scaglione advances: The predicament of literary history — that "a comprehensive understanding of any phenomenon cannot prescind from all its multiple dimensions" — "characterizes not only every scientific field but even the question of science as a whole, as shown by the ongoing arguments concerning the correct way to analyze, understand, and explain the history of science itself" (1988: 160-61).

What occurs when well-read native informants in cultures that have already developed a strong composite tradition of literary history renew, extend, or modify it? Such a readership 'shares' a repertory that includes some works distanced in cultural time or space. A major condition that colors the act of writing 'serious' literary history is the supposition that, even if some imaginative works may present us with distant or radically fictive realities, we read such works in relationship to a world or worlds relatively better known to us. Collectively, groups of readers recognize as their contemporaries those who in significant measure experience a somewhat similar temporal and/or geocultural nearness to some and distance from other works. The mean distance from literary texts that is normative at a particular juncture in a literary system will lie somewhere between what experts and ordinary readers think is readily accessible.

Let us stipulate that this sense of 'distance' is relative to all the modifying factors that obtain in the complete communicative framework and that the framework is not static but shifting. Specialized readers, mainly literary critics and historians, direct our attention to works conceived in or for other times or places. Their contrastive specialist knowledge, as David Perkins argues, can be wielded as a potent instrument for critical assessment of any "present" cultural situation and stance (1992: 186). For this reason alone, general history must count among the important discursive practices which enable a richer literary history. The tie is nowise nullified by the obvious fact that, in some periods and kinds of literature, fictional narrative and literary history, and even general history, show extensive overlappings. For example, to a considerable degree, novels like Huysmans' *À Rebours*, Rilke's *Die Aufzeichnungen des Malte Laurids Brigge*, and Joyce's *Ulysses* are concatenations of philosophical meditations and cultural essays, openly strung as many-splendored beads along fictional wires. The competent reader senses that the details are related to an enormous referentiality reaching back in time and out into other cultural and discursive realms (for instance, the Middle Ages, the natural and the human sciences, etc.). Yet we recognize that 'standard' kinds of literary history constitute a separate generic set from those fictions which massively appropriate literary history among their materials.

Competent Western readers have long since absorbed from major fiction-writers like Laurence Sterne all the complaints that are raised against literature and history (for instance, literature and history operate with arbitrary categories based on cultural prejudices and contingencies, cannot be complete or objective, are just collections of speech acts, etc.). Thus these ideas, too, have become distinctive elements in the arsenal of motifs registered and weighed by literary history. Acknowledgment of a marketplace of traded values and ingrained habits does not overpower, rather it enhances, the need and purpose of having a supple analytic instrumentarium that helps sort out the governing factors and the fictional repertory.

In the long haul and on balance, extreme selectivity, misprisions, and knowledge gaps do not obliterate the effective habits of competent historians. Just as historians will appreciate historical consciousness in creative artists and will seek to place it in appropriate frameworks, so they will deal in general with the referentiality found in the language and in the forms of creative imagination. Theoreticians like Hayden White may assert that, because all modes of discourse have in common a rhetorical structuring that relates them as created narratives, types of history (including that of science) pertain to the genres of fiction. But real-life reading experience teaches us that the existence of gradations of fictionality or of structural similarities does not mean that reading communities cannot distinguish between works that on balance are constructed primarily as histories or primarily as fictions.

Cervantes has illustrated the point with Quixote's confusion of such distinctions in numerous episodes such as his attack on a stage villain who is about to abduct a damsel in the puppet theater. Nor does it matter that some human beings deliberately manipulate the semiotic conventions to deceive us or to fight back against deceivers, a fact De Laclos explores in *Les liaisons dangereuses* and Poe in "The Purloined Letter." Counter-efforts by critics to expose falsifications, much like those manoeuvres by characters inside a work of fiction, can and do contribute to re-establishing the larger, complex communicative siuation. This Cervantes illustrates with Sancho's progressive education in the subtleties of interpretation as he attempts to cope with the mind and behavior of Quixote. It is on the basis of the presumption that fictions can be contrasted or checked against a known body of materials that readers in any age assert that the representation of certain persons, acts, and circumstances in imaginative texts is highly fictionalized, or relatively less fictionalized.

Obviously, unusual cases may crop up where no such self-evident, adequate historical corpus or virtually none exists, and great uncertainty may prevail. There may then be doubt over whether some elements in a work refer to real persons and cultures, and this will affect literary history, too. This was the case with respect to many elements of Homer's *Iliad* and *Odyssey*, until Schliemann's excavations of Troy and Mycene gave an archaeological foundation for a myriad of specific details. Many nineteenth-century Positivistic critics found it hard to believe that a single (blind!) author could have composed works so spiced with materials from yet earlier times than Homer's reputed century and they were suspicious of the names of things not known from other records — until these very things were dug out of the tumulus of Troy! Today it is common knowledge Joyce aspired to make *Ulysses* shadow Homer's *Odyssey* partly in the fancy that, just as scholars had reconstructed the lost pre-Hellenic world and Troy itself from Homer, a future age digging around in Irish ruins could reconstitute the Dublin of 1904 out of his novel, even though his pictured world might well seem 'unreal' to later scholars.

Internal clues in texts often reveal degrees of fictionality and historicity. Individually and collectively, we discern these internal clues because they are derivative largely from a repertory and relate to a particular culture or set of closely related cultures. Without belief in some referential capacity of literature and of history, however limited, we could not make finer distinctions of such categories as 'agitprop' or 'fantasy' or 'science fiction.' The commonsensical approach can be highlighted by looking at actual instances of literary falsification of history. I shall pass over here the weaker sort of falsification — when a general prejudice or ideology programmatically foreshortens the picture of actual life, but historians who are not materially or spiritually beholden to the political rulers quite easily expose the distortions. An example would be the debunking of sanitized versions of Soviet life in so-called 'Socialist Realism,' when literary historians trained in the European critical tradition subjected the evidence to the simplest tests and saw that Socialist Realism had little to do with realism and more with state-sponsored romance. Instead, I shall consider a stronger sort of falsification, when a notable writer deliberately recasts historical materials that are fairly well-established.

This is certainly the case in Schiller's play *Don Carlos*; and Verdi expands the distortion in his opera based thereon. Thus it came about that the reinforced Schillerian falsification of the character and political ideas of the protagonist Don Carlos shown by Schiller and Verdi tended to block out awareness of the historical account even for relatively competent readers at the start of the twentieth century. For my argument it does not matter that the widespread misprision of Don Carlos' 'actual' role has been far more influential *on* the shaping of history (by helping to promote interest in Schiller's libertarian values among the European public) than the historians' 'accurate' version would have been. What counts here is that in writing a relatively detailed history of the fortunes of Schiller's play and noting echoes of it in other works of imaginative literature, no literary historian jealous of his or her reputation would make the claim that Don Juan, son of Philip II of Spain, was endowed with the key heroic attributes which Schiller assigned to him just before the French Revolution. The literary historian may with right place the play in the generic stream of German Classicism and Romanticism and in many other contexts, but he or she cannot in good faith ignore that Schiller bent the historical record to suit his own libertarian purpose. Today even operagoers ordinarily find a mention of the different 'real' historical personage in the playbill. This corrective acknowledgment is a product of the gradual self-adjustment of the literary system whereby competent readers reaffirm the existence of a historical referentiality with which literary referentiality is associated, even though in many instances imaginative and/or propagandistic works tell (historical) 'lies.' Our desire to acquire accurate knowledge about significant 'lies' and to bind supposedly powerful 'meta-narratives' is today one of the cornerstones of historical referentiality.

The Postmodern notions that writers/critics should actively engage with history and alter its terms, that academic researchers and artists should effectively terminate (the tyranny of) literary history and create in an immediate present, indirectly acknowledge the existence of a referentiality that seems an obstacle to the contemporary exercise of interpretive will. The psychodynamics of this drive is nothing new, and as Bloom (1973) has shown poets and critics will use any and every strategy to fight for a place in the sun. The Postmodern turn was to be expected after so many great Modernists boldly and effectively exhibited the insides of the semiotic creature and its confabulatory tricks to the complicitous twentieth-century readership. In essence, Postmodern revisionists accuse the Modernists of doing that to which the Modernists have already explicitly confessed. This turn permits the Postmodern critic to hold onto the literary system, the only thing available, while pretending to alter it radically, even to end it. Not surprisingly, one of the most frequently discussed Postmodern 'paradoxes' — now already enshrined in literary history — arises from a programmatic desire to overcome history at large and literary history with it. We are invited to believe we are passing out of (Western codifications of) history in general, but we cannot relate to such a happening without awareness of history. Although such referentiality is sometimes constituted by deliberate acts of silence, these signal (as if in an unconsciously post-Symbolist vein) the existence-in-absence of what is being ignored or refused.

References

Bloom, Harold. 1973. *The Anxiety of Influence: A Theory of Poetry*. London: Oxford University Press.
Fokkema, Douwe. 1989. "Questions épistémologiques." In Marc Angenot, Jean Bessière, Douwe Fokkema, and Eva Kushner (eds), *Théorie littéraire*. Paris: Presses Universitaires de France, 325-351.
Perkins, David. 1992. *Is Literary History Possible?* Baltimore: Johns Hopkins University Press.
Scaglione, Aldo. 1988. "Comparative Literature as Cultural History: The Educational and Social Background of Renaissance Literature." In Clayton Koelb and Susan Noakes (eds), *The Comparative Perspective on Literature: Approaches to Theory and Practice*. Ithaca: Cornell University Press, 147-161.
White, H. V. 1978. *The Tropics of Discourse: Essays in Cultural Criticism*. Baltimore: Johns Hopkins University Press.

The Parnassus of the Twenty-First Century Turns into a K2

Frank de Glas
Utrecht University

In literary studies over the past few decades a great deal has been written and said about the process of literary canon formation, with particular attention paid to the dynamic character of this process. Old reputations fade away, new reputations establish themselves. As the ranks of older generations of writers are thinned, new ones take their place downstage. Over the years, moreover, there is a rigorous selection process at work: of the many hundreds, even thousands of fiction authors in any given language area who publish a first novel, only a small list of names will survive. This will be the select group of writers whose work will be recognized by future generations, whose names will enter the anthologies and whose work will remain in print.

A crucial condition for this process to continue is the existence of a dynamic *République des Lettres*, which depends not only on the constant generation of creative talents, but also on specific social and economic conditions. It is not surprising, therefore, that in recent years more attention has been paid to the healthy functioning of both production and distribution machinery for the (literary) fiction book as a condition for the smooth development of the work of new generations of writers.

Another important condition for the building of new literary *oeuvres* and for the establishment of emergent literary reputations is the accessibility of the *République des Lettres*. On the one hand, this means that existing publishing houses must be open to young authors, to new artistic opinions and experiments, while on the other hand newly formed houses should be able to enter the literary market and to present younger generations of writers who may have been denied access to the lists of the established houses. Both the old and the new houses have to be able and willing to take the risk to invest in new authors. This risk especially occurs in issuing first novels of new unknown writers. When publishing a first novel, it is still unclear to a house whether the writer in question is likely to produce subsequent manuscripts and whether a reading public for his/her work can be found. All publishers of literary fiction therefore apply the technique of so called internal subsidy, i.e., the best-selling titles of the list enable them to earn the money to publish other, more risky manuscripts, for example those offered by young, unknown authors. As a rule of thumb it is reckoned that less than half the titles published cover their costs (Balkin 1994: 57), while only a small percentage turn into real best-sellers. The problem for the publisher, however, is that no one can predict which titles these will be. In the case of many past writers who gradually built up a solid reputation, it took several years, even decades before their publishers received material compensation for their confidence in these writers and for the investments they had made by publishing their early works (Röhring 1992: 176).

As things are at the moment, it seems that in most developed countries the *République des Lettres* is a relatively open system, where at regular intervals new literary generations, movements and opinions can emerge and find their way onto the literary market. In France, Jean-Marie Bouvaist did some empirical research into the opportunities for new publishers to enter the literary publishing scene in the seventies and eighties (Bouvaist 1991: 298-316). Despite the somewhat unstable trends in this process of renewal, and in spite of the limited book production of these new imprints compared with the overall book market, Bouvaist's findings showed that there was still room for them. With regard to the openness of already existing publishing houses, young writers seem to have substantial access to the lists. Publishing houses indeed feel that they must be alert to the constant need to renew and rejuvenate their lists: that if they cannot tap new sources of talent, their lists will dry up on them, and therefore they put up with the economic risks that this process of renewal implies.

Yet there are indications of a change in the accessibility of the literary market, a change that will make the climb to Parnassus considerably steeper for the coming generations of writers. In the last few years we have seen a number of mergers and take-overs in the publishing business. This has not only concentrated a number of literary fiction publishers under one roof, but has also placed literary fiction imprints within larger conglomerates that have previously concentrated on the production of either non-fiction books, text books, newspapers and magazines, commercial television or on fully different economic activities.

Meanwhile, in many developed countries, important changes have occurred in the distribution of books, including works of literary fiction. The rentability of the 'classical' bookshop with its wide range of titles on the shelves is decreasing (Cahart 1987: 91). Not only the rents in the shopping complexes are going up, but also salary costs and distribution costs. In the sixties and seventies, public authorities backed the publishing business by buying books for public libraries on a large scale in many countries. In some countries with a longer tradition of state intervention in the social and cultural area, specific aid to literary writers and publishers was added to this support, especially if they formed small-scale language regions that needed additional protection (Danielsen 1995). In the eighties and nineties however, there has been an international trend of diminishing state involvement, and the support of government and local authorities for, amongst others, public libraries, having achieved a maximum development, often began to decrease. This decline in government support for the public libraries, especially in the U.K. (due to Thatcherian politics), was felt as a blow for the publishing business (Owen 1988: 42).

In several countries, overall sales of books no longer show economic growth. In addition, we can observe an international trend of sharp concentration in the outlets for books, whether through the rise of huge retail chains or through the increase of book clubs. When purchasing books from the publishers, both book clubs and retail chains insist on extra high trade margins. As part of this profit drive, they make a drastic selection from the flood of titles that are issued every month, giving high regard to the 'sales potential' of a given title as an important criterion for its selection. In many countries, the decision as to which books eventually land up on the bookshop's shelves is made by a increasingly smaller number of persons. The "Book Club Syndrome" (Yrlid 1990: 137), a maximum exposure of a restricted number of relatively well-selling titles, affects the publishing policies of the houses themselves. At the same time, a range of costs for book production and distribution are going up and the life cycle of new titles is getting shorter and shorter. It is generally assumed these days that a new title has to prove itself in the first few weeks after publication, after which, if it has not been sold, it will be pushed aside in the stream of the hundreds of other books that are published every month. The changing conditions for publishing put more and more restrictions on the room for manoeuvre of literary fiction publishers. They affect selection policies, such that publishers become more cautious with new authors. Is s/he promising enough to be worth the investment in a first novel? Is the author willing to cooperate with the publisher in gaining extra media attention? Is s/he photogenic? Is the story suitable for an adaptation for the screen? What are the odds on the author winning some prestigious literary prize?

When Françoise Verny, editor of some of the most famous literary imprints in France (Grasset, Gallimard, Flammarion) wrote her memoirs some years ago, she offered some remarkable insights into the extraordinary levels of intrigue that the French literary publishing world has reached when it comes to influencing the juries of the most coveted literary prizes (Verny 1991: 124-132). But it is not only in French publishing houses that the demands of marketing departments interfere more and more with the considerations of editors when selecting manuscripts. Publishers undergo a shift in their priorities: in various countries there have been complaints that the traditional publishing house is neglecting its traditional tasks of the careful editing and improving of the raw material it has to work with, the writers' manuscripts (Gross 1992: 30).

Finally, there is the impact of the new media on publishing literature. Over the past thirty years, at regular intervals the end of the traditional printed book has been predicted. Until now, however, this prediction has been constantly disproved. It has been stressed that the book as a carrier of information has certain advantages that cannot be easily rivalled by the electronic media. But even that situation is currently changing. Publishers of scientific journals and books are increasingly opting for the electronic media, offering information both on-line and off-line. Moreover, publishers of other types of nonfiction books such as reference works, hobby manuals, books on cooking, childrens' care, sports and travel are experimenting in issuing these products on CD-ROM or CD-i. Even if literary fiction texts in electronic form have been scarce until now, this shift from paper to bytes will have an immediate double consequence for literary publications. Within the large publishing companies with many different imprints (those companies that in any case must be considered first in this context) huge investments will be required, and this will certainly not make it easier for their literary imprints to spend large sums on new authors with an uncertain future. Second, within the book trade, an important shift in consumer spending is anticipated from the traditional book to information on diskette, CD-ROM and CD-i. So far it remains uncertain whether the future customers of electronic information products will buy these on top of or *instead* of their monthly book purchase. In any case, this will again not make things easier for literary fiction publishing.

In the context of this book it might seem odd that the continuation of a national literature might depend on such trivial factors as the rent prices of shopping malls, the retail margins that publishers and book chains agree upon, or the production costs of a CD-ROM. What I want to suggest is that in the field of literary canon formation, as in others, literary studies should be aware of those extra-literary factors that can substantially influence the literary market.

References

Balkin, Richard. 1994. *A Writer's Guide to Book Publishing*. New York: Plume.
Bouvaist, Jean-Marie. 1991. *Pratiques et métiers de l'édition*. Paris: Éditions du Cercle de la Librairie.
Cahart, Patrice. 1987. *Le livre français a-t-il un avenir?* Rapport au ministre de la Culture et de la Communication. Paris: La Documentation française.
Danielsen, Øivind. 1995. *Staten i den litterære republikk*. Oslo: Noregs forskningsråd.
Gross, Gerald (ed). 1993. *Editors on Editing. What Writers Need to Know about What Editors Do*. New York: Grove Press.
Owen, Peter (ed). 1988. *Publishing: The Future*. London: Peter Owen Publishers.
Röhring, Hans-Helmut. 1992. *Wie ein Buch entsteht. Einführung in den modernen Buchverlag*. Darmstadt: Wissenschaftliche Buchgesellschaft.
Verny, Françoise. 1991. *Le plus beau métier du monde*. Paris: Olivier Orban.
Yrlid, Rolf. 1990. *Litteraturens villkor*. Lund: Studentlitteratur.

Daughter of Theology

Jaap Goedegebuure
Catholic University of Brabant

Using a variation on Aquinas' well-known characterization of philosophy (*ancilla theologiae*) one might say that literary interpretation is the daughter of biblical exegesis. Attaching significance to texts, insofar as this has a place in the intellectual culture of the Western world, is rooted in the interpretation, determined by traditions and doctrines, of one type of text: those of the Old and the New Testament.

The oldest form of textual interpretation in this context is the Talmud, the body of commentary on the Torah. This could be considered an archetypal reception history, but one with a fundamentally open and dynamic nature. Pivotal in the Talmudist practice of exegesis is the awareness that the potential of meanings of the text to be interpreted is inexhaustible. This awareness has survived up to the present day in hermeneutics. It was already articulated by Friedrich Schlegel, who wished to measure the value of literary writings in terms of the number of possible interpretations. The literary work which is immortal in the true sense of the word, was taken to be characterized by its semantic inexhaustibility. Herein lies a possible explanation for the situation that nowadays the enigmatic art of the nineteenth and twentieth centuries (and Symbolistic and Modernistic poetry in particular) is the most often interpreted and most highly valued art form in academic circles. The poetics of important Symbolists such as Baudelaire, Mallarmé and T.S. Eliot have contributed considerably to this situation.

In later years these views will also affect the field of literary theory in the shape of the idea, formulated by, among others, Iser, that the essence of the literary text not only remains unspoken, but, in the final analysis, cannot be articulated. The efforts of interpreters to break the silence of the text constitute the defining aspect of literary communication. Iser, closely following Romantic poetics, refers to the cognitive faculty that is deployed to this end as *Einbildungskraft*, a concept which originally carries strong religious connotations. Wordsworth speaks of "Heaven's gift, a sense that fits him to perceive / Objects unseen before," Poe makes mention of "a lesser degree of the creative power in God" and Joubert refers to "l'imitation du divin."

The high status acquired by literature, especially since the middle of the eighteenth century, which statements such as those made by Iser show, are supported within the fields of literary criticism and literary theory even today, is related to the fact that it is approached from the same hermeneutic principles as those which have applied to the Bible for centuries. The authority of the sacred texts, in and through the approach used, is imparted to literature. In close connection with this process a development occurred in which literature replaced the sacred texts of Judaism and Christianity.

From this perspective, Schleiermacher's switch from the *hermeneutica sacra* to more general hermeneutics is far from arbitrary. This theologian, who calibrated the term "Kunstreligion" in his *Rede über die Religion*, proclaimed from the professorial *cathedra* the same viewpoint as his contemporaries Novalis and the Schlegel brothers: *qualitate qua* religion is imbued with poetry. Later, in the transition from Romanticism to Symbolism, we perceive a contrary movement. After religion is first partly or completely identified with poetry, in a second phase poetry (or literature, or the totality of art) is perceived as the contemporary equivalent of religion. Alfred de Vigny very clearly and concisely states: "L'art est la réligion, le spiritualisme moderne: tendance vers une autre foi." Carlyle calls poetry "another form of Wisdom, of Religion." Emerson is so much aware of the historical development which has had an impact on the alternation between religion and poetry that he writes: "Poetry is inestimable as a lonely faith, a lonely protest in the uproar of atheism." Even the atheist Flaubert, who prided himself on the pursuit of scientifization and objectivization of literature, wished to consider the writer as a priest.

It is fairly simple to gather from the past two centuries of literary history dozens of poetical statements that endorse this point of view, obviously with the necessary variations and modalities. For now, two quotations in which representatives of the academic profession of literary theory arrive at similar opinions, will suffice. First, a fragment from Cleanth Brooks' famous essay on Keats's "Ode on a Grecian Urn." In the conclusion to this essay we read the following characterization of the previously analyzed poem: "It has the validity of myth — not myth as a pretty but irrelevant make-belief, an idle fancy, but myth as a valid perception into reality."

One might say that the New Critics, the school of thought to which Brooks belongs, ascribed to literature a status of almost metaphysical proportions. In an era dominated by Poststructuralist relativization, voices can be heard that clearly echo Romantic notions. In *De lust tot lezen*, for instance, Maaike Meijer writes about the reflective possibilities of poetry. "We silently contemplate a small, finite piece of text, which, surrounded by white, draws all attention. There is something ritual and religious in the interaction with poetry."

I am willing to state that deep down most literary theorists concur with what Brooks and Meijer acknowledge openly. To them, literature is not an object like other objects, but the irreplaceable cornerstone of their image of man and their philosophy of life. Like Brooks, they were moulded in an era when Modernism was the dominant artistic movement. It was the Modernists who, in the wake of Romanticism and Symbolism, awarded art the position which had until then been reserved for religion. Douwe Fokkema would never have engaged in the interpretation of Modernistic novels in such a probing manner, had he not been convinced of the high value of literature.

Naturally, hermeneutics has drawn from other sources as well. The influence of the philology of Greek and Latin, with its textual criticism based on fact and linguistics, is undeniable. However, the fact that Gadamer in his *Wahrheit und Methode* awards a central position to the notion of *applicatio*, provides food for thought. In the first instance this concept is related to the application of a scriptural passage or section of the law to a specific situation here and now. Of the two fields of knowledge mentioned by Gadamer, i.e., jurisprudence and theology, the latter is closest to the interpretative practice with regard to literary writings. The magistrate applies the law *ad hominem* in each case. Clergyman and literary critic, on the other hand, focus on a community of individuals, irrespective of whether they are readers of literature or believers. Similar to the minister or priest who every Sunday tries to apply a *locus* from the Old or the New Testament to the situation of his congregation here and now through an actualizing explanation, the interpreter of literary texts attempts to show through his commentary that a writer from the past still has something to say that is of fundamental importance to the community, whose interpreter and intermediary he has appointed himself. In this respect

Bourdieu's term *consecration* is appropriate: the interpreter makes a decisive contribution to the consecration, preservation and communion of the literary text.

In addition to the writer, critics, essayists and literary theorists are the ones who, in their capacity as interpreters, bring literature's function of attaching significance to the attention of the reader. Statements that, through reading poetry or novels, one can obtain if not certainty, then a certain peace of mind, which before was only possible through faith, are frequently heard. One regularly encounters statements that reading really great literature can lead to comfort and enlightenment. Here we also detect the influence of the Romantic tradition. It was Schopenhauer who ascribed to art a salutary effect which he had long since denied religion.

In the work of philosophers like Heidegger, Levinas and Ricoeur, who occupied themselves intensively with the epistemological and existential aspects of the hermeneutic process, it is also obvious that the interpretation of a text undergoes a religious hypostasis. Of the three, Levinas provides an interesting case because of his orientation on the Judaic exegetic tradition and the Romantic literary notion that hermeneutics is the pre-eminent signifying function anyway. Levinas even goes so far as to say that the act of reading determines the human experience in its totality.

> The experience is a reading, a comprehension of meaning, an exegesis, hermeneutics, and not intuition. *This if that*: meaning is not a modification that is applied to an existing content separate from language. Everything remains incorporated in a language or a world, in which the structure of the world resembles the order of the language, with possible meanings no dictionary can fix. In *this if that* neither *this* nor *that* surrender to us from the start and without discussion.

No wonder that in this view art is considered 'the celebration of existence.'

Here I have let Levinas speak, but it would have been equally possible to quote Heidegger, Rorty or Nussbaum. As far as Nussbaum is concerned, it is, again, very clear that there is nothing new under the sun: in presenting the tragedy as a medium that can contribute to a fuller human existence she falls back on Aristotle's theory of *catharsis.*

Not so long ago, an interesting discussion took place in the Netherlands, the main issue being interpretation. Slavist and essayist Karel van het Reve, referring to the existing practice of literary theory, wondered if interpretation served any purpose. "If the writer had meant to say something else than what he says, then why did not he write that," he sneered. He was applauded by novelist and critic Maarten 't Hart, who insinuated that *subtilitas applicandi* was nothing more than a way for literary theorists to declare themselves initiates and expose all others as outsiders.

Common sense tells us that the remarks made by Van het Reve and 't Hart sound like acceptable reasoning. However, the practice of interpretation is different, because it depends on a subject-related and therefore variable constitution of meaning. Where literary theory and literary criticism have searched for the explanation of this variability or lack of univocality in concepts such as 'ambiguity,' multiple connotations and 'Leerstelle,' the exegesis of the Church Fathers (Origenes, Tertullianus and others) has preceded them with its system of the four complementary ways of reading. In addition to literal reading, which viewed the account as the registration of what had at one time occurred in this way and no other, the allegorical, anagogical and symbolic ways of interpretation were practised. In my opinion it is evident that these four types of reading stood, like fairies, at the cradle of literary hermeneutics. This was undoubtedly a development that took place in the course of many centuries. Already in the early Middle Ages, for example, people started to read Classics such as Homer and Virgil, no doubt encouraged by accepted exegesis, allegorically. (In the case of Virgil an added factor is that he was attributed the status of pre-Christian prophet based on the second *Ecloga*.) The later tradition in classical philology enhances this trend, especially during the Renaissance, in which Bacchus and Christ are considered two manifestations of one single type. The preference of Friedrich Schlegel, one of the godfathers of literary hermeneutics in its modern form, for a symbolical interpretation, builds on this tradition.

One often hears that literary theory should become a real science, i.e., subordinate to the logical-empirical standard paradigm. This may be a valid claim for certain parts of literary theory, but interpretation carries the principle of *noblesse oblige*, which it was given by virtue of its origins. It implies the obligation to continue seeing the function of signification as a social assignment, which retains its relevance even without a blessing from above. Because interpretation has a crucial place in the diverse whole of literary theory, its mission has consequences for the task of literary theory as a whole. This task is and remains focused on the preservation of the existing culture and humanistic values.

Literary Genres and Intercultural (Mis)Understanding

Rik van Gorp
Catholic University of Leuven

I would like to discuss here Bakhtin's concepts of dialogism and monologization in relation to the notions of speech genres and intercultural (mis)understanding. My point (hypothesis) is that misunderstanding is inherent to the diachronic and intercultural transfer of literary genres, because of the 'loss' of their original "Sitz im Leben." In Bakhtin's words: the life of literary genres necessarily implies a sort of "monologization." I will try to illustrate this (hypo)thesis with some examples from the history of the modern novel. Finally, I will make some critical remarks on Bakhtin's concept of monologization.

Bakhtin's concept of speech genres and monologization

My starting points are some passages from Bakhtin's essay on "speech genres" in which he tried to explain the major aspects of the genre concept, i.e.: (1) the well-known dialogic principle (implication of the addressee, responsiveness, achievement); (2) the pre-existence of the genre before the particular use of it; and (3) the co-existence of first and second speech genres.

Speech genres, according to Bakhtin, are speech acts that presuppose a speaker and an addressee, as well as a concrete historical and ideological situation. In order to interpret a speech genre it is, thus, necessary to take into account not only data such as: who speaks? who is spoken to? in which particular situation?, but also, what is mostly forgotten, which question (even not expressed) does the speaker answer or fail to answer, and for whom and for what reason?

Speech genres, moreover, already exist as a sort of "language system." In other words, one does not invent a genre, but one "sub-scribes" oneself in an already existing type of discourse. A number of speech genres manifest themselves as fairly stable and even prescriptive, so that the personal intention of the individual speaker is limited to the boundaries of the genre in question. Other genres are more free, so that there is plenty of room, within the given boundaries, for a creative restructuration.

In the global field of "relatively stable types" of utterances (Bakhtin 1986: 60), Bakhtin makes an important distinction between primary (or simple) and secondary (or more complex) speech genres. Primary genres are specific forms of individual and spontaneous discourse, characterized by its alternation of interlocutors. Typical examples are the everyday dialogue, the report (question-answer; order-execution), the description, and the exchange of letters or correspondence. Secondary genres are more complex, arising in a comparatively higher developed and organized cultural, primarily written, communication. Bakhtin mentions novels, dramas, major genres of commentary, and so forth (Bakhtin 1986: 62). Secondary genres usually absorb and digest various primary genres, which will lose, therefore, their immediate relation to actual reality. For example, traces of everyday dialogue or letters found in a novel acquire a new existence in the novel as a whole. But this "localization" in a higher order of cultural exchange tends to a sort of "monologization." As Bakhtin notes in a reflection on "the human sciences":

> le texte participe d'un dialogue [...] Dès que nous faisons du dialogue un texte compact, en d'autres termes, dès que nous effaçons la distinction des voix ... le sens profond ... disparaît. [...] Le mot d'autrui devient anonyme, familier (sous une forme retravaillée, bien entendu); la conscience *se monologise*. On oublie complètement le rapport dialogique originel au mot d'autrui [...] Après quoi, la conscience monologisée ... s'insère dans un dialogue nouveau (avec, désormais, de nouvelles voix d'autrui, extérieures). (Bakhtin 1984: 384-386)

Literary genres, monologization, and intercultural (mis)understanding

Against the background of this monologization process, I would like to stress that the historical and intertextual situation in which specific secondary genres, in this case narrative literary genres, have emerged, is important to understand the 'generic' utterance. Indeed, it is generally accepted that literary genres function in literary history as a sort of problem solving models (Wesseling 1991: 18). They suggest specific solutions — whether consciously or not — to problems of form and content at that time. The formal problem concerns all sorts of topoi, stylistic devices, and strategies intended to instruct, entertain or persuade the reader. In order to achieve this, authors normally select appropriate primary forms as well as successful secondary forms. As far as content is concerned, specific problems of the time are often focused on or referred to. For the reader these literary genres constitute sets of expectations which direct the reading process. Thus, generic repertories may be regarded as bodies of shared knowledge in a certain historical and cultural context (Wesseling 1991: 19).

These repertories can be explicitly codified in various kinds of metatexts, such as poetic treatises, prefaces, reviews, etc., but they are always implicitly present in the creative works themselves, i.e., in their specific plots, characters, setting and world view, since a genre, as any speech act, is an answer to or a polemic with other utterances on the same topic or in the same tradition. This fact in particular makes readers aware of a genre. Bakhtin speaks in this respect of utterances "filled with dialogic overtones" (Bakhtin 1986: 92), which must be taken into account in order to fully understand the style (and thus the full meaning) of the utterance in question. But their knowledge gradually diminishes in the transfer from primary to secondary speech genres and, further on, to imitations, adaptations and translations. That is a well-known phenomenon in the existence and evolution of literary genres. I would like to illustrate this with examples from two successful literary text types in seventeenth- and eighteenth century Western Europe, i.e., the travel narrative, and the picaresque novel.

Monologization in the travel story

The travel story is a secondary genre based upon and integrating primary speech genres such as the logbook, the description and epistolary forms. These primary genres presume a certain objectivity, an answer to precise questions, a piece of information about new events, etc. In the case of a voyage of discovery, they include, moreover, specific documents like maps, which by their nature demand a spatial and 'objectal' approach. By using and integrating these simple speech genres, the travel story tries to represent and model a foreign world. Although the primary speech genres lose their direct relation to their "Sitz im Leben," their influence remains: they are, so to say, 'romanticized' in a higher type of discourse within the cultural exchange, by an individual author with his own intentions. This kind of monologization explains at the same time the travel story's ambivalent position between objectivity and subjectivity, which may lead to different interpretations. Anyway, the point of view of a non-participating 'third person' strips the above mentioned primary speech utterances of their original multivoiced context, in favor of an exotopic story, i.e., a monological discourse about (not by) the others (Zavala 1990: 84).

The dilution of the picaresque novel

My second example concerns the transfer, not from primary to secondary speech genres, but from a prototypical literary genre to its imitations, adaptations and translations. The picaresque novel, which relies itself on primary forms such as the (auto)biography, the confession, the portrayal of character-types and the battle of wits, found its "Sitz im Leben" in sixteenth- seventeenth-century Spain. The prototypical representatives that gave rise to the genre of the 'novela picaresca,' show, in spite of major differences, a number of common formal and thematic characteristics. As far as the plot is concerned, the 'typical' picaresque novel presents an episodic story line, in which events are largely determined by chance. The motifs that constitute the plot are mostly of a materialistic nature, although they also touch — and that is very important as socio-cultural background — on the Spanish concept of 'honra.' They are held together by the central theme of disillusionment (*desengaño*). The picaro-narrator-protagonist is a lonely figure, badly treated even by his/her social equals, and generally leading a somewhat shady existence. The world s/he is confronted with, consists of a series of stereotyped lords and masters (gallery of character-types) and by representatives of all social classes. The relation between the picaro and his/her antagonists, often marked by dishonesty on both sides (cf. battle of wits) embodies the central theme of disillusionment and underlines a highly critical view of society. These summarily sketched characteristics are common to a large number of novels published in Spain between 1600 and 1645, following the spectacular success of Mateo Aleman's *La vida de Guzman de Alfarache* (1599-1604). This novel led to a renewed interest in the anonymous *La vida de Lazarillo de Tormes* of 1554, which is said to be the prototype of the genre.

What happened to the genre in its evolution during the seventeenth and the first half of the eighteenth century? Because of the success of the genre, many authors felt attracted to write, imitate or translate similar works (genre awareness). The monologization phenomenon is, by the way, typical for adaptation and translation processes: the 'dual' aspect of most literary (secondary) texts, i.e., the tension between its denotative meaning and its connotative context, is often, for clarity's sake, strongly simplified, so that the stratified actual meaning of the original is lost. As a matter of fact, this monologizing process developed, in the case of the picaresque novel, in two directions. On the one hand, a number of so-called picaresque novels appeared that stressed the adventurous character of the plot at the expense of the original Spanish themes. The result was a tradition of hybrid picaresque adventure stories, especially in France and England, culminating in Lesage's *Gil Blas de Santillane* and Smollett's *Roderick Random*. On the other hand, the confessional element, clearly present in *Guzman*, led to a tradition, especially in Germany, in which picaresque and didactic elements are combined. These two forms of "monologization" are clearly influenced by cultural (national) traditions: the initial (Spanish) structure and thematic are adapted to the norms of the specific national literary systems at that time. One could thus say that the evolution of the genre is a clear manifestation of one-sided (mis)understandings and interpretations of the prototypical examples, furthered by socio-cultural factors (Van Gorp 1981).

Some concluding remarks

Some critical remarks on Bakhtin's interesting ideas on monologization are necessary, since it seems paradoxical that the transfer from primary to secondary utterances and the evolution of speech genres is reduced to such a process. Bakhtin is right in putting that the initial "Sitz im Leben" with all the voices (dialogic overtones) involved, is taken up by an individual author (a third person) who dominates the entire story. However, his stylization would be considered an essential aspect of what we expect 'literary' texts to be, so that they can function in all sorts of contexts (cf. the well-known notions of "decontextualization" [Riffaterre] and polyvalence convention [Schmidt]).

Bakhtin's monologization could be seen as the price one has to pay for another dialogism, i.e., the never-ending interpretation and "redialogization" by successive readers in their socio-cultural contexts as new addressees of the "monologized" work. In that perspective Bakhtin's opposition between dialogism and monologism must not just be understood as referring to different kinds of primary and secondary texts, but also, and in my view chiefly, to different kinds of intertextual configurations and evolving reading practices. This implies that the same text(s) might function dialogically in certain historical situations, and monologically in others; that they might sometimes function as innovating text types, and at other times as conservative ones (cf. Even Zohar). Bakhtin has apparently overlooked in this sphere the impact of those reading practices, influenced by political, ideological and psychological factors, as well as by cultural institutions, especially since different understandings and misunderstandings of literary texts are often caused by a conjunction of these factors.

References

Bakhtin, M. 1984. *Esthétique de la Création verbale.* Paris: Gallimard.
— . 1986. *Speech Genres and Other Late Essays.* C. Emerson and M. Holquist (eds). Austin: University of Texas Press.
Even-Zohar, I. 1990. "Polysystem Studies." *Poetics Today* 11(1).
Gorp, H. van. 1981. "Traductions et évolution d'un genre littéraire: Le roman picaresque en Europe au 17e et 18e siècles." *Poetics Today* 2(4): 209-219.
Wesseling, E. 1991. *Writing History as a Prophet.* Philadelphia: Benjamins.
Zavala, I.M. 1990. "Bakhtin and Otherness: Social Heterogeneity." *Critical Studies* 2(1/2): 77-89.

Brutalization of Cultural and Universal Values in Marlene van Niekerk's *Triomf*

Relativity of Cultural Relativism or Redefinition of Universal Validity?

Ina Gräbe
University of South Africa, Pretoria

Through a reading of Marlene van Niekerk's controversial Afrikaans novel *Triomf* I shall examine the usefulness of Douwe Fokkema's redefinition of the concepts of cultural relativism and universal validity in literary studies. I shall argue that Van Niekerk's novel induces a critical examination of the principles underlying an Afrikaans cultural identity, which indeed supports Fokkema's insistence on the "*relativity* of cultural relativism" (italics mine). However, I shall attempt to show that the novel also simultaneously questions universal values, in that it places an apparently counter-intuitive construction on the principles underlying so-called universally valid moral and ethical values.

Whilst acknowledging the usefulness of the concept of cultural relativism, defined by Fokkema as "a way of perceiving things within their own cultural context" (1992: 119), he argues that its limited explanatory value necessitates both a recognition of the *relativity* of cultural relativism and the consideration of universally identifiable values. Fokkema is careful to point out that although not all shared values may be universally upheld, they could nevertheless "be *declared* to have universal validity" (1992: 122). These distinctions are relevant for an understanding of Van Niekerk's depiction of a working class Afrikaner family (or "poor whites"), confronted with the inevitability of a new political dispensation on the eve of South Africa's historical transition from white minority to black majority rule early in May 1994. Firstly, the manner in which the destiny of the Benade family is shown to be inextricably linked to Afrikaner history and culture confirms the usefulness of the notion of cultural identity, defined by Fokkema as an emphasis on "the cohesion of group cultures, based on ethnicity or the use of a particular language or a common history" (1992: 123). Secondly, the extent to which the fictional characters both differ intraculturally from Afrikaners and show intercultural affinities with working class people from other cultural groups, substantiates Fokkema's claim regarding the relativity of cultural relativism and, consequently, the danger of overemphasizing cultural identity at the expense of an awareness of universal values. Finally, the depiction of certain forms of behavior, which though a universal phenomenon are not necessarily universally acceptable, supports Fokkema's argumentation in favor of an occasional reliance on universal validity in literary communication.

The concepts of cultural identity and cultural relativism are relevant for an understanding of the socially determined codes of behavior associated with the Benade family, in that the 1994 publication date of the novel explicitly links the economically destitute and socially isolated Afrikaans speaking family to a certain moment in the history of the Afrikaner people generally. This becomes evident in those instances where an awareness of political debates permeates the thoughts, dialogue and actions of the Benades. For instance, Treppie, the cleverer of the two Benade brothers, ridicules a political slogan intended to allay the fears of minority groups, thereby simultaneously exposing the insecurity of the Benade family on account of their intracultural Afrikaans relationship: "Ons praat hier oor minderhede, minder héde, minder verlede, minder toekoms" (*Triomf* 1994: 51). Freely translated, Treppie's word play on the Afrikaans term "minderhede" (minorities) concerns the anticipated diminished present, past and future prospects of minorities in a new political dispensation. By means of references such as these, the reader is sure to recognize the Afrikaans speaking Benade family as representatives of a minority culture. This brings to mind the cultural relativist position advocated by Ruth Benedict, who maintains that the individual should be regarded "as a member of the social group of which he is part, whose sanctioned modes of life shape his behavior, and with whose fate his own is thus inextricably bound" (quoted by Fokkema 1992: 118).

If the concept of a minority culture is linked to the story of minorities, it becomes apparent that the fictional characters in *Triomf* are doubly marginalized: they belong to the politically disempowered white Afrikaner group within the broader South African society, but within that group they occupy the position of social outcasts, shunned because of their unacceptable lifestyle. It is precisely this position as outcasts within a minority culture which provides the possibility of explaining the Benade family's situation in terms of universal values. An interesting interdependence between Fokkema's concepts of cultural relativism and universal validity is suggested: on the one hand, the Benade family's destiny is linked to the interests of one particular minority group; on the other, their status as outcasts attains universal validity, since their behavior would have been evaluated as despicable by any standards in any community. Even though the norms of acceptable behavior change continuously, especially in liberal and permissive Western societies, any reader confronted with the excesses of verbal and physical abuse of the Benade family, will surely condemn a lifestyle punctuated on a regular basis by violent incidents usually triggered by incestual relationships between the two brothers and their sister on the one hand, and their illegitimate epileptic offspring and the mother on the other.

The positive aspect of their lifestyle emerges in the mastery of the art of survival in the face of considerable obstacles. In this respect, the isolation of the Benade family within the Afrikaans minority also relates to Fokkema's concept of the relativity of cultural relativism, the assumption being that the Benades would probably have more in common with society's outcasts generally, than with the minority culture to which they supposedly belong. This is borne out, for instance, by the incident where Lambert finds it possible to negotiate a trade with a black fellow scavenger of rubbish heaps, suggesting that he would be at home in a sort of 'brotherhood' of the homeless and hungry in the struggle for survival. Although Fokkema has in mind the correspondences between different cultures, the increasing bonding across cultural boundaries becomes evident in the common ground discovered between Lambert and his black acquaintance from the rubbish heap, or in Treppie's relationship with his Chinese employers. It is certainly true that, their Afrikaner heritage notwithstanding, one may concur with Fokkema that there seems to be a greater degree of differentiation within the Afrikaner group between the Benades and representatives from a middle class, than exists between the Benades and people from different cultures who share their position of social outcasts. This supports Fokkema's observation that "[t]he other cultural conventions can be found next door, in another cultural community, in another subculture or in another social class" (1992: 120).

All of this might initially tempt the reader at best to remain untouched by the plight of the Benades, or at worst to be repelled by their unacceptable behavior. Indeed, at a first assessment the fictional strategy of concentrating all possible misdeeds within one family takes on the semblance of a calculated brutalization of the bleak existence of the members of an 'ordinary' family who, to a large extent as a result of circumstances beyond their control, have become outcasts in society. However, the novel requires a far more serious commitment from its readership than merely a tacit approval of the marginalization of the Benades. A number of fictional and narrative strategies are skilfully employed gradually to get the reader to recognize, as a first step in a process of reorientation, that the deviant behavior of the main protagonists is not confined to an easily recognizable section of the community, set apart from civilized members of a middle class on account of universally unacceptable behavior. This reorientation of the reader becomes possible because the Benades mature from being objects of focalization to themselves becoming focalizing agents: Treppie is able to expose the hypocrisy underlying empty political promises; and Lambert, the most violent and destructive sexual abuser within the family, is given the opportunity to observe and comment upon the deviant sexual behavior of some of his neighbors.

However, the reader is required to mature to an even more surprizing realization: the possibility that the excesses of unacceptable conduct may conceal some intrinsic human values, that goodness may, in fact, be found beneath the excesses of brutality. This more profound reorientation becomes possible because the repulsive story of the Benades reveals unforeseen intrinsic qualities, such as genuine care for one another and the dogs, a desire for peace, a reconciliation to their circumstances and the realization that, despite their suffering, they can find reasons to be grateful, since they can rely on one another's support and, unlike the homeless, they are privileged in having a roof over their heads. The resigned but nevertheless courageous acceptance of their fate lends some dignity to the generally despised members of the Benade family. Such a disclosure of adherence to some intrinsic values, despite the totally unacceptable abusive behavior, requires a reversal, or at least a reconsideration, of institutionalized values.

This is precisely the stage in the reading process where the concept of universality becomes pertinent: on the one hand, the impression that the general degradation of the Benade family could be viewed as a marginal phenomenon is countered, in that it is shown to implicate the entire South African society. On the other hand, the reader is led to discover hidden universal values, which may even be seen to be realized more sincerely amongst untouchables from a lower class than is the case amongst the so-called intellectually advanced, culturally refined or morally elevated representatives from economically more privileged classes in society. It is this surprising exploration of the observation of intrinsic human values, not only *despite* deplorable human practices prevalent within the Benade family, but also apparently precisely *as a result of* their destitute situation as social outcasts, which problematizes Fokkema's notion of universal validity as a necessary complement to cultural relativism in literary interpretation and evaluation.

Clearly, then, the novel questions established codes of behavior by means of a rediscovery of intrinsic values precisely in that which is normally rejected or despised by society, without an understanding of precisely what it entails to be rejected, unemployed and poor. Marlene van Niekerk depicts characters who, strictly speaking, find themselves outside societal norms and values, in order to launch a critique of institutionalized values. It is this aspect which necessitates some modification of Fokkema's concept of universal validity: whilst I would agree that there are some universally shared values that may not be viewed as relative to a particular culture, it is precisely such apparent universally shared values which are redefined in *Triomf*. Thus, whilst the usefulness of universal values for literary interpretation and evaluation is not to be denied, the reader of literature would be well advised to keep in mind that even universal values may be affected by the literary experience.

In conclusion, then, one may say that Fokkema's distinctions between the concepts of cultural identity, cultural relativism and universal validity may certainly be useful in literary interpretation and evaluation. It is important, however, to realize that their interdependence in the process of reading a novel, which often both relies upon and transgresses its cultural context, may require a reorientation of conventions determining the distinction of universal values in what Fokkema calls our "global literary village."

References

Fokkema, Douwe W. 1992. "The Relativity of Cultural Relativism." *Journal of Literary Studies / Tydskrif vir Literatuurwetenskap* 9(2): 117-124.
Van Niekerk, Marlene. 1994. *Triomf*. Kaapstad: Queillerie.

The Conventions of Interpretation

Elrud Ibsch
Free University of Amsterdam

In 1992, Douwe Fokkema and I published a book in Dutch, the title of which in English would be *The Study of Literature and Cultural Participation*. We argued in favor of a clear distinction between on the one hand *empirically* valid research projects in literary studies aiming at explanation, and on the other *argumentationally* valid commentary aiming at interpretation or making sense. The former requires an observer's position of the researcher, who uses methods of the social sciences; in the latter case, on the contrary, the scholar acts as a participant in the literary system, who is engaged in hermeneutic understanding. Our concept of observer, it must be added, does not imply an objectivist or positivist epistemological point of view, but one that has its point of departure in the post-positivist notion of theory-guided observations and the cognitive-constructivist emphasis on our mental input in "world making."

Our book provoked a lively discussion and, happily, was received with criticism which stimulated us to rethink some aspects. The critical voices centered on two main arguments:

1. We were supposed to marginalize interpretive activities which had always been central in the academic study of literature.
2. In making the distinction between explanation and interpretation, we were supposedly reserving all methodological considerations for the empirical branch of literary studies. The interpretive "freedom" we were advocating left hermeneutic interpretation without any standard and, consequently, invalidated it as a serious scholarly discipline.

In this brief essay in honor of my co-author and husband Douwe Fokkema, I will try to respond to some of the critical arguments, elaborating predominantly on the standards of interpretation.

I have to admit immediately, that in our effort to express our conviction that in literary studies we are in need of empirical validation of the numerous intuitions we have at our disposal, we have emphasized research problems which can be solved in an empirical way. In our book we encourage literary scholars to undertake research, and we report on some results (see ch. 8, "Vormen van empirisch onderzoek").

Coming now to the problem of interpretation, it is certainly justified to assume that we conceive of the study of literature as comprising more than interpretation. It is far less justified, however, to accuse us of excluding interpretation from the discipline or marginalizing it. In fact, we have devoted two chapters on criticism (including the interpretation and the evaluation of literature). The answer to the first objection, therefore, is an easy one: We believe that interpretation and any kind of critical commentary belong to literary scholarship, but are not its only and exclusive task. We conceive of interpretation as a necessary and unalienable part of the university curriculum, because interpretive skills, reflection on interpretive frames of reference, tolerance with respect to the variety of interpretations and judgments, and discussion about the different ways of making sense have to be learnt in a systematic way.

The answer to the second objection is more complicated and requires a more extensive discussion. It is true, we plead for an interpretive practice that is free from the claims of the standard-model of scientific research. An interpretation is not a hypothesis, as it cannot be empirically tested and possibly falsified. Efforts to submit interpretations to testing procedures have proven to suffer from severe inconsistencies (see the discussion in Fokkema and Ibsch 1992: 35-50).

The criterion for judging interpretations was phrased globally by us as "argumentational validity." This means that for an interpretation to be accepted the arguments on the basis of which it is defended are of crucial importance. Without any doubt, interpretations are judged and not all of them are accepted or evaluated as equally plausible. Some receive almost no attention, others provoke counter-arguments, to again others authoritative value is attributed. It happens that some interpretations submitted to the editors of a journal for publication are not accepted, whereas others are immediately welcomed and published.

I propose to conceive of the regulative principles for the acceptance/non-acceptance of interpretations as conventions. Douwe Fokkema repeatedly elaborated on the characteristics of conventions. He stresses their arbitrary, non-foundational basis. Conventions are open to change and to reflection upon their adequacy at a certain moment. At the same time, however, once a conventional behavior is accepted as being suited to solve a coordination problem within a certain domain of social life, participants are expected to behave accordingly (Fokkema 1989).

There are, however, differences with respect to the sanctions following nonconventional ways of acting and behaving, depending on the strength or weakness of the institution involved. The institution of jurisdiction, for example, is a strong one, which expects a high degree of observance of the penal code and has a repertory of sanctions at its disposal in case of violations. The literary institution, on the contrary, is a rather weak one, dependent partly on the whimsicality of the market, partly on the professional community which is hierarchically organized according to the degree of professionality assigned to its members.

Douwe Fokkema has devoted a number of books and articles to the change of conventions in literary production (Fokkema 1984, 1989). In the domain of modern literature, violation of conventions, i.e., attempts at innovation or 'originality,' is usually more appreciated than conventional behavior, to an extent that "the well-known tenet of the uniqueness of the literary text [...] is, in fact, incompatible with the idea that the text relies on conventions" (Fokkema 1989: 3). Robert Weninger expresses the tension between individual originality and convention as follows: "eine private Konvention [ist] ein Oxymoron. [...] Konvention steht dem Individualitätsgedanken damit konzeptionell diametral entgegen" (Weninger 1994: 37).

The reception of literature, and in particular that part of it that results in professional interpretation, follows the innovative pursuit at considerable distance. Although a new interpretation has to be innovative to some extent in order to distinguish itself from earlier ones, its posteriority with respect to literary creation requires a recognizable relationship between text and metatext. This fundamental requirement is responsible for the existence of a set of interpretive conventions.

With the exception of classroom situations, a refusal of interpretations which is based on systematically listed arguments is not the normal case in the literary institution. In general, non-acceptance is expressed by means of offering a 'better' interpretive proposal, a counter-argument.

Nevertheless, if we take a closer look, it can be observed that interpreters respect certain conventions in order to invest their meaning attribution with a sufficient argumentational validity.

As far as I see, we may distinguish the following interpretive conventions. An interpretation is expected:

1. to be *consistent*, i.e., free from contradictions between framework and argument.
2. to respect *the primary linguistic level of a text*. (An interpreter will not easily read 'horse' if the word 'cat' occurs in a text. That s/he may conclude that 'cat' *signifies* 'woman' is the outcome of another convention discussed below).
3. to have *a balanced relationship between argument and example*. (A comprehensive meaning attribution is in general supported by a number of well-chosen examples in the text. It occurs rarely that an interpreter defends his/her argument by using only one textual example).
4. to reassure the reader that the interpreter has *knowledge of other existing interpretations* of the same text. (S/he uses them to confirm his/her own reading or to develop a counter-argument).[1]

The first four conventions are based on the requirements of *descriptive plausibility*. They are to a large extent respected and rather stable and can be conceived of as the basic conventions of an interpretive argument.[2] The other conventions I will discuss imply a choice related to the theory of interpretation to which a scholar subscribes, and are pertinent for the requirements of *referential plausibility* (i.e., the relationship between text and metatext).

These interpretive conventions differ according to the factors which are held responsible for the final comprehensive meaning of the text. This may be: (a) the author and/or the authorial communicative context (the position of E.D. Hirsch and, more recently, of scholars who subscribe to systems theory); (b) it may be the text as a repertory of signifiers which are related to each other in a more or less transparant way (the position of Structuralism — Jakobson, Genette — and with some qualifications of Poststructuralism); (c) finally it may be the reader, who constructs meaning in an interactive process with the text (the position of reader-response, and psycholinguistics).

If the choice is made in favor of (a) an interpretation based on the authorial intention or the authorial context, the basic conventions are completed by the following ones.

The interpretation is expected:

5a. to place the text within a specific genre;
6a. to place the text within a specific period;
7a. to refer to the problem situation to which the text is probably an answer.

If the choice is made in favor of (b) an interpretation based on the textual structure, the interpretation is expected:

5b. to subscribe to the principle of functionality: "all identifiable parts of a literary work should be artistically relevant" (Olsen 1978: 146);
6b. to clarify the pattern of segmentation of the textual structure.

If the choice is made in favor of (c) the reader's construction of meaning, the interpretation is expected:

5c. to reflect on the relevance of the interpretive framework (psychoanalytic, religious, feminist, philosophical, thematic etc.);
6c. to give a systematic account of the basic concepts of the framework;
7c. to be explicit about the metaphorical reading process to which the primary linguistic meaning is submitted;
8c. to reflect on the partiality of the interpretation, which may be conceived of as competitive but not as exclusive.

Although interpretation, in principle, is free, this freedom does not resemble anarchy or irrationality. It is based on conventions which are rational choices. They are open for discussion and judgment and we possess conceptual instruments which can be used in the discussion. "Freedom" signifies: free from the claims of scientific methodology, and free in the selection or "Verortung" (Weninger 1994: 40) of the conventions which are responsible for the referential plausibility. "Freedom," finally, refers to the contents of the interpretive arguments. The conventions I discussed are limited to their argumentational structure. They do not deal with the argumentational content. This is the reason why I can only make some very general remarks about the change of interpretive conventions.

I do not quite agree with Kermode who links such change almost exclusively to the change of canons: "The intrusion of a new work into the canon usually involves some change in the common wisdom of the institution as to permissible hermeneutic procedures" (Kermode 1983: 180). It may be, in fact, the other way round: the change of interpretive conventions may provoke a change of canons.

The general shift from (a) authorial conventions via (b) textual conventions to (c) reader's conventions which took place during the last sixty years can be explained by the influence of changes in poetics and literary production in the first case (a-b), and by the cognitive turn in psychology and linguistics in the second one (b-c). Philosophy, linguistics, politics, poetics, they all contribute to interpretive conventions and to their dynamics; (see the various explanatory hypotheses offered by Andringa 1994: 184-193). The anthropological and aesthetic need for a degree of innovation (that, however, does not completely disturb our cognitive balance) may be responsible for the desire to present a new reading of a well-known literary work. In dealing with the change of interpretive conventions, I purposely do not use the concept of successive paradigms. The 'older' conventions are not replaced but are still alive, and play a role in the recent debates (as is the case, for example, with Eco 1992).

Notes

1. Els Andringa (1994) comes to a more skeptic conclusion with respect to mentioning previous interpretations. In an empirical study on the interpretation(s) of Kafka's *Before the Law* the references to other interpreters appear to be rather poor.
2. Stein Haugom Olsen distinguishes two criteria used for the level of description: "completeness" and "correctness" (1978: 126). Olsen's chapter "The Validation of Interpretative Conclusions" is an example of a text-based validation procedure and therefore in my opinion one-sided.

References

Andringa, Els. 1994. *Wandel der Interpretation. Kafkas 'Vor dem Gesetz' im Spiegel der Literaturwissenschaft*. Opladen: Westdeutscher Verlag.
Eco, Umberto, et al. 1992. *Interpretation and Overinterpretation*. Stefan Colloni (ed). Cambridge: Cambridge University Press.
Fokkema, Douwe W. 1984. *Literary History, Modernism, and Postmodernism*. Amsterdam / Philadelphia: Benjamins.
—. 1989. "The Concept of Convention in Literary Theory and Empirical Research." In Theo D'haen, Rainer Grübel, and Helmut Lethen (eds), *Convention and Innovation in Literature*. Amsterdam / Philadelphia: Benjamins, 1-16.
Fokkema, Douwe W., and Elrud Ibsch. 1992. *Literatuurwetenschap en Cultuuroverdracht*. Muiderberg: Coutinho.

Kermode, Frank. 1983. *The Art of Telling: Essays on Fiction*. Cambridge, MA: Harvard University Press.
Olsen, Stein Haugom. 1978. *The Structure of Literary Understanding*. Cambridge: Cambridge University Press.
Weninger, Robert. 1994. *Literarische Konventionen. Theoretische Modelle, Historische Anwendung*. Tübingen: Stauffenburg Verlag.

Post-Totalitarian Culture in a Postmodern Labyrinth

From the Perspective of Poland

Halina Janaszek-Ivaničková
Silesia University

There are at least three reasons, in my opinion, why Postmodernism in post-communist countries can be regarded as a Copernican breakthrough for the reconstruction of social and philosophical consciousness. These reasons are:

1. The victory of the so-called weak thought (Lyotard 1979, Vattimo and Rovatti 1983) over strong thought, which reduces reality and renders it homogeneous. Translated into the language of concepts and employed in our part of the world this means toppling the principle of the 'sole correct reason' of a single party and a single viewpoint.
2. The rejection of determinism, which becomes supplanted by the concept of indeterminism (Hassan 1982 and 1987). Chance is no longer the question of our ignorance (as several generations have been taught in our schools in accordance with the Leninist theory), but as the theory of Heisenberg, René Thom or the model-like comprehension of the dispersion of dissipative structures in physics maintain — a mode for the existence of the world, and an opportunity for its development or disappearance (Prigogine and Stengers 1984).
3. Pluralism — the "essence of the postmodern" (Welsch 1991) — takes into account the diversity of the world and the multitude of options and languages of statements which make debates possible (Lyotard 1983).

In the post-communist countries of Central and Eastern Europe the role of pluralism which in the West is the outcome of the uninterrupted existence of democracy (regardless of the manner in which its meaning is undermined by technocrats and managers who manipulate postindustrial society) is interpreted differently — as a simple consequence of overthrowing the principle of the 'sole correct reason' which allows also the development of the reasons of others; in the domain of culture this signifies, for example, emancipation from the terror of Marxism, Socialist Realism, etc.

The theses which I have articulated in various contexts and in a paper read in 1994 at the XIV International ICLA Congress in Edmonton (Janaszek-Ivaničková 1995) apparently disturbed one of the participants in the discussion who, Douwe Fokkema assumed, was a representative of South Korea, a country distant from enclosing itself in the pantheon of the 'single correct thought' of Kim Ir Sen. I was astounded and, at the same time, amused to hear the Korean speaker publicly ask:

Does the Polish government support Postmodernism?

The absurdity of this enquiry consisted of the fact that the period when the sole coherent state-party ideology was imposed as an article of universal faith had come to an end in 1989, and that a government which would once again attempt to decide what its citizens should or should not think would simply ridicule itself, not to mention the fact that Postmodernism as a cognitive anti-fundamentalist discourse whose strength lies in doubt, is highly unsuitable to play the role of a state-creating world outlook.

I replied, therefore, quite truthfully that the government is simply uninterested in Postmodernism. This response did not satisfy my interlocutor who pressed on and asked whether Postmodernism is present in the mass media and whether it influences the development of social consciousness.

These questions have made me aware of the fact that their author was concerned with something more than was signalled by the first question, namely, with the force of the impact and place of Postmodernism in the post-communist vision of the world. His cardinal query has become an impulse for re-approaching the entire theme, albeit this time from another point of view.

Postmodernism is present, 'although negatively,' in the mass media, predominantly television and radio. Such a presentation is caused by the fact that these institutions are basically interested in superficial sensation and, as a result, propagate everything which in Postmodernism is regarded as extravagance and which could shock the *mass* member of the Polish public, for example, a new unfamiliar form of the avant-garde (in the meaning granted to this concept by Lyotard 1983), style in art (literature) or life itself and its cultural forms. Compositions and architecture which combine various styles in the form of quotations from the past could appear to be shocking, especially against the backdrop of the heretofore dominating functionalism and sterile constructivism of the masters of the Historical Avant-garde and their theories about the superiority of the simple solid and abstract line over the often ridiculed columns, arches, and canopies (which, nota bene, are frequently and willingly chosen by private owners of houses who have been absolved by a fashion that has come to us under the impact of the international celebrity of Jencks and his books which have appeared also in Poland (Jencks 1977).

A member of the public could be, and is, shocked primarily by the cult of the minority, enrooted in the Postmodern vision of the world (Lyotard 1979, Rorty 1979, Baumann 1991). Up to now, life in countries subjected to totalitarian pressure was dominated by the majority. It is, after all, in the name of the proletarian-peasant majority that revolution was carried out; it was also the majority to which reference was made while liquidating the right of other strata or classes to articulate their arguments. Respect for this imaginary, absolute subject of history inclined intellectuals to deprive themselves of the right to independent thought, to condemn Julien Benda's "clercs" and to repent for their individualism.

Under the slogan of Postmodernism television demonstrates not the essence of the problem but chiefly that which in Polish and Slav conditions appears to be unusual, strange, extravagant and newest — the sexual minorities of gay men and women, with attention drawn to the diverse deviations of various spiritual communities.

The mass media do not examine the cultural minority of women, which in Poland is not engaged in a struggle for sexual pleasure as is the case in the West but for fundamental issues such as life and survival, in categories of Postmodern feminist deconstruction although the ideas propagated by feminism are distinct among many women's groups. The activity pursued by the cultural minority of women is depicted on television screens more in political categories such as the battle waged against the Catholic Church, its paternalism and the re-relegation of women to the bedroom, nursery and kitchen.

The discussion concerning national minorities which in the multi-national

Poland of the past were numerous and whose number today is slight, is by no means new; although at present it refers to novel principles of conduct, defined by new international legal acts (mentioned by Jagiello 1995), it takes place — at least on television — outside the range of Postmodernism. Emotions come to the fore only when it appears that a certain minority is supported by a powerful majority, a mighty neighbour or a lobby dominant on a global scale which question the very category of a minority.

What is the opinion of politicians and businessmen as well as their successive governments? They too, or perhaps above all, make pragmatic and avaricious use of the freedom of activity provided by democracy, free market economy and, last but not least, the downfall of great narrations, although they have never heard of Lyotard. In Poland and other post-communist countries the end of great narrations was not generated by Postmodern philosophy, but it seems that it is in the latter that it discovers its legitimacy, although the authors of these theories are frequently philosophers deeply disappointed with capitalism who with the aid of paralogy wish to find cracks indispensable for shattering the sealed and insufferable system (Lyotard 1979).

This stage will inevitably also occur in Poland. At the moment, the country is experiencing the joy of emancipation from onesidedness and a conviction, shared by all the leaders of transformations that, to cite the words of Welsch, the most differentiated and dynamic society is the most stable one (Welsch 1991). This is not to say that those who think so have actually read Welsch. It does mean, however, that the group of views, here conventionally described as the "spirit" of Welsch, soars above together with the spirit of Lyotard, Vattimo and, last but not least, Fokkema who, while studying the socio-code of Postmodernism and its diffusion throughout the world, was one of the first to notice, appreciate and stress the international significance and alliances of Postmodernism (Fokkema 1984 and 1995).

A reply to the question posed by my Korean interlocutor about the place of Postmodernism in the totalitarian vision of the world should mention that by capturing and accumulating signals of essential changes which have already taken place in the West, and which could be summed up in the slogans of 'open society,' 'civic society' or 'feminist destruction' (propagated from 1989 also by consecutive governments in post-totalitarian countries), Postmodernism has become decisive for the period in which we and our governments live. It provides both of us, in various doses and by various ways, with philosophical self-knowledge that makes it possible to understand the world in categories of constant change, game and surprise, and not of an earlier decreed path of progress which has not proved to be successful. A deeply enrooted distrust towards every type of rhetoric, even the most recent, of a 'wonderful new world,' produces additional buffers against the abuse of magnificently sounding words. This does not, however, exclude the use of bombs instead of arguments once the latter are rejected in current and future debates. In accordance with Tom's catastrophe theory, tested on rabid dogs (Lyotard 1979: 95) the outcome of such differences and controversies is simply unpredictable.

The phantom of terrorism soars over the world with increasing speed and points to the practical effects of the supremacy of dissension over consensus. This is the dangerous other side of lofty metaphors about multiplicity and variety as well as a dramatic challenge towards embarking upon a true dialogue.

References

Baumann, Zygmunt. 1982. *Intimations of Postmodernity*. London and New York: Routledge.
Fokkema, Douwe W. 1984. *Literary History: Modernism and Postmodernism*. Amsterdam / Philadelphia: Benjamins.
—. 1995. "The Metamorphosis of Postmodernism: The European Reception of an American Concept." In Halina Janaszek-Ivaničková, with the cooperation of Douwe Fokkema (eds), *Postmodern Literature and Culture of Central and Eastern European Countries*. Katowice: Slásk. (In press.)
Hassan, Ihab. 1982. *The Dismemberment of Orpheus: Toward a Postmodern Literature*. Madison: University of Wisconsin Press.
—. 1987. "Pluralism in Postmodern Perspective." In Matei Calinescu and Douwe Fokkema (eds), *Exploring Postmodernism*. Amsterdam / Philadelphia: Benjamins.
Jagiello, Michal. 1995. *Partnerstwo dla przyszlosci. Szkice o polityce wschodniej i mniejszościach narodowych* (Partnership for the Future: Sketches about Eastern Policy and National Minorities.) Warszawa: Wydawnictwo Bellona.
Janaszek-Ivaničková, Halina. 1995. "Postmodern Literature and Cultural Identity of Central and Eastern Europe." *Canadian Review of Comparative Literature* (Revue Canadienne de Littérature Comparée.) September. (In press.)
Jencks, Charles. 1977. *The Language of Post-Modern Architecture*. London: Academy Editions.
Lyotard, Jean-François. 1979. *La condition postmoderne. Rapport sur le savoir*. Paris: Minuit.
—. 1983. *Le Différend*. Paris: Minuit.
—. 1988. *Le Postmoderne expliqué aux enfants*. Paris: Galilée.

Prigogine, Ilya, and Isabelle Stengers. 1984. *Order Out of Chaos*. Toronto and New York: Bantam Books.
Rorty, Richard. 1979. *Philosophy and the Mirror of Nature*. Princeton, NJ: Princeton University Press.
Vattimo, Gianni and Pier Aldo Rovatti (eds). 1983. *Il pensiero debole*. Milano: Garzanti.
Welsch, Wolfgang. 1991. *Unsere postmoderne Moderne*. Weinheim: VCH, Acta Humaniora. (Quoted from the Czech edition: Naše postmoderní moderna. Selected by Jolana Polaková, Trans. Ivan Ozarčuk and Miroslav Petříček, Praha: Zvon, 111.)

Theory, Theories, Theorizing and Cultural Relativism

Eva Kushner
University of Toronto

In his *Les morales de l'histoire* (1991), Tzvetan Todorov pinpoints the reason for which the human sciences forever will fail to reach a healthy division of functions between 'subjectivity' and 'objectivity,' the more they try to avoid deformations in both directions. No matter how careful we are to treat the object of our study scientifically, it will at some point want to 'speak' to us; such is its specificity. This kind of statement confirms the trajectory of many contemporary scholars who have been profoundly concerned with establishing the validity of our knowledge prior to attempting any new construction.

Admittedly, the process of self-legitimation has been highly therapeutic in that it has destabilized and (intellectually at least, if not in actual library catalogues) swept away works, trends and probably entire sub-disciplines based on insufficiently analyzed assumptions. 'Positivistic' literary history, a favorite example, was ready for a sound whipping in that regard. It was duly chastized. But literary history did not die. Rather, it has tended to renounce vast syntheses, to become more inductive, less reliant on preconceived periodizations, more content with the fragmentary, the particular; more reconciled to being what it had always been without knowing it — a discourse of its own time; the difference being that, in Postmodernity, it can view being a discourse of its own time as an exciting opportunity.

What neither historians of literature nor their critics had fully realized was that the criticisms directed at literary history might in fact have been applicable to other forms of exposition within literary studies as well as to other areas of historical exposition than literature; that the flaw did not lie in the historicity, but in the totalizing, 'foundational' character of traditional literary history, including comparative literary history. It was — and often still is — in that kind of connection that critical theory became the intellectual 'goad,' not only of literary studies but of the human sciences in general.

It is not my purpose here to describe historically the process whereby theory pursued a double path; on the one hand, a critical one, negative at least in appearance, undoing established constructions by revealing presuppositions and forces at work in them (remember Freudo-Marxism?); and, on the other hand, a pro-active one, generating constructions of its own. Any attempt to periodize this set of phenomena would lead to oversimplification, especially if we seek to gain an international perspective. The various formalisms, new criticisms and structuralisms as well as their legacies have tended towards construction and systematicity (once they had dismantled traditional literary history). One would hear them grandly define literary theory as the science of discourse. They have also helped pave the way to far greater interdisciplinarity in the human sciences, which in turn demands constant theoretical attention lest any falsely foundational concept come to predominate. As Poststructuralism, Deconstruction, feminist and Postcolonial readings, readers' responses gain ground, destabilization of meaning appears to be their common pursuit while new signification and interpretation tend towards the singular; in the process, theory itself loses its privileged domain of unlimited generalization. It, too, is (and has it not always been?) part of the social discourse of its day; it, too, can be regarded as a cultural practice among others, the special calling of which is reflection upon discourse. At that point, of course, the very concept of theory has to be reexamined; we have to venture, ever so briefly, into theory of theory.

This leads to the question: has the function of theory within our studies changed significantly in the recent past? Or are we not simply seeing an attitudinal change away from the construction and application of *theories*, and towards *theorizing* the object of our studies? In my view this has long been the case in vast sectors of literary theory, without being explicitly so stated by its main exponents. Yet what are, for example, speech act theory, pragmatic studies, empirical studies and what is hermeneutics if not imperative calls to immerse our investigations into the concreteness of process? Like philosophy (cf. Vattimo among others) literary theory appears to have renounced systems; or, where it actively claims the advantages of systematicity, as in semiotics or in the polysystem theory, it will favor descriptive rather than prescriptive strategies.

The proceedings of a recent conference on *The Point of Theory: Practices of Cultural Analysis*, edited by Mieke Bal and Inge E. Boer go much further in dealing with the changing role of theory: they announce its death....and resurrection. But is it theory that is dead, or its caricature in various academic circles? The kind of academic circles which heralded the death of literary history at the hands of literary theory, and more recently have sacrificed literary theory on the altar of cultural studies? No scholar is quite innocent of proffering (or just presupposing) such generalities; when we critically analyze the perspective of others we should also let them correct our own. The above-mentioned conference appears to have struck precisely the open-minded and experimental vision which I would advocate. It started from theory being a set of attitudes, rather than the accustomed attempt to universalize upon a state of theory which inevitably will change tomorrow (or will already have changed today). It favored interdisciplinary reflection of the kind that tries out conceptual tools drawn from one discipline to solve problems in another, without ceasing to focus on the area of knowledge the researcher knows best. It saw theory as interacting with the objects of knowledge rather than, ultimately, with itself.

Jonathan Culler offers many insights into the manner in which theory has been, and currently is, perceived. He deals with theory the panacea, or "organon of methods" as Wellek and Warren designated it; and with theory the scarecrow of many a student. Let us note in passing that these two opposite extremes have in common an excessive expectation of the potential benefits of theory. He also deals with the attraction and perils of juxtaposing many theoretical problems, vistas, methodological approaches as is often done in a host of courses which again embody extremes or at least are in danger of doing so: some tend to isolate literature from other pursuits and from life itself by encouraging self-reflexivity; others look at the widest possible range of discourses in order to let them learn from one another...

Are the latter two connotations mutually incompatible? Not if one accepts Culler's concluding remark according to which new understanding will stem precisely from the fear of the unfamiliar. On the strength of this observation we should, however, go much further. Re-humanizing theory, especially by making it into an adventurous experience, is undoubtedly a gain. We should, however, beware of letting it become just another return of the pendulum (for instance, from excluding any consideration of humanism, humaneness, subjectivity, because they might interfere with the scientificity of the literary discourse, thus spoiling the forever lurking prospect of comparability with the exact sciences; to excluding any consideration of, or hope for objectivity on methodological, philosophical, or moral grounds). "Swings of the pendulum" is at any rate a deceptive metaphor because, given the complexity of the field we are attempting to describe, the next phase is far from predictable even if we can safely venture to forecast that it will be a reaction against the previous phase.

By the same token, sweeping 'either/or' choices between oversimplified theoretical stances could be eliminated as false choices. For example, today, we can see in perspective that it was not necessary for scholars to opt between literary theory and literary history, two complementary dimensions of reflection upon literature. Douwe Fokkema was among those who propounded this complementarity (cf. ch. XIV, *Théorie littéraire; problèmes et perspectives*). Since the moment of the false choice between theory and history, theory has plunged into historicity as part of its object. Also, the historicity of theory, if and when it turns its gaze upon itself, has become far more visible. This is where we encounter cultural relativity if not necessarily relativism: theoretical discourse, as any other discourse, originates in a given place at a given time. It cannot but belong to the intellectual history of that place, of that time. Yet its very constitution is centrifugal; it always demands to be validated at a higher level of generality than other forms of discourse, ultimately for the sake of an overall coherence which may be utopian, but cannot be denied existence as an ideal goal. Thus, while it is necessary to recognize the diversity and heterogeneity of theoretical issues among the human sciences, there is no excuse for not allowing diverse disciplinary domains to exchange experiences, parameters, methodological advice.

But a new obstacle arises when we probe another, more recent 'either/or': the opposition between literary and cultural studies. This cannot be lightly dismissed as another false opposition, though ultimately, it may well be an ill-conceived one, for many reasons such as the variability of the denotation and extension of the concept of literature, the astounding heterogeneity of what, in the United States at any rate — as opposed to the historically more cogent British experience — is subsumed under cultural studies, the obviously political agenda of numerous cultural studies problematics. Yet who is to throw the first stone? It should not be forgotten that, in the sixties and seventies, it was theory that was cast in the negative, investigative, destabilizing role that cultural studies assume today!

But a deeper and greater problem arises from the fact that, whatever label we may adopt for our particular field of reflection within the human sciences, the metatheoretical apparatus for any procedure whatsoever must be examined for cultural variability. To not subject it to such questioning would invalidate chances for wider applications; to do so will always imply the risk that a theoretical insight cannot be universalized, or at least that equivalents will have to be sought from culture to culture. It is, for example, reasonably safe to assume that everywhere, at all times, and among all peoples, human experience becomes enshrined in symbolical narratives. Cultural anthropology has been supplying us with models making intelligible the relationship, say, between mytheme and mythologem and we have been blithely demonstrating that the relationship between these two structures is as arbitrary as that of signified and signifier so that mythologies of widely separated times and regions can be superimposed into more and more universally valid models. Yet I suspect that an assumption governs these orgies of comparability, namely that (as was so well understood in the *European* Middle Ages) not all meanings are literal. But if it is assumed that meanings are literal, which cultures with fundamentalist attitudes may well assume, the model may not lose its heuristic value, but it will not work pedagogically in such an environment.

Why cultivate theory at all if any attempt to universalize is so fraught with difficulties? There are more reasons than previously for doing so. Agreed upon truths do not require demonstration; emerging truths do, and as the pace of discovery quickens, the intensity of the need for authenticating them also increases. Therein lies the ongoing need for shared theoretical reflection.

References

Angenot, Marc, Jean Bessière, Douwe Fokkema, and Eva Kushner (eds). 1989. *Théorie littéraire: problèmes et perspectives*. Paris: Presses Universitaires de France.
Bal, Mieke, and Inge E. Boer (eds). 1994. *The Point of Theory: Practices of Cultural Analysis*. Amsterdam: University of Amsterdam Press.
Todorov, Tzvetan. 1991. *Les morales de l'histoire*. Paris: Grasset.

Literary Theory and the Dynamics of the Media Age

Static versus Dynamic Models

José Lambert
Catholic University of Leuven

At the end of the twentieth century it has become common among literary scholars to approach literature as a kind of communication. They do so either implicitly, when taking into consideration that audiences and distributors as well as writers or texts may play a role, or explicitly, when discussing the basic rules of literary communication. It is not clear, however, to what extent they realize what the final implications may be of this use of communications frames. First of all, literary research generally refers to one particular communication model, known mainly (in fact incorrectly) as Jakobson's model. In many cases this model is in fact used in a reductionist way: the sender, the message and the receiver are often the only components. On the other hand, scholars in literary studies generally ignore the resources and constraints of (the many) other models for the study of communication, as demonstrated by specialists in communication studies (McQuail and Windahl 1982). Could we then really claim that we treat literature as communication?

It is not impossible, by the way, that theorists of communication may have excellent reasons for imitating our example, i.e., for looking into linguistics, into translation studies or into literary studies in order to examine whether they have not (too much) excluded language from their field of study. But let us focus on our own discipline first.

One of the most embarrassing consequences of the openness to the question of communication within literary studies is that it renders absurd any (further) reduction of literature to the written/printed traditions. From the moment we accept that literature is (only?) linked with verbal communication, we are supposed to differentiate between oral, written, printed and other sign systems. The truth is that the traditions of literary research are much richer in the area of printed communication than in the other ones.

It has been said that literary theory and literary research are narrowly linked with Western culture and with a very Eurocentric world view. (In fact it would be very naive to include the rich body of research on China, India, the Middle East and other Asian cultures in our — indeed — 'Eurocentric' concepts: what is meant is the reduction to the written/printed traditions, which confirms that communication criteria are being used.) In case such a statement is relevant, the question remains whether all areas of literary studies deserve to be stigmatized as Eurocentric, and to what extent particular options may have succeeded in overcoming cultural barriers.

At first sight it would be strange if comparative literature would also be submitted to this kind of Eurocentrism since it has been developed mainly as a reaction against a narrow-minded view on societies and cultures. But many congresses on comparative literature — long before the one in Tokyo (Miner and Haga 1995) — have illustrated how colleagues from Asia or Africa want to react against the remnants of colonialism within scholarship. If comparative literature struggles with colonialism, how then could literary theory — in general — be successful in its attempt to provide models with universal relevance, the more since it is not a very common habit among researchers in the humanities to test out their models worldwide?

This is another aspect of the communications problem. The organization of worldwide testing — if requested at all — would not be simple, given the fact that it would require the organization of a certain kind of scholarship, which itself requires a certain degree of compatibility in the organization of societies. In case literary studies appears to be Eurocentric, it may be simply due to scholarship as such, i.e., to socio-cultural factors rather than to intellectual ones. This may sound as a consolation for the individual scholar (say: "a consolation devoutly to be wished," in Hamlet's terms), but not as a consolation for scholarship as such. Whatever cultural skepticism may teach us in matters of scholarship, the question of worldwide relevance for theoretical models offers new challenges to scholars of the media age.

Let us dig into the question of sign systems. Among the rather basic objections against the traditions of literary studies we ought to mention that we are in trouble as soon as other kinds of literature than the written/printed one are involved (Ong 1990; Lambert 1989a; Lambert 1989b). In the dominant models of literary theory and literary history a few centuries and a few continents are cut off from our concepts since it is (often implicitly) assumed that *littera*-ture is necessarily written and/or printed, hence linked with the book-form. Semioticians like Lotman have widened our concept of text while demonstrating that we cannot (can never) reduce it to its verbal component. There is a widespread unawareness among literary scholars of the interaction between 'audiovisual' and verbal worlds of communication, even in the case of printed (narrative) texts and texts written long before printing had been created. It might be relevant to suggest extending Ong's distinction between "primary" oral communication (in societies that ignore written communication) and "secondary" oral communication (in societies where written communication is common) to the world of audiovisual communication: references to auditive and visual communication are common in all societies, but they have quite a new function in societies where (electronic) audiovisual communication has been institutionalized. No written (literary) communication would ever take place without audiovisual communication.

Such an extension of our text concept due to insights borrowed from semiotics and communication studies compromises our traditional view on literature along the so-called Western model. Since oral literary traditions — of the primary and the secondary type — have always been a problem for literary studies, it is a fascinating question how the discipline will be able to cope with literature in the multimedia age. The difficulty is not really whether literature will survive: traditional communication has survived several technological revolutions through the ages. The difficulty is rather how scholarship will deal both with the technical and with the functional-institutional problem, i.e., (1) with the new combinations between verbal and, say, multimedia art, and (2) with the — inevitable — less central position of the written/printed literary traditions. The answer to the first question is predictable on the basis of the interactions between film studies and literary studies: film studies has become a discipline in its own right and the interaction between film and literature is a much neglected area among specialists of cinema and among specialists of literature (Cattrysse 1992).

One of the consequences of our traditional language and literature concept is the — more or less explicit — idea that literatures — and/or literary "systems"! — coincide with particular (national) languages, especially with some of them, and hence also with nations (Lambert 1989a). Although not many linguists accept that linguistic borderlines coincide with political ones, most specialists in literary studies keep assuming that the languages of literature can only be national ones, especially those of the Western world, even in the case of literatures from Africa and Latin-America. This is another aspect of the so-called Eurocentrism, since the traditional distinction between (standard) language and dialect appears to be heavily indebted to modern European societies. Not only the various oral traditions in Africa and Latin-America, but also the various new written literatures in these languages seem to be at least incompatible with many key concepts (author, genre, audience, etc.) from our dominant scholarly models, because they have (also) been generated within particular models of communication and society.

In case my criticism of the eclectic treatment of so many chapters in the history of mankind is relevant, there are strong chances also that the theoretical assumptions underlying them need a radical revision. Not only our image of literature from the past needs to be updated, but also our picture of contemporary and future kinds of literature, which simply means that our very idea of literature and literatures is probably too artificial.

We may assume that the first serious symptoms of the conflict between scholarly concepts and their object of study have been the crisis of canonization. At a given moment in our twentieth century the established categories applied to literature have appeared to be much too narrow to account for the dynamics of literary life. Many new genres (detective stories, crime stories, science fiction, comic strips, etc.) have developed outside of the strict literary frame. Scholars have adapted little by little to the new literary landscape. Hence the more or less common distinction between canonized and non-canonized (less-canonized) kinds of literature. The trouble is that many among these new genres have penetrated our literary world via the TV screen and little by little also via the computer screen. How can we keep distinguishing between literature and the media? Or should we simply accept, with Siegfried J. Schmidt (1987), that literature itself belongs to the media world, simply because it is (also) communication?

From the moment we really are aware of the fact that literature is a kind of communication, it is not only contemporary literature that changes but also literature from the past: the entire conceptual frame applied to literary phenomena needs to be updated. One of the first consequences is that scholars are now supposed to take seriously the very conceptualization of literature through the ages: what kind of a communication is it exactly, and why is it only in relatively recent times that it has been given a name of its own, namely "literature"? (Culler 1989: 33; Meletinsky and Bessière 1989: 13-29) The conceptualization of literary phenomena within culture is itself part of the problem. But more particular concepts such as 'authorship,' 'originality,' 'copyright,' 'text,' 'individual versus collective,' 'conscious versus unconscious' need to be redefined in a similar (more global) anthropology, as indicated by Bourdieu (1994). Much less than before, literary research can be carried out in isolation, as a self-sufficient activity.

While entering the age of virtual societies, literary scholars may also realize how the concept of 'fiction' is conditioned by extra-literary communicational and societal frames and, especially, by their institutionalization. Hence the national frames that are still in use as basic structures for the approach to literature and language are more outdated than ever because they are too static and too narrow. In case literary scholars do not care about the basic changes in our communicational frame, it might turn out that the survival of literature is less at stake than the survival of literary research.

References

Angenot, Marc, et al. (eds). 1989. *Théorie littéraire. Problèmes et perspectives.* Paris: Presses Universitaire de France.
Bourdieu, Pierre. 1994. *Raisons pratiques.* Paris: Seuil.
Cattrysse, Patrick. 1992. *Pour une théorie de l'adaptation filmique. Le film noir américain.* (Regards sur l'image, série II: Transformations.) Bern: Lang.
Culler, Jonathan. 1989. Angenot 31-43
Lambert, José. 1989a. "À la Recherche de cartes mondiales des littératures." In Janos Riesz and Alain Picard (eds), *Semper aliquod novi. Littérature comparée et Littératures d'Afrique.* (Mélanges offerts à Albert Gérard.) Tübingen: Gunter Narr, 109-121.
—. 1989b. "La Traduction, les langues et la communication de masse. Les Ambiguïtés du discours international." *Target* I(2): 215-237.
McQuail, Dennis, and S. Windahl. 1982. *Communication Models for the Study of Mass Communication.* London and New York: Longman.
Meletinski, Eleazar, and Jean Bessière. 1989. "Sociétés, cultures et fait littéraire." Angenot 13-29.
Miner, Earl, and Toru Haga (eds). 1994. *The Force of Vision. Proceedings of the XIIIth Congress of the International Comparative Literature Association.* Tokyo: University of Tokyo Press.
Ong, Walter, 1990. *Orality and Literacy. The Technologizing of the Word.* (New Accents.)

London and New York: Routledge.
Schmidt, Siegfried J. 1987. "Skizze einer konstruktivistischen Mediengattungstheorie." *Spiel* VI(2): 163-205.
Schmidt, Siegfried J., and Peter Vorderer. 1995. "Kanonisierung in Mediengesellschaften." In Andreas Poltermann (Hrsg.), *Literaturkanon — Medienereignis — Kultureller Text.* Berlin: Schmidt, 144-159.

Censorship and Literature in a Democratic South Africa

Margreet de Lange
Utrecht University

Censorship can play an important part in the process of canon formation. The first and most obvious effect a ban can have is barring a book from potentially entering the canon. But a second, indirect, effect can also be quite the opposite: sometimes a literary work becomes part of the canon *because* it is banned. That happened to a number of works written by South African authors in the 1970s when literary censorship was still widely practised in South Africa. *Kennis van die Aand (Looking on Darkness)* by André Brink, for example, gained fame as the first novel in Afrikaans that was banned (in 1974) and still derives its reputation more from that fact than from its literary qualities.

When one considers not the fate of separate works but that of literature as a whole, a similar ambiguous effect can be discerned. It is common to consider every form of publications control as a stifling factor in the creative process. There is a legal consensus — at least in the Western world — that freedom of expression is a constitutional right. However, when the political situation in their country changes authors in totalitarian countries often become disoriented in making the transition from a situation of almost complete control to one of freedom. What becomes apparent then is that censorship and the political context that necessitates it have functioned as a focus for creative efforts. One can think of the complaints heard from the former Communist countries of central and eastern Europe that after the fall of the Wall there is nothing left to write about. Lev Loseff talks about the "beneficence of censorship." I would not go this far — too many authors are killed and too many works never published — but that severe control can become a decisive factor in the creative process cannot be denied.

South Africa is another example of a country that is making a transition from a totalitarian state to democracy. This transition took on momentum in 1990 with the release of Nelson Mandela and the unbanning of the ANC and has since inspired a fierce debate on the future of South African literature. "What should South African literature be when it is no longer an arm in the struggle?" was the question Albie Sachs asked in a seminal article that has elicited numerous reactions. (See, for example, *Spring is Rebellious*, which reprints Sachs' articles together with a number of reactions.)

More recently, another debate has been added to the literary one, a debate on the nature, need and form of censorship in a democratic South Africa. The current censorship law dates from 1974 and is a legacy of the apartheid era. Some articles of this Publications Act have already been suspended as unconstitutional under the interim-constitution. Mindful of the need to repeal or replace this law the Minister of the Interior, Buthulezi, appointed a Task Group who formulated a proposal for a new censorship law. This Film and Publications Bill was published for comment in the *Government Gazette* of March the third, 1995, but has to date not been discussed in Parliament. The following paragraphs offer a few arguments that may help one to decide on the nature of the Bill.

The existing censorship apparatus would remain largely intact. There will be a Film and Publication Board and a Film and Publication Review Board to replace the Directorate of Publications and the Publications Appeal Board. The function of these bodies generally stays the same as under the current law. The Bill would reinstate the avenue of judicial review closed in 1974. Review Board decisions would be appealable to the Supreme Court. This possibility had been removed when the Publications Act replaced earlier law. Nevertheless, the major part of publications control would remain in the hands of officials who are appointed by the President and who could use their power for political purposes.

A system of classifications would replace the banning of publications and films. Claims are being made that censorship is being abolished. According to Task Group member Dr. Braam Coetzee "what we went for is classification rather than censorship" (*Star Tribune* 19-3-95). Chairman Van Rooyen states that "the emphasis falls on regulation rather than prohibition" (*Weekly Mail and Guardian* 10-3-95). The gap between the desire to eliminate censorship and the real possibility of continued censorship under the proposed new system is illustrated by the lead article in the *Sunday Times* on February 19,

1995. The banner shouts "END OF CENSORSHIP" but in the ensuing article one can read: "There will be no pre-censorship on magazines, but distributors can voluntarily apply to have their magazines classified to avoid risking *censorship* after they have appeared." (emphasis mine.)

Under the current law, publications can be declared undesirable. Publications declared undesirable cannot be distributed. In some cases there is also a ban on possession. The Bill would create a rating system that allows for classification into 4 categories: XX, X18, R18, and F18. Restrictions on distribution and, in some cases possession are based on the classification system's categories. The category XX is aimed at sexually explicit and violent material and at material that promotes religious hatred. Under the terms of the Bill, works classified as XX would be, for all practical purposes, banned. As far as X18 material is concerned, that too could be practically impossible to obtain. It can only be purchased in adult premises that need a license from the local authorities. Opponents of the relaxation of censorship in the Bill have already suggested the denial of such licenses as an effective strategy to ban X18 material from their communities. These same opponents have also called on people to restrict the availability of R18 and F18 material through consumer actions. In *Die Kerkbode* Horace van Rensburg, founder of 'Stop' (Stop Pornography):

> versoek die publiek om briewe te skryf, fakse te stuur, telefoon oproepe te maak, om politieke-, gemeenskaps-, kerk- en sakeleiers te besoek en om op elke moontlike manier protes aan te teken teen pornografie. Boikot winkels wat pornografie verkoop en laat hulle weet waarom hulle geboikot word. Ondersteun winkels wat weier om pornografie te verkoop en bedank hulle vir hulle standpunt. (23-6-95)

> ask the public to write letters, send faxes, make telephone calls, visit political, community, church and business leaders and to protest in every possible way against pornography. Boycot stores that sell pornography and let them know why they are boycotted. Support stores that refuse to sell pornography and thank them for their stance. (Translation MdL.)

The grounds on which a publication can be classified would be reduced. The Publications Act permitted banning on political, moral and religious grounds. In the Bill, there is no provision for classification on political grounds but the moral and religious ones remain in modified form.

After extended debates racial speech has not been included as ground for classification in the new Act. The Task Group recommended leaving that area to the courts to avoid the risk that the new Act would be used for political purposes. The Task Group report makes the following argument:

> The accent of the new proposed legislation is on morality and, to a certain extent, religion. These are issues which, we believe, could and should be dealt with by administrative and quasi-judicial structures with specialised knowledge in these fields, and not by the Courts.
>
> *The matter of race relations has a legalistic air and it would be much more appropriate for a Criminal Court to deal with it: here the matter of intention and concomitant rules of procedure would be central to the procedure and once a Court finds that the intention of the accused was to promote or incite racial hatred the requirement of intention could be regarded as a reasonable and justifiable limit to free speech in an open and democratic society.* (Report, 52, emphasis in original.)

The distinction the Task Group makes between religion and race seems questionable. Religiously offensive speech, and even morally offensive speech, can also be used for political purposes. In the past, moral and religious grounds, sections 47 2(a) and 47 2(b) of the Publications Act, were often used to ban politically undesirable literature. Much of the Afrikaans literature banned in the seventies was banned on moral and religious grounds (for example, *Kennis van die Aand* and *Magersfontein O Magersfontein*).

The reduction in the number of grounds for publications control covered by the administrative process is a positive development. In quantitative terms alone, the number of publications which may fall under this quasi-judicial system may be expected to decline. However, the danger that the law will be used politically still exists. As in the past, there is no bright line dividing the moral and religious from the political.

Literature and the arts would be exempt from classification. There is a special exemption for literature. It falls under schedule 5: *Art and Science exemption for publications*:

> The XX or X18 classification shall not apply to a *bona-fide* technical or professional, educational, scientific, documentary, literary or artistic publication, or any part of a publication which judged within the context of the publication is of such nature.

Not literature in general is exempt but 'bona-fide' literature. What the term 'bona-fide' means is not defined in the Bill, nor is it explained in the Task Group report. It is understandable that the Task Group has not attempted to define the term, as a definition would inevitably have elicited strong criticism. The use of the term does, however, imply that there is also 'mala-fide' literature that is not exempt from classification.

The attempted distinction brings to mind the discussion surrounding the introduction of the first censorship law in 1963. Writers protested loudly then that literature would suffer severely. The legislators responsible for the law responded that *good* writers had nothing to fear. The law was not meant to ban *good* writing. But as we have seen, *good* writing *was* banned. Later, after 'literary' quality had been made a mitigating factor, it still proved to be a subjective and flexible term. At one and the same time, one book could be unbanned because it was poorly written (Gordimer's *Burger's Daughter*) while another could be banned for the same reason (Matshoba's *Call me not a man*).

Not defining 'bona-fide,' however, can also be a problem. One is reminded of the US Supreme Court justice who, when asked what his definition of pornography was, answered: "I cannot define it but I know it when I see it." As one of his colleagues, Justice Brennan, has pointed out, relying on intuition is not a sound basis for justice. People should know beforehand what the rules are.

This touches upon the ultimate dilemma in publications control. It seems impossible to reach an absolute level of objectivity in defining the rules. One wonders therefore whether it would not be better not to have any such control at all. Censorship's role in literary canon formation in South Africa will probably be significantly reduced in the near future, but it remains unfortunate that the opportunity for a clean sweep has not been taken.

Against Interpretation

Hermeneutics and Empirical Studies

Geert Lernout
University of Antwerp

If the nineteenth century was the era of history, the twentieth will be known as the century of interpretation. Born as a daughter and handmaid of history, hermeneutics needed the first half of the twentieth century to kill her mother and she has reigned supreme the last fifty years. There are some indications that a change is at hand, but it is not clear who or what will replace interpretation. The advent of New Historicism has heralded a return to history, but it does so in a way that would not be recognized by any of the old historicists. Other — and equally political — reading strategies have attempted to locate the study of literary texts in their sociological and ideological contexts.

There is a completely different approach to literature which takes many forms and goes by many names but which politicized literary theorists usually lump together under labels that refer to a supposedly right-wing 'backlash.' Some theorists call for a literary pragmatics, an approach to literature that would be critical and scientific, and even, if possible, empirical. What these critical approaches have in common is some form of contextualization designed to counter the effects of what Richard Rorty has called the "textualism," or literary idealism, of the preceding generation of Poststructuralist critics. According to one of its defenders, literary pragmatics sees

> the writing and reading of literary texts as interactive communication processes. Like all such processes, literary writing and reading, even though they do not function face-to-face, one-to-one or even contemporaneously with each other, are inextricably linked with the particular sociocultural contexts within which they take place. (Sell 1991: XIV)

The two camps can then be distinguished in terms of text versus context, language versus history. On the one hand, critics believe that the literary text should be read intrinsically, as a piece of language that does not refer to an outside world. Pragmatics, on the other hand, claims that both writing and reading are historical processes.

If we take a linguistic point of view, we can only applaud the gradual zooming out from the text-and-nothing-but-the-text, to the reader of the text, to the society/culture of the reader or to the society/culture of the author. Literary criticism has only belatedly discovered that linguistics did not end with Saussure.

The irony is that neither the New Critical *cum* Poststructuralist school nor the pragmatic-empirical school seem to have any doubts about the nature of the literary text. Unfortunately, the opposition between 'decontextualization' and 'recontextualization' does not really help us understand what the literary text is. The feeling of both groups of literary critics and theoreticians that at least we agree on what constitutes the text, is shared by those writers who would dismiss most of the mountain of commentary we have built around it. In the most outspoken defense of literature against usurping commentators, *Real Presences*, George Steiner exempts the philologists who establish the literary text from its comprehensive condemnation of all commentary and criticism.

The blind spot in most theories of literature and criticism goes beyond the facile dichotomy between decontextualization and recontextualization. Theorists and anti-theorists alike, Postcolonialists and George Steiner, share a disturbing naivety about the central object of their study. All of them seem to assume that the literary text is an objective and fixed fact, ironically even when their theory of language is firmly based on floating signifiers and *différance* and when their philosophy tells them that objectivity and facts do not exist.

As a rule, literary scholars assume that the literary text they work on is the sequence of black marks on a page. These marks form words and a text is a sequence of such words. It is this text that the literary critic takes as the basis of his inquiry. It is strange, to say the least, that the question of how this particular sequence came into existence seems to be beyond the limits of inquiry. In the new approaches that followed New Criticism in the late sixties and seventies, the issue was never addressed because it was assumed that the preceding generation of scholars had once and for all dealt with the issue. This is not yet the case in a book like *Theory of Literature*, in which Wellek and Warren still had to argue the case of New Criticism against what they call "textual critics" whom they fought for control of both departments and the profession as a whole. Evidence of the former battle field surfaces when the authors warn that bibliographical studies "need to be criticized adversely only when they usurp the place of other studies and become a speciality mercilessly impossed on every student of literature" (1973: 57). Chapter Six of the book, "The Ordering Establishing of Evidence," makes it clear that what textual critics do does not really belong to the proper study of literature. The two kinds of literary study, based on the famous division in extrinsic and intrinsic approaches, is dealt with in parts Three and Four. Chapter Six forms the whole of part Two: "Preliminary Operations." The problem with textual studies is that they "often become ends in themselves" (57), of interest to textual critics and to nobody else.

Wellek and Warren were still fighting against what they saw as the dominance of textual studies in the discipline. When the battle had been won, new generations of critics were not even exposed to the principles of textual editing, so that the very specific concept of text that New Criticism had developed could enjoy the untroubled success which led to the complete 'decontextualization' in the seventies and eighties.

But textual critics had not simply disappeared, the most that can be said is that they had gone into inner exile until in the early eighties a new generation began to challenge the supremacy of literary theory. Maybe influenced on the one hand by French genetic critics who had earlier married Derrida to philology, and on the other by New Historical approaches, textual studies suddenly became a 'sexy' discipline. Young scholars have begun to ask their elders, "Where do texts come from?"

In *The French Joyce* I have tried to assess the role James Joyce and his work have played in the development of French criticism and philosophy and I hope I have succeeded in showing how *Ulysses* and *Finnegans Wake* are crucial texts in Poststructuralism. Since then, most newer brands of criticism have continued to influence Joyce studies, but one development occurred in the mid-eighties that nobody could have predicted. The publication of Hans Walter Gabler's new edition of *Ulysses* and especially the attacks on it by John Kidd, forced Joyce critics, boring old New Critics and trendy post-everythings alike, back to the issue of what exactly constitutes a literary text. It is impossible to understand the disagreements between Kidd and Gabler (let alone to participate in the debate about the new edition), without at least a working knowledge of textual studies and bibliography.

One of the results of this movement back to textual problems, might be a return to a radical reassessment of the relative values of the different types of critical activity and I would like to offer a suggestion for this discussion here. I believe it would be beneficial if we could simply turn the current hierarchy of values on its head. Rather than being the alpha and omega of literary studies, interpretation is its least important part. In a hierarchy of disciplines, textual studies would come first, if only because nothing can be done until the textual critic or editor has established a text. Next comes annotation or what the Swiss Joyce critic Fritz Senn has called "pre-quotation." Its opposite is "post-quotation": showing that the literary text confirms what you claim. A pre-quoter or annotator, on the other hand, isolates a difficulty in the text and then proceeds to elucidate the obscure passage. Both textual critics and pre-quoters cannot avoid using both intrinsic and extrinsic evidence. This is also true for the third discipline: a translator uses the text established by the textual scholar and all the annotations he can find in order to produce as close an equivalent of the literary work in a second language. The fourth and hierarchically lowest discipline is interpretation.

It should be clear that one of the reasons that the first three disciplines are crucial is the fact that they cannot avoid considering the whole of the text. Another element is that they can also not avoid using authorial intentions at least as "a regulative ideal." This formulation was first suggested by Alexander Nehemas (1981). Interpretations can easily (and usually very elegantly) disregard large parts of the text and they certainly, in the last fifty years, let themselves be regulated by anybody's intentions *except* those of the author. In E.D. Hirsch's terminology in *Validity in Interpretation*, the main difference between an annotation and an interpretation is that the former has as its object the meaning of the text, whereas the latter concerns itself with the text's significance.

It seems to me that only the first three disciplines share a number of characteristics with the historical sciences: revisability, communicability, falsifiability, objectivity (or if you will, intersubjectivity), which are completely (and almost by definition) lacking in interpretation. Whether universities are the best places to pursue or to teach interpretation, is a question I am not prepared to answer here. I can only express the hope that the current reign of interpretation will end soon. Let me end by misappropriating the words of one writer, quoted by a second writer in a novel by a third writer: "As for interpreting, our servants can do that for us."

References

Nehemas, Alexander. 1981. "The Postulated Author: Critical Monism as a Regulative Ideal." *Critical Inquiry* 8: 133-49.
Sell, Roger D. 1991. "Literary Pragmatics: An Introduction." In Roger D. Sell (ed), *Literary Pragmatics*. London: Routledge.
Wellek, René, and Austin Warren. 1973. *Theory of Literature*. Harmondsworth: Penguin.

Justifying the Canon

Paisley Livingston
McGill University

It is relatively uncontroversial to observe that the literary canon is a *publically recognized* collection of works believed to have some kind of value, such as artistic merit. What is far more controversial, of course, is the idea that the canon is or could be justified. In this brief essay, I delineate and assess some of the arguments surrounding this difficult topic.

Consider a first, schematic thesis, versions of which are defended by many literary scholars:

(1) The existence of the canon is justified, and some existing literary works intrinsically deserve to be included in it.

In a fairly standard version of thesis (1), the canon is conceived of as a publically recognized collection of especially valuable literary *works of art*. To be *literary*, a work of art must have been produced in one or more written or spoken natural languages. To be a work of art, some item must have been made with the right sort of intentions and under the right conditions, or it must serve artistic functions in the right sort of way. The literary canon is then conceived of as a publically recognized collection that includes literary works of high literary merit, where a work's literary merit is a matter of its combined artistic and aesthetic value. It is usually conceded that the boundaries of the literary canon are fuzzy and a matter of degree. But there are instances of works that are clearly not canonical, just as there are clear-cut cases of works that definitely are and should be canonical. As time passes, new items are included in the canon. It is also possible to recognize that some work that was previously canonical was overestimated and should now be removed from the collection.

Proponents of thesis (1) may also wish to distinguish between the overall canon and various sub-canons. For example, the overall canon includes all works having a certain degree of merit, but other factors, such as linguistic and cultural ones, serve to single out a number of distinct subsets of valuable works.

It should be noted that the basic position identified as thesis (1) is often maintained when critics assert that the canon should be revised, claiming, for example, that certain political and ethical values should supplement or replace aesthetic ones in our selection of canonical works. But if this tendency is carried too far, blunt but persuasive manifestoes, treatises in political philosophy, and position papers take the place of poems, novels, and plays in a canon that is only 'literary' by name.

Is thesis (1) correct? Attempts to justify the canon along these lines usually begin with arguments about the merits of particular literary works and the valuable functions these works serve. The next step is to point to the valuable consequences that follow from the canon's existence; they also evoke negative consequences that would likely follow should there be no publically recognized collection of prized literary works. One strong argument in this vein points to the canon's valuable function of helping agents with limited cognitive capacities negotiate the extraordinary complexity of literary history. As Will van Peer has noted, "even the most wealthy and most literary minded culture cannot afford to continually store, let alone distribute and have read, all that is written or printed in the literary mode. Hence only a tiny subset of literary works plays a role of any significance in the culture at large" (1994: 185). A publically identified canon of valuable works helps agents to identify the right subset, which is one good reason for the canon's existence.

Yet one may grant that the canon serves useful functions, while doubting that it is the case that works of high literary quality are in fact selected — or even *can* or *should* be selected. Douwe Fokkema has advanced the intriguing idea that the canon is an arbitrary (i.e., 'conventional') solution to a social coordination problem where there is more than one possible equilibrium. In other words, there is in principle more than one adequate decision about which restricted collection of works could serve as an adequate basis for a common (literary) culture, and what matters is not that this or that collection be chosen, but that one of them be made to play that beneficial role. Agents' preferences for a work's inclusion in the canon must be *purely conditional*, that is, justified only by the belief and preference that the other relevant agents share that same preference. This argument is compatible with thesis (1) if it is assumed that the works' features weigh significant constraints on which items can be included in the various possible canonical collections: high literary merit, for instance, is held to be a necessary criterion for inclusion in the canon, but it turns out that there are too many excellent works for this condition to determine a single equilibrium. If it is assumed, on the contrary, that the works' features do not constrain canon formation, then the idea that the canon is a useful but arbitrary selection of works is an instance of another thesis:

(2) The existence of a canon is justified, but no existing literary works intrinsically deserve to be included in it (for instance, because literary value is an illusion or an arbitrary construction).

Note, however, that according to this view, the *global* existence and justification of the canon as such is not necessarily a matter of convention in David Lewis's sense: our preference for there being *some* shared collection of works is not conditional if it is supported by our belief that the existence of such a collection is a necessary means to certain valued ends. The underlying idea, then, is that we would be worse off, artistically if not in other ways, if we lacked a publically identified collection of 'central' literary works. To revert to one of Lewis's examples, we do not care too much where we meet, as long as we make the *rendez-vous*, but we do have a strong, non-conventional preference for meeting as opposed to standing each other up (Lewis 1969).

It is important to distinguish, then, between *local* issues related to the merits of particular works (or groups of them), and *global* questions concerning the canon *per se*. It is one thing to argue that particular works do or do not merit a place in the canon, and something else to give sufficient reason for there being a canon at all, and differences between particular works do not in themselves suffice to justify the existence of the literary canon. One could coherently argue, for example, that the negative consequences of the existence of a publically recognized collection of valuable literary works far outweigh the positive ones, and this in spite of the existence of genuine differences in merit. One might then defend the following thesis:

(3) The existence of a canon is unjustified and/or unjustifiable, even though particular works otherwise merit inclusion and exclusion.

Thesis (3) only looks attractive to those who think that people's literary and other interests are today suffering from the imposition of a restrictive, common literary culture. There is, of course, evidence for such a view, but its proponents tend to overlook the evidence for the opposite problem, i.e., the strife, confusion, and waste fueled by cultural differences and divergence.

Doubts about the global justification of the canon can, of course, be joined and motivated by doubts about the merits or value of particular works. Versions of a fourth schematic thesis have many adherents today:

(4) The existence of a canon is unjustified and/or unjustifiable; no works merit inclusion or exclusion, because literary works are of deficient, equal, or non-existent merit.

Theses (3) and (4) both involve global critiques of the canon. It is important to recognize the different forms such critiques can take. *Skeptical* critiques challenge the sufficiency of others' decisions, without attempting to provide sufficiently grounded alternative conclusions. All that is claimed is that the existence of the canon has yet to be *justified* by decisive arguments. Skepticism, we should recall, leaves us with a standoff. Properly handled, it serves as a spur to further enquiry and debate; when misused, it deadens the mind and fosters intellectual and institutional carelessness and inertia. Often, skeptical questions rhetorically serve *substantive* critiques, which defend the stronger thesis that the existence of the canon, or the inclusion or exclusion of some work or works, is in fact *unjustifiable*, presumably because all possible grounds have been shown inadequate. As this is no mean feat, it is usually best to be skeptical about such sweeping and negative substantive positions. *Cynical* critiques, which appear in the service of both skeptical and substantive arguments, amount to the claim that the reasons said to justify canon-related decisions are not in fact those that actually motivated the agents, as when it is shown that personal ambition, as opposed to authentic literary reasoning, has motivated some reader's or critic's choices and actions.

There is some confusion in the literature over the import and strength of cynical lines of critique. The intuition behind these critiques is that agents are either hypocritical or deluded about what motivates them when they defend the existence of the canon and make decisions about the status of particular works. Typically, the cynical argument runs like this. Step 1: the cynic observes that the relevant agents have claimed that the justifying *raison d'être* of the canon is essentially a matter of singling out works of great artistic and/or aesthetic merit. Step 2: the cynic observes that the relevant agents' real reasons range from beliefs about the political consequences of canonization to more grimy

Justifying the Canon

and short-sighted personal motives and interests. Literary reasons are either a screen for, or are in fact determined by, other underlying motives. Step 3: the cynic concludes that the canon is unjustified; and in a bold inductive leap, the conclusion is sometimes reached that the canon is in principle unjustifiable.

One problem with such cynical arguments is that they tend to conflate such significantly different questions as the following:

Q1: What reasons did some agent offer as a justification of a decision about the canon?
Q2: What attitudes/reasons in fact guided that agent's canon-related decision?
Q3: Was the agent's decision in fact justified?
Q4: Would we today be justified in making an analogous decision?

What the cynic often wants to argue for is a negative response to Q4, and answers to Q1-Q3 are presented in support of such a conclusion. The cynic tells us that the good reasons for a literary judgment, if there are any, were not the agent's *real* reasons. The answers to Q1 and Q2 diverge, so the reasons cited in response to Q1 do not warrant a positive response to Q3. Even if the cynic's answers to Q1-Q3 are perfectly correct (and often they are not), the cynic's overall argument is not valid. It would also have to be shown that we could not have any good reasons for making a similar literary judgment, a rather strong thesis that amounts to a direct answer to Q4. The reasons relevant to Q3 and Q4 may overlap, but they are not logically equivalent. It is one thing to explain why some past agent did something or held some belief, but it is something else to ask whether an analogous activity would today be justified. Sometimes we are right to decide that some previous critic reached the correct conclusion for the wrong reasons.

What the cynic has to show is that we, today, are somehow 'fated' to make unjustified decisions whenever we ratify or revise the canon. Such a claim of course follows trivially from the thesis that none of our human decisions is ever rational, but I fail to see how anyone could be rationally persuaded by that self-defeating argument. Nor do I think that it has been shown that our canon-related activities *cannot* or *should not* help us to solve some of the basic literary problems that we face, such as the problem of singling out for our attention and common concern works of great merit. And this is surely a central problem for short-lived creatures who are confronted by a long and complex art, and who have much to gain, when dealing with that art, from the cooperative and competitive activities that only a shared literary culture can make possible.

References

Lewis, D.K. 1969. *Convention: A Philosophical Study*. Cambridge, MA: Harvard University Press.

Van Peer, Willie. 1994. "Das erste und das zweite Gesetz der Literaturgeschichte." In Achim Baursch, Gebhard Rusch, and Reinhold Viehoff (Hrgs). *Empirische Literaturwissenschaft in der Diskussion*. Frankfurt am Main: Suhrkamp.

Canons and Comparatists

Earl Miner
Princeton University

"In the beginning," Bacon said, "God planted a garden." Then there was some problem with a canon of trees, and now we have comparative literature. Since there is no literature written in comparative, the question, "What is the canon of comparative literature?" is useful precisely for its lack of practical application, theoretical sense, and historical existence. These constraints have greatly hampered our consideration of 'the canon.'

Another problem is that a canon does not stay put under our critical microscopes. It seems we must try the kaleidoscope and admit to what we have known ever since those trees. Viz., concepts of the (single) canon are basically useless and decidedly unhistorical. They ignore: reselection (addition) for new inclusion from without a set corpus; exclusion of the preselected; and constant interpretive redefinition of what is chosen. For that matter, 'the canon' of any of us is a constantly altering thing.

Discussion of canons, even in the necessary plural, are often conducted with a sacral hush befitting the great masterpieces being weighed and our importance in conducting the rites. Let us confess that each of us sins by committing these virtues. And next recognize that many readers have canons that "Plato's airy burgomasters" (Milton) forbid. University book stores stock some dubious titles, and airport shops are not filled with books from Gallimard or Insel Verlag but with mystery stories, science fiction and mildly to steamily erotic love stories: with canons.

One academic analysis of those popular paperbacks is the dire accusation of (capitalist) commodification. Since the writings saying so are also mercenary, the analysts are "not worthy of rational opposition" (Jane Austen). We form and change our lifetimes' various literary canons from multiple canons of resource: besides the designated elite and the popular there are the religious, the anti-semitic (or other hate literature), the pornographic, the didactic, the mystic, and those we stole from parental top shelves. We have every right to detest or sneer at foolish canons because our own are not rationally formed and might be no better if they were. But canons they all are.

There is also traffic between canons. A science fiction writer like H. G. Wells or Ursula K. Le Guin becomes taken seriously. Often there is shady traffic, as when 'serious' writers plagiarize ideas, plots, and motifs from examples in 'lesser' kinds. Sometimes the traffic is Postmodern, as when the hifalutin is hybridized with trash. The shady and the Postmodern are especially interesting for their tacit recognition of various canons and codes in the very stealth or glitz that seems to seek evasion of distinctions. Since stealth and spectacle, along with other literal transgressions are as old as the Chinese *Classic of Poetry* (*Shijing*), the hour for protest would seem to have passed.[1]

Canons have other reasons for being nomadic. They expand, contract, and mutate as literature varies in conception. It is not news that 'literature' has meant different things at different times, although some reminder that there have been other times and that there are some other places does seem necessary sometimes. We comparatists are especially sensitive to the existence of canons in literatures we have not got around to. There are also niggling nuisances. What is written in English or Chinese is not, ipso facto, part of English or Chinese canons. Eighty-five per cent of extant pre-modern Korean literature is in Chinese but almost none of it is included by Chinese in, say, *The Complete Tang Poems*, which is vast and incomplete.

Then there is India, exemplifying a vast ignorance shared in culpable equanimity by me with almost anyone likely to read these words. How many canons can there be in a country with fifteen constitutionally recognized languages? How many kalpas would be necessary to inventory them? Our abilities include (too little) intelligence, (faulty) memory, and (underused or misplaced) knowledge. Some of these human charms belong to the category of things one can do nothing about and need not concern us further here. We *could* enter Indian plays and their assumptions into the midstream of comparative study. That would rearrange, reidentify, and enlarge more than our canons. We could, we should, and probably won't. Thought about canons is irritating in its resemblance to those troublesome devices that go on but cannot be turned off, until the battery — or something closer — dies.

Although there is literally no conclusion (before the energy gives out) in these matters, we owe to our fellow dying animals reassurance that, whatever the symptoms, we are still alive, helping assure our plurality of canons. Talk of 'the canon' is a meaningless luxury of pampered wits. Let them on their soft pillows sound alarms about dire threats from rampant viragos or dead white males. That will assist the craft of literary study by diverting them from more important matters.

Our many canons testify to those signs of life, disagreements. Real danger comes less from prescription than its twin, proscription, as Korea strikingly shows. Like other peoples, when there were no problems from the outside Koreans have skillfully devised their own, prescribing this and proscribing that. Dissension between the Confucianists and the Buddhists might make a choice between the *Analects* or *The Lotus Sutra* one of life or death. An especially bad hour — and for Korea that is saying a lot — came with Japanese occupation early in the twentieth century. The Korean language was banned, Koreans were made to take Japanese names, they were educated from Japanese textbooks, they had to read Japanese classics, and their poets were forced to sing alien songs in their own land. In such cases, prescription is indistinguishable from proscription. The censor's heart delights in both.

There is no dearth of examples, commonly involving the political or religious fist in the velvet glove of ideological purity. *In extremis*, religifying the aesthetic leads to the stake, as politicizing leads to the gulag. For the most part, Hollywood and TV defeat waking minds. Religious zeal would ideally reduce the canon to a holy writ, as leftist zeal has produced Socialist Realism, whose only known intrinsic side effect (gulag apart) is somnolence. It is exasperating that most of the putatively greatest works were written in repressive regimes like Augustan Rome or Le Grand Siècle. Dante's and Spenser's bad ideas exasperate us, not only because we fail to learn enough about them, but also because things we abhor also generate the wonderful things in their writing. *The Tale of Genji* provides the apex of Japanese literature and is remarkable for its authorship by a woman who lived a millennium ago. Of low rank, she still was part of perhaps one per cent of the population and little concerned with the other ninety-nine.

We are no less able to fail to recognize what is unfamiliar than skilled at ignoring what we know. Literary problems commonly turn on what we agree is obvious, and then act as if it did not exist. Every comparatist knows that there are some few moments at which great shifts in canons occur, but by theorizing (about The Canon) unhistorically we may belittle the extraordinary. To take another Asian example, from late in the nineteenth century Japan did with literary tides what Xerxes and King Canute failed to do with their bodies of water: they reversed the direction of the literary tides in east Asia. Japan released a tremendous literary energy when it set about to adapt Western culture to its purposes. By deliberately enlarging its canons to include Western thought and practices, Japan took over the centuries-held Chinese role as teacher and intellectual strongarm. New education, new terminology, and new literary practices were absorbed into old to produce Modernism for east Asia. (Lu Xun, usually called China's greatest modern writer, is but one of many Chinese who received his education in Japan.)

The counterpart enlargement of the Western canons with Japanese and Chinese infusions is a lesser thing, but not negligible. It is a commonplace that like a Mori Ōgai in Germany, an Ezra Pound sacking foreign realms of gold found in the foreign what they sought for the native, often making the straight crooked. Pound was remarkable for the freedom he exercised and the headlines he wrote as he proved what Theseus said about the lunatic, the lover, and the poet. And yet, as Qian Zhongshu has put it, Pound's assaults on Chinese canons are marked by felicitous howlers.

To compare small things to those great, critics and other readers have sorted and resorted Modernist writing into various canons with various assessments as to their wholesome or poisonous natures. Some dons refuse to flow quietly about their anger over the sins of quasi-fascist Modernists. In that quarrel with the Moderns there is no other side of the Ancients. It must be particularly trying for certain politically puristic critics of Modern literature to have to choose between sinful but interesting Modernists or pink-cheeked peasants and heroic tractors. The devoutly humorless and the altitudinously trivial are counterparts with the lazily careless and irresponsibly solipsistic. They make it very difficult to be genuinely serious about canons and not laugh with Democritus.

The latitudinal and longitudinal plurality of canons raises a problem difficult enough to put an end to this discussion. In debating issues about our multiple, ever-shifting canons we too steadily ignore the making of canons: selection. What are the grounds for selection? This issue is so integral to our lives that we forget that it is as simple as the choice of the next book we read.

Most of our choices are made without deliberation. Others we take more seriously because our interests are at stake. Do we choose to devote our professional lives to Renaissance or Romantic literature? How can we choose (i.e., judge justifiably) between a Georges Sand and a George Eliot, between a Ming or a MHG narrative? The more we theorize about the issue, the more clear it is that our theories themselves are part of the problem. The more we historicize the issue, the more we sink into seemingly incomparable examples that multiply and perplex.

There are two other issues difficult enough to have merited our ignoring them. One concerns the grounds of comparison adequate for selection. The other involves historical, cultural, and in fact logical relativism. Until these issues are fully discussed, canonicity seems likely to be one of the few things still assignable to free will.[2] We need only account for the act of selection, justify it by principled comparison, and devise means at once to admit and control relativism. As these tricks show, the game of canons can be played by any number, and the only danger lies in playing the game seriously by oneself.

Notes

1. My selection of Asian examples and concern with issues of canons, selection, comparison, and relativism reflects personal interests. But since they are topics that have often concerned Douwe W. Fokkema, they exemplify the sincerest form of flattery for the occasion of this book. I regret the editorial necessity for so brief a discussion. A georgic task has had to be treated in the small space of a sonnet.

2. Attempts like Fokkema's to deal with relativism are rare, and with comparison rarer still; mine (in *Comparative Poetics*, Princeton 1990) are all too inadequate. Perhaps some headway might be made with those problems as well as with canonicity by inquiry into scientific, legal, and other counterparts.

Canons in Context

Jozien Moerbeek
Utrecht University

Since a number of years canon formation has been considered from a communicative point of view and no longer as a result of the intrinsic qualities of a literary work. From a historical perspective some important shifts based on changed opinions about the meaning of the canon concept as a result of social modifications can be pointed out. One of these changes concerns the constellation of social groups which influence the construction of canons. Moreover, the availability of texts has increased enormously, just as the number of information channels has. Popularization and pluralization are the main issues which characterize the developments of the recent decades.

Popularization and canon formation cannot get on together very well. On the one hand there is suspicion or at least skepsis towards a canon prescribed by a cultural elite, on the other hand one fears that cultural standards will fade away, that the individual art experience will be lost in mass culture. The principal complaint of culture pessimists like Bloom, Hirsch, Finkielkraut or Postman concerns the fact that people do not know their 'classics' anymore. They are afraid society might grow superficial if the cultural basis would be reduced. According to them the decrease in the extent of reading of students and adults is especially due to the shortcomings of literary education. In the Netherlands too this lack of knowledge — even on the part of university students — is noticed as a problem. More than ever school is seen as the only place left for the structural transmission of culture. With unremitting concern one is looking for possibilities to cope with the threatening crisis within education. On an increasing scale teachers ask for more specific objects and sometimes the lack of explicitness about the canon is held responsible for the general cultural devaluation.

However, it is not clear how *the* canon should be defined. The concept is not sufficiently clear to be scientifically useful. Inevitably we will meet with the problem of valuation and quality awards, as the definition of Fokkema (1986) shows:

> a selection of well-known texts, which are considered valuable, are used in education, and serve as a framework of reference for literary critics.

No decisive answer is given to the question as to who is to decide that some texts are valuable. Still a canon cannot be empirically established whithout relating that canon to a clearly defined social group. In a society, where 'taste cultures' which are no longer bound by social class are dominant (Lewis 1981) there can no longer be question of universal validity.

The idea that the development towards a multicultural society should result into the formation of several canons is shared by various theorists. Gaiser (1983), for example, proposes a pluralization of the canon concept by connecting literary canons to homogeneous groups, like literary critics, feminists, "Grünen," etcetera. In this way pluralization leads to a specification as well as to a broadening of the canon concept. An interpretation like this implies that there can be as many canons as canon composers. This view also implies that consensus is an important factor that determines the course of the selection of texts from the past. On the basis of this group-bound canon concept we can formulate the following definition:

> A canon is a collection of texts and writers which are considered valuable by a/one social group or literary circuit and which serve as a framework of reference for (in publications of) that social group or literary circuit.

For each situation the social group or the literary circuit will have to be defined, as the function of a canon is context-bound. Thus it will be possible to speak of a canon of a reading-club, a canon of a literary magazine, an academic canon or a school canon. From this point of view 'canon' equals selection.

When we see canonization as a dynamic process we shall have to investigate how selection is enacted, for example by analyzing literary criticism, actions of the media or the real reception of literary works by the general public consisting of readers and buyers. Analyzing schoolbooks and selections of texts used in the classroom can also give an insight into the selection system influencing the process of canonization. For this purpose the standards underlying the selection in literary education have to be revealed. One can assume that not only literary aspects count in judging whether a writer or text will be fit for discussion in the classroom. Undoubtedly external factors (like notions concerning literary education) also influence the choice from the variety of titles available.

The concept of what a canon is has changed in accordance with the rise of new theoretical concepts in literary studies. Various interest groups insist on canon-adaptation, for example: taking on more female writers and recent literature. Besides, one wonders if by now the time should not be ripe for an international, at least a more European oriented, kind of literary education. Moreover, one holds the view that in secundary education texts should be offered which are geared to young people's perception of their environment. One of the results of such an opinion is that for the different levels and directions of education various canons can function next to each other or even be mixed up together.

Analyzing school canons

Against the traditional concept of a prescriptive canon a more pluralistic concept has been introduced which connects canons with social groups. Meanwhile it is also admitted by theorists that the assumption of a system of universal standards and values is based on an illusion. Each canon has its own quality and function. Therefore *the* canon does not exist, Gaiser emphasizes.

The new canon concept which Gaiser introduces can be described as follows. Each canon has a relative constant 'core' which has gained a general consensus. Round about such a collection a series of works gather themselves. The selection of these works depends among other things on historical, political and geographical factors. A concrete work can have a different position in different canons or through various times: from a dominant position the work can even move towards the periphery. No canon will remain unchanged during a number of years. On the one hand, in each period people set different standards towards literature, not seldom based on changing criteria of valuation. On the other hand, a canon has at all times to be able to select and integrate the contemporary literary production.

One of Gaiser's assumptions is that canon variation will be effected by international or regional differences. Northern German curricula will rather take on certain writers than Southern German curricula and vice versa. The canon of English literature and the canons of Irish, American or Australian literature will not be the same, although the texts are written in the same language. Such secondary differences appear especially in the periphery; the central elements will remain largely constant. A study of literary canons in the highest three forms of secondary schools in the Netherlands and Flanders (the Dutch speaking part of Belgium) can point out whether this assumption is tenable.

If we want to form a canon from the selections of the three groups which are involved in literary education — teachers, students and authors of schoolbooks — we will have to make the notion operational. After all, it does not suffice to distinguish core and periphery, as Gaiser does, without any further description. Which percentage of the answers has to correspond in order to be able to speak of a core? Gaiser does not offer any solution, no more than any other theorist does. One does not speak of percentages, and titles are not mentioned, as if people are equipped with feelers for canonical works: when you meet a canonical work you will recognize it. However, it should be emphasized that canons are context-bound, constructions afterwards based on selections by a certain group on a certain moment with a certain purpose. Consensus is the key notion.

In order to uncover the differences and similarities between the various canons within one country as well as between two countries, the Netherlands and Flanders, I sent out a questionnaire to three hundred teachers. Among other things I asked these teachers which five texts and writers they dealt with most thoroughly and which five texts and writers were read most by the students (in the school year 1992-93). Arranging the titles mentioned in tables in order of frequency revealed little consensus with regard to the selection of writers and texts, neither in Flanders nor in the Netherlands, not with the teachers and even less with the students. Not a single title or writer approaches a consensus of 75%, which in statistics is considered as a limit for consensus.

The fact that some works were not mentioned does not have to mean that they are not discussed or not considered worthwhile. In principle teachers have an unlimited choice from the inexhaustible literary domain. It would be a coincidence when two respondents would make similar selections from this enormous reservoir. In this respect one could rather expect that all titles were mentioned once.

Although a canon in the strictest sense may not exist in actual literary education, the results may nevertheless show certain tendencies. Hierarchical shifts do occur, depending on country, region, education level or denomination. We shall have to design a model which can visualize these shifts. Point of attention are the *similarities* (names or titles mentioned by different groups) and *frequencies* (the number of times that a certain name or title is mentioned: high/low). Highly frequent texts or writers have the strongest position in the hierarchy. Highly frequent ánd similar texts indicate a consensus in the direction of a core collection. It is not necessarily the highly frequent texts in the individual categories (the Netherlands-Flanders, teachers-pupils, authors of schoolbooks) to be the similars at the same time. In other words: texts or writers frequently mentioned in Flanders may take a much lower position in the hierarchy in the Netherlands and the other way round. It is even possible that they are not mentioned at all in the Netherlands. Anyway, the periphery will consist of a number of *singulars* (names and titles only mentioned once). Finally, we must confront the selections of teachers and students with the selection of the schoolbook authors, in order to verify to what extent the 'vivid' practical canon and the canon of schoolbooks correspond and differ.

Conclusion

From an empirical point of view a canon can be considered as a selection of works and writers by a certain group or literary circuit. This choice is context-bound and a reflection of a certain moment. The effect of the renewed canon concept is that a school canon for secondary education does not necessarily have to be equal to the academic canon. Even within one type of education several canons may appear. Canons in Flemish literary education will differ at some points from those in Dutch education and a catholic canon will not completely be the same as a protestant canon, etc.

By interpreting the concept of 'canon' as a relative measuring result the problem of quality will for the greater part disappear. In this way we will get a concept which can function on a meta-level, which can be studied empirically and make comparisons possible. Academic research can be focused on the mechanism of the acquisition of reputation: which books are read and considered valuable by which readers; which role do the several literary institutions play in the selection process; to what degree do the various literary circuits differ from one another? Eventually, on the basis of a range of synchronic and diachronic descriptions we might be able to get an idea how canons have changed in the course of time, in other words: how canon and context are related to each other.

References

Fokkema, Douwe W. 1986. "The Canon as an Instrument for Problem Solving." In János Riesz, Peter Boerner, and Bernard Scholz (eds), *Sensus Communis, Contemporary Trends in Comparative Literature; Festschrift für Henry Remak*. Tübingen: Gunter Narr Verlag, 244-254.

Gaiser, Gottlieb. 1983. "Zur Empirisierung des Kanonbegriffs." *Spiel* 2: 123-135.

Lewis, George H. 1981. "Taste Cultures and their Composition: Towards a New Theoretical Perspective." In Elihu Katz and Tamás Szecskö (eds), *Mass Media and Social Change*. London / Beverly Hills, 201-217.

Interpretation and Explanation

Hans Mooij
University of Groningen

The problem of the validity of interpretation has been arousing a large amount of interest during the last decades in several countries. According to Paisley Livingston this very problem has been the key issue of literary theory, the subject of its central debate. The solutions differ, of course, as well as the terminology and the frames of reference. Sometimes the problem has been couched in terms of scientific method: is the interpretation of literary texts a matter of scientific, scholarly research, or is it rather the outcome of subjective and collective preferences?

This way of stating the problem has a remarkable feature which I find difficult to accept, namely the opposition between interpretation and explanation. In this opposition, interpretation is the suspect activity, whereas explanation is above suspicion as it counts as an evidently scientific activity, if not the scientific activity *par excellence*. And so, according to several participants in the debate, the science of literature should abstain from interpretation, which has no legitimate place in it, but strive after explanation instead.

The historical background of this opposition is clear enough. It derives from Wilhelm Dilthey's distinction between the natural sciences ("Naturwissenschaften") and the human sciences ("Geisteswissenschaften"). The structure of the former category is geared to explanation, the latter being essentially based on understanding ("Verstehen"). Many scholars of the twentieth century were wary of this methodological dichotomy, which could most easily be done away with by doing away with understanding. And so explanation has been opted for as the core of a common methodology.

What Dilthey had in mind, however, was not explanation *tout court*, but causal explanation on the basis of universal laws, briefly: nomological explanation. It is not at all clear that this is what the study of literature, along with the other human sciences, is able to supply. I even think that Dilthey might have used 'explanation' as his generic term, making a distinction between nomological explanation on the one hand, and understanding or interpretative explanation on the other. Indeed, something like this is what explanation in the study of literature and similar disciplines typically amounts to. Here there are hardly any precise universal laws which could generate nomological explanations.

So explanation in itself cannot be taken as an evident warrant of scientific respectability in the sense intended here, because there are different methods of explaining phenomena, different ways of answering why- and how-questions, different explanatory claims. The laborious, drawn-out debate on the validity of the covering law model for historical explanations in itself provides a reason to doubt the general validity of that model.

But there are also different ways of understanding or interpreting phenomena. To mention some fundamental possibilities: one may tell how one understands something, one may state how something can be understood, one may state how something must be understood, and one may propagate how something should be understood. It follows that some interpretations are true or false, others are not; some can be rationally defended, others cannot.

How is it that the dichotomy of explanation and interpretation has maintained itself for so long? I believe that there is a widespread rhetorical structure in defending this dichotomy and the different cognitive and scientific status of explanation and interpretation connected with it.

On the one hand explanation is confined to nomological explanation as specified in the covering law model. According to that model, explaining a phenomenon is showing that it follows from a general law, or more precisely: explaining a phenomenon amounts to constructing an argument in which a description of that phenomenon (the explanandum) logically follows from a set of premises (the explanans) that includes at least the statement of a valid general law and the description of a specific, particular condition.

On the other hand interpretation is confined to highly dubious or otherwise defeasible instances of understanding. The subject can be a historical event or a social configuration, but the preferred subject is a literary work of art. The core of the manoeuvre is the idea that interpretation is the conferment of meaning rather than the assessment of meaning.

The upshot seems to be that explanation is unmistakably part of the scientific enterprise, whereas interpretation is unmistakably not. The former would be a suitable object of testing procedures in the strictest sense, the latter would be devoid of testability even in a looser sense. And so a wide gap yawns between explanation and interpretation. They are like two opposite cliffs in the high mountains.

What disappears from sight in this way, however, is the region of the valleys in between, where there may be some less sublime kinds of explanation and some less creative kinds of interpretation. At most, these valleys can be vaguely observed as obscure or misleading levels of cognition.

But this top-down approach, although it has been useful, is *itself* misleading. In any case, it has to be complemented with a bottom-up approach, where we look from the low level phenomena and only dimly observe the nature of the cliffs.

What we do see clearly then, are continuities. Kinds of explanation blend into kinds of interpretation and the other way round. A historian discussing a historical trend or change normally switches between the explanation and the interpretation of actions and of utterances, and so does an anthropologist discussing a society, or an art historian discussing an artistic or critical movement. Think, for instance, of the many attempts at explanation of the decline and fall of the Roman Empire. (I guess that there are no fewer competing explanations here than there are competing interpretations of, for instance, *The Waste Land*.) I feel that one may very well say that in such explanations the countless events amounting to the decline and fall of the Empire are also interpreted, in the sense that they are presented and characterized in the light of the supposed cause. And would not this apply even more evidently to trends that, to a larger degree, depend on intentions of the people directly involved, like the *creation* of the Roman Empire, not to speak of biographical studies?

In suchlike cases understanding and explanation are cognate and complementary activities, and they often go together. They only separate under further conditions. Accordingly, there would be no convincing reason to suspect interpretation as such, nor to embrace explanation unconditionally.

Now back to literary interpretation. Let me indicate two continuities which show to what degree literary interpretation is connected with other activities that have a clearly rational character. First there is the continuity both with common linguistic and with pragmatic interpretation. Some time ago I read a comment on "The Rime of the Ancient Mariner" stating that at the end the Mariner is said to have become a sadder and a wiser man. This, I think, is clearly wrong. The mistake may be useful, though, as a reminder that the understanding of a poem essentially involves the correct application of grammatical rules. Moreover, in assessing the meaning of 'sadder' and 'wiser' there is no necessary flight of fanciful imagination. Even in asking why the Wedding-Guest should have become sadder and wiser, and more in particular, what is the wisdom to be gained from the Mariner's tale, one need not step beyond the sphere of rational, justifiable knowledge. Is this wisdom based on insight into the universe as being "grim and forbidding," inclusive of an inescapable contrast between marriage and religious devotion (Edward E. Bostetter), or is it based on the notion of "universal charity," "the sense of the 'One Life' in which all creation participates" (Robert Penn Warren)? To be sure, there is textual evidence for both views, but, it seems to me, more for the former than for the latter. The idea that the relevant wisdom is Cartesianism, however, is certainly mistaken.

Part of the understanding of any text is the assessment of meanings that are present, plus (perhaps even more importantly) the rejection of meanings that are not present. It is true, of course, that one may suggest overall interpretations of a poem that are only loosely connected with meanings to be assessed or ascertained and that depend largely on meanings conferred. Even then, however, there remains a difference between fanciful overinterpretation and responsible overall interpretation. In so far as they are dependent on perspectives, the link between the perspective and the outcome may be more or less convincing, and the perspective itself less or more farfetched.

Another example: in reading H.G. Wells's *The First Men in the Moon* (1901), one finds that the narrator, Mr Bedford, tells how he enjoyed (and possibly still enjoys) the killing of a number of Selenites. This may convincingly be construed as unreliable narration. For part of the message of the novel is that violence is wicked, and it is Cavor rather than Bedford who suggests that message.

But when it comes to interpreting the Selenites' society, things become more doubtful. Surely, this is not a utopian society. The grotesque professional specialization and the excessive social control are (and are meant to be) appalling. But neither is it simply dystopian. Several aspects of the Selenites' society seem to be intended as rational and/or peaceful alternatives to irrational and/or violent features of terrestrial societies. They serve as a positive model rather than as a deterrent example. Indeed, even the thorough specialisation and the hierarchical power structure are not too far removed from Wells's own social and political values as presented in his contemporary non-fictional writings, from *Anticipations* (1901) to *First and Last Things* (1908).

As to the question which is which, though, there is room for differences of opinion. In particular, present-day readers will tend to be much more critical of this Platonic construction of government and social hierarchy than the first readers (including the author) evidently were. A Popperian or Orwellian dislike of closed societies may easily be projected by us onto the meaning of this novel.

Again, although different interpretations as to the degree of its dystopian character are possible, some of them are less reasonable than others, some may even be definitely wrong, and some may be quite defensible.

Proposing those partial or overall interpretations is suggesting explanations for textual features at the same time: why those features are there and how they are related to other features. To be sure, these explanations are not nomological. But why should they?

This brings me to the second continuity. Interpretation in the study of literature is continuous with interpretation in a number of related disciplines. Some I have mentioned already; the set includes history, art history, parts of sociology, parts of psychology, parts of political science. Banning interpretation and the cognate kinds of explanation from the region of scholarly activities would play havoc not only with the study of literature, but also with a lot of neighbouring disciplines. I wonder whether this would be a sensible strategy. The price seems to be too high.

References

Barnes, Annette. 1988. *On Interpretation: A Critical Analysis*. Oxford: Basil Blackwell.
Eco, Umberto. 1990. *The Limits of Interpretation*. Bloomington / Indianapolis: Indiana University Press.
Eco, Umberto, et al. 1992. *Interpretation and Overinterpretation*. Stefan Colloni (ed). Cambridge: Cambridge University Press.
Fokkema, Douwe W., and Elrud Ibsch. 1992. *Literatuurwetenschap en Cultuuroverdracht*. Muiderberg: Coutinho. (Esp. ch. 3.)
Livingston, Paisley. 1988. *Literary Knowledge: Humanistic Inquiry and the Philosophy of Science*. Ithaca-London: Cornell University Press. (Esp. ch. 6 and 7.)
Margolis, Joseph, et al. 1995. "Symposium: Relativism and Interpretation." *The Journal of Aesthetics and Art Criticism* 53: 1-18.

Influence Versus Intertextuality

Ulla Musarra-Schroeder
University of Nijmegen

In recent comparative literature studies the concept of 'intertextuality' has been extremely successful, whereas other traditionally prominent terms, such as 'analogy' and in particular 'influence,' have lost their originally privileged position as comparatistic key terms. Undoubtedly the introduction of the concept of intertextuality and its application to a wide range of stylistic, rhetorical or semantic phenomena have been of great use to the analysis of interliterary relationships. In numerous studies the concept has proved to be highly operational. Where traditional comparative studies, especially when concentrated on relations of influence, were characterized by a certain vagueness and terminological inexactness, in numerous studies of intertextuality the concept, with its various sub-categories or sub-species, has proved to be an exact and heuristically fairly efficient instrument of textual analysis. Nevertheless I will argue in favor of a rehabilitation of the concept of influence, a concept or a term which ought to be maintained, the more so because the phenomenon as such belongs to what may be considered the reality of interliterary relationships. However, a necessary condition for a rehabilitation is a revision of the concept, a restriction of its import and a determination of the manner in which we may distinguish it from the various forms or sub-categories of intertextuality.

From the perspective of the theorist of intertextuality the concept of influence seems in general to be a matter of minor or marginal importance. Within the Poststructuralist model, according to which intertextuality is of general and universal nature ("the very idea of textuality is inseparable from and founded upon intertextuality," says Michael Riffaterre), there is no definite space for the category of influence. When concerned with influence, the attitude of the Deconstructivist theorist is rather polemical or disparaging. The concept may be discussed in the negative terms of Harold Bloom's "anxiety of influence," it may be mentioned incidentally to illustrate what intertextuality is *not* ("The study of intertextuality is thus not the investigation of sources and influences as traditionally conceived; it casts its net wider to include anonymous discursive practices of later texts," Jonathan Culler writes) or it may be parted with as being nothing more than an inaccurate metaphorical formulation of an outdated, positivistic idea of interliterary relationships (Paul Claes).

A similar discrimination of the concept of influence occurs also in recent Structuralist-oriented studies. Here intertextuality is treated not as a phenomenon common to literature or to texts in general, but as a particular property of specific literary texts. Intertextuality may then, as indicated by Manfred Pfister in the introduction to his and Ulrich Broich's *Intertextualität*, function as a sort of blanket term which can be split up in various sub-categories, among which you might expect, next to quotation, allusion, imitation, parody, etc., also the concept of influence. The system of classification proposed by Pfister is, however, different. On the basis of six criteria he distinguishes various types of more or less "strong" and more or less "weak" intensity. A quotation may be weak or strong. Important is the foregrounding of, for instance, referentiality, communicability, "dialogism." The phenomenon of influence, which Pfister inappropriately ranges with that of imitation, is, by way of contrast, mostly weak: "Von geringer Intensität sind [...] meist auch die intertextuellen Bezüge, die sich mit Begriffen wie Einfluss und Epigonentum verbinden: Sie sind oft dem Autor nicht bewusst und werden von ihm weniger intendiert und passiv erfahren." Also according to Broich the relation of influence is unknown to the writer. Moreover, in opposition to that of intertextuality, it constitutes no essential part of the act of literary communication: "So kann z.B. ein Text durch andere Texte beeinflusst sein, ohne dass der Autor sich dieses Einflusses bewusst ist oder ohne dass er die Erkenntnis dieses Einflusses durch den Leser als Voraussetzung für das adäquate Verständnis seines Textes ansieht." I may agree with the second part of this statement, although I am of the opinion that some texts (a novel of Albert Camus, for instance) will be more adequately read or interpreted if the reader is able to recognize certain structures, certain themes or certain philosophical concepts (in the case of Camus certain ideas of Nietzsche, as stated by Peter V. Zima in *Komparatistik*), which in some way may have had an impact on their process of creation. With the notion of "unconsciousness," however, I cannot agree at all. Literary history knows numerous examples of writers who acknowledge to have been "profoundly influenced" by another author (Adriaan Roland Holst, for instance, when talking of W.B. Yeats). But also writers who (in the terms of Harold Bloom) attempt to efface the traces of the work of one or more precursors, are highly conscious of whom they are indebted to. Sometimes a writer will conceal these traces behind the mask of explicit intertextual references to writers, who have been less important to him or her and by whom he or she has certainly not been influenced.

Also in Gérard Genette's *Palimpsestes* the phenomenon of influence is of marginal importance. None of the categories of the immense catalogue of possible relations between hypo- and hyper-text points to what might be considered as indications of influence. In the commentaries, however, as well as in the practical illustrations of the various categories the phenomenon is not completely absent, although the term or the concept does not occur. In the paragraph dedicated to Tom Stoppard's *Rosencrantz and Guildenstern are Dead* Genette describes the thematic relation between this hypertext and its hypotext *Hamlet* as a specific form of intertextuality, but the stylistic and dramatic reminiscenses of Beckett are described in terms which seem to indicate a process of influence:

> Il serait peut-être plus exact de définir *Rosenkrantz et Guildenstern* comme une continuation paraleptique ou comme une transfocalisation (c'est souvent la même chose) d'*Hamlet*, écrite dans une large mesure *à la manière de* Beckett, et plus particulièrement du Beckett de *Godot* [...] Mais à quoi peuvent bien s'occuper ces deux personnages lorsqu'ils ne sont pas sur la scène d'Hamlet? Telle est la question génératrice de cette pièce, et l'on peut alors imaginer [...] que *le caractère quelque peu beckettien*, dès l'origine, de ce couple de fantoches interchangeables *s'impose à l'esprit* de Tom Stoppard, et lui fournit une solution à ce problème: Rosenkrantz et Guildenstern s'occuperont, lorsqu'ils seront seuls, *comme pourraient s'occuper en pareille occurence* deux héros de Beckett, et spécialement Vladimir et Estragon. (The italics are mine.)

The quoted passage suggests that the terms of intertextuality are not sufficient for giving a satisfactory description of Tom Stoppard's play and that other forms of interliterary relationship should be considered, such as those of influence. The conclusion seems obvious: Stoppard not only makes use of Shakespeare's *Hamlet* as a hypotext, but uses also a style and a dramatic situation in which there are undeniable traces of the work of Beckett, traces which indirectly indicate the impact that Beckett has had on Stoppard before and during the elaboration of the play.

The dismissal of the concept of influence seems to me to have led to a deadlock in the theory and study of interliterary relationships. In my view a rehabilitation of the concept would be desirable. A revision and a delimitation of the concept is, however, a prerequisite. In the first place we should notice that a process of influence, different from a relation of intertextuality, may often originate from certain philosophical, psychological, sociological or scientific ideas. Rather than by one or more concrete (literary) texts a writer may be influenced by the work of great thinkers such as Kierkegaard, Nietzsche, Freud, Bergson, etc. In such a case the starting point of the process of influence may be represented by the concept of a general and more or less comprehensive model text or discourse, which — possibly through specific thematic or semantic clustering — will manifest itself on the structural surface of the target text. In some cases, those of Proust and Bergson or Svevo and Freud, the traces of influence will be accompanied by sporadical intertextual indications. To this type of influence we may add the frequent case of writers who have been inspired by the way of thinking of other writers, or in more concrete form, by themes or motifs used by these writers. A second type of influence is constituted by relationships on the level of formal, stylistic, structural and compositional principles. The model text may be represented by a genre, a style, certain structural devices. In the third place, and this seems to me to be a necessary condition for a distinction between intertextuality and influence, I will propose a restriction of the concept. The concept of influence includes only those phenomena which in some way have directed the process of creation of a text, the writing process, phenomena which consequently may be considered as preceding the text. On the level of the textual structures, however, the process of influence, as indicated above, may manifest itself in various ways: in certain schemes or patterns of semantic, stylistic, compositional or formal order and sometimes also in concrete intertextemes such as quotations or allusions. It is not inconceivable that writers explicitly refer to texts which have served as models or examples, though often the opposite situation is the case. The specific features of intertextuality and the traces of influence do not converge, the first pointing in the direction of hypotexts different from the texts which have functioned as positive examples.

This is the case in *Rosencrantz and Guildenstern*, as indicated above. In Postmodernist fiction in general the tenor of intertextual references deviates considerably from what may be regarded as representing the model text. In *Invisible Cities* by Italo Calvino, for instance, a great deal of the numerous intertextual passages refer to texts which belong to the classical and modern tradition of the Utopia and Anti-Utopia (from More, Campanella, Bacon, Fourier to Huxley, etc.), a whole tradition to which Calvino responds in his own Postmodern way, proposing a "perfect city, made of fragments mixed with the rest, of instants separated by intervals." But the origin of the book in the terms of influence is another: a model text namely, which, next to semiology or structural semiotics, is constituted by the experiments made by the members of the Parisian *Oulipo* with literary writing as a combinatory game. There are no intertextual references to Pérec or to Queneau, whereas allusions to the field of research first mentioned, the Saussurian game of chess, for instance, are not totally absent. In Douwe Fokkema's novel *Zichtbare steden* ("Visible Cities") one of the intertexts is evidently Calvino's famous book. But the various possible model texts are of an entirely different order. One might think of Modernist essayistic fiction, of Valery Larbaud's *Barnabooth*, which, however, functions at the same time as one of the most prominent intertexts, and eventually of Postmodernist intertextual montage.

Thus in Postmodernist fiction the relation between the various devices of intertextuality and the phenomenon of influence is rather complex. Whereas in classical and traditional texts the traces of influence and the intertextual references are often on a par with one another, in Modern and Postmodernist texts they will mostly diverge. It is, moreover, especially in Postmodernist narrative that intertextuality as a specific device becomes itself influential. In this sense intertextual practice in itself constitutes a trace or an indication of influence. The text as intertextual network is therefore a result not only of the impact of certain trends in contemporary narrative and criticism, but also of the influence that other contemporary writers, from Joyce to Borges or from Barth to Calvino and Eco, may have had on its author.

The Structure of Literary Revolutions

John Neubauer
University of Amsterdam

> My heart leaps up when I behold ...
> *The Child is father of the Man.*
>
> Wordsworth (1802)

Wordsworth suggests, anticipating Freud, that childhood experiences shape the life of the adult. He does not mean that descendants determine the identity of their forefathers. The evolutionary theory of Wordsworth, Coleridge and others, which still continues to shape our thinking about literary history, moves chronologically forward, even if it assigns creative power to memory.

Yet questioning the priority of the prior, the defining role of genesis, is not just a fashionable Postmodern idea. It motivated New Criticism's attack on biographism and the intentional fallacy, and it informed T.S. Eliot's influential essay "Tradition and Individual Talent." Eliot demanded that poets write with a constant awareness of the "Western tradition," but he endowed the present with defining power by adding that every new author and work redefined the meaning of that tradition. He proposed that the meaning of the past does not reside in its very texts but is constantly redefined by an evolving future.

Eliot and New Criticism had little interest in readers and their psychology, but their critique of intentionality shifted the locus of meaning from genesis to text. Reception theory and reader-oriented approaches took the next step and located meaning production in the recipient. This well-known story need not be pursued here further. Most literary scholars of today will agree, however much they may differ on other matters, that neither the reconstruction of authorial intention nor textual analysis alone will suffice to give texts an intersubjective meaning.

To what extent has the conceptualization of literary history into periods, styles, and movements capitalized on these newer insights? Few scholars would subscribe today to the older belief that a full assemblage of facts from the past would yield coherent historical periods. In the decades after mid-century, the generally accepted view was that periods were to be understood in terms of general "systems of norms" (René Wellek), which left the questions open, who determines the norms and how enduring they are.

The most frequently used term for literary history and periodization today, 'construction,' goes further than 'norms' in suggesting that periodization is a-posteriori rather than historically given, but its wide use has made it a catch-all. Perhaps the most important contemporary meaning of 'construction' originates in 'narrativist' approaches to literary and general history. Hayden White, Frank Ankersmit, and others have powerfully argued that the historian selectively chooses from the raw historical data and applies to it pre-existent linguistic and narrative patterns. The past has no intrinsic coherence, it is constructed by means of the historians perspective, which selects the relevant facts and interconnects them by means of the mechanisms implied by the linguistic and narrative patterns. Such narrative approaches to historiography recognize that the historical data can be 'glued together' differently, but they leave the question open whether we have any means to choose between the various alternatives, or at least rank them with respect to plausibility. Would terms like 'Romanticism,' 'Realism,' and 'Modernism' not become empty if we allowed for limitless ways to define them and not seek for selection criteria? Is there a way to 'save' such terms without reanchoring their meaning in presumed facts of the period?

Narrativist approaches to history have performed an important function as they question the traditional demarcation of literature and history, but now that we have become sensitive to overlappings and the grey areas between them we need to find residual, more flexible demarcation criteria, for the distinction seems intuitively plausible. But what kind of constraints can one impose on the historical imagination? Can the raw historical data itself represent a constraint and determine which narrative structures and period concepts are relevant?

Fokkema and Ibsch, for one, admit that the polyinterpretability of texts and the high abstraction of the concepts we apply to literary history allow for a great latitude in period concepts. In their view, the periodization of literary history is not fully objective but is partly based on pragmatic and normative principles and determined by the choice of the individual scholar. But

Fokkema and Ibsch seek to retain an intersubjective component in the construction of history, and they remark, not unjustly, that the narrativists confound history with fiction by neglecting the representational dimension of historical narratives. More specifically, they suggest that we ought to correlate the narrative structures with the ways in which the relationship between the past events were experienced (however differently) by their "actants." They regard historical constructions like Romanticism as schematic models based on (implicit or explicit) theoretical principles, which can be tested against those "clusters" of literary and cultural conventions that historical, geographical, and sociological research of the past offer.

This is a reasonable approach to a complex problem, and an admirable attempt to 'save' the intersubjective respectability of literary terminology. But will these two propositions suffice? The perspective of the historical "actants" on their own experiences is one, but only a single factor in the historian's construction. Their epistemological value is actually less than the interpretation that authors give to their own work. Actants tend to have a limited view of their world, and historians have to weigh their testimony against empirical data and theoretical views that were not available to them. We should ask how artists and critics used the term 'realism' in the nineteenth century or how the literature of 'decadence' was received in the fin de siècle, but the meaning we give to these terms cannot exclusively rely on the answers.

Histories of literary conventions rely on models that we apply to the historical texts as well as to biographical, institutional, sociological and other materials. This data limits the choice of models but is far from decisive, for no model can use all the data, alternative models select different subsets of it, and we have no universal and enduring criteria for deciding which subset is more important. The very generation of data depends on the interests and values of the research community, which shift with the conventions and paradigms of the field. As Thomas Kuhn and the post-Kuhnian theorists of science have argued, different paradigms focus on different sets of data, and they actually define what constitutes relevant data. Similarly, literary historians working in different theoretical schools will construct their periods and movements out of different sets of data.

I have argued elsewhere against a simple importation of a Kuhnian model into a theory of literary history. I am evoking it here merely to suggest that paradigm models of history, in science as well as literature, must recognize that each paradigm shift involves a redefinition of the past paradigm and, by means of this, all past paradigms. Kuhn himself believes that the subsequent

The Structure of Literary Revolutions

paradigms are "incommensurate." According to him, the history of science is written by those who won the latest scientific revolution; their paradigm defines what the legitimate problems and research goals are. But in my view, a restatement of problems and goals not only defines the new paradigm, it also redefines the old one, which now will have to be read as the foil of its successor, not merely in terms of its own problems and goals. What holds for a single revolution holds for the whole chain that constitutes history: each revolution redefines its immediate predecessor and *mutatis mutandis* all the previous ones: in light of the latest, all the past changes its meaning, the new paradigm lays bare hitherto hidden features of the past. Subsequent paradigms, far from being incommensurate, are interrelated by means of retrospective reinterpretations.

What does this imply for periodization in literary history? By extension of my Wordsworthian motto I am claiming that "children define their elders," that the self-image of Romanticism, Realism, Modernism and other periods is redefined by the next periods and movements, which set up their predecessors as strawmen to satisfy their own needs. In some cases the term crystallizes for the first time only once the successor has appeared: Modernism, for instance, has assumed clearer terminological and epistemological features only once Postmodern ideas needed a marker of things past, of ideas and conventions superseded. By extension, every new period and movement rewrites literary history, defines itself by reaccentuating the past.

I am suggesting a constructive view of periods, in which the construction of past periods is understood as a means for the present to define itself. Since reconstructing the image of the historical Other is in the service of self-construction, period construction is neither fully determined by the past nor terminable. But since it can be analyzed in terms of elements in the past on the one hand and the needs and perspectives of those who construct on the other, it is not arbitrary either.

The model may be called a hermeneutics of historical periods in the sense that it attributes a shaping role to the interpreter's perspective, but it does not involve the kind of empathy with the interpreted object that is sometimes attributed to hermeneutics. We may also regard it as an institutionalized and gender-neutralized extension of that psychoanalytic father-son conflict that Harold Bloom has dramatized in *The Anxiety of Influence*. For if Eliot has claimed that new texts and authors redefine the tradition, Bloom has added that rewriting the past is the late-comers way to assert themselves against the predecessors. I am suggesting, by extension, that the actants of periods and currents define themselves by (re)defining past periods and currents, by assigning the reigning powers to the rubble of history.

This may sound like a fanciful exaggeration? Are we ignorant of the dominant styles, conventions, and literary practices of our own age? Do we need to wait for the arrival of some ultra-Postmodernism to come to a definition of our literary culture? Surely not — and I am not claiming that we need to. What I am suggesting is that our self-view is but one way to conceptualize our culture and that this self-view will be modified by later literary and critical currents. This view has been generally accepted with respect to individual texts, but in writing literary history it has, in spite of some recent innovative histories, not even been tested.

Take for instance Romanticism. Although each twentieth-century critical current has defined itself to a considerable degree by reconstructing Romanticism, studies of this period still tend to look for its permanent features, preferably for features that the Romantics applied to themselves. I know of no study that would characterize the period in terms of the successive images that subsequent periods and movements have constructed of it. The same holds for Realism, Naturalism, and even Modernism, although in the latter case the approach is more self-consciously historical because of Postmodernism's need to define itself in opposition to it.

A relative neglect of the insight that historical periods are constantly redefined seems to me also the major weakness of the series on the comparative literary history in European languages that is appearing under the aegis of the ICLA Coordinating Committee. These volumes on periods and movements have admirably enriched literature's synchronic breadth by crossing national boundaries and, in recent volumes, by placing literary periods into their cultural environment. But defining their historical units they disregard diachrony, by which I mean not the internal history of the movements and their transnational migrations but the history of their reinterpretations. At best, we occasionally find traditional but unsystematic and theoretically unfounded comments on the period in terms of its reinterpretation of the past, for instance on the Romantic revival of Medieval literature and culture, or on Eliot's Modernist revaluation of the metaphysical poets and devaluation of Romanticism.

Will the literary historians of the next period perhaps define themselves against us by seriously entertaining the idea I have presented? I would not presume to be a prophet of the future, but the idea deserves empirical testing.

Cultural Relativism and Models for Literary Studies

Ziva Ben-Porat
Tel Aviv University

Contemporary studies of culture are characterized by:

a. The universal conceptualization of the nature of culture, defined as the complex of patterns of behavior which are not biologically inherited;
b. The attempt to overcome the popular evaluative use of the term through the functional approach (i.e., different cultural practices are shown to be successful responses both to the same basic human needs and to context specific needs);
c. The growing awareness and concomitant interest in those patterns which are the responses of specific groups of people to specific needs;
d. The claim that all cultural practices are in some way ideological, hence manifestations as well as practitioners of power relations.

The direct result of the new insights is Cultural Relativism, which, in its more recent conceptualization as Multiculturalism, requires a rethinking of our attitudes towards the study of literature and our models for literary research. I would like to propose a comprehensive model for literary studies in the age of Multiculturalism, based on a new definition of units of culture.

In view of the recent anthropological and sociological approaches, the notion that the basic unit of culture is an ethnic or national group — the notion which underlies the two basic models of cultural relations: the relations within one culture and the relations between different cultures — is no longer sufficient. It needs to be expanded and modified to include the new insights about the potential cultural variety within any ethnic/national group as well as insights about the parameters involved in determining the relative homogeneity of any cultural grouping.

I propose to see the basic cultural unit as a group whose members at a given time share a language, a repertoire of representations (concepts, cognitive models) and an ideology (in the widest current sense). A modern state is a dynamic conglomerate of such cultural units which can be distinguished from other similar conglomerates by some cultural practices common to all its members (including of course legal identification). This conceptualization suggests three concepts — which implies models and terms — of cultural relations.

1. 'Intracultural relations' refer to the relations obtaining between the cultural subsystems of the basic cultural unit — a cognitively, linguistically and ideologically defined cultural (poly)system. This complex system is by definition culturally homogeneous. Its components derive from the hegemonic ideology. The notion of derivation is important here because it allows us to include many peripheral and counter-culture phenomena within the 'homogeneous' picture. The notion of 'Hegemony' is important, for it guarantees the dynamic conceptualization of this homogeneous entity.
2. 'Intercultural relations' refer to the relations obtaining between the cultural subsystems of a heterogeneous, usually national, (poly)system. An official national entity, which consists of various ethnic, national or other cultural groups (for instance, French, English, and native Americans in Canada; Arabs and Jews, or even Russian Jews and members of other Jewish communities in Israel) provide paradigmatic examples of such heterogenic (poly)systems. Obviously, youth, women, gay and other groups are part of this heterogeneous unit.
3. 'Crosscultural relations' refer to the relations obtaining between distinctive cultural conglomerates.

Models of studying literary relations

Applying this tripartition to literary studies, we come up with three different models for the study of literature, corresponding to the cultural state.

Intracultural literary studies

Disregarding the fact that homogeneous cultures as defined here are more theoretical than factual, it is possible to describe the literary system of such a society and the appropriate methodolgy for studying it.

In a homogeneous culture the definition of the field of study and that of the object of study pose no problems. The culture offers one — and not a number of rivaling — definiton of literature. Similarly, there is a concensus around the canon, aesthetic norms, the cultural role of the literary product, the social role of its producer, and the like. Literary studies need to concern themselves with any of these issues only in descriptive terms, if at all. The major task of literary studies is the preservation and perpetuation of the successful texts and models respectively, a task which can be achieved by copying, restoring and interpreting canonic texts, by compiling anthologies and writing histories of the encyclopedic type, in which the 'intracultural relations' are 'static,' i.e., rather fixed temporal and hierarchical relations.

The fact that this has been until quite recently the paradigm of literary studies in our heterogeneous societies proves that such imaginary communities are historical facts. Ideological hegemony can combine or coerce very different socioeconomic and ethnic groups into a homogeneous culture. Also, as I will propose later, intracultural literary studies of this type may be politically and culturally useful even in today's most advanced multicultural pluralistic society.

Intercultural literary studies

'Intercultural relations' which by definition are the relations characterizing a heterogeneous cultural system posit a different model for literary studies, one, which I believe can be successfully developed along the lines of Even-Zohar's functionalist "Polysystem Theory."

The literary study of intercultural relations focuses on the dynamics of the literary system, whether it emphasizes, like (the early) Even-Zohar, intrasystemic forces which transform for their special needs other cultural processes of change, or whether it emphasizes the actual power relations and struggle for cultural dominance which is manifested in the literary field as well as in all other cultural practices.

In the intercultural study of literature the object of study is the literary polysystem and not an inventory of more or less canonic texts. The canon looses its static nature and becomes either the problem of canonization or the battle for canonicity. Literature is defined ad-hoc and as widely as possible, because the literary system is conceived as a network of texts and models whose interrelations make them a cultural whole. The relevant questions are no longer those of interpretation but those of general rules governing literary processes: the transfer of models from center to periphery or vice versa, relations between change and permanence, stratification of sub-systems, changes in the repertoire, and so forth. Even-Zohar's key concepts here are: center and periphery, hierarchical stratification based on cultural oppositions (for instance, canonic and noncanonic, elite and popular/trivial), productive versus secondary models, and available admissible repertoires — as well as his key metaphor, the battle for control of the center — are useful tools for the study of interrelations in the literature produced by a heterogeneous culture.

Crosscultural literary studies

The study of two or more autonomous literary systems (autonomous only in the sense of not being defined in relation to each other), the products of two or more distinct cultural conglomerates, entails (like the other two types of cultural relations) a methodology of its own. However, because of the autonomous nature of the parties involved, we must take into account here two different methodologies.

The first method is unique to autonomous entities and is based on the assumption of analogical relations between cultures (literatures), where actual contacts can be treated as irrelevant for a specific topic of study. Its object of study is any phenomenon common to both literatures or any generalization about the nature of literary texts or systems (including assumptions about generating or interpreting texts) which aspires to a universal validity. The relevant research problems are similarities and dissimilarities in the functions and manifestations of the phenomenon in the two systems.

The second methodology deals with relations of contact. It can, like that of intercultural literary studies, be developed along the lines of Even-Zohar's polysystem theory in its discussion of literary contacts and interference and Toury's studies and theory of translation. In this case, the object of study is usually the 'target system' — that literary system which through its contacts with another system imports models or other elements in the repertoire. The relevant research problems are the reasons for import, its channels, and the acculturation of the imported elements. Direct power relations, in which the target system is controled by the source system (the exporter), though played down by Even-Zohar, fit easily into this model for studying crosscultural relations.

The pragmatics of model-based applications

Presenting the three methodologies not only as corresponding to, but actually derived from the three types of cultural relations, might create the impression that it is mandatory/natural to apply to each system the corresponding methodology. This is not the case.

Cultural groups, or rather hegemonies, construct their self images. In that case research carried out from inside the system might prefer a methodology which an outside researcher might deem unfit. For example, at the stage of crystalization a cultural group might wish to create a canon, not to challenge it; it might at the same time wish to adapt oral or imported-translated texts into its canon. Thus where an outsider might see clashing cultures (oral versus literate) the group's self image is one of a homogeneous culture, whose literature should be studied from the intracultural angle.

A second example might be that of groups competing for cultural (and political) hegemony, which may choose either the intracultural or the intercultural model. If their literary system is not yet fully developed the members of one group might prefer the intracultural approach. Conceiving of their literature as an autonomous system might serve their political ends better than asking admission to the larger system. But if the competing systems are equally developed, and if there is enough common ground (i.e., cognitive repertoire, cultural institutions, etc.) for two literatures to be seen as belonging to the same heterogeneous cultural system, the intercultural model might be preferable. Its methodology suits better the analysis of models in competition, of challanged canons, of actual fights over resources and recognition.

Obviously such choices are not theoretically but pragmatically based. The motivations for a particular study influence the choice of a model more than the specific cultural state. All three methodologies are applicable to any literary system, and if a comprehensive multicultural picture is the aim all three should be employed.

Where Invention and Representation Meet

Ann Rigney
Utrecht University

*You're in Dawson street, Mr Bloom said. Molesworth street is opposite.
Do you want to cross? There's nothing in the way.*

Pavement Inscription, Dawson St., Dublin

Can Leopold Bloom be said to 'exist' in the same way that I do? Does the Dawson St. in Joyce's *Ulysses* differ from the Dawson St. his readers may walk down? Metaphysically hair-splitting questions like these have long been of importance for philosophers. But for literary scholars, among whom there has been a surge of interest in fictionality, questions regarding the ontology of fictional beings are becoming increasingly subordinated to questions regarding the attitude of those involved in the production and reception of fictional utterances. Giving primacy to the pragmatics of fictionality makes sense when it is considered that the existence of a Sherlock Holmes or a Leopold Bloom, walking the streets of their respective cities, is dependent on people's capacity to imagine them; or more generally, the capacity to invent information about non-existent beings, and the social acceptability of doing so. What distinguishes a lie from a fiction, and fiction from error, is not the ontology of the entities referred to, but the attitude of the parties engaged in the communicative exchange. Whereas in the case of error the speaker is misinformed, and in the case of a lie s/he violates the 'sincerity principle' by knowingly misleading someone else, in the case of fiction s/he knowingly makes false statements in the understanding that the receiver will recognize this intention and react accordingly.

The fact that this sort of acceptance is forthcoming, and that inventers can presume it will be, is generally attributed to the existence of something like a 'fictionality convention,' i.e., a traditional model of the behavior conducive to mutual coordination in certain situations (*in casu* the situation in which one party invents imaginary entities and tells a story about them). Thanks to such a convention, the parties reponsible for the invention can indicate their intentions through a variety of contextual and textual signs which, when recognized, will bring the reader to adopt an "as-if" attitude (Vaihinger 1986), or a readiness to "make-believe" (Walton 1993). The general assumption among theorists is that once the conventional behavior has been brought into play, it is plain sailing from then on. In other words, once the fictional intentions of the writer have been identified and admitted, the crucial border into make-believe is crossed, all reference to the actual world is suspended, and the readers become "immersed" (for instance, Ryan 1991: 21) in the fiction which has been prepared for them, only to re-emerge again at the other end of the book. This image of immersion and emergence is supported by the persistent notion that the fiction is congruent with the utterance and, like it, autonomous (see, most recently, Ronen 1994 *passim*). Thus, although fictional narratives usually incorporate elements from the real world and combine these with elements which have been invented, the convention-theory assumes that the reader will not correct deviations from fact (for instance, Hrushovski 1984: 237). What is presented in the text is considered as an autonomous 'fictional world,' which will be treated by the reader *en bloc* as such.

But communicative practice would seem to be more complex than the 'autonomy' principle (admittedly greatly simplified here) allows for. Just as ontological approaches to fiction were dogged by the problem of the mixture of real and imaginary in so-called 'mixed sentences,' so too the problem of the relationship between fact and invention inevitably begs to be treated in any pragmatics of fiction.

In 1829 Sir Walter Scott published a collected and revised edition of the Waverley novels incorporating new footnotes and prefaces written in response to the many unsolicited letters he had received from the public. Among these responses were a letter from a certain John Christian of the Isle of Man demanding that the view of one of his ancestors presented in *Peveril the Peak* be corrected (this letter was subsequently included in the revised edition); a letter from one of the descendents of Anne of Geierstein correcting an error in the portrait of her in the eponymous novel (Scott 1833: III, 352-53); letters offering additional information regarding some of the historical figures or places mentioned in the novels (a certain William Hamper having provided him with a complete inventory of all the furniture in Kenilworth, the list was included in a new footnote to the novel of that name; II, 226); above all, letters identifying the prototypes of his fictional characters (the sister of the purported prototype of The Black Dwarf was apparently plagued by enquiries from the public; I, 356; see also 178-79; 182; 188).

Between June 1842 and October 1843, while Eugène Sue was writing and publishing his best-selling serial *Les Mystères de Paris,* famously execrated by Marx, he received more than 400 letters in response to the various episodes (see Thiesse's excellent analysis of this correspondence). While some of these letters were straightforward demands for money (on the principle that the writer must resemble his philanthropic protagonist!), others involved recognitions of the prototypes of his fictional characters and praise for the accuracy of the portrayal (thus a certain Mme A. Lichtenauer, *portière*, wrote in praise of his portrait of the honest workman Morel, in the belief that "le mérite d'un auteur et [sic] d'approcher du vrais [sic] le plus possible," [Thiesse 1980: 55]). Finally, a large number of the letters involved comments on the social implications of Sue's portrayal of the *bas-fonds* of Parisian society, urging him to propound certain courses of action and engage with current debates, offering him extra information in the form of economic treatises or accounts of local credit-union initiatives. As a result of these interventions, the novelist not only began to incorporate long passages of commentary into the later instalments (for example, on the prison-system, currently being debated in the parliament), but also became involved in setting up a liaison system between the philanthropic rich and the deserving poor.

A number of things are remarkable about these cases. Firstly, there is the fact that the novelists' public, rather than being passively immersed in a ready-made fiction after their initial acquiescence in the game, became involved in the elaboration of the text itself. Secondly, there is the fact that, even as the readers acknowledge and accept that the plot as a whole is invented (no-one seems to deny this), they do detach certain details, episodes, and characters, and comment separately on these; in other words, the reaction is discriminating, tangential, and fragmentational rather than monolithic. Thirdly, in commenting on parts of the story, the readers are persistently interested in the relationship between particular episodes, characters, places, and their prototypes or analogues in reality. Indeed, one could see the urge to intervene in the production of the definitive text as a reflection of the belief that the text was simultaneously the vehicle both for invention and for the representation of a collectively shared reality. Finally, the reader's emphasis on the representational function of the text may be so strong that it even runs counter to the avowed intentions of the writer himself to be presenting 'merely' a fiction (a somewhat limp disavowal given the fact that the novelists in question have clearly taken pains to locate their stories in a recognizable reality). According to Thiesse, Sue was more than surprised by the reformist tendencies attributed to him (his initial plan was simply to write a rattling good tale), but went along with his readers' view of his intentions; as his notes and letters indicate, Scott was at times irritated by the extent to which his readers insisted on reading his narratives, not only as romances or novels, but also as representations of those parts of historical reality which interested them (see, for example, Scott 1833: II, 115-16; Grierson 1932-37: XI, 371).

One swallow, even two swallows is no guarantee that it is springtime. But if the two cases examined briefly here do not allow us to draw any general conclusion, they do provide further support for the notion that an utterance may have both a representational and a fictional function, that make-believe and belief are not mutually exclusive but rather complementary in ways which have yet to be fully explored (though hinted at in passing by Pavel in his brief discussion of the interaction between "relevance" and "distance," 1986: 145-46). In other words, there are grounds for taking the familiar "No reference to any living person is intended or should be inferred," not as proof of the general tendency to divorce invention and fact, but rather as a symptom of the tendency of both writers and readers to conjugate them.

Once the notion of a double function is recognized and taken seriously, it becomes important for theorists to take account of the contextual factors which influence the reader's emphasis of one function or another, even to the point of almost over-riding the fictional convention altogether. A number of such factors are suggested by the cases glanced at here. A text may address or find its way to a public with little knowledge of, or respect for, literary conventions. The text in question may not fit into a recognizable genre, hence allowing for greater improvization on the part of the public. The text in question may be a historical novel which, as such, invites foregrounding of the representational function. The readers may have little alternative to novels for access to information about the world (what might be called the *faute de mieux* principle in cultural participation). Finally, and most importantly perhaps, there may be something like an *auto-recognition* principle at work whereby readers take the fact of being able to recognize their own locality, acquaintances or experiences as a value in itself. As Thiesse suggests, many of Sue's non-bourgeois readers were thrilled to find representatives of the class with which they identified themselves figuring in a novel, as presumably Scott's Scottish readers were gratified to see places and 'local heroes' they recognized figuring in a published work (the equivalent of being 'on the telly' nowadays). Whatever may have been the precise combination of factors influencing the responses mentioned here, it is clear that a future pragmatics of fiction cannot proceed on the assumption of a homogeneous, and politely passive reading public always more interested in art than in reality.

References

Grierson, H.J.C. (ed). 1932-37. *The Letters of Sir Walter Scott.* 12 vols. London: Constable.
Hrushovksi, Benjamin. 1984. "Fictionality and Fields of Reference: Remarks on a Theoretical Framework." *Poetics Today* 5(2): 227-51.
Pavel, Thomas. 1986. *Fictional Worlds.* Cambridge, MA: Harvard University Press.
Ronen, Ruth. 1994. *Possible Worlds in Literary Theory.* Cambridge: Cambridge University Press.
Ryan, Marie-Laure. 1991. *Possible Worlds, Artificial Intelligence, and Narrative Theory.* Bloomington, IN: Indiana University Press.
Scott, Sir Walter. 1833. *Introductions, and Notes and Illustrations, to the Novels, Tales, and Romances, of the Author of Waverley.* 3 vols. Edinburgh: Robert Cadell; London: Whittaker.
Thiesse, Anne Marie. 1980. "L'éducation sociale d'un romancier: Le cas d'Eugène Sue." *Actes de la recherche en sciences sociales* 32/33: 51-63.
Vaihinger, Hans. 1986 [1927]. *Die Philosophie des als ob: System der theoretischen, praktischen und religiösen Fiktionen der Menschheit auf Grund eines idealistischen Positivismus.* Aalen: Scientia Verlag.
Walton, Kendall L. 1993 [1990]. *Mimesis as Make-Believe: On the Foundations of the Representational Arts.* Cambridge, MA: Harvard University Press.

Should We Have Insured Ourselves Against Nietzsche?

Frans Ruiter
Utrecht University

During the past ten years, the rules of literary criticism seem to have changed. Whereas Formalist, Structuralist and Marxist critics sailed under the flag of objectivity, critics nowadays brag about their partiality and perspectivism. Many identify with groups that are (or feel themselves to be) culturally excluded: women, blacks, homosexuals, ethnic minorities. They have seized upon the fashionable relativism which, in the eighties, spread in the wake of Poststructuralism, to exercise their cultural politics of emancipation. On the whole, literary studies have gained by this. Well-known literary texts are read differently, which is instructive, and new texts are added to the literary canon, which is enriching.

One advantage of these developments is that the ethical dimension of literary communication (for too long neglected in literary studies) has been brought back into prominence. Positive as this is in itself, it is at this point that I am having a bit of a problem. To put it succinctly: emancipatory concerns (which are primarily directed towards the recognition of a *collective* identity) do not always combine easily with ethical ones (which are *individual* by 'nature'). From an ethical point of view, cultural politics have gone astray as soon as literary works are branded as ideologically dangerous and politically incorrect, and are removed from the curriculum or, even worse, from the library shelves.

In the Netherlands, cultural politics are just emerging and the library shelves are still well filled. There has been some sabre rattling recently, though. In 1991, two emancipation inspired scholars, Ernst van Alphen and

Maaike Meijer, edited a book with what they called 'contrary interpretations' of well-known Dutch literary texts. Rather belligerent, the book is titled in Dutch *De canon onder vuur*, which can be translated as 'the canon under fire.' In the introduction, Van Alphen and Meijer duly pay respect to their Anglo-Saxon examples. As they put it: in England and the United States all 'great' writers have already gone and been cut open. They do not hesitate to put the word 'great' between quotation marks, leaving little room to guess what, at least in their view, the result of this surgical intervention has been.

As things went, not the canon, but their book itself came under pretty heavy attack. Interestingly enough, it was not the 'contrary interpretations' which elicited furious critical reactions, but the moralizing tenor of the bulk of the essays. Especially the contribution of Mieke Bal, professor of Literary Theory at the University of Amsterdam, succeeded in needling everybody. Bal analyzes *Het land van herkomst* (Country of Origin), an important Dutch novel written by E. du Perron (1899-1940) and published in 1935. It is one of the few Dutch novels which Douwe Fokkema and Elrud Ibsch, in *Modernist Conjectures* (1987), had judged worthy of their European Modernist canon, side by side with *Der Zauberberg*, *Ulysses* and *À la Recherche du temps perdu*. Clearly, this did not impress Bal. She reaches the highly unfavorable conclusion that the main character in *Het land van herkomst* is guilty of racism, sexism, and homophobia. Because the content of the novel is more or less autobiographical, the author E. du Perron is also declared guilty of these sins. But Bal did not stop there. As the majority of the Dutch literary intelligentsia holds Du Perron in high esteem (he functions more or less as a role model, because of his intellectual independence and 'political correctness' *vis à vis* the threat of fascism and communism in the thirties), all these admirers are guilty by association. Needless to say, the literary critics did not follow Bal's casuistry. Unanimously, they declared it absurd to screen literary texts for moral abuses in such a crude and anachronistic way. The reactions were rather emotional, and on the whole not very well substantiated. Still, the critics had a point.

A closer look at a rather peculiar institution in the Dutch literary field may help us to gauge how kindred this present-day criticism is to a seemingly outlived form of moralizing criticism. I allude to the — nowadays almost forgotten — Roman Catholic Information Service Concerning Reading, which, from 1937 till 1970, functioned in the Netherlands as a semi-official Catholic censorship board. It became known as *Idil* (an abbreviation of the

Dutch name, Rooms Katholieke Informatie Dienst Inzake Lectuur; in the following I base myself on the highly informative article by Evert Peet in *Jaarboek Katholiek Documentatiecentrum* 15 [1985]: 50-80). Since the anti-authoritarian and liberal movements of the sixties, *Idil* has been considered a reprehensible organization of rather narrow-minded moralizers. But how much is the difference between the practice of present Postmodern critics (who are an offshoot of these very sixties) and that of those Catholic moralizers? Let us take a closer look.

Idil was founded by Catholic booksellers, librarians, publishers, and laymen with a professional interest in literature. Their aim was to interpret the Catholic canon laws as far as they had a bearing on books. Only in exceptional cases did the Church ban books and place them on the notorious *Index*. The problem was that one never could be sure that a book, which was not placed on the *Index*, was not forbidden. In fact, every book that went against doctrinal authority or was just morally off-color, was forbidden for Catholics, even if the Church did not explicitly forbid it. This meant that every Catholic reader who took up a book had to ask himself whether it could jeopardize him spiritually. If so, the book was forbidden territory. In case of doubt, or if the reader felt he could not judge by himself, he had to call in the help of an expert. *Idil*, now, wanted to advise the multitude of common 'innocent' readers, who could not trust their own reading power. In fact, one was discouraged from reading a book before it was properly reviewed by the information service.

To enable reviewers to do their work properly they got special episcopal reading-permission. This was crucial. Without such permission a reviewer had to lay down a book as soon as he suspected that it was a forbidden book. Reviewers were advised, though, to hide review copies away at home. "Don't let the poison cabinet wide open!" the instructions ran.

Book reviews in the *Idil*-periodical ended with a Roman numeral. *V* meant: this book is fit for everybody; *IV*: only for adults; *III*: only for educated readers; *II*: may be read only by exception and for sound reasons; *I*: forbidden for Catholic readers. It is interesting to see the judgment the reviewers passed on modern Dutch writers who later secured themselves a place in the canon. Simon Vestdijk, Willem Frederik Hermans, Harry Mulisch, Louis Paul Boon, and Hugo Claus (to mention only the most famous of the postwar Dutch writers) fluctuated between Roman I and Roman III. This simply meant that the common Catholic reader had to leave the works of these writers unread. The emerging canon of postwar Dutch literature was already coming under severe fire when Ernst van Alphen and Maaike Meijer were still in their cradles. Nowadays we know the canon hardly suffered from it.

Idil was just a small part of a "politics of recognition" (Charles Taylor), which tried to reach its aims by way of culturally isolating the different sections of the population according to confessional allegiance — what in Dutch is known as 'verzuiling.' Ideally, the 'politics of recognition' covered all domains of life: politics, religion, the media, education, commerce, leisure, etc. Even though such total control was never effectuated, confessional segmentation has been the hall-mark of Dutch society from the twenties to the sixties.

The Postmodern emancipation movements of today do their work far more subtly. Of course, the fundamental tension between the cultivation of one's own cultural identity and participation in the dominant culture is still there. But the old, defensive parochialism and narrow-mindedness is avoided nowadays.

Maaike Meijer, who is a prominent advocate of Women's Studies in the Netherlands, would never contemplate issuing a reading ban on sexist literary texts. In her opinion, (female) readers have to learn to fight. To avoid becoming victims of "cultural rape" (her phrasing), they have to develop into resisting and rebellious readers. It is clear that feminists like Meijer opt for able-mindedness, where *Idil* chose ignorance.

Nevertheless, there are some puzzling similarities. Both anti-modern and Postmodern critics attribute extremely strong power to literary texts. For *Idil* texts could be poison (which, by the way, implies they can also be a medicine or even a placebo). The cultural critics of today also hold that the unlicensed consumption of certain texts can cause damage to the mind. This damage, then, has to be prevented by educating people into combative readers. In a hostile cultural climate (white, male, Eurocentric) this kind of readers have to be nurtured and coached. This explains the flood of exemplary feminist and anti-racist interpretations. Exceptions left aside, sexist and racist texts are not taken out of circulation: they are rather 'cut open.' A politically correct interpretation supposedly puts a stop to sexist and racist effects: the evil spell will be broken. Hopefully, in the long run non-professional readers will be able to make their own correct interpretations.

In *De canon onder vuur* Van Alphen and Meijer claim that it is not history that produces the text and its interpretations, but it is the text and its interpretations that produce history. Needless to say, someone who takes this view (and is not happy with the course history has taken), has a vital interest in deactivating the detonator of potentially explosive texts. Every time this is pulled off successfully, the spreading of evil is hampered. But does such a view, in the end, not legitimize (or rather make mandatory) a total and unremitting surveillance of the imagination?

"Contrary interpretations are necessary," so we read in the *De canon onder vuur*, "not to astound, not out of a need to do something new, but to break out of the compelling grip of the tradition of interpretation, which has the tendency to persist endlessly." This statement deserves some reflection because of its almost Christian rhetoric. There is a clear hint of a fall into the tradition of interpretation (meaning into history, which, as we have seen, is only a derivative of texts). But there seems to be hope of salvation: there are possibilities for breaking out of the compelling grip of interpretation and history. What kind of agent, one wonders, is able to remedy the fallen state of interpretation and history? He or she must have been touched by grace (which, in the Christian doctrine, is a special privilege of the wretched of the earth). Maybe we do not have to take all this so literally. But then, that would imply that the grip of interpretation and history is not so compelling after all. Which makes it wholly unnecessary to choose such a pathetically rhetorical mode to speak about texts and their readers.

Van Alphen and Meijer seem to waver between dependence on some kind of irrational leap out of the tradition and an urge to get the tradition under total control. In an earlier book — *Bang voor schennis? Inleiding in ideologiekritiek* (Afraid of Violation? An Introduction to the Criticism of Ideology) — Ernst van Alphen draws up a complete checklist with which the would-be cultural critic can assess the harmfulness of a text: what exactly are the dangerous elements of a text, for whom are they harmful, how big will the damage be, how long will it take before the damage is effectuated, etc. This looks suspiciously like a form for an insurance claim. Should (and could) we have insured ourselves against Nietzsche?

Both for the critics of *Idil* and for the cultural critics of today the self-responsible reader seems to be a source of concern. *Idil* made the choice not to expose the reader to harmful modern influences. Their Postmodern successors want to get the reader into a maximum state of alert. They believe it is imperative that all incoming cultural information be screened for harmfullness. Every moment of weakness will continue the rule of evil in the world. In my opinion, this extremist (and even paranoid) view threatens to set the recent reflections on the place of ethics in literary studies on a wrong and worn track.

Northrop Frye and the Problem of Cultural Values

The Case of Canada

Roseann Runte
Victoria University, Toronto

If, for Nietzsche, it is an illusion that truth exists as an unattainable entity, then for Northrop Frye, Canada is a reality, not an illusion. Indeed, he is seen by David Staines as a "cultural theorist, mythmaker, and mapmaker of and for his own country." Frye had "a vision of Canada and a hope for the future of a tolerant and cosmopolitan country" (1994: 160). Yet the very quote from Frye which Staines employs in support of his thesis, denies the existence of a nation, of Canada. "The Canada to which we really do owe loyalty is the Canada we have failed to achieve. It is expressed in our culture, but not attained in our life" (Frye 1971: 122-23). Is Canada then an illusion, the creation of the critic, a non-state and non-culture? How can culture be separated from life and life from culture?

Hayden White points out that the most distinguished proponents of cultural studies, such as Althusser and Habermas, tend to dismiss Frye because of his Formalism, Structuralism, and idealism. Frye was put down because he believed literature was paradigmatic of culture and that culture was autonomous of society. Thus, culture and society must be ahistorical (28ff.). Yet, when it came to the elusive notion of his own country, Frye appeared ready to make an exception. Indeed, he wrote in *The Modern Century* that culture is, in part, "historical memory" (125). Linda Hutcheon finds such tensions in Frye's work as possible evidence of his "Postmodernism." She views the conflict between his assertion that Canadian literature should be seen as part of

Canadian life more than as a part of an autonomous world of literature as well as his claim that literature should be viewed as disinterested (what she terms Frye's "militantly non-referential view of literature") as symptomatic of the conflict which is found elsewhere in Frye's work. It is the apparent conflict posed by his opposition to Romantic genius and his support of imagination. This is a Postmodern tension in that it posits the local or the particular against the universal. Hutcheon sees Frye's Canada as "postmodernly open and provisional [...] becoming, trying, not quite there" (1994: 109ff.). This represents yet another Postmodern query about the ontology and epistemology of history itself. How can literature be ahistorical when it is evolving?

Frye's position as a cultural critic is extremely intriguing for he knew personally many of the poets whose works he reviewed. He was, perhaps, even aware that his own criticisms would affect their next productions and that he was an active participant in the creation, not only of a new literature, but of a new country. Frye represents the simultaneity of past and present, of criticism and creation, and the juxtaposition of myths denied and recreated in a culture which he saw as evolving but which, in actuality, reflected not society but the individual. Rather than a literature separate from world literature, in a country of fortresses separated from nature, a country sketched out by a series of stops on the Intercontinental and Canadian Pacific rail lines, Frye imagined a literature which would become qualitatively an integral part of a universal literature, replete with universal myths. For, as I have noted elsewhere, if Frye's Canadians tried to understand nature, their reading was essentially a text they invented. And, if Frye listened to the music of Canadian verse, the symphony or cacophony was of his creation. Terry Eagleton wrote, in speaking of Yale Deconstructionism, "literature becomes the truth, essence or self-consciousness of all other discourses precisely because unlike them it knows that it does not know what it is talking about" (104). It is perhaps in this respect, then, that Canada exists, as a country. It is an entity only when it is described in literature, defined in criticism. Thus, Frye was indeed a creator of Canada and perhaps, more than a cultural critic, he was a creator of culture, a barometer of culture in a land where the barometer is still rising.

As Dennis Porter points out, like the tale of Bougainville's voyage, which provoked Diderot's *Supplément*, Lévi-Strauss's *Tristes tropiques* prompted its own response by Jacques Derrida who criticized Lévi-Strauss for failing to posit a structure without a "transcendental signified." His work was like a globe without a center. He did not practise systematically his own Structuralist theory. Derrida wrote:

> as a turning toward the presence, lost or impossible, of the absent origin, this Structuralist thematic of broken immediateness is thus the sad, negative, nostalgic, guilty Rousseauist face of the thinking of freeplay of which the Nietzschean affirmation — the joyous affirmation of the freeplay of the world without truth and without origin, offered to an active interpretation — would be the other side. This affirmation determines then the non-center as otherwise than the loss of the center. (1970: 264)

Roland Barthes pursued Derrida's logic in *The Empire of Signs* (1970) in attempting "to go beyond essentialism in the European relation to otherness through a practice of 'writing' that was intransitive" (Porter 287). This was what Porter termed a "kind of poststructuralist beyond of theory" (287) and what we might compare, finally, to Hutcheon's Postmodern Frye. Both attempted to turn their backs on Europe and to discover a new world on its own terms. Both were extremely creative in attempting to alter the basis for inquiry (i.e., changing the question from "Who am I?" to "Where is here?"). However, the difference is essentially that Barthes attempted unsuccessfully to erase the slate and to interpret the new signs to which he was exposed without bias. Frye, on the other hand, erected his own sign posts in the Canadian desert and then, albeit dismissing the past, read them against an imagined future, a future which would contain traces of the great myths which join this culture to all others. Frye's Canada stemmed from the pioneering literature of the nineteenth century which "continually conveys the feeling that Canada was a kind of non-criminal penal colony, designed for remittance men and Irish housemaids" (Frye 1991: 126). He compared the present-day Canada to the United States. The latter had, he asserted, "developed from barbarism to decadence with no intervening civilization" while Canada had evolved from a "pre-national to a post-national state without ever having become a nation" (1982: 15).

Frye pointed out in *The Critical Path* that "as culture develops, its mythology tends to become encyclopedic, expanding into a total myth covering a society's view of its past, present and future, its relation to the gods and its neighbors, its traditions, its social and religious duties and to its ultimate destiny" (1971: 36). He then traces the development of literature from orality to its written state and the creation of the myth of concern, the fully developed encyclopedic social myth. In an address he gave shortly before his death, entitled "The Cultural Development of Canada," Frye posits that the country will indeed develop its myth and a rich, cosmopolitan, intellectual and cultural life in which new Canadian writers would bring with them the languages and cultures of the world and weave them into a new literature which would be of world quality. He even meditates on the possibility of, for example, a person of Sri Lankan origin, achieving great literary acclaim. One might wonder if he were indeed thinking already of Michael Ondaatje, whose brilliant novel, *The English Patient*, won not only the Trillium Award in Ontario and the Governor General's Medal in Canada but also the Booker Prize on the international scene.

Yet, Canada is composed of more than a symphony of immigrant voices. It contains two cultures: one French and one English which joined together to create one country rich in natural resources and subject to the economic exploitation of more developed nations. This was Frye's reading, his vision. It was, like the literary canon debated so hotly in recent times, like the curriculum we establish in our teaching, limited by the agenda and concerns of the day. It totally excluded the aboriginal peoples. Indeed, Frye saw the nineteenth-century traveller arriving in an Arcadia, unblemished by the Fall and thus, *sans mythe*. *Hélas*! Would that that reading had been without flaw! Not only did the settlers bring with them the tares of the garden of the expulsed, but the original inhabitants had their own myths and the conjuncture of the shared existence of resident and visitor in this harsh clime was, in itself, a myth which grew from the first day. Frye cites F.R. Scott's translation of Lescarbot's 1606 poem which was addressed to the men who were about to return to France,

> To you who go to see congenial friends
> In language, habits, customs and religion
> And all the lovely scenes of your nation,
> While we among the savages are lost
> And dwell bewildered on this clammy coast

(cited in Frye 1971: 21)

as an example of the somewhat-less-than-heroic voice of the early settler/writer. While Lescarbot does pull himself together sufficiently to recall his mission: to "bring conversion" to a "nation that has no god, no laws, no religion" (1971: 21), Frye sees in this passage yet another demonstration of the lack of fondness for the land so characteristic of the builders of garrisons who were Frye's early Canadians. However, the passage and Frye's interpretation both bear testimony to the imperialist reading of the European who discovers and civilizes the Other. Like Barthes, Frye reads the signs in his own language.

Frye disagrees with the American poet, Wallace Stevens, who in "Description Without Place," a poem, indicates that man does not live directly in the world but inside his own constructs of the world. He concludes that nationality has no existence within nature. But Frye reminds us that when we travel to Spain, everything looks Spanish. He doubts it is all in our minds. For, should we see a windmill in a field of sunflowers in the middle of Tokyo, we would immediately question its congruity.

Frye used this logic to argue that there must indeed be a Canadian identity. However, by this logic, there can only be a Canadian identity inasmuch as there are other nations to provide contrast and inasmuch as there is a beholder who knows of them. Thus, Canada's existence depends on that of other nations and on the ability of the viewer to notice differences.

This means that the responsibility for creating myths lies with the reader, not with the text. In this case, Frye as reader was appropriately active in contributing to the creation of the Canadian myth of concern. Furthermore, he was perfectly accurate in positing that the creation was incomplete, for as long as there are readers for the text, the process of creation will continue.

However, each reader brings his or her own experience to the text and like Frye and Barthes, we interpret the signs according to our own linguistic and cultural experience. Thus, the definition of Canada is as multiple as the readers of its texts and the country exists in reality but a reality which is our individual construct, thus an illusion. Frye, as cultural critic, succeeds both in deconstructing culture and in writing and reading his own work, providing us a new text which is part of the process of the creation of the myths of a new culture.

References

Barthes, Roland. 1973. *L'empire des signes*. Geneva: Skira, and Paris: Flammarion.
Derrida, Jacques. 1970. "Structure, Sign and Play in the Discourse of the Human Sciences." In Richard Mackay and Eugenio Donato (eds), *The Languages of Criticism and the Sciences of Man*. Baltimore: Johns Hopkins University Press.
Eagleton, Terry. 1984. *The Function of Criticism: From the Spectator to Poststructuralism*. London: Verso Editions and NLB.
Frye, Northrop. 1971. *The Critical Path*. Midland: Indiana University Press, and Toronto: Fitzhenry and Whitehead.
—. 1982. *Divisions on the Ground: Essays on Canadian Culture*. Toronto: Anansi.
—. 1991. *The Modern Century*. Toronto: Oxford University Press.
Hutcheon, Linda. 1994. "Frye Recoded: Postmodernity and the Conclusions." Lee and Denham 105-21.

Lee, Alvin A., and Robert D. Denham (eds). 1994. *The Legacy of Northrop Frye*. Toronto: University of Toronto Press.
Porter, Dennis. 1991. *Haunted Journeys: Desire and Transgression in European Travel Writing*. Princeton: Princeton University Press.
Staines, David. 1994. "Frye: Canadian Critic/Writer." Lee and Denham 155-63.
White, Hayden. 1994. "Frye's Place in Contemporary Cultural Studies." Lee and Denham 28-39.

Empirical Studies of Literature — What Else?

Siegfried J. Schmidt
University of Siegen

Today most literary scholars agree upon the insight that it is inadequate to study literary texts in isolation from actors and sociocultural contexts.

Whatever is said is said by an observer to an observer. Observers are living systems endowed with a cognitive apparatus. Like any other system, living systems, too, can only be defined in relation to an environment. The respective environment of cognitive systems is the result of their sense-constructive activities because cognitive systems are operationally closed. Consequently, symmetry breaking happens exclusively in the cognitive domain of the systems.

As active participants in the social construction of reality, observers are conditioned by biological, psychological, sociocultural and media instances. The basic operation applied by observers consists in drawing and naming distinctions. These distinctions are observer-relative, they are not contained in the environment. Thus, cognition does not provide us with a picture of reality, but with a picture of our activities in environments. Operating (in) system-specific environments, we never encounter objects ('as such') but only the results of our highly conditioned activities (= experience, knowledge). According to H. von Foerster, objects and events are not primary experiences but representations of relations.

It follows from these assumptions that literature is what observers deem literary according to the concepts by which they establish and handle the difference between the literary and the non-literary. These concepts are acquired by experiencing prototypical cases of both sides of the difference in the course of literary socialization. Normally, these concepts remain implicit, as blind spots of the cultural domain of first-order observers.

First-order observers, i.e., actors operating in their "socio-natural" environments, automatically interpret their experiences of pragmatic, logical, or social stabilities in terms of an evident intrinsic order of reality. If the intuitive faith in experiencing reality is disturbed or blamed, questions pop up concerning reality, empiricity, objectivity or truth. These questions are typical for second-order observers observing other observers' observations, including their blind spots. Of course, the observations of second-order observers, too, are dominated by blind spots of the cultural distinctions they apply in their observations.

Since these kinds of observation can, in turn, be observed by a third-order observer (with his/her blind spots) we know for sure that we live in a contingent world of experiences. Cultures, i.e., semantico-epistemological communities, serve as (more or less unquestioned) ordered systems of distinction together with their normative interpretation and emotional loading. As long as a society, based on culture and reproducing itself via culture, survives, constructor and construct form an inseparable unity. It is unreasonable to assume that the observer is categorically separated from the world observed. If we forget or neglect this intrinsic relation, we are tempted to perceive our environments and other observers therein as trivial machines (following H. von Foerster) whose function we are to uncover.

In the past, the concept 'empirical' was always related to 'experience.' In order to avoid an empiristic reading of this relation we have to enlarge the concept of experience beyond sensory perception alone. Experience integrates sensory/perceptual, motoric, and conceptual elements; it interweaves operational as well as "ontological knowledge" (after G. Rusch). Experience and knowing is effective acting in cultural traditions. Knowledge is action which, as a social event, happens in communication. Signs, too, do not refer to objects in reality, but to consensually interpreted activities in culture, i.e., to communication. This is the reason why observers succeed to communicate, although their cognitive systems are operationally closed. What is often called the 'mental representation of reality' must be regarded as co-ordinating relation, not as images. We do not mirror things, but our handling of those things.

If — by equally respecting system and environment as mutually defining instances — we define 'reality' as the domain determined by the actions and interactions of observing systems, or if we follow B.C. van Fraassen's argument that what counts as an observable phenomenon is a function of a/the epistemic community, then the objectivity of experiences has to be determined in terms of making, communicating, and evaluating experiences.

Today most philosophers of science agree that scientific behavior can be modelled as theoretically determined production of knowledge and experience through the applications of explicit methods. This happens primarily on the level of communication in the framework and under the conditions of the social system 'science.' From a communicative point of view, scholars do not handle stable realities, but communicatively stabilized distinctions and descriptions in the experiential world of a community of investigators.

Empirical research generally means the production of logical, pragmatic and social stabilities. Stability, i.e., a systems-dependent aspect, may be regarded to be a central criterion of/for 'reality' on all levels of observation. Knowledge is evaluated as adequate to reality if it allows relevant predictions and thus provides a stable basis of action. Whatever successfully supports the construction of stability (according to ceteris-paribus-conditions) in scientific communication serves as a datum or document.

From these assumptions it follows that the intuitive and traditional reference of 'empirical' to 'reality' in an ontological sense and to the experience of first-order observer has to be transferred to:

1. cognitive and communicative activities embedded in sociocultural contexts;
2. the construction and evaluation of knowledge according to sociocultural criteria developed by observers;
3. the level of second-order observation.

If these observations are explicitly directed by theories and methods toward the solution of explicitly formulated problems, I speak of scientific, empirical research, because the results can be stabilized in (inter)disciplinary communication, and because concepts, criteria and results of systematic experiencing are consensual — in a scientific community.

H. von Foerster has described the methodically controlled production of data as trivialization, i.e., as a procedure to construe stable distinctions under conditions which — in many cases — drastically reduce ecological complexities (for instance, in laboratory research). Trivialization is further specified by procedures of isolation and reduction — procedures which turn out to be highly inadequate when applied to complex, non-linear cognitive or social systems, whose essential feature consists in the interaction between their components. They are, in Foerster's terminology, non-trivial machines, i.e., they are synthetically deterministic, historically dependent, analytically indeterminable, and unpredictable.

Although, for practical reasons, in empirical research we cannot avoid reducing complexity via standardization of procedures, we should regard human beings as self-organizing, creative and autonomous world-constructing machines who are responsible for their constructions of realities; i.e., we should always try to de-trivialize them. De-trivialization characterizes a research strategy that tries to reach two goals: to incorporate the observer into the observed, and to operate in a manner oriented to systems, i.e., to avoid the methodological and methodical shortcomings of isolation and reduction.

Literary scholars do not talk about objects (in the traditional sense). They talk about phenomena which emerge from the application and interpretation of distinctions deemed relevant by a community of investigators in the social system 'literary studies.' As scholars, they talk about literary phenomena in order to solve problems they deem relevant together with other members of the academic community, according to commonly shared cultural convictions, norms, and goals.

The solution of problems requires procedures. In a scientific context, where problems have to be explicitly formulated, and where problem-solving has to follow theoretically defined strategies in order to obtain results which can thus be systematically checked, empirical studies of literature may be modelled in terms of a reflexive experience of literary phenomena. It consists of reflexive second-order observations of the social system literature, as well as of the symbolic system literature, i.e., the set of literary phenomena.

If the notion 'empirical' is related to specific procedures of observers making experiences with literature, then we may draw two final conclusions:

1. "Hence, I submit in all modesty, the claim for objectivity is nonsense!" (H. von Foerster).
2. "Empirical Studies of Literature — what else?" (S.J. Schmidt).

Cultural and Literary Identity: Disease or Medicine?

A Dialogue with Douwe Fokkema

Rien T. Segers
University of Groningen

Sometimes I dream the dream about the social validity of literary studies occupying a prestigious status in the Western world. The utopian world where we have discovered the new alphabet. Politicians, economists and journalists are waiting in line before the doors of literary scholars to hear the latest news about a new Hamlet interpretation, the results of a just completed research project or the most recent publication on literary and cultural identity...

The reality, however, is different. How different, can be inferred from an interesting, though relatively unknown publication by Douwe Fokkema (1990). This presidential address, delivered at the Twelfth Congress of the International Comparative Literature Association and hidden in one of the five voluminous *Proceedings* volumes, may still serve as a *pièce de résistance* in the debate concerning the validity of literary scholarship. It shows a deep concern for the relevance of literary studies in a world which is predominantly preoccupied with economic progress. This paper has an additional advantage: it clearly shows the reader the three significant public dimensions of Douwe Fokkema: scholar, organizer and defender of reason.

By concentrating ourselves on the scholarly aspects of this article we receive a clear vision concerning the status of literary studies in a rapidly changing world. It contains a plea for a non-speculative literary theory, deplores the lack of continuity in literary scholarship, and condemns the search for national or regional characteristics.

Cultural and Literary Identity: Disease or Medicine?

Douwe Fokkema's timing to deal with a particular scholarly topic has always been very precise. In fields that interested him he published generally speaking at the right moment. Also in this case: the timing to attack the concepts of cultural and literary identity was almost perfect. At that time, in 1988, these two concepts started to receive some response in literary studies, after years of victory in many branches of the social sciences especially in North America.

Whereas most of Fokkema's observations expressed in that paper are still valid, his view on questions relating to cultural and literary identity should be updated and revised, I think. Fokkema starts out to defend the universal character of literature with which every comparatist would agree. But my disagreement begins with the implication that the similarities among the several literatures are much more striking than the differences. How would you prove that? The similarity feature is characteristic for the practice of comparative literature until the mid-eighties. Different cultures were supposed to produce literatures which are to be investigated on similarities rather than on differences. Now, more than a decade later, the similarity feature of literature is questioned. One might wonder to what extent this is due to the awakening of nationalism almost all over the world.

Fokkema posits that the "search for national or regional characteristics is a disease that has also affected the scholarly debate" (114). Does that mean that he pushes cultural identity aside at the very moment when it is gaining relevance for literary and cultural studies?

Research that takes the concepts of cultural and literary identity as points of departure, may result in a number of advantages for literary studies: new insights into old problems and the discovery of other research domains. Here I single out three of such advantages.

First of all, the concept of *cultural* identity requires a well-grounded and adequate definition of culture. In recent years several important publications have appeared concerning the two elements of the concept: 'culture' and 'identity.' For instance, the book *Cultures and Organizations* by Geert Hofstede (1991) gives an interesting view on the former concept. His book encountered a remarkable reception in some branches of the social sciences and business administration over the last years. Now it has entered the gates of literary studies, and not without reason.

Hofstede's definition of 'culture' is interesting and useful. I subscribe to his view, because his definition unites three important elements. It shows the decisive value of culture, the importance of cultural relativism and the constructed character of culture. Hofstede distinguishes two meanings of the word culture. There is culture one, which refers to civilization, refinement of the mind which can be found in education, art and literature. This is not the description of culture I would like to refer to. I shall select here Hofstede's culture two, which

> deals with much more fundamental human processes than culture one; it deals with the things that hurt. Culture (two) is always a collective phenomenon, because it is at least partly shared with people who live or lived within the same social environment, which is where it was learned. It is *the collective programming of the mind which distinguishes the members of one group or category of people from another.* (45)

Hofstede has a systemic (*in sensu* Niklas Luhmann) conception of culture. He does not see 'culture' as a vast unspecified domain, but as an entity consisting of different levels, which are interrelated. At the same time a person always belongs to a number of the following levels, indicators of identity, for instance: a national level according to one's country; a regional / ethnic / religious / linguistic affiliation; a gender level; a generation level; a social class level; an organizational or corporate level for those who are employed. The implication is that it is impossible to speak about 'the' identity of a person or of a group; it may vary according to circumstances.

For the concepts of 'cultural identity' or 'literary identity' this implies that the identity of a particular group or people is only partly determined by their national identity. The other part may be determined by international conventions, international flows of information.

Through the concept of cultural identity a second, heavily debated topic comes within reach: the well-known discussion about the opposition between globalization and nationalization. A 1989 report by the OECD formulated this opposition rather clearly:

> on the one hand, there is the search for cultural authenticity, the return to origins, the need to preserve minor languages, pride in particularisms, admiration for cultural self-sufficiency and maintenance of national traditions; on the other hand, we find the spread of a uniform world culture, the emergence of supranational myths and the adoption of similar lifestyles in widely different settings. Modern technological societies have generated a transnational, composite, mass culture with its own language whose linguistic imprint is already universally evident. (OECD 1989: 16)

This paradox between nationalization and globalization can be found in many parts of the world and in many different ways.

By concentrating on cultural or literary identity we meet a third 'hot' issue: nationalism. Nationalism is back today with a vengeance all over the world, from Canada to India, from the former USSR to Iraq, from Japan to Turkey. For the time being I belong to those who believe that nationalization will dominate globalization at least in the foreseeable future, and not only outside Western Europe as some critics want us to believe, but also to a considerable extent in the countries that belong to the key group members of the European Union. Helmut Dubiel (1994: 896), for instance, recently described new forms of German nationalism. But similar tendencies are alive and well in many other countries of the European Union.

I fully agree with Rolf Dahrendorf's (1994: 760) conclusion after his fine analysis of the future of the nation state. He is convinced that also in the coming decades the nation state will stay on as the framework of individual rights and the center from which international relations will be constructed. The nation state will not be touched by all kinds of new political and social developments. To phrase this in well-known German words: 'Europa ist eine Kopfgeburt und die Regionen sprechen das Herz an.'

Another advantage of research within the domain of cultural and literary identity has an idealistic nature. I believe with Douwe Fokkema (1995) in the concept of cosmopolitanism, despite its naive connotations referring to the early days of Comparative Literature in the fifties. In my view, however, cosmopolitanism can be achieved only by an awareness of the fundamental differences between cultures and their literatures. Only on the basis of the acknowledgement of the otherness of a certain culture, one is able to practise 'code-switching' between two or more cultures. If the cultural identity of a foreign nation is not perceived as such, the need for code-switching is absent. The consequences of sticking to one's own code in foreign cultures lie on a scale between impoliteness and war.

Is the search for cultural identity a disease? The answer to this question is dependent on the aim of the search. If the aim is, as has been the case so many times in the past, to legitimize one's own superiority, then it is a disease and a rather malignant one. But the search for cultural and literary identity can also be undertaken in view of the fostering of understanding for the 'otherness' of foreign countries or cultures. The aim is then merely irenic: an attempt to make undeniable cultural differences visible and, at the same time, an attempt to bridge these differences by the understanding of similarities. And is this not the supreme justification and the ultimate goal of comparative research into the concept of cultural identity?

Obviously, I realize that the study of the cultural or literary identity of a nation or a group within that nation does not constitute a direct highway to the utopian world I sometimes dream of. On the one hand there are severe scholarly problems in using the concepts of cultural and literary identity: they are tricky and vague and the description of the cultural specificity of a community is a rather complex phenomenon. On the other hand there is the problem of the impact of our scholarly endeavors. Politicians, especially those in countries where two or more cultural identities compete with each other, will probably find scholarly analyses of cultural identity too multi-dimensional and too complex for use in the political arena. Usually they tend to favor constructions of reality that do not do justice to its complexity but are based on easily applicable and rather superficial analyses.

Moreover, there is an additional reason to be skeptic and critical, which is also true for similar concepts such as 'tradition,' 'culture,' 'nation,' and 'ethnic group.' As Richard Handler (1994: 28) correctly observed in this respect: "Identity has become a salient scholarly and cultural construct in the mid-twentieth century, particularly in social-scientific scholarship in the United States. Its prominence in that context, however, does not mean that the concept can be applied unthinkingly to other places and times."

To deal with all these and similar points of justified criticism would imply writing a much longer essay. For the moment, however, let me conclude by stating my conviction that concentration on studies concerning cultural and literary identity will enhance our insight into the major contemporary and social issues. Could that approach help in developing a medicine against the fear of literary studies to get marginalized? Could it also be a medicine which helps to combat the growing nationalism by showing that cultural identity is just a construction and not an innate property?

References

Dahrendorf, Rolf. 1994. "Die Zukunft des Nationalstaates." *Merkur, Zeitschrift für Europäisches Denken* 48(9/10): 751-761.
Dubiel, Helmut. 1994. "Über moralische Souveränität, Erinnerung und Nation." *Merkur, Zeitschrift für Europäisches Denken* 48(9/10): 884-897.

Fokkema, Douwe W. 1990. "On Theory and Criticism in Literary Studies: The International Point of View." In Roger Bauer, Douwe Fokkema, and Michael de Graat (eds), *Proceedings of the XIIth Congress of the International Comparative Literature Association*. 5 vols. Munich: Iudicium Verlag, vol. I, 111-119.

—. 1995. "Western, Eastern, and Multicultural Canons of Literature: Comparative Literature and the Problems of Canon Formation." Plenary lecture International Congress "Cultural Dialogue and Cultural Misreading," 9-11 October, Peking University, Beijing, China.

Handler, Richard. 1994. "Is 'Identity' a Useful Cross-Cultural Concept?" In John R. Gillis (ed), *Commemorations: The Politics of National Identity*. Princeton, N.J.: Princeton University Press, 27-40.

Hofstede, Geert. 1991 [Paperback ed. 1994]. *Cultures and Organizations: Software of the Mind, Intercultural Cooperation and its Importance for Survival*. Hammersmith, London: Harper Collins.

OECD. 1989. *One School, Many Cultures* Paris: Organization for Economic Cooperation and Development; Centre for Educational Research and Innovation.

Literary Studies, Media and Low Culture

Some Minor Clues for a Major Topic

Maria Alzira Seixo
University of Lisbon

It seems that literary studies, considered in a cultural relation with the development of the mass media, may take position, for the moment, in two directions: (1) scholars may keep an attitude of cultural elitism that must face social and economic individual differences as a way of maintaining recognized levels of aesthetic perception and canonical works of guided reading; (2) conversely, they may open other perspectives by considering new modes in the emergence of the literary object, accepting mixed manifestations in the artistic intents, and creating adequate methodologies in the teaching of literature. In so doing they may enlarge the field of literary performances realized and accepted, such as reading literature as entertainment, reading literature as a professional need, reading literature as a cultural habit and, as a new trend they may in that way develop, reading literature as a single activity supported by other surrounding activities. In that multiple cultural complex, the literary fact may lose some of its specific marks and forms of traditional communication but, on the other hand, literature can eventually emerge in a stronger way in our contemporary cultural practice.

It is a matter of fact that the traditional views, in the first attitude, can only be sustained in order to preserve cultural values, which may not mean that the criteria for evaluation are something *sub specie aeternitatis* but must configurate a set of common human implications (aesthetic, ethic and emotional) that can determine a majority of similar effects in the act of reading. Those similar effects happen to be usually concentrated in canon-formations (not only for inclusion but also for exclusion), which depend on identical forms by which the community perceives cultural and literary values in the same objects. This is in fact contradictory with the conditions of basic differences (especially economic and social) and of superior-inferior (elitist) criteria of distinction. Nevertheless, these effects, swinging between similarity and difference, have the possibility of balancing themselves in a conservative position, as far as they are determined by a dynamic where the values of permanence, socially and emotionally secure, and most of all converging with a classic ideal of beauty, often alternate with the wish to gain access to the universe of "distinction," in Bourdieu's word.

Of course the school keeps this ideal in mind, and has in it its real justification. But the question is exactly whether the permanence of this ideal, nowadays, with a concept of modernity that is precisely defined by change, by new perceptions of time as passage, and by operating infractions to the regular concepts of beauty, signifies the supremacy of school or not. We can recall here the emergence, in some European countries, of new courses, of new universities, and new institutions of teaching in all modalities, and most of them encouraged by governments, although they sometimes are private. (And for good reasons do governments themselves encourage them). If the forms of teaching at school do not change, that means that the very relation with education must naturally change, and school supremacy might be lost. Moreover, some practical changes in schools are not established by a theoretical reflexion, but by bureaucratic needs and institutional directions that contribute to nullify the specific values of the teaching of literature.

For the second attitude, there are maybe three manners in the way we can take it. First of all, we may follow contemporary times, adapting techniques, adding new works and texts to our analytic work and adapting topics to present needs. I believe that this attitude of adjunction does not change anything and is more conservative than cultural elitism effectively assumed. But we could find another manner, and that is the complete change of matters, canonical prescriptions, critical methodologies and participation of students in academic activities. That manner will undoubtedly develop interesting ways of teaching and important innovation in the syllabuses, but this way of turning things into their opposite may become simplistic and not satisfactory in its results. It can be argued that this is a mere question of words, but with some precaution we could also say that it is really a question where important intents turn just around words, and where words, sounds and images are equally the matter of complex reactions. So, let us accept that the cultural system may appear to us at present as a discontinuous whole, and yet never evasive or insignificant, and that the university, in literary studies, could try a kind of practice of, let us say, 'accommodation' between a systematic way of teaching and the different forms of the world outside (which on a psychological level is always simultaneously inside and outside).

Maybe a third positon could simply be that of considering (that is, of looking at) the world while we are teaching, and trying to establish a network of directions (developed by meaning, by social input and by multiple kinds of reception) that could reintegrate a phenomenon of creation called literature (which develops disruptions against the temptation of fixed models) and a situation of instability called society (which, on the contrary, develops its own conventions in search of permanent values), accepting that reproduction and creativeness remain in both, but in different proportions and to different goals (cf. Rigney and Fokkema 1993).

And then one of the most urgent things that we should see is how different forms of culture involve our crystallized notion of literary studies, and that what makes it possible for literature and art to be involved by these different forms of culture is exactly the media, and other means of reproduction that (since the nineteenth century, and especially since Baudelaire) have been changing the effects of creation, as Walter Benjamin has argued. One could even think that what we call low culture is not a stratum of dishonorable features constituting a human level of knowledge and emotion, but a mixture of several levels, including high cultural levels, and starting from this modern idea (and democratic too, execrated by Baudelaire) that to reproduce art is good for humankind. In a similar way, high culture depends more and more on this 'modern' invention of low culture, from 'kitsch' to some very elitistic productions coming from Duchamps' inventions, which can be found in the literary domain nowadays in some parodistic thematizations of detective stories (Kurt Vonnegut, Jean Echenoz) or, in an even more sophisticated way, in several attempts at creating in literature the visual effect obtained by comics or by television (Mário de Carvalho, Luísa Costa Gomes), and where Michel Butor, to my mind, holds a very important place as a writer who breaks the traditional and conventional idea of the book in order to open it to the most diverse cultural practices, preserving a very high cultural level, as we like it.

Low culture is thus a whole set of artifacts and ways of thinking or feeling produced by modern art, and fostered by the media. Of course the media also bring to us high culture, and literature, and everything else (at least some media do). I would like to emphasize the place of television because it is undoubtedly the most prominent means of mass communication nowadays (which can absorb others, like journalism and radio), and where literature is practically non-existent and low culture most prominent. The works presented on TV are particularly representative, as we know, of ideological forms of alienation and stereotypical devices. And yet we can observe this peculiar mark, which is that a large proportion of audiences watch them regularly.

The question is: why do all these people watch television? And also, why are all these people satisfied with low culture? We know the common answer: it is because low culture is easier to consume, it is because these people are not cultivated, it is because the political and the cultural system in the media do not want to offer better productions; but this last point is justified by the fact that TV productions are looking for large audiences, and large audiences prefer low culture, what brings us to the previous two points. And those two points are strong arguments, not in favor of high culture but against school. Because all those people have gone through school, and the school did not prepare them for high culture; on the contrary, it seems that the school has precisely led people to low culture, since even teachers are not aware that they are doing so, and that they are dominated by the low culture system.

This leads me to my essential point, namely that if we agree on the description I have provided, we must discuss our responsibilities in the teaching of literature, art, culture, and the humanities in general; moreover, we have to decide whether we want to work in literary studies with our students with conventional and artificial syllabuses, separating our teaching from our behavior in everyday life, as students separate theirs, at least because we constitute an example for them, or whether we want to bring some real life and breath into our teaching, making it part of common behavior and experience, and, starting from here, developing criticism and evaluation, effectively building a body of cultivated people related with their contemporary society. For this, analysis and criticism of the media must not be a simple rejection of them or a demagogic inclusion in the syllabuses, but a discussion of the consistent points they present to be validated in contemporary life, and especially of art forms, and new art forms they are allowed to create.

The place of literature, and particularly literary studies, does not emerge clearly from this argument; and it is so if we consider literature as a product of writing inactively waiting in books, and its teaching as a function of tradition and convention; but if one takes literature to be a production of meaning which partially breaks and reconstructs systems, and the teaching of literature as a social and cultural function that increases the capacity of learning as an activity, and the possibility of evaluation as a way of criticism and transformation, one necessarily needs to situate literature, not exactly in a context (which is a vague way of supposing that texts lie in constraining and sterile grounds, that can mostly signify more than them) but in some precise social, cultural and artistic situations that effectively structure the text, like a sermon in a church, or a speech in a meeting, like a poem read on the radio, or a narrative accompanying images in a serial drama.

In general, TV does not care about literature; and it is generally painful, for literary scholars and amateurs to look at daily information about politics, business, sport, and sometimes art, that is, about money, and realize that there is no place in it for literature; however, more distressing is the fact that literature can sometimes be a TV topic, but only for telling the life of a writer, or for preparing adaptations from texts to images. One rarely sees on the screen attempts at the manifestation of writing, regular statements coming from authors and cultural debates on literary subjects. To complain about it means nevertheless to accept the situation, and attests to the mediatic disadvantage of literature, *quod erat demonstrandum*. In fact, insisting on our teaching (with concrete examples and specific methods) that literature is mediatic as any other subject; and teaching literature conceiving it *also* as a component of a multiple complex of arts, systems of communication and mediatic instances — are tasks that scholars should accept, if professional ethics is not only in this case considered in the administrative sense, but also in an appealing way of expressing the fascinating power of the art of writing.

Reference

Rigney, Ann, and Douwe Fokkema (eds). 1993. *Cultural Participation*. Amsterdam: Benjamins.

Traveling Theory: A Twisting Movement

Dan Shen
Peking Univeristy

In his influential article "Traveling Theory," Edward Said proposes a model for the way any theory or idea travels from one culture to another, a model that consists of four distinct stages: (a) the birth, (b) the movement, (c) the reception (including resistance to), and (d) the transformation of the theory (1983: 226-227). Insofar as the first stage is concerned, the model seems to involve a confusion between a discussion of the travel and the travel itself. In investigating what happens to a theory when it moves from one place to another, the theorist or critic may first of all be obliged to explain how the theory comes to birth or enters discourse in the initial circumstances. But the birth of the traveler surely does not constitute a stage in the traveling process proper. It also seems problematic to treat transformation of the theory as the final stage, which occurs only *after* the movement and the reception of the theory. By separating 'transformation' from 'movement' and 'reception,' the model has played down the transforming function of the latter two stages. In the traveling of theory from Lukács to Goldmann, as illuminatingly discussed by Said, whatever transformation of the theory is involved, it takes place exclusively during the movement itself (see Said 234-238).

Generally speaking, if we are merely concerned with the traveling of a theory, there is only one discernible stage, that is the movement of the theory from the original writer to the new writer in the new culture. If we are interested moreover in the reception of, including resistance to, the transplanted theory and take the reception as an extension of the primary intercultural travel (since many secondary intra-cultural trips are involved when the transplanted theory reaches different readers within the new culture), the model will consist of two stages. At the first stage, the theory goes from the source culture to the receptor culture, a movement which is often, if not always, accompanied by various transformations of the theory. At the second stage, the transplanted theory is received in the receptor culture, a reception which is again accompanied by further transformations of the theory.

A movement usually involves a continuous process of progression in time and place until the destination is reached. What is pertinent to the present movement, however, are, generally speaking, only two points in time and place: the original writer in the original situation and the new writer in the new situation. While the distance between the two situations, which accounts for their differences, matters a great deal, how this distance is traversed — whether by surface mail or airmail or by some other means — is usually irrelevant. The central issue is the new use of the theory in the new situation, which not only marks, in terms of distance, the destination of the journey but also marks, in terms of relevance, the beginning of the journey, for the travel cannot be considered to have begun until the theory is translated, introduced, expounded or applied by a new writer in the receptor culture. In terms of relevance, that is to say, the new use in effect constitutes the whole movement. By this is meant that, to see how twisting a movement is, we need only measure the new use against the pre-travel original theory, without paying attention to the intermediary process.

There is no theory, as pointed out by Said, that is capable of covering, closing off, or predicting all the situations in which it might be useful (241). A theory or idea conceived in a Western language may not be applicable to Chinese. In *Comparative Literature and the Interpretation of the Novel*, Zhou Yingxiong applies, as many other Chinese theorists or critics have done, Jakobson's principle of binary opposition quite mechanically to the Chinese language. According to Zhou, the difference in meaning between the two Chinese characters '被' (bèi) and '配' (pèi) resides in the fact that 'b' is unaspirated and 'p' is aspirated (16). This explanation fails to take into account a peculiarity of Chinese, a language that is characterized by its ideographic written form. Scores of Chinese characters composed of different radicals may be identical in sound — not only in the combination of consonants and vowels but also in tone. It is true that in the two characters '被' and '配' cited above, an opposition can be found between the unaspirated 'b' and the aspirated 'p.' But this opposition surely does not suffice to account for the difference in meaning between the two words since '被' has more than twenty homophones

Traveling Theory: A Twisting Movement 215

(备,倍,背,贝,辈,钡,狈,惫,焙,孛,邶,蓓,悖,碚,褙,鐾,輩 etc.) and '配' has at least six (佩,沛,霈,旆,辔,帔). Generally speaking, Chinese relies much less on sounds in making a distinction between individual characters, which are ideographic in nature and which are *invariably monosyllabic*. The difference in sound, including that in tone, serves merely to mark off one group of monosyllabic homophones from another. Within the group, what distinguishes one sign from another are the dissimilarities of form between the ideograms.

In spoken Chinese, however, one can only resort to collocation or the context to differentiate a monosyllabic word from its homophones. Interestingly but not surprisingly, in spoken Chinese, what we often encounter are not monosyllabic signs but disyllabic or polysyllabic ones, usually made up of two or more monosyllabic morphemes. Whereas verbal distinction in written Chinese (of which classical writing forms an orthodox example) essentially leans upon the graphic contrasts obtaining between the monosyllabic ideograms, in spoken Chinese (of which vernacular writing can be taken as a kind of record), verbal distinction is principally dependent upon the phonic differences between the disyllabic or polysyllabic words or phrases.

One may suppose that, as far as written Chinese is concerned, the problem of differentiation can be easily solved by further applying the binary principle to the graphic differences between the homophones. But this is in effect an area where binarism often fails to function. For instance, except for two cases, the homophones that share the sound 'pèi' cannot be organized by binary oppositions since there is no paired contrast between any two of them. If we leave aside sounds and go straight into the Chinese graphic system, we will be in a much better position to apply the binary principle to the written signs. Although a large number of paired alternatives can be found in the code, such as the presence versus the absence of a given radical, we are still left with some cases which cannot be organized by binary oppositions. Now, what is the fundamental reason for the partial failure of binarism in the Chinese graphic system? I would venture the point that Chinese characters, which are made up of several hundreds of radicals and are typically based on pictographic or ideographic images, are less arbitrary than English words and, further, that Chinese characters therefore depend less heavily on interrelations and oppositions within the linguistic code for meaning.

It seems that, apart from calling into question the Western phonetically-oriented binarism, the Chinese language presents, as far as the *decontextualized monosyllabic* signs are concerned, an even greater challenge to Western phonocentrism. Saussure refers to the written form of a word as "the written image of a vocal sign" (1960: 24). He only considers the sound-image to be essential and illustrates this point vividly by comparing the sound-image to a person and the written image to that person's photograph. In his assertion that "the linguistic sign unites, not a thing and a name, but a concept and a sound-image" (66), the written image is completely left out of consideration. Saussure is in fact aware that written Chinese is an ideographic system. He says, "To a Chinese, an ideogram and a spoken word are both symbols of an idea; to him writing is a second language" (26). It is nevertheless not sufficient just to grant the monosyllabic ideograms the position of a second language. In Chinese, where an ideogram on average has more than five homophones, many with more than ten or twenty homophones and some with more than thirty, fifty or even eighty homophones (for instance, the sound 'yi'), it becomes doubtful whether we can still talk about *decontextualized monosyllabic* spoken signs at all. According to Saussure, "the important thing in the word is not the sound alone but the phonic differences that make it possible to distinguish this word from all others, for differences carry signification. [...] [A] segment of language can never in the final analysis be based on anything except its noncoincidence with the rest" (118). Owing to the abundance of coincidences in the Chinese phonetic system, sounds often fail to distinguish one monosyllabic word from another. Generally speaking, the graphic form constitutes the sole distinctive linguistic identity of a decontextualized monosyllabic Chinese sign.

This fact has so far escaped the attention of both Western and Chinese theorists and critics. Zhang Bingzhen and Huang Jinkai have, for instance, mechanically carried over Saussure's phonocentrism in introducing his theory of the linguistic sign into Chinese. They observe that any linguistic sign unites a sound-image and a concept and they exemplify this point with the character '树' (shù), which is the Chinese equivalent for the English 'tree.' They claim that the sign '树' is formed by the combination of the sound 'shù' and the concept involved (7). This rigid replacement of Saussure's Latin word 'arbor' (67) by the Chinese character '树' is undoubtedly misleading. While there is only one Latin '[arbor]' (arbor), one English '[tri:]' (tree), and one French '[arbr]' (arbre), there are at least eighteen Chinese characters which share the same sound 'shù' (数, 述, 术, 戍, 束, 恕, 庶, 墅, 漱, 竖, 沭, 澍 etc.). The sound simply fails to differentiate the sign in question from nearly twenty totally different signs. Leaving aside collocation or the context, the sound 'shù' has no way to function as a signifier for a given concept and cannot therefore be regarded as a spoken sign.

In applying any Western theory of the linguistic sign to Chinese, one has to keep in mind the fact that, for various reasons, graphic contrasts constitute the sole differentiating means in the case of most *decontextualized monosyllabic* Chinese signs. In such a case where the original theory is inapplicable, the movement of the theory cannot be a straight one but has to twist in one way or another to accommodate the new object.

The issue of theories traveling is an important and much-discussed one in the present globalization of comparative literature. So far critical attention has focused on how traveling theories are transformed or resisted in new cultural contexts. In *Crossing Borders*, for instance, Robert Holub concentrates on various aspects of the transformations and difficulties involved in the traveling of German reception theory to the United States, or in the traveling of Poststructuralism to the German context. Similarly, Edward Said, in his influential discussion of traveling theory, is concerned with how theories are transformed in different social-historical contexts. Interestingly, Said and Holub take quite different stands towards the transformations involved. To Said, transformations in the traveling process are quite necessary, since a theory "is a response to a specific social and historical situation" (237). Such "critical consciousness" or "critical recognition" of the limitations of theories is taken by Said as helpful and indispensable to critics. By contrast, Holub is much more bothered by transformations involved in the appropriation of foreign theories, transformations which typically arise from the "biases" of native social, political, intellectual traditions, or "an already established constellation" in the importing country. Holub's goal is to establish a framework "designed to insure that future border crossings will not be susceptible to the types of distortions and misunderstandings" as discussed in his book (1992: xi).

While "distortions and misunderstandings" also occur in the traveling of Western theories into China, what is most lacking in the Chinese context seems to be what Said calls "critical consciousness" or the "critical recognition" of the inherent limitations of the Western theories concerned. It would surely be going a bit too far to say that the cases of mechanically applying Western distinctions to Chinese invariably suggest submission to the domination of Western theories. But the fact that many highly competent specialists in Chinese would totally neglect the characteristics of this language when introducing a Western theory does seem to point to the existence of such a kind of (perhaps only subconscious) submission. The new writer in Chinese tends to take an influential Western theory on trust and apply it straightway, failing to notice its inapplicability in the new culture. As shown above, such a straight movement of the traveling theory runs the risk of distorting the new object, for instance, unwittingly 'transforming' ideographic written Chinese into an alphabetic system of writing.

References

Holub, Robert C. 1992. *Crossing Borders: Reception Theory, Poststructuralism, Deconstruction*. Wisconsin: University of Wisconsin Press.
Said, Edward. 1983. "Traveling Theory." *The World, the Text, and the Critic*. Cambridge, MA: Cornell University Press. 226-247.
Saussure, Ferdinand de. 1960. *Course in General Linguistics*. Trans. Wade Baskin. London: Peter Owen.
Zhang, Bingzhen, and Huang Jinkai. 1987. *Structuralist Literary Criticism*. Shenyang: Liaoning University Press.
Zhou, Yingxiong. 1990. *Comparative Literature and the Interpretation of the Novel*. Beijing: Peking University Press.

Uniqueness and Contingency

Horst Steinmetz
University of Leiden

> *Emphasizing the uniqueness of an event soon brings the debate to a grinding halt. Nor can anything be learned from the unique aspects of events.*

These sentences of Douwe Fokkema's are taken from the chapter "Literary History" in the book *The Study of Literature and the Transmission of Culture* (*Literatuurwetenschap en Cultuuroverdracht*) which he wrote together with Elrud Ibsch. I cite these particular sentences because they contain an important aspect of Fokkema's views on literary theory and literary history. As such, they will serve as a starting-point for several considerations on his views. I will not concern myself as to the truth of his claim, although I would like to say here that I do not believe he is right: perhaps some events remain unique exactly because people *have* learned from them.

Fokkema's aversion to events in literature and literary history being labeled as unique phenomena, arises from his efforts to make a true science of the study of literature. This science is ideally to be a science grounded in theory, a science that allows objective control ("empirically verifiable" is his favorite term for this) at every step — and these steps should, moreover, be repeated by all researchers — and, finally, a science capable of making predictions. Fokkema has defended the need for such a science in numerous publications, always emphasizing that it should be a concept with general laws and rules. Indeed such a design for a science (which comes very close to that practised in the natural sciences) has no use for uniqueness as unique phenomena are in principle opposed to generalizations, make repetitions impossible and are devoid of any predictive qualities.

The problem confronting Fokkema once he has required that literary theory have a scientific character, is caused not only by his fellow researchers' various judgments and prejudices, but also by the nature of the object that literary theory and literary history study. Of course Fokkema knows, like everyone else, that history does not and never will repeat itself, despite the well-known adage to the contrary. History as such means change, and change prevents repetition in the sense of the same thing coming into existence again. And literary history repeats itself no more than history does. History and literary history constitute a series of one-time events: history being an infinite series, literature perhaps a finite series of unique events. Phenomena in history and literary history are not the end-products of established processes like televisions or automobiles.

Neither are literary works end-products of processes which repeat themselves and lead to predictable results. Every literary work is a unique document. Therein lies the particularity of literature and of art in general, but also the resistance of art and literature to all approaches that desire to be scientific, that would apply general laws and rules to them. If one wants to break down this resistance, then one is forced to do something which is in essence inadequate: one must deny the uniqueness of literary works, and thereby also deny a significant part of their specificity.

Consequently, literary theory as Douwe Fokkema conceives it manoeuvers itself necessarily into an insolvable dilemma. On the one hand it must do justice to the object of study and therefore leave the uniqueness of literary and historical phenomena intact, on the other hand it must comply with its own principles of generalizations supported by laws and rules, and this is only possible at the cost of the object of study.

In this situation Fokkema tends to go ahead and favor the demands of a scientific basis. He chooses an approach that aims at developing theories which process the commonalities, similarities and analogous characteristics of unique entities and which in this way make it possible to arrive at generalizations and, in the most fortuitous cases, the formulation of laws. Naturally such a science of literature is conceivable and can be implemented for studies in literary theory, and equally for studies in literary history. The uniqueness of separate phenomena does not make them impossible to compare; individuality does not preclude relationships and family traits. Uniqueness does not therefore render general statements about unique specimen pointless in advance.

There are indeed innumerable publications on literary theory which go about things in this way. Genre studies, style analyses, reception studies and the like are regularly conducted with this kind of approach, whether or not based upon an explicit theory. Under certain conditions even the analysis of historical periods can be included here. Characteristic for these studies, however, is that they are limited to systematic research. Historical aspects have to be ignored, for history does not allow itself to be systematized.

The question then is this: must a scientific ideal as pictured by Fokkema be abandoned when studying history and literary history? This is indeed partly unavoidable because uniqueness only tolerates a partial bond with generalizations. On the other hand, Fokkema's science can without doubt be applied to historical and artistic phenomena, namely in the sense that the origin of phenomena in each separate case can be explained with the aid of theories, empirical tests, etc. One restriction does, however, apply: every individual phenomenon requires its own explanation. We can investigate, describe and explain the appearance of all separate phenomena, works, and events in a scientific way. But we are not capable of deducing laws from one or more analyzed events which would hold true for other, let alone for all other events. We can only discover what happened and under what conditions. We can analyze the Battle of Waterloo but we can not draw any conclusions as to the outcomes of other battles. The same is true for literary works. One can analyze their particular history of origin and their characteristics (individually and also in a wider historical or literary connection) and thereby satisfy the demands of a scientific approach. But we can do no more than that. We can determine all the characteristics of Romanticism, all the characteristics of the conditions of Romantic authorship, but this does not enable us in any way to make plausible the necessity of Coleridge writing the "Rime of the Ancient Mariner."

History and literary history occur as series of contingent events. Being contingent events, they are unique. No science and no law can breach contingency. Contingency can at best be explained in retrospect, once it has become part of the past. Hence it is possible for historical analysis, conducted retrospectively, to describe the continually occuring contingency, for example as the consequence of causal chains. This certainly ought to be done with the aid of theories, and the results can be 'empirically tested' against the facts which the theories use as evidence (once we have agreed as to what ought to be considered a fact).

The conclusion all this is leading to is that we, in our efforts to make a 'true' science of literary theory, must not change the objects of our study in order to bring them in line with our concepts of science. Studies in literary history, too, must proceed from the 'fact' that everything in history could have come out differently than it has. Uniqueness and contingency belong to the foundations of history and literary history. And our research designs need to keep that in mind.

An Ambiguous Story

Sartre's *Dépaysement* Between Modernist and Existentialist Conventions

Hans van Stralen
Utrecht University

In 1981, when the Pléiade edition of Sartre's prose appeared, the reader could for the first time lay eyes on the complete text of *Dépaysement*, the story the French author wrote around 1937. For in 1938, Sartre had published parts of this text in the magazine *Verve*, under the title *Nourritures*, but this never resulted in a complete publication.

Initially Sartre wanted to publish *Dépaysement* separately and he interpreted his story as an intensification of the problem he had concentrated on in *La nausée* (1938). Although some themes are indeed treated in both *La nausée* and *Dépaysement* (for instance, the busy city life, the reflections on the work of art, the desire for adventure, and especially the feeling of redundancy) there are differences too. In contrast to *La nausée*, the theme of food plays an important role in Sartre's story. Besides this, the emphasis in *Dépaysement* falls on the efforts of the protagonist, Audry, to make contact with Naples, the city where he is staying. In that sense the tourist problem is highlighted; we observe Audry trying to escape the customary way of seeing the sights. Thus Sicard sees Sartre's story as a description of a city through the vicissitudes of a "personage déculturé, et qui veut saisir une culture autre" (Sicard 1989: 171). And: *La nausée* describes in particular Roquentin's reflections on existence, while in *Dépaysement* the *actual* existence of 'l'homme seul' is the central theme.

Sartre discarded his later idea to incorporate *Dépaysement* in the collection of short stories *Le mur* (1939), because he felt the difference in tone between these texts would be too great. Sicard observes: "Sartre a choisi de parler des lieux, du voyage, changeant ainsi considérablement d'orientation" (Sicard 1989: 170). In *Le mur*, more than in *Dépaysement*, the subject matter of the oppressive presence of the other person dominates.

It is immediately visible that *Dépaysement* shows considerable autobiographical tendencies. Sartre and his life partner, Simone de Beauvoir, undertook a journey to Italy in 1936 and the impressions they gave later can be connected to certain parts of this story. Besides this, the type of hallucination that also characterizes *La nausée* can be read between the lines of *Dépaysement*. According to Sartre this was related to his experiments with mescaline. Around 1936 he wanted to gain more insight in the nature of the phenomenon 'consciousness' by means of this drug.

Not a trace of political engagement is to be found in *Dépaysement*, although this might have been expected from a writer who always stressed involvement in the social world. Sartre later claims that his political understanding was markedly underdeveloped in the thirties. The only thing De Beauvoir mentions in *La force de l'âge* is that she and Sartre packed uneasily for the Italian trip, because of the developments in Spain. The sole political reference in *Dépaysement* is the instance when Audry remarks that Fascism forms no real part of Naples.

Dépaysement takes up a special place in Sartre's work. Although Sicard makes intertextual links between *Dépaysement* and the 'Voyage en Orient,' as worded by Flaubert, for example, it should be observed that Sartre's story occupies an autonomous place within his own work. Naturally *Dépaysement* shows Existentialist characteristics, a fact we might have expected, considering Sartre's literary and philosophical status. Nevertheless, the Modernist characteristics as described by Fokkema and Ibsch in *Modernist Conjectures* are also manifest in this early text. Therefore, *Dépaysement* may well be considered to be a story in which both Modernist and Existentialist conventions have been thematized.

Dépaysement is about a young man Audry who is staying in Naples and who wonders what it means to be there, i.e., "Sentir cette existence" (Sartre 1981: 1537). He does not want to reside in Naples as a tourist, "dans un monde abstrait, dans un livre de morceaux choisis" (Sartre 1981: 1538). The sights begin to bore him and he feels an intense need for food, sleep and eroticism.

Audry concludes that only an erotic adventure can really link him to Naples and he allows himself to be led to a brothel by two sailors. Once there, a love scene between two women is enacted before him. The protagonist of *Dépaysement* is overcome by feelings of estrangement when he finds himself out in the street again. Nevertheless, Audry feels genuinely free, especially after the sailors have been singing songs. He then experiences the sensation of actually being in Naples.

In order to situate *Dépaysement* in a literary historical way, we should first consider the year of production. Sartre wrote his story around 1937, the time described is 1936. Fokkema and Ibsch situate Modernism between 1910 and 1940. So in this respect *Dépaysement* finds itself near the borderline between this school and literary Existentialism (1935-1960).

Modernist tendencies are still easy to discern in *Dépaysement*. The title itself may well be combined with the semantic field of 'detachment' as formulated by Fokkema and Ibsch. Moreover, we read that Audry has a cosmopolitan outlook; the travel impressions he provides bear witness to that. His being detached is reinforced by the fact that nobody in Naples pays any attention to him. Thence perhaps his tendency to kill time. In the brothel Audry unfolds a specific combination of detachment and observation when he is not directly involved in the love scene of the two women. After his experiences in the brothel Audry still feels 'depaysé,' but his mood rapidly changes to one of joy. However, while in Modernist literature detachment is considered as a condition for the autonomous functioning of the individual, in *Dépaysement* Audry experiences this status as undesirable. In this story (in contrast to *La nausée* too) the feelings of detachment and redundancy are overcome by submission to the erotic adventure.

The second semantic field distinghuished by Fokkema and Ibsch, 'observation,' shows itself in Audry's wish to come to a "retournement de soi" (Sicard 1989: 172) by intensive observations of the surroundings. We may recognize Sartre's philosophical background in the elaboration of this semantic field. That is to say, Audry wants to collect 'views' of Naples by observing the city from various vantage points. The philosophically interested reader may here see relations with the work of the founder of phenomenology, Edmund Husserl (1859-1938). Sartre had studied his work with interest in Berlin in 1934 and 1935. Amongst other things, Husserl claims that the essence of the object observed can never present itself by intensive observations alone, as these are limited. It is the unifying consciousness, detached from empirical reality which can finally define adequate judgments about reality. The narrator of *Dépaysement*, however, in the spirit of Proust the Modernist, writes the following: "Ce n'est pas ainsi [by means of observations from various vantage points, HvS] que les villes se dévoilent. Il suffit parfois de regarder un pavé déchaussé, de respirer une odeur, ça y est, la ville est là, autour de vous" (Sartre 1981: 1537). Another philosophical notion unfolded in *Dépaysement* concerns the work of Henri Bergson (1859-1941), which was important in the first phase of Sartre's thinking (1927-1934). Bergson postulated the "élan vital," a vitalist principle said to be manifest in all forms of matter. Initially Bergson thought that this stream of energy showed itself as temporally homogeneous, but later he changed his mind about this. Consequently he felt that the speed of the "élan vital" is dependant upon the nature of the matter in which it is released. In *Dépaysement*, this idea is thematized in the following reflection of Audry: "Ils [les gens, HvS] ne vieillissent pas assez pour ressembler aux pierres" (Sartre 1981: 1540).

Not only observation, which concerns the here-and-now, but also memory plays an important role in Modernism. Remarkable in this respect is the moment when Audry has come out of the brothel and realizes that his adventure has already become "Un souvenir absurde et poétique qui chercherait en vain sa place parmi les autres souvenirs" (Sartre 1981: 1556). Furthermore, there is a link with the well-known 'Madeleine-experience' from Proust's *À la recherche du temps perdu*. In the first part of this series of novels — *Combray* — the narrator describes how Marcel, the protagonist, is enabled to re-enter the domain of his youth after tasting a small cake (a 'madeleine'). The 'madeleine' which Marcel used to eat as a child precipitates the memory of the past. In *Dépaysement*, Audry elaborates on various kinds of cake; one of them reminds him of the novels of D'Annunzio (Sartre 1981: 1544).

Concerning Modernism's final semantic field, 'consciousness,' a certain tension between Modernist and Existentialist tendencies may be discerned. Audry's reflections on himself are Modernist, but his consciousness is also focussed on others and on the city; therefore — in contrast to the Modernist code — his reflections do not solely serve the search for his own inner self. The thought of his redundancy is unfolded within the circuit of the reflexive consciousness, but conforming to the Existentialist code that the solution of the problem lies with the *other person*. It is the inhabitants of Naples who form the cause of Audry's problem, but they also liberate him from his position of detachment.

The Existentialist tendencies in *Dépaysement* concentrate on the contrast between 'being there' and 'existing.' 'Existing' refers to an active involvement in the situation motivated by moral sense. 'Being there,' on the other hand, is the uncolored indication of the fact that man is a phenomenon in the universe, like trees and animals are phenomena. Refusal to depart from this anonymous way of life is considered to be bad faith within Existentialism. In *Dépaysement* the attitude of the tourist is connected to this superficial and risk-free life. In contrast to the tourist, Audry wishes to be actively involved with his situation by means of adventures. In addition to this, a sense of redundancy is tangible in *Dépaysement*. This 'être de trop' we already knew from *La nausée*, but in this novel it relates especially to the material reality. In Sartre's story, however, redundancy mainly concerns the city and its inhabitants. The desire to change this situation predominates. Initially, this does not succeed. The buildings in Naples manifest themselves as massive and defensive things, just like the objects in *La nausée*. It is said of one of the sailors in *Dépaysement* that he has a face like a rock. The feeling of being unable to make contact with the situation, and the feeling of redundancy also show up in contact with the body of man's fellow-being. Thus Audry feels sickened by the sight of a sick woman and he is frightened by the nakedness of the whores in the brothel. Similary the moment when Audry sees himself in the mirror and notices that he is a little red is an uneasy one. Once outside again, he speaks of "un souvenir absurde" (Sartre 1981: 1556); it seems as though he is referring to the superfluity of the event itself. Nevertheless, a reversal also takes place. In many Existentialist texts, closed spaces appear which may lead to a confrontation with others. In *Dépaysement*, those fellow human beings are, of course, the whores. But also the fact that they are outsiders — and this goes for the sailors as well — may be understood in the light of Existentialist conventions. After all, the outcast is often sought out in literary Existentialism, because it is felt that he has escaped from the ethics of those who only want to *be* perfunctory or unthinking.
(Translated by A.M. Iken)

References

Fokkema, Douwe W., and Elrud Ibsch. 1987. *Modernist Conjectures: A Mainstream in European Literature*. London: C. Hurst and Company.
Sartre, Jean-Paul. 1981. *Oeuvres romanesques*. Paris: Gallimard.
Sicard, Michel. 1989. *Essais sur Sartre*. Paris: Galilée.

Genology: In Search of Adequacy

Leon Strydom
University of the Orange Free State

What follows, involves research planning rather than research results, and consequently deals with potential rather than fact.

If one accepts that science has the potential to function as a cognition and problem-solving system which brings about the standardization of knowledge and know-how, i.e., which has the potential to generate knowledge and to solve problems in a distinctive way, then, amongst others, one also has to accept the following.

Firstly, that universities are there because of science, i.e., that continuation of the science process is a university's main concern and that the functional hierarchy of campus activities is determined to the extent of their support of this distinctive function.

Secondly, that the exclusively rational basis of the science system, on the one hand, is a condition for continuation of the science process and as such for the standardization of knowledge, and on the other hand, results in science as not capable of producing final answers and absolute truths, because scientific knowledge — being rational and objective, explicit and falsifiable, tested and testable — is always theory-bound and as such relative, i.e., valid only in terms of the specific, conceptual frame which generates that knowledge (academic freedom, one could say, is that very freedom to go and determine the consequences of any theoretical presupposition).

Thirdly, that the research process therefore does not merely comprise the compilation of information, but has to develop as an argumentation which begins with the (scientific) identification of a problem, followed, in the first place, by a hypothetical solution of the problem, and in the second place, by systematic testing of that tentative solution. The process of testing is in principle endless. However, the scientific productivity of the solution is measurable at any time on account of the extent of coherence (logical consistency), correspondence (agreement with empirical facts, also intercultural / international for the sake of greater validity) and consensus (agreement with the independent perceptions of other scientists, also interdisciplinary for the sake of greater validity) of which the argumentation gives evidence, and in terms of the distinctive identification and the predictable explanation made possible — or not — by the standardized knowledge.

In the light of these directives, exploration of the genre realm soon makes it clear what exactly curbs scientific productivity. In the first place: the existing state of genre research does not guarantee the objective identification of poetic, narrative and dramatic presence. There is no intersubjective consensus on the distinctive features of a genre. That which is characteristic of the narrative genre for A, is just as emphatically pointed out by B as activator of meaning in a poetry text. What is typical of a certain genre for someone, is for somebody else distinctive of literature. A contributory factor is also that terminology used in this regard often is the product of common sense and not of systematization. In the second place: the erroneous impression is made that genre theory is merely a taxonomy, a classification encyclopedia, because its explanatory potential — if any — is usually minimal. The cause of that is insufficient systematization, i.e., the argumentation fails to establish enough causal relations. Investigators, for example, tend to reduce genre to only one component of literary communication (for instance, to text at the expense of reader, or vice versa), or they try to define one genre without reference to another, or they do not consistently exploit the potential of a conceptual frame to generate knowledge, or they confine themselves in their argumentation to one way of thinking instead of approaching the problem in an interdisciplinary way.

I expect my research to develop a model which would make possible the objective identification and explanation of generic presence. And I expect that model to be developed by way of an interdisciplinary argumentation which utilizes the analytical potential of at least the following three conceptual frames: Structuralism, since to structure in a literary way is, ideally, to create meaning; semiotics, because genre features obviously involve signs to which meaning is accorded by reason of knowledge of the system in terms of which those signs function; and the cognitive approach which analyzes the literary processing of texts as a cognitive activity, assuming that literariness is determined by both cognitive, top-down factors and textual, bottom-up factors.

For the sake of a more adequate systematization I present a few theoretical points of departure. I assume that the manifestation of literature since ancient times in the threesome of poetry, narrative and drama cannot be arbitrary and I expect my research to try and explain why that is the case. Apparently these three represent distinctive modes of literary cognition which are, in principle, not replaceable by any means.

I assume that experience is culturally creative in so far as it satisfies man's seeking after truth. In this regard I expect my research to explicate the respective contributions of science, religion and art as cognition systems, problem-solving systems — epistemes, to speak in Foucaultian terms for the time being, i.e., configurations of relations which function as frameworks of particular forms of knowledge, as the conditions for the production of certain sets of statements and not others — through the ages developed by man in order to organize and understand his life-world. Evidently each system is essential; one can say that each system has the potential to produce new information in a distinctive way and as such to complement the other. The science system seems to be objective, confining the subject to standardized logic; on the basis of rationality and by way of testable argumentation it explains man's life-world, creating knowledge of causality. The art system seems to be subjective, implicating the subject in the cosmic association, the analogy of all being; on the basis of imagination and by way of implicit communication it explains man's life-world, creating knowledge of recognition. The religion system seems to be mystical, substituting the subject by holiness; on the basis of faith and by way of revelation, epiphany, it explains man's life-world, creating knowledge of salvation.

I assume that the literary processing of texts is, in principle, a distinctive actualization of the aesthetic cognition system. My research should prove that and also make explicit the informational potential of generic organization, i.e., the logical possibilities for maximal informativity. Apparently the tendency toward optimal informativity characteristic of the culturally productive imagination takes shape by way of implicit communication which is organized by the principle of parallelism. And as thematization, i.e., the functional semantization of rules and strategies of organization, seems to be a condition for maximal informativity by way of implicit communication (cf. in this regard concepts such as polysemy, Jakobson's "focus on the message for its own sake," iconicity, self-actualizing communication, literary text-processing as production of knowledge rather than expression and transmission of knowledge), it follows that the medium of each art has the potential to effect distinctive text-processing, and thus distinctive actualization of aesthetic cognition, not replaceable by any means. This entails that in literature, where the tendency toward maximal ordering and informational saturation manifests itself, not in the annihilation of language, but in the secondary modelling system being superimposed on the primary modelling system, genre rules ought to be deduced from the cognitive possibilities of the principle of parallelism being superimposed on the paradigmatic and syntagmatic axes respectively, and that textual strategies should be explicable in terms of either paradigmatic parallelisms (similarities) or syntagmatic parallelisms (contiguities).

I assume that the notion of literature, like that of genre, pertains to a system and not to a text, i.e., to the invariant which organizes the text and functions as deciphering code, and as such gives the text a significant part of its meaning, but which cannot replace the text as variant and as particular manifestation of the system. As a result the concepts of literature and genre should be formulated in my investigation, not as observational results, but as exclusive, theoretical constructs which retain their systematic structure while being confronted with texts, and as such with predictability as their primary characteristic.

If one accepts that literature (art) does not replace the other cognition systems developed by man, but that it complements them in order to extend man's ability to organize and explain experience, then one must also accept that — in like manner — different genre systems as distinctive modes of literary cognition complement each other during text-processing for the purpose of enlarging literature's informational potential. The informational potential, according to cybernetics, is proportional to the number of systemic alternatives; the more choices available to the recipient, the higher the informational potential. Consequently it seems that optimal informativity by way of generic organization is possible only, on the one hand, if generic ordering satisfies the condition stipulated by the epistemic concept of literature, namely the thematization of the rules and strategies of organization, and on the other hand, if the implicitness of literary communication is accomplished by different genre systems de-automatizing and complementing one another, because the informational potential of literary text-processing is relative also to the number of genre systems being integrated.

In conclusion I mention the distinctive rules of the three genre systems as they appear to me, as well as a few obvious strategies in terms of which generic manifestation (and thus scientific identification) can be expected to take place.

Function of the *poetry* system is to identify for the reader a state of consciousness by thematizing strategies of similarity. Conditioned by the thematization principle that means implicit communication, recognition by the reader him- or herself, the preclusion of communicational distance and heterogeneity, i.e., identification *of* the reader *with* a state of consciousness. However, it is predictable that the organizing principle will be repetition, that reading-time in its entirety will be devoted to a moment of existence, a lasting mental state, that discourse will proceed in the first-person singular and in the present tense, that prominence will be given to the emotive (expressive) function of language, and that the state of consciousness will not be contextualized and explained, i.e., presented in historical or logical terms.

Function of the *narrative* system is to demonstrate to the reader the cognitive function of history, i.e., of the time-space continuum by thematizing strategies of change. As this implies history as surveyable and significant, and as such a perspective which is synoptic and empirical, it is predictable that the organizing principle will be historical causality (sequential contiguity, action and reaction, cause and effect), that reading-time will be devoted to an occurrence (or occurrences) and to the account of the occurrence (or occurrences), and that a narrator will mediate between the reader and an observed event (or events), referred to in the past tense and in the third-person. Representations of time and place will explain the event (or events), and will as such lend credibility to the demonstration. Obviously the thematization of narrative strategies will entail the demonstration becoming implicit, i.e., actualized by the reader.

Function of the *drama* system is to confront the reader with alternative possibilities of choice by thematizing strategies of contrast. As this implies divergent points of view of equal validity as well as the absence of an intermediary, it is predictable that the organizing principle will be logical causality (consequential contiguity, presumption and conclusion) which will manifest itself, on the one hand, in dialogue — i.e., discourse oriented toward the second-person and strongly involving the conative function of language — which synchronizes production and reception of text, and on the other hand, in an appeal to the future as the reader's choice will still be pending. Owing to the principle of logical causality, the reader may (dis-)approve of — but not identify with — a point of view, and motivation of all perspectives will take place exclusively in logical terms. Analogous to the other two genres it is to be expected that optimum organization of dramatic communication for purposes of optimum informational potential will result in the confrontation of the reader being effectuated in an implicit way.

I expect my investigation to argue and to test these rules and strategies, logically and empirically. Productivity of the model would increase in so far as more strategies are generically classified because of the logical relatedness of genre rule and textual strategy. If the model eventually indeed does guarantee the objective identification and explanation of generic presence during text-processing, it would also serve in helping to explain the fluctuating generic preferences in literary history.

Diary as Narrative: Theory and Practice

Susan Rubin Suleiman
Harvard University

My reflections on the diary as a narrative form will be in the performative as well as in the analytic mode; part of this paper will consist of excerpts from a diary I kept while living temporarily in Budapest, my native city, a few years ago.

The challenge of a diary, for both reader and writer, is that it is a loose form, weaving together a large number of different themes, and stories, that emerge only gradually. This is true of fictional diaries, or so-called diary novels, as well as of real diaries. But real diaries present some added features and problems that make them particularly interesting, and I want to dwell briefly on two of them: factuality and contingency.

By factuality (one could also call it historicity), I mean that aspect of the diary which claims for itself the condition of truth — that a verifiable congruence exists between the written text and one or more events occurring in a specific time and place. "Sunday, 9 March, 1941. Here goes, then. This is a painful and well-nigh insuperable step for me: yielding up so much that has been suppressed to a blank sheet of lined paper." So begins the diary of Etty Hillesum, a young Jewish woman living and writing in Amsterdam (Hillesum 1985: 1). "Sunday, 14 June 1942. On Friday, June 12, I woke up at six o'clock and no wonder; it was my birthday" (Frank 1972: 1). So begins the diary of Anne Frank, a young Jewish girl living and writing in Amsterdam. Whether the event is external, occurring in the world of people and things (a birthday, involving celebration and presents) or whether it is internal, occurring only on the written page (the blank sheet is about to be transformed into a page covered with words that expose the writer's hitherto secret feelings and thoughts), the diary guarantees that an event took place, on the date indicated. Something happened to somebody, and I who am writing now was there to witness it or hear about it or experience it.

The fascination of another person's diary for a reader is, I think, in large part due to its factuality or historicity, its 'being there'-ness. More exactly, its 'having been there'-ness: one rarely reads a diary, not even one's own, the moment it is written. This fascination becomes all the stronger when the writer of the diary is dead, definitively absent. Aside from the rich inner world and the external drama revealed to us in the diaries of Anne Frank and Etty Hillesum, there is our knowledge, at once bitter and poignant, that these young women never lived to see their diary published, much less to continue it. Theirs are interrupted narratives in the most literal sense of the term.

Fictional diaries may, of course, simulate the factuality and historicity of real diaries — that is one of their traits as a fictional genre. But I contend that the experience of reading a diary novel is qualitatively different from that of reading a real diary, not only because in the case of the latter we know that the writer of the diary was / is an actual person whose existence has a historical reality outside of the diary, but also because of our expectation, or trust, that what the writer reports is the truth as she or he knows it or experiences it at the time. This explains my own sharp sense of betrayal when I learned a few years ago that one of the most memorable passages, for me, of Anaïs Nin's diary had altered the facts: what she had recounted as the painful experience of a stillbirth, having to labor to expel a baby that she knew was dead, had in fact been an abortion (revealed in the unexpurgated version of the diary). What I had read as the immensely moving account of the pain of a woman deprived of motherhood became, by this simple change, a lie. Yet, the emotional pain she experienced was no doubt just as real — and if she had reported it in the first place as an abortion, I might have found the passage equally moving. What made me feel betrayed was the fact itself that she had lied; and consequently, that I as a reader had shared in the wrong kind of grief. In short, it was a category error. But the difference between fictional diaries and real diaries is precisely a categorical difference.

No sooner have I said this than I realize just how complicated the question is. What if the writer, or the editor (most posthumous diaries have editors) does not alter the facts but leaves some things out, whether for aesthetic or personal reasons? The editor of Etty Hillesum's diary tells us that he was forced to shorten the text, for "to publish a 400-page diary by an unknown woman was too much of a risk, even in the eyes of this most faithful admirer." He assures us, however, that he has "tried to convey the contents of the exercise books as carefully as possible, taking out repetitions and many quotations." Above all, he affirms that "No word has been added" (Hillesum 1985: xvii). This kind of scruple seems indeed necessary in the case of a diary whose author is dead. But what about a living author? Is it all right for the living author to 'add words' to a diary she is planning to publish, even if those additions are made after the date of the entry? Is it all right for her to *change* words, revising her reports for coherence and style if not for the events reported? At what point do such changes transform her diary into a novel? These are questions I am currently struggling with from the point of view of a diary writer. But I contend that the question of factuality ("Was this really written on the day indicated by the person indicated, and is the report true?") hovers in the background for every reader as well.

The second trait of the diary as a (nonfictional) narrative form is what I call contingency: the day-to-day unfolding of the story, which necessarily escapes the foreknowledge and control of the writer. Contingency in this sense is obviously linked to factuality: it is because the story I am telling is my own, existing in a place and time outside my text, that I literally cannot foresee one day what I will write the next. Furthermore, I may report on a single day many pieces of different stories, some of which will end up going nowhere. Here again, fictional diaries can duplicate the nonlinear, open-ended nature of real diaries, but their teleology is reversed, since the author presumably knows where she or he wants to end up and must simply find the most effective way to get there.

Upon reflection, however, things again become more complicated. The author of a 'real' diary (suddenly, I feel the need to use those derealizing quotation marks) must also make choices, both in the actual moment and process of writing a given entry (one cannot record *everything* that happens in a single day) and also as the accumulation of entries produces, gradually, the sense of several stories unfolding for the writer herself. It is because I have already written about X or Y on previous days that I will continue to write about them today, perhaps at the expense of other people or events or memories. As I begin to realize that my diary is producing a series of stories, I allow those stories to determine the further direction of my diary. In so doing, I am moving closer to what a novelist does.

This is all the more so if I decide to publish the diary and to put false names on real people in order to protect their identities — or even endow them with false physical traits or professions in order to prevent them from being too easily identified, if what I write about them could prove embarrassing to them. Conversely, a novelist does not always know where he or she is going in writing a novel, whether in diary form or not. The novel's direction may emerge only gradually, and in a sense contingently. In this aspect, then, I see a much more blurred line between fictional diaries and 'real' ones. Maybe the important distinction is not between fictional and real, but between published and private. Because the minute you make your diary public, or the minute you write with a public in mind, you necessarily shape and preen your story, your image, and your style. Of course, that activity of self-construction is not specific to diary writing; it may be part and parcel of any writing in which one says 'I,' as Montaigne well knew.

In lieu of a conclusion, I shall offer a very short excerpt from my own "Budapest Diary," itself part of a longer autobiographical book (the provisional title of the book, forthcoming from University of Nebraska Press in 1996, is *Budapest Found: A Jewish-American-Hungarian Memoir*.) This fragment will, I hope, confirm my theoretical observations — and will also make clear why it is extremely difficult to publish short excerpts from a diary. The full effect of a diary, whether 'real' or fictional — and that is undoubtedly one of its chief features as a narrative form — is gradual and cumulative. You can appreciate its parts only by reading the whole.

Saturday, March 6
For the first time since I arrived here, this morning I pulled out the folder marked "A Return to Budapest." The first thing that caught my eye was a letter from Mother, dated July 23, 1984 — she sent it to me in Paris, giving some addresses and advice. Next to it in the folder was the old document I found in the safe in Miami Beach after she died, an official copy of her and Daddy's marriage certificate. I had read this document before, and found it very moving with its spidery handwriting and its 'authentic aged' look. It has been folded and unfolded many times, and there is even a small hole in the middle.

Looking at the document again this morning, I found a lot more to interest me. First, the date of this copy is November 19, 1947 — they must have gotten it as part of their preparation for leaving Hungary, when they were requesting the exit visa that never came. There are separate columns on the certificate for information concerning the bride and the groom. The abbreviation "Izr.," for Izraelita, Jewish, appears in both columns. Her address is listed as Akácfa street 59, in the 7th district; his as Szinyei something street 1, in the 6th district. This latter piece of information was completely new to me — I had never noticed it before. Just for the fun of it, I looked under the S's in the street list of my Falk map, tenth edition — and there, in clear letters, was Szinyei Merse utca: a side street off the upper end of Andrássy Avenue. Number 1 had to be on the corner.

All previous plans for the afternoon were scrapped, and I ended up walking the length of Andrássy Avenue from where I got off the bus. At number 88-90, the avenue broadens out into a circular piazza, with space for four grassy plots and statues of great men. At the four 'corners' of the circle are large and very ornate buildings which wrap around into side streets. Szinyei Merse is one of those streets. The courtyard of Number 1 is a bit smaller and more irregular than the one on the avenue, which has a nice big staircase as you walk in; but by now both courtyards look badly in need of renovation, as indeed does the whole once-splendid round of buildings on the piazza.

While I was examining the courtyard at Number 1, I could see a woman in the shadow near the staircase, evidently the concierge, looking at me. After a few seconds she asked: "Can I help you with something?"
"I'm afraid not. I used to know some people who lived here long ago," I answered. I went over to where she was standing, in the doorway of her apartment.
"Well, I've lived here for forty years, so go ahead and ask me. What's their name?"
"Rubin. But they were here even before your time. When my father got married, this was the address he gave — in 1936." Her face fell.
"That was before my time."
"Have most people in the building lived here very long?" I asked. "Yes, everybody."
"Well, thanks anyway." I noticed three large plastic garbage cans near the door on the way out, marked in big white letters: Szinyei Merse 1.

References

Frank, Anne. 1972 [1947]. *The Diary of a Young Girl*. Trans. B.M. Mooyaart. New York: Pocket Books.
Hillesum, Etty. 1985 [1981]. *An Interrupted Life: The Diaries of Etty Hillesum 1941-43*. J.G. Gaarlandt (ed). New York: Washington Square Press.

Universalism and Cultural Relativism

Mihály Szegedy-Maszák
University of Budapest

In 1990 Jacques Derrida gave the following definition of cultural history at a conference on European identity: "l'histoire d'une culture suppose sans doute un cap identifiable, un *telos* vers lequel le mouvement, la mémoire et la promesse, l'identité, fût-ce comme différence à soi, rêve de se rassembler" (Derrida 1960: 22-23). This characterization reveals the self-contradictions of comparative studies as they are pursued at the end of the twentieth century.

While the eighteenth-century idea that the role to be played by a literary work is "de renforcer le caractère national" (Rousseau 1960: 137) can no longer be regarded as a normative paradigm in West-European and North-American culture, the emergence of new literatures in Africa, Asia, and Canada warns us that it may be too early to insist on the desirability of globalization. What is more, cultural diversity seems to increase not only because of Postcolonialism but also as a result of post-communism. After the collapse of the Warsaw Pact and the decline of the international communist movement, more national literatures are alive in Europe today than ever before.

It is easier to condemn ethnocentrism and cultural nationalism than to have a more than superficial knowledge of other cultures. While no legitimate interpretation can be given by scholars whose reading is limited to texts in one language, some literary works — especially those in which ambiguity and polyvalence can be traced back to the signifier, or in which connotations are based on etymology — can be understood only in the original by those who have a full command of the language in a very broad sense, including the history of the language. Interpretive communities and practices cannot exist without an intimate knowledge of certain conventions. The relative absence of great orchestral conductors in the late twentieth century, for example, may suggest that interpretive traditions built up gradually by several generations may die out if radical changes occur in the cultural climate.

A scholar's awareness of the limitations of his knowledge of other cultures may lead him to the belief that he can develop historically relevant interpretations only of the literature written in his mother tongue. It is only in such cases that a true reading occurs or takes place — in the sense the words "Es ereignet sich aber das Wahre," taken from Hölderlin's late hymn *Mnemosyne*, have been applied to interpretation (De Man 1978: 221). The few references made by Western scholars to the culture of Eastern Europe may indicate that it is difficult to speak from the centre about peripheral cultures. To what extent can it be taken for granted that the substance of such historical concepts as Romanticism, Realism, or Symbolism is the same when applied to literatures other than those in which their definition had been originally developed? Does it help any reader understand the poetry of Endre Ady if he is called a Symbolist, and is it possible to speak of Postmodernism in countries that have not experienced the advantages and disadvantages of a consumer society? The answer to such questions is by no means simple. The danger is that the reading process is stopped too early and too easily when the unfamiliar is quickly reduced to the familiar. The so-called minor literatures are often treated as imperfect replicas, their history is viewed in terms of *décalage*.

It seems somewhat problematic to conceptually deduce progress or delay or to define the contemporaneity of the contemporaneous unless you can locate a center with absolute certainty. The assumption that a culture is either central or marginal is closely related to a Classicist legacy — the manners of the court are opposed to those of the provinces — and it is by no means obvious that this ideal can be used in the interpretation of the literature of the last two centuries. If Mallarmé is considered to be the crucial figure of Symbolism, it may seem doubtful whether a poet who used verse as an instrument of political message can be associated with this movement. When a Hungarian scholar is asked about Symbolism in his culture, he may try to 'sell' Ady as a representative of that movement and thereby avoid the old realist-nominalist debate, but the question whether the concept of Symbolism is helpful for the understanding of Ady's political or religious verse remains unanswered. The interpretation may be so reductive that it can hardly be called a form of historical understanding. In a similar way, it is possible to have doubts about the legitimacy of calling Postmodern narrative fiction which affirms Christian values. The works

György Lukács wrote in his middle period, between the two world wars, his frequent use of the labels progressive and reactionary, might serve as a warning that the teleological concept of *Weltgeschichte* may give rise to totalitarian consequences. The interpretation of *Epochenschwelle* as developed by Blumenberg, Koselleck, or Jauß is incomparably more sophisticated, but even this concept implies a universalism that may relegate some cultures to the periphery.

Of course, I would accept the view that comparative literature has legitimacy only if there are degrees of translatability. It is more possible to read *Bleak House* in translation than *Atemkristall*, a sequence of short and cryptic lyrics by Celan. However tempting the universalism of some Enlightenment thinkers, the Romantics may remind us that works are language-dependent. In the early twentieth century there were avant-garde journals in most parts of Europe and in America which aimed at the creation of an international literary climate. My guess is that the illusion of the generation of Ivan Goll and Lajos Kassák has been lost by now. While in music and possibly even in the visual arts it is easier to speak of an international canon, in literature there are no institutions that are comparable to concert halls or museums. There exists a public which can equally appreciate the works of Hokusai and Giovanni di Paolo, Lassus and Cage, but it would be difficult to find many readers with a historical understanding of the works of both Tu Fu and Shakespeare. I admire and enjoy *The Dream of the Red Chamber* more than many European or American novels, but I cannot claim to be able to develop a historical interpretation of this work.

The self-contradiction in Derrida's definition — culture as identity and *différance* — suggests that history is knowledge of alien experience, yet it is also constituted by memory. "Zuletzt kann niemand aus den Dingen, die Bücher eingerechnet, mehr heraushören, als er bereits weiss," wrote Nietzsche (1969: 297-298), and one of the possible implications of his remark is that if the distance between the text and the reader is too great, no continuity, ellipsis, or disruption of tradition can be felt and no historical understanding seems possible. It may be easier to learn about the place of a work in history than to acquire a sense of history in that work. "Durch sein Gedicht stiftet der Dichter Gedächtnis," says Gadamer (1986: 131). The historical nature of understanding is closely related to intertextuality and may be the main reason why there are limits to the fruitfulness of creative misinterpretation. When reading in Hungarian, I can have an awareness of intertextuality that is natural, almost instinctive, whereas if I read Celan, my memories of Hölderlin and Rilke will depend on my studies which relate to ideas about the text rather than to the text itself. When perusing Keats or Ashbery, Milton or Stevens are not in my ear, so I am at a disadvantage in comparison with a native speaker of English who has a kind of organic contact with texts in that language and therefore it is less difficult for him / her to sense the contest that takes place between texts in English. If you know more, you can afford to be more flexible, relaxed, and spontaneous, whereas if you know less, your reponse might be somewhat stiff. It is not difficult to see a failure of historical understanding in the way the verse of Poe was read by Baudelaire, Mallarmé, and Valéry. Value judgments have to be based on a sense of continuity and discontinuity in the history of a culture, some assessment of the relation between precursor and ephebe. You cannot enter a tradition; you have to stand in it. "Tradition ist nichts, was Einer lernen kann, ist nicht ein Faden, den er aufnehmen kann, wenn es ihm gefällt; so wenig, wie es möglich ist, sich die eigenen Ahnen auszusuchen" (Wittgenstein 1984: 76).

If cultural relativism is manifest in musical interpretation, it plays an even more crucial role in the historical understanding of literature. The relations between the unfamiliar and the familiar are complex. Otherness may be a liberating force and source of inspiration but if it serves merely as a pretext for self-understanding and there is no merging of horizons, no historical understanding takes place. Reading implies that there are always limits to understanding, just as there are different degrees of translatability. A Baroque concerto can be interpreted from a Romantic perspective but cannot be transformed into a symphonic poem, just as a sonata cannot be read as a twelve-tone composition or as *Das Cabinet des Dr. Caligari*, *Der letzte Mann*, *Our Hospitality*, or *The General* cannot be transformed into sound-films without a fatal distortion of their message. The organizing principles underlying German Expressionist films directed by Robert Wiene and F.W. Murnau or the art of Buster Keaton are incompatible with the rules of talking pictures.

Reading in one's mother tongue necessitates interpretive strategies different from those followed when reading in a foreign language or in translation. The distance between the source and the target language may be one of the reasons for the different degrees of translatability. The international status of a language undoubtedly affects the reception of literary works. English, French, German, Russian, and Chinese are taught as second or 'foreign' languages. This makes it easier to view the literature in these languages from the outside.

In the case of Estonian or Albanian it would be difficult to speak of the perspective of the outsider, since the community of readers with Estonian or Albanian as a second language must be very small. There is no international discipline of Estonian or Albanian literary studies. Intercultural hermeneutics is a fascinating field for future research, but in some cases it seems more possible than in others. Colonization may remind us that cultures may be not only assimilated but also ignored. As Goethe wrote to Herder in 1796: "Die Fremde hat ein fremdes Leben und wir können es uns nicht zu eigen machen, wenn es uns gleich als Gästen gefällt" (cited in Wierlacher 1990: 59). The range of reading positions in the case of an Estonian poem is so narrow in comparison with a novel originally written in English that the interpretive strategies might be radically different in the two cases and it is virtually impossible to use the methods of *Wirkungsgeschichte* or *Rezeptionsästhetik* in the first case.

The world is extremely fragmented and yet the canons, highly institutionalized and based on accessibility, are very rigid. Some European literatures have become no less marginalized than certain cultures which developed on other continents. When we teach comparative literature in Europe, we tend to focus on works composed in English, French, and German. Italian, Spanish, and Russian play a less central role in the teaching and research of those who are not specialists of these cultures, and relatively few of us can cope with Scandinavian texts. Except for native speakers, hardly any literary scholar could claim to have a systematic knowledge of Czech, Hungarian, Polish, or Romanian works. In most European countries there are more specialists of Chinese or Arabic than of Estonian or Albanian. Although it is tempting to believe that great literature is produced by large linguistic communities, the assumptions underlying such a hypothesis would need further analysis. Moreover, the relative insignificance of Victorian music may remind us that economic growth and political power cannot guarantee artistic excellence.

Although comparative literature scholars can do more than specialists of national literatures for a dialogue of different cultures — a goal still far from reached at the end of the twentieth century — the difficulties of such a task are considerable. Collective projects can be a solution only if they go beyond the juxtaposition of contributions that are too diverse in material and method to help intercultural understanding. To make some progress, it would be advisable to deconstruct the opposition between Western and non-Western cultures and examine the distinction between 'great' and 'small' literatures. Without a radical opening up of the international canon comparative literature research cannot justify its legitimacy in the future.

References

De Man, Paul. 1989 [1978]. "Foreword to Carol Jacobs, 'The Dissimulating Harmony.'" *Critical Writings, 1953-1978*. Minneapolis: University of Minnesota Press.
Derrida, Jacques. 1960. *L'autre cap, suivi de La démocratie ajournée*. Paris: Minuit.
Gadamer, Hans-Georg. 1986. *Wer bin Ich und wer bist Du? Ein Kommentar zu Paul Celans Gedichtfolge "Atemkristall."* Frankfurt am Main: Suhrkamp. (Revidierte und ergänzte Ausgabe.)
Nietzsche, Friedrich. 1969. *Ecce homo*. Berlin: Walter de Gruyter and Co.
Rousseau, Jean-Jacques. 1960. *Lettre á M. D'Alembert*. Paris: Garnier.
Wierlacher, Alois. 1990. "Mit fremden Augen oder: Fremdheit als Ferment: Überlegungen zur Begründung einer interkulturellen Hermeneutik deutscher Literatur." In Dietrich Krusche und Alois Wierlacher (Hrsg), *Hermeneutik der Fremde*. München: Iudicium.
Wittgenstein, Ludwig. 1984. *Culture and Value. (Vermischte Bemerkungen)*. Chicago: University of Chicago Press.

Flaubert and the Transformation of Idyll

Joachim von der Thüsen
Utrecht University

There is probably no other author in the nineteenth century whose stance is more fiercely anti-idyllic than Gustave Flaubert. To Flaubert, all forms of the pastoral were part of that 'Romantic' literature, which, by nourishing illusions about the world, could "poison" immature souls. The famous sixth chapter in *Madame Bovary* describes some of this 'Romantic' reading material. None of the books young Emma is reading is identified by title, except for the very first one: it is *Paul et Virginie*, the famous tragic tale about love and innocence on a subtropical island. Written in 1788 by an ardent follower of Rousseau, Jacques-Henri Bernardin de Saint-Pierre, it became the most widely read book in early nineteenth-century France. Its exotic setting fired the imagination of its — mostly young — readers, while its scenes of tenderness, virtue, and untimely death moved them to tears. In *Madame Bovary*, reading *Paul et Virginie* denotes the stage of initiation: the book introduces Emma to that realm of elation and otherness, which will forever alienate her from the mediocrity and *ennui* of the world around her.

There is a second reference to *Paul et Virginie* in the works of Flaubert. In "Un Cœur simple" (1877), a boy and a girl are named after Bernardin's heroes. They are the children of Madame Aubain, a widow living in a small town in Normandy. Flaubert's text, which is short on motivations, does not reveal whether Madame Aubain herself has read the novel *Paul et Virginie*. Perhaps, in giving her children these famous literary names, Madame Aubain simply succumbed to the fashion of her day. Sainte-Beuve once said that "all children" born around 1800 were christened Paul and Virginie, just as one generation earlier "all children" had been named Émile and Sophie.

At first glance, then, the names 'Paul' and 'Virginie' in "Un Cœur simple" seem to be little more than ironic details, giving an additional touch of historical accuracy to the depiction of life in early nineteenth-century France. Indeed, there is nothing idyllic about the life of these children. Growing up in a provincial town, the Aubain children are harnassed to a thoroughly bourgeois type of existence. They do not even seem to have some of the illusions and dreams of Emma Bovary.

This is all the more astonishing as Flaubert claimed that he had written "Un Cœur simple" for George Sand, his friend and "vieux maître." George Sand died after Flaubert had embarked on his project. When, after six long months of writing, the story was finished, it had become a most peculiar epitaph. "Un Cœur simple" showed no trait of the Rousseauistic vision of country life, for which George Sand had been well-known.

In her first novel, *Indiana* (1832), George Sand had expressly mentioned *Paul et Virginie* as a model for her own two heroes, an English baron and his Creole cousin Indiana. They grow up together on an island in the West Indies and, after years of wanderings, they return to their island and find happiness there. The novel, with its sharp dividing line between natural goodness and corrupt society, has all the features of a Rousseauistic confession. Although in her later works George Sand did not return to this model of the exotic pastoral, she continued to depict rural worlds of virtue and compassion. There could hardly be a sharper contrast between this arcadian view of countrylife and the anti-idyllic perspective adopted by Flaubert.

One has to look at Flaubert's story more closely in order to learn something about this puzzlingly complex textual relationship. Since space is limited, I will confine myself to a few observations on the conventions of idyll, as they appear in *Paul et Virginie*, and on their radical transformation in Flaubert's tale.

The family structure in Flaubert's text bears a strong resemblance to the one in Bernardin's novel. Madame Aubain, like Madame de la Tour in *Paul et Virginie*, marries a man below her station. Monsieur Aubain is a bourgeois who leads a dissipated life and dies early, leaving his wife with just a small portion of her former property. The young widow is joined by Félicité, a maid of humble origin who, in her devotion to Paul and Virginie, becomes a motherly figure herself. The matriarchal family pattern, which Bernardin had placed at the centre of his idyll, is thus mirrored in the structure of the Aubain household. Yet while Bernardin's novel opens up a space in which the very principle of *mésalliance* becomes the foundation-stone of social harmony,

Flaubert's story presents a world in which none of the social barriers is breached. Madame Aubain is a harsh woman, embittered by her fate, while Paul and Virginie are not particularly grateful children. Kindness and pity would be in short supply, were it not for Félicité's inexhaustible capacity for love. This asymmetric relationship leads to grotesque situations when, for instance, Félicité is rebuffed for her motherly urge to caress the little ones. Yet even under these unfavorable circumstances, there comes a moment of emotional closeness. Both 'mothers' lose their dearest ones: Virginie dies at the convent of Honfleur, while Victor, the beloved nephew of Félicité, perishes on a voyage to the Americas. When, some years later, both women open the wardrobe in which Virginie's clothes are still hanging, they kiss each other in a spontaneous embrace: "Leurs yeux se fixèrent l'une sur l'autre, s'emplirent de larmes; enfin la maîtresse ouvrit ses bras, la servante s'y jeta; et elles s'étreignirent, satisfaisant leur douleur dans un baiser qui les égalisait" (1989: II, 611).

This is the first time Madame Aubain shows any sign of affection for Félicité, and the reader does not get the impression that such a scene will repeat itself. Yet precisely because Flaubert is such a severe critic of the sentimentalist anthropology of Rousseau and Bernardin, this scene of mutual consolation is remarkable. In this one instance, the realist author allows his text to become an echo of the harmony of mothers in the sentimentalist novel.

The fact that it is the death of Virginie which brings these two women together points to another textual parallel. In Flaubert's tale, as well as in Bernardin's novel, the name 'Virginie' has an ominous ring. In both texts, a class-conscious mother sends her daughter away for her 'proper education,' but what is intended to lay the foundation for a happy future leads to premature death. Both Virginies return as corpses; they become the very image of womanhood preserved in its virgin state. Not surprisingly, the memories of both girls circle around the word "angel."

Whereas Flaubert's text preserves part of Bernardin's arrangement of characters, its descriptions of nature differ sharply from those of Bernardin's idyll. In *Paul et Virginie*, the little community is embedded in a lush and benevolent nature. In keeping with the idyllic tradition, nature constitutes the wider matriarchal horizon: Nature feeds and preserves human life. Correspondingly, in Bernardin's novel one can find an abundance of plant metaphors referring to human beings, confirming the underlying symbiotic relationship between man and nature.

By contrast, Flaubert's Normandy is a land of austerity. The immediate surroundings of Pont l'Evêque show the harsh and forbidding side of nature. The valley of the Toucques river is full of marshes, undermining the health of its inhabitants, while on the higher grounds, where most of the farms are situated, man has to toil to survive. Here, living 'close to nature' does not mean being surrounded by plentiful vegetation, but living close to animals. In this dire world man shares the plight of beasts.

In an environment determined by such hardship, the names 'Paul' and 'Virginie' are indeed misleading. The values of virtue and compassion evoked by these names are not upheld in the bourgeois sphere, nor can they thrive under the difficult conditions of rural life.

Perhaps Bernardin would have agreed that, in Europe, both the climate and the oppressed life of the peasants do not allow for credible depictions of rural happiness. Thus, even from his viewpoint, Flaubert would have been right in stressing the deprivation and monotony of country life in Normandy. For the realist, however, there is no easy way out: an idyllic island on the other side of the globe is just as much a product of fantasy as an arcadian valley in France would be.

Ever since his journey to Egypt and Palestine (1850-51), Flaubert had been conscious of the omnipresence of boredom and misery. That experience had strenghtened his conviction that one could not, as the writers of idylls did, remove a small part of the world from the universal network of affliction: no human domain was exempt from the laws of history. The writer of idylls, by allowing his microcosm to be governed by different rules, showed his belief that man could return to an archaic experience of time: by obeying the rhythm of seasons and adopting a cyclical 'view' of time, man could create a bulwark against history. Yet even Bernardin, who had pleaded for such a return to an older form of time-consciousness, had let his story end in a tragic clash of the idyllic with the historical.

Even the staunchest defender of Realism cannot deny that human beings yearn for a harmonious and peaceful form of existence. Every observer of human behavior has to accept such feelings as part of a basic anthropological truth. But whereas the sentimentalist transforms ideals into actions, the realist has no similar recourse. He has to confine himself to the representation of ideals and visions as an inner reality. He knows that it is not possible for ideals to survive in the world of action: as soon as they become part of the complexities of the social world, they will be deformed, corrupted, and even destroyed.

The realist is condemned to represent a world in which — as Hegel formulated it — "the poetry of the heart" collides with "the prose of circumstances."

In *Madame Bovary* and *L'Éducation sentimentale*, Flaubert gives us two powerful representations of this collision between the realm of desires and the forces of the historical world. "Un Cœur simple" contains a more subtle treatment of this conflict. By making the simple soul Félicité the focus of his story, the author greatly reduces the tension between the inner and the outer world. Félicité has few desires. Although, at an early stage in her life, she is thwarted in her hope for marriage, she soon acquiesces in her fate and finds all of her happiness in the serving of others. Most of Félicité's actions meet with approval, since they gratify others and help stabilize existing social structures. Thus there is little cause for conflict with the outer world.

Her deeds equal those of the sentimental hero, yet Félicité has no sentimental ideals. In Flaubert's tale, she is the only person who leads a life true to its roots, never forgetting the essential knowledge she acquired on a farm, in the community with animals. It is precisely this life of humility and toil which, unexpectedly, leads to the reappearance of virtue and kindness.

In creating the figure of the maid Félicité, Flaubert resurrects part of the traditional idyll and rewrites it at the same time. Félicité has that essential quality of the idyllic character: innocence. Yet in Flaubert's world, there are no others left who are equally pure of soul. Everybody else belongs to that other group: the harsh and the scheming. This makes Félicité a rather lonely dweller in the realm of idyll. What was once a small community of peaceful souls has been reduced to its smallest circumference: the consciousness of a single person. The idyllic island has become one person's horizon.

References

Flaubert, Gustave. 1989. *Œuvres*. Texte établi et annoté par A. Thibaudet et R. Dumesnil. 2 vols. Paris: Gallimard (Pléiade).
Saint-Pierre, Jacques-Henri Bernardin de. 1964. *Paul et Virginie*. Texte établi, avec une introduction, des notes et des variantes par Pierre Trahard. Paris: Garnier.

Political Satire in Hungarian Exile Literature

Systemic Considerations

Steven Tötösy de Zepetnek
University of Alberta

Theoretical Postulates

Exile, or emigré(e) literature can be studied successfully, in my opinion, with the systemic and empirical theoretical and methodological framework. This, I think, would achieve meaningful results among which I rate highly the framework's ability to avoid the mistake of downgrading the literary, indeed, polyvalence and consequently canonical value of some, if not all, exile literature. Most importantly, the systemic approach allows us to take into account extra-literary factors which often mark, indeed, designate, the perception of exile literature. This perception in general, I contend, designates exile literature as marginal. Also, to frame my introduction to some characteristics of political satire in Hungarian exile literature with this theoretical approach is appropriate not only because of my general approach to literary analysis drawn on the systemic and empirical approach to literature (see, for example, Fokkema 1991; Schmidt 1994) — but also because exile literature in general and Hungarian exile literature in particular appears to be more often than not having difficulties in the overall canonization process. The theoretical importance of the systemic and empirical approach with reference to the canonization process has been argued for previously by Douwe Fokkema (1991). (See also my theory and application of cumulative canon formation in Tötösy 1994, and 1996a.)

I would also like to point out, again from a systemic point of view, that owing to political and ideological structures and mechanisms until recently in power in Hungary, it is only since the mid-1980s that Hungarian literary scholars began to pay more sophisticated attention to literature produced abroad, that is, in Western Europe and in North America (see Czigány 1994; Pomogáts 1994).

On the analytical side and with reference to the question of literary critical sophistication Robert S. Newman writes:

> it is safe to say that we normally expect exile or refugee literature to be transparent. That is, we assume that those who encounter it will accept it at face value and perhaps even understand its subtextual implications. But the varying reception of exiles and refugees over the years should make us wonder about this model of transparency. (1992: 87)

Newman underlines what I experienced during conversations with Hungarian scholars during my recent visits to Hungary and that, in turn, correspond to the perception of Hungarian exile literature in Hungarian literary histories. To reproduce the opinions I encountered bluntly, the general opinion expressed was that authors such as Stephen Vizinczey or László Kemenes-Géfin are "simply second-rate" writers, because their writing is autobiographical and lacking multi-layeredness and sophistication. I will attempt to show that such perceptions are void of precisely the systemic perspective I postulate. Francesco Loriggio explains that

> One of the more interesting aspects of ethnic literature as a field of study is the obligations it entails. The critic is forced to work on many levels simultaneously. S/he must name the texts, disseminate them, and, at the same time, at this particular stage of the game, define them, situate them within the agenda of the century and the debate it has forstered. (1989: 575)

This *a priori* positioning of the study of ethnic literature — I argue that exile literature is to be categorized in the domain of ethnic literature — is in essence what I designate as 'systemic.' More to the point, once the 'systemic' positioning of the exile text is performed, it already obtains a higher order of perception with regards to its more sophisticated analysis, and hence, possible canonization. So, because in a systemic context the text is located within the framework of the interrelation between its function as an exile text related to both the 'home' literature *and* the literary origins based in its location of production. Following Loriggio's argumentation that the positioning of an ethnic text involves historical strategies, in which "ethnicity is active disemia, disemia congenital to one's biography and behaviour, historically and institutionally overdetermined" (1989: 585), the systemic positioning of ethnic minority writing with reference to what appears to be the criticized historical and autobiographical element in exile literature, becomes, evidently, multi-layeredness and creative sophistication.

Some Examples of Hungarian Exile Literature

Following the context of the suggestion above, I will look at some aspects of satire in Stephen Vizinczey's *In Praise of Older Women* (1965) and in László Kemenes-Géfin's *Fehérlófia* (1978-1991). Vizinczey entertains his readers with the erotic and sexual adventures of an adolescent boy, and later, of the same person as a young man. In Vizinczey's case this is fictional autobiography and it is thematic on the surface. However, a closer referential reading will reveal that much of these adventures contain a politico-satirical dimension involving elements of pre-1945 Hungarian society and mores, and more intensely, a satire of societal parameters with reference to the politics of the Rákosi era. For example, his description of his love affairs when a high school student, resulting in his teachers recognizing his suddenly developed "qualities of leadership" (79), represent the underlying authorial implication that the dominant parameters of the new 'communist' society yet to be built do not differ from misinterpretations party to the older generation. In other words, Vizinczey suggests that the new world, as much as its representatives would have liked to believe, reacts to life and youth no different than before, from a historical perspective. This experience and his reading of it is often reinforced, as in his descriptions of "civil disobedience" (for instance, 88-89).

The protagonist's life and adventures are framed in the historicity of the period, expressed by phrases such as "This was the time of capricious terrorism in Hungary" (100). The framing is, of course, an important element in the understanding of Vizinczey's satire of the politics and ideology of the pre-1956 period. For example, his description of the machinations of the Hungarian Secret Police is closely related to the erotic and sexual life of those affected by the Secret Police (102-103) and the terror of the times is parodized and satiricized by the suggestion of the availability of an affair. To illustrate my point further, see the following passage: "I would have gone to prison to be torn apart by the Security Police if I could go to bed with her first" (118). More,

Vizinczey succeeds in providing a satire of the Rákosi regime by drawing an analogy of the coming of age of young András as opposed to the not-coming of age of the early-Hungarian Stalinist era, so with depicting the impact of sexuality in a slice of life. At the same time, young András' sexual exploits represent the author's satire of contemporary dominant ideology where sexuality represents a release from terror, as opposed to the sexual repression he later experiences in the 'free' worlds of Italy and Canada.

Kemenes-Géfin's *Fehérlófia* is a larger and more serious work, consequently with more elements and layers. It abounds with similar strategies of eroticism and sexuality in a satirical framework on politics, history, ideology, and literature. The work contains a higher order of historicity as it makes continuous references to overdetermined and fictionalized historical facts and factors of Hungarian history. For example, the 1956 Revolution is 'fictionalized' by poetic mutations of history and sexual autobiography:

> Egész jól indult a reggel, az asszony azt hiszem már nem sokáig bírja a szobában, kiéheztettem, körömvágás, körömreszelés, K. Attilától telefon, öregem, a diszkóban nem tudtam fölmarni senkit, mi van Katalinnal, mondtam este jöhetsz a szögesdrótvirgáccsal, megpuhítjuk együtt fehér bőrét. (16)

> The morning started well enough, I think the wife is not going to stand it much longer in the room, I starved her, cut my finger nails, filed my finger nails, then the phone call from Attila K., my good buddy, I couldn't pick up anyone in the disco, how is Kathrine, I told you you could come by in the evening with the barbedwirerod, together we will soften her white skin. (My translation.)

The section of the novel then progresses into a verse-report on the Revolution in Western Hungarian cities, thus connecting the autobiographical with the historical. Géfin's depiction of Hungarian realities is deeply historical with thoroughly imbued and explicitly ordered sexuality. I would suggest that this strategy is an innovative satiricization of Hungarian history — with a red thread of continuous references to the Stalinist Rákosi period — with the author's employment of sexuality, more, with sexual and erotical pornography. (By this I mean his explicitness and his transgression into a hitherto nonexistent genre in Hungarian literature.) Granted, there is a profound *honvágy* (home sickness) in Géfin's writing but this does not prevent him to exploit the possibilities to build satirical layers of historicization through pornographic descriptions. His satirical and hence *alternative* historicization of Hungary extends history to politics but also to religious history and religion as an ideology and historical force. This basic aspect of his work alone makes it a Postmodern text before its time — let us not forget that most of the work was written and first published in Toronto and Montréal in the 1970s! — highly charged with innovation in Hungarian literary history. His satire of history, politics, religion, and Hungarian literature on a basis of pornography and eroticism is not, I contend, a curious expression of dissatisfied yearning for a different Hungarianness. Rather, it is the expression of a Postmodern understanding of humanity which, at the same time, is regionally conditioned. The political and historical satire of the work resides in Géfin's debunking of Hungarian parochialism in its literary representation. I suggest that his inversion of the quintessential and forever instilled and installed mode of the still all-prevalent dictum *Extra Hungariam non est vita si est vita non est ita* — so by his satire of everything Hungarian — is the innovation of an incipient coming-of-age in Hungarian literature.

In contemporary, that is, post-1989 Hungarian literature, there are, however, signs of similar trends. For example, the poet Endre Kukorelly's work, although not containing the vocal exuberance of Géfin, expresses at times similar perceptions, including eroticism and sexuality. Kukorelly's work is a layered verisimilitude of what remains in contemporary Hungarian literature mostly on the level of an *Erwartungshorizont* or implicitness. In my opinion, one difference between Kukorelly's, for example his *A memória-part* (1990) — an equally historical work both in the autobiographical and in the political and ideological (see Tötösy 1996b) — and Géfin's *Fehérlófia* is exactly the lack of satire in the former and the magnitude of it in the latter.

It is in this attention to the systemic and to innovation in literary studies that Newman's postulate becomes evident: the political, ideological, and historical satiricization in the work of Vizinczey and Géfin becomes a potent and innovative literary device, worth our serious attention.

In conclusion, satire in Hungarian exile literature, at least in the works of Vizinczey and Géfin, but also, for example, in the work of the second-generation British-Hungarian Tibor Fisher in his *Under the Frog* (1992) or in the writings of Robert Zend's *Nicolette* (1993), marks an important departure from the traditional narratives of historical fiction, autobiographical or other.

References

Czigány, Lóránt. 1994. *Gyökértelen, mint a zászló nyele. Írások a nyugati magyar irodalomról*. Budapest: Szabad Tér.
Fokkema, Douwe W. 1982. "Comparative Literature and the New Paradigm." *Canadian Review of Comparative Literature / Revue Canadienne de Littérature Comparée* 9(1): 1-18.
—. 1991. "Changing the Canon: A Systems Theoretical Approach." In Elrud Ibsch, Dick Schram, and Gerard Steen (eds), *Empirical Studies of Literature: Proceedings of the Second IGEL-Conference, Amsterdam 1989*. Amsterdam / Atlanta, GA: Rodopi, 363-69.
Kemenes-Géfin, László. 1991 [1978]. *Fehérlófia*. Budapest: Szépirodalmi.
Loriggio, Francesco. 1989. "History, Literary History, and Ethnic Literature." *Canadian Review of Comparative Literature / Revue Canadienne de Littérature Comparée* 16(3/4): 575-99.
Newman, Robert S. 1992. "The Reader of Exile: Skvorecky's *Engineer of Human Souls*." In James Whitlark and Wendell Aycock (eds), *The Literature of Emigration and Exile*. Lubbock, TX: Texas Tech University Press, 87-104.
Pomogáts, Béla. 1994. *Nyugati égbolt. Tanulmányok a nyugati magyar irodalomról*. Budapest: A Magyar Írószövetség és a Belvárosi Könyvkiadó.
Schmidt, Siegfried J. 1994. *Kognitive Autonomie und soziale Orientierung. Konstruktivistische Bemerkungen zum Zusammenhang von Kognition, Kommunikation, Medien und Kultur*. Frankfurt: Suhrkamp.
Tötösy de Zepetnek, Steven. 1994. "Toward a Theory of Cumulative Canon Formation: Readership in English Canada." *Mosaic: A Journal for the Interdisciplinary Study of Literature* 27(3): 107-19.
—. 1996a. "Factors in a Theory of Cumulative Canon Formation: Contemporary Hungarian and English-Canadian Literature." *Literatura Comparada: Novos Paradigmas / Comparative Literature: New Paradigms*. Oporto: Associação Portuguesa de Literatura Comparada. (Forthcoming.)
—. 1996b. "Urbanity and Postmodern Sensuality: The 'Post-Magyar' Endre Kukorelly." *World Literature Today* 70(2). (Forthcoming.)
Vizinczey, Stephen. 1965. *In Praise of Older Women: The Amorous Recollections of András Vajda*. New York: Ballantyne.

Between *Prise de Position* and *Habit-Taking*

The Contribution of Operative Semantics to the Semiotics of Culture

Horst Turk
University of Göttingen

Douwe Fokkema oftentimes enjoys to play out the card of institutionalism against hermeneutics. However, in the following short contribution I shall try to decide the point in question in my favor.

In the following, I shall first adopt the praxeological view of cultural units. Then, two further steps will help me to discuss the premises of this view. A certain deviation with respect to the texts I discuss, will be that I always speak of processes of symbolization, histories, cultures, and human beings in the plural and in the sense of general interdependencies. Terminologically, I presuppose that symbol systems may be interpreted by behaviorial habits and corresponding actions just as much as behaviorial habits and actions may be interpreted by symbol systems. What are the characteristics of the reciprocal relationship between institutions, behaviorial habits and processes of symbolization, actions and historical developments, if we choose culturally organized human societies as our field of observation?

Cultures are not merely systems of interpretation, but mainly systems of conviction. Behavioral habits and actions are inseparable from symbolizations, but symbolizations may not be separated from behavioral habits and actions, either. If they were separated, one could hardly speak of processes in the sense of historical developments any more. It is also true that neither is conceivable without the impact of institutions. Institutions transform the field of structural relations into a "field of power" (Bourdieu 1983: 325), a "field of positions" (316). The field is handled by way of the sanctioned formation of convictions with the help of deliberated habitualization. The control and consistence of adopted attitudes is contingent upon this deliberated habitualization. In the process, empirical facts and material interests play a role as much as symbolic interests and cultural values. Symbolic orders function as a medium of this reflected practice. They may be used for different purposes. The adjustment of empirical circumstances to traditional interpretations may receive priority, or so may the adjustment of traditional interpretations to empirical circumstances, or the adjustment of both to institutional regulations and vice versa. Myths and paradigms constitute the repertoire for the reproduction as well as for the change of structures. In each case, the process is subject to the set of rules of the constitution of convictions.

The driving forces are to be located in the field of social powers and positions, with its conflicting and controversial positions of the exercise of influence. Among these, the positions of disposition formation play an outstanding part. The prospective plausibility of available modes of behavior and convictions hinges upon them. Cultural units may well be conceived as semiotic units, though their unity depends upon an operative semantics. The latter's most prominent characteristic is that it does not merely focus on a dispositional and a real, but also on a reflexive plausibility, that one does not merely understand *according* to it, but in *itself*. But then, what kind of conditions make up the tools of a semiotic theory of culture? I will begin with the point of reflexivization in the versions of Charles Peirce and Ernst Cassirer.

In their semiotic analyses, Peirce and Cassirer presuppose a certain final state of the reflected relation of signs. Cassirer does so by viewing the "vague demand for a similarity of content" as substituted by "a highly complex logical relation," a "general intellectual condition" — "Its value lies not in the reflection of a given existence, but in what it accomplishes as an instrument of knowledge" (Cassirer 1955-57: I, 75). Peirce conceives of the "intellectual" or "rational" meaning content of concepts or of symbols in general as located in their "effect."

The relevance of both approaches for cultural history lies in the fact that Peirce as well as Cassirer favor an embedding in the comprehensive process of symbol and sign formation. As a result, a certain stage in evolution stands for the reflexivization of the sign relation in the distinction between the "knower" and the "known" (Cassirer: II, 175) or between the three "dimensions" of the sign relation, respectively. In either case, we might speak of a process of symbol and sign formation analyzing itself, while the main difference seems to be that we are offered different versions as to how the change takes place.

In the case of Cassirer, the embedding seemed important mainly for the theory of culture. He registers that the "symbolic form" — the text elaborates on different "forms" such as language, myth, knowledge, but also religion and art — "does not *have* the limit between I and reality as pre-existent and established for all time but must itself create this limit — and that each fundamental form creates it *in a different way*" (II, 156): "It would not be possible to speak of a discovery of the subjective in myth if the widespread view that the concepts of the I and the soul were the *beginning* of all mythical thinking were justified" (155). Rather, one would have to start from the idea that the "essential achievement" of the respective symbolic forms "is not that they copy the outward world in the inward world or that they simply project a finished inner world outward, but rather that the two factors of 'inside' and 'outside,' of 'I' and 'reality' are *determined* and delimited from one another only in these symbolic forms and through their mediation" (155f.).

Peirce closely ties this embedding to the founding problem of semiotics. In knowledge, a distinction between the knower and the known occurs in such a manner that knowledge conceives of itself as a part of the process of designation. Peirce and Cassirer view subjective reality as mediated by the process of designation.

The third and final correspondence between Peirce and Cassirer is that in the course of the acts of designation (in Cassirer's words: of "distinctions and connections"), man is brought to himself. Cassirer's text declares that "It is not mere meditation but action which constitutes the center from which man undertakes the spiritual organization of reality" (II, 157). In place of this thought, Peirce uses the concept of "habit-taking." The "relation *to* some thought" leads to the "deliberately formed, self-analyzing habit" as a "living definition" and a "veritable and final" interpretation. It is the "logical interpretant" — "self-analyzing because formed by the aid of analysis of the exercises that nourished it." The "logical" is supplemented by the "energetic interpretant" of the testing of the adopted behaviorial habits in action: "The habit, conjoined with the motive and the conditions has the action for its energetic interpretant" (Peirce 341f., nr. 5.491).

This runs dry all the options of correspondence and difference in point of view. But two questions remain. Firstly, to what extent is the pragmaticist analysis compatible with the historico-genetical analysis under the aspect of the recollected succession of such binding convictions? Secondly, the question should be raised whether the institutionalistic approach may be applied especially to the position last mentioned, which then creates an 'image' of the action of cultural units that conforms with reality. Concluding, I shall concentrate on the act of position-taking — a "prise de position" in Bourdieu's sense (Bourdieu 1974: 316) — as it has been practised in the *Philosophy of Symbolic Forms*.

According to the *Philosophy of Symbolic Forms*, it is the task of cultures and of culture as such to transform "the passive world of mere *impressions*, in which the spirit seems at first imprisoned, into a world that is pure *expression* of the human spirit" (Cassirer 1955-57: I, 81). Thus, the primacy of doing in relation to observing is taken into account, but in the way that the processes of the genesis of the sign may be read retrospectively from the position of the "individual feeling and consciousness of self" (II, 175) as its own doing or action. In retrospect, consciousness discovers its production in all symbolic forms, even though it qualifies only with reservations as the originator of the forms. After all, it has been brought to itself by the forms in the first place. Still, the processes (or the process as a whole) assume the character of a self-determined activity, whereby evolution becomes emphatically endogenous, but also increasingly prospective and — this is the crucial point — also increasingly differentiated. The previousness of the symbolic forms does not rule out that man is brought to himself in the execution of the symbolic forms. But it does rule out that this 'to himself' should always be the same, irrespective of the diversity of possible starting points.

At this point, not only the weakness, but also the strength of the historico-philological approach shows. It does not dismiss prospectively the theoretical reflexion on culture into the plurality of operative semantics (or self-discoveries). Instead, it tries to capture this plurality in a universal historical development, thereby binding it to this development or launching an act of conviction in its favor. Cassirer's text on the universal historical self-discovery is at the same time a text *about* the unity of culture, a unifying text *of* culture, and a unifying text of a *specific* culture or a complex of cultures reflected upon historically. Thereby, it is in accordance with the introductory demand made for the "new view of the 'symbol'" (II, 258), that it should establish from within itself the "unity of phenomena" (I, 75) it thematizes — dispositionally: in the same way in which it thematizes them. In this respect, the text may be viewed not only as a text *on* operative semantics, but as a *document* of operative semantics.

Finally, it may serve as an example for the executed "interplay of [...] assimilated basic patterns" (Bourdieu 1974: 143) on the level of literary discourses, if the objective in question is not to defend philosophical reflexion as such, but rather its importance for the exploration of "unconscious (or deeply dug in) schemata," where "Bildung" or the "habitus" are "rooted." If one were to follow Bourdieu in this matter, it would solely be an affair of institutions, for instance, of "the school" as a place where norms of behavior are induced, to implement the schemata and generate the habitus.

It was not the purpose of my argument to question the validity of this statement. But my argument was meant to raise skepticism concerning the further conviction that the interplay of discipline-transgressing "basic patterns" or the "system of interiorized patterns" as a whole would simply be cases of "basic patterns assimilated in advance," which could furthermore only be handed down as such. To put it briefly: that the "explicit function of the school" would be to "transform the collective heritage into an individually as well as collectively unconscious" (Bourdieu 1974: 139). Here, the concept of habitualization lacks exactly that element which is capable of explaining the increased abilities in perseverance as well as in irritation. The methodological principle to treat "a specific case as a 'singular case of the possible'" (1991: 11), on the other hand, enjoys unrestricted approval even after I have finished my argument.

References

Bourdieu, Pierre. 1974. *Zur Soziologie der symbolischen Formen*. Trans. Wolfgang Fietkau. Frankfurt am Main.
—. 1983. "The Field of Cultural Production, Or: The Economic World Reversed." *Poetics* 12: 311-356.
—. 1991. *Die feinen Unterschiede. Kritik der gesellschaftlichen Urteilskraft*. Trans. Bernd Schwibs and Achim Russer. Frankfurt am Main.
Cassirer, Ernst. 1955-57. *The Philosophy of Symbolic Forms*. 3 vols. New Haven and London: Yale University Press.
Peirce, Charles Sanders. 1960. *Collected Papers of Charles Sanders Peirce*. Vol. V. In Charles Hartshorne, Paul Weiss, and Arthur W. Burks (eds). Cambridge, MA: Harvard University Press.

Hermeneutics *and* Empirical Studies

Mario J. Valdés
University of Toronto

Douwe Fokkema's "Concluding Observations" in his *Exploring Postmodernism* gives me an excellent starting point: "We need empirical research," he writes, so that we can better "judge the merits of the various constructions of Postmodernism. As both Eibl (1976: 12) and Schmidt (1985: 125) have argued, however, precision in our observations largely depends on the way our perception is guided by theories" (238). Not only do I agree, but I agree within the inquiry of hermeneutics.

The argument I will begin to outline draws primarily from *Philosophical Investigations* of Ludwig Wittgenstein and *Time and Narrative* of Paul Ricoeur, but will also seek to establish a common cause with empirical studies, especially the work of Siegfried J. Schmidt.

Wittgenstein reminds us of the essential flexibility of language usage which is central to this inquiry, "For I can give the concept 'number' rigid limits in this way, that is, use the word 'number' for a rigidly limited concept, but I can also use it so that the extension of the concept is not closed by a frontier" (1953: par. 68). The actual usage can vary as widely as "the probability of an event in the absolute square of a complex number" (Feynman 1967: 63) to "my number is up," the popular metaphor for anticipated death, or Wallace Stevens' "A swarming of number over number, not / One foot approaching, one uplifted arm" (296). Wittgenstein in effect points out that meaning is determined by the rules of the game and not by the nature of things and, since there are more situations than the rules cover, the possibility of polysemic expression is greater than univocal sense, but both are part of our reality. We can begin to work on our response by saying that meaning can be determinate or indeterminate depending on the criterion one is using in the designation and that both determinate and indeterminate meanings can be shared.

The determination of meaning can never be considered fixed. The meaning we construe to any statement or any text is tentative; indeterminacy is controlled by a system of signs we accept as determinate in order to establish a temporary identity to the text. This question of variable and stable identity of texts becomes a matter of political concern since nothing remains as absolute; every text can be subverted from the inside (Hutcheon 1989: 2-10; Valdés 1985: 297-311). I am, therefore, proposing that the common denominator of Poststructuralism is that *order* is an open-ended catalytic agent rather than an isomorphic referential parallel.

I am well aware of the rhetoric of excess that has been used by some empiricists to denounce the purported obscurantism of the "hermeneutic paradigm" and, on the other side, the facile dismissal by some in hermeneutics of the "German bean counters," but I am also aware that one of the most prominent empiricists, Siegfried Schmidt, has never ruled out dialogue with hermeneutics, although he has at times been in despair that the apparent impasse was due to more than intellectual differences. Without going into details in this brief position paper, I can outline some of the most important points of agreement between empirical studies and hermeneutics. Foremost is the proposition that meaning has an intersubjective foundation. Both phenomenological hermeneutics and empirical studies have developed analogous approaches to the study of the production of meaning. For both schools of thought meaning is determined through perception by the socially conditioned individual. This idea does not rule out idiosyncratic and highly personalized interpretations of phenomena, but these exceptional views are variations on what is socially possible. The major differences between hermeneutics and empirical studies are those of disciplinary formulation and terminology. While empirical studies are closely allied to biological research, hermeneutics draws its main support from the Heideggerian concept of language as the common habitat of human existence. The coming together of the philosophical linguistics of Emile Benveniste and the Heideggerian hermeneutics of Hans-Georg Gadamer, in what we now recognize as Paul Ricoeur's hermeneutics has given literary theory the common ground for the dialogue with empirical studies and, as I hope to point out here, also with experimental physics.

The most evident common direction of research is the development of the literary text as a forum, a meeting place of sociocultural determination rather than as a depository of fixed meanings. The validity and significance of literary studies and studies of literary history lies in this proposition that I am sure both Schmidt and I can take as a starting position.

The concept of order as a factor in human action functions as a paradigm for control over contingent circumstances. Some years ago in conversation with Jorge Luis Borges we discussed the idea of order. I asked him about his sense of order and randomness. His answers have remained an important part of my thinking. We were sitting in a near empty classroom in the university where he was scheduled to speak. He turned to a wastebasket which was located near the door, it was half full with debris. He asked if there was any order in the wastebasket. I said that if there were, it was not apparent to me, that it appeared to be the normal random collection of mid-day garbage. He said that my response in itself could be construed as a sense of order in what I considered to be normal mid-day garbage, but then he took the basket and turned it over on the table. The empty milk and juice containers, the empty lunch bags, folded newspapers, etc. spilled out. "Look at it now on the table. Have I not created a special order by putting it on the table?"

Order, therefore, is an imaginative configuration that deals in systems and totalizes things. Without the things, garbage in this case, or a system like language, there can be no order except as an idea, a mental need for sense-giving configuration. Furthermore, Borges stated, "there can be no order unless there was, and is, the possibility of disorder." The two are dialectically linked. "Now, then," he added, "if we were to put up a mirror to our table display of garbage we would have begun the process of duplication that is art." It was only a few months later that I read a paper by Paul Weiss in the volume edited by Paul G. Kuntz, *The Concept of Order*. He writes: "Disorder is an excess of order; it occurs when there are too many orders imposed upon a set of entities. [...] Order is selective and restrictive; it provides a channel through which to move from one entity to another; it helps to organize things in such a way that they can be understood. Disorder instead provides too many channels through which to move from one entity to another, too many alternative ways in which to understand" (16-17). Weiss then proceeds in the next paragraph to make an observation about the sense of order and disorder much in the way I had discussed with Borges:

> A case of disorder would be a heap, a miscellany, a heterogeneity of entities which are not similar in color, origin, shape, place, meaning, or value. These entities logicians call members of a class; mathematicians say that they make up an aggregate or a set. Though distinct, they are sufficiently joined to be together in one group. But the ways in which they can be related are too many. It is a disorder, contrasting with the usual arrangement of the positive integers 1, 2, 3, 4, 5... which offers only one way to move from one number to another. (17)

Of course, Weiss was not concerned either with the spacial order created by Borges or with mirror duplication, which as I have suggested are part of the imaginative order of configuration. Therefore, when we speak of order we are also speaking of disorder and order is always a configuration of something actual or virtual. Although no one particular order is required, there must be some way of grasping the whole. Order "is a means by which we can move clearly and easily from one entity to another. If we get rid of all particular orders we are left with a set of aggregated elements which can be interrelated in an endless number of ways" (17).

The spacial order of the debris on the table is an order of spacial configuration as in the plastic work of art: a configuration of space. The mirror duplication brings into the discussion the whole spectrum of representation and the inversion of the double. The idea of order is imposed by the knowing imagination of those who look upon it as spacial configuration. Why, we should ask, need this be so? Why do we impose order on objects? This imposed order does not invent relationships but rather takes up one aspect of things and ignores others. Again Weiss comments: the order one tries to impose is an order that is present in the original conglomeration of orders. The imposed order is selected out of the indefinitely many that are present. My response to the above query is that sense demands order. As Wittgenstein states, where there is sense there must be order (1953: par. 105) or when he writes: "confusions which occupy us arise when language is like an engine idling, not when it is doing work" (1953: par. 132) or, in our terms, making sense.

The problem of meaning is in fact the problem of representation — the problem of representing the heterogeneous diversity of types of knowledge in the different contexts of understanding. We understand and interpret texts to the extent that we are able to contextualize them. On this most important point, semiotics, hermeneutics and experimental physics are very close. The common concern is to connect understanding to contextual pre-understanding through the work of the process of inquiry (Ricoeur 1984-88: II, 155-56).

The Postmodern intellectual revolution of the end of the millennium, which has been subject to journalistic caricature as a breakdown of all rules and norms, is in fact a time of realism and an acutely self-conscious use of reason. If Modernism was the age of arrogance and, in literary studies, the ultimate arrogance was the fable of definitive interpretations, then Postmodernism will yet come to be known as the age of acknowledged limitations. The latest inclusion into the spirit of Postmodernity is mathematics. John Horgan of *Scientific American* writes:

> Mathematics, that most tradition-bound of intellectual enterprises, is undergoing profound changes. For millennia, mathematicians have measured progress in terms of what they can demonstrate through proofs — that is, a series of logical steps leading from a set of axioms to an irrefutable conclusion. Now the doubts riddling modern human thought have finally infected mathematics. Mathematicians may at last be forced to accept what many scientists and philosophers already have admitted: their assertions are, at best, only provisionally true, true until proved false. (1993: 93)

As I have argued here, there is a strict complementarity between hermeneutics and empirical studies. Postmodernity, therefore, should be construed as a time of a questioning of authority, an increased conflict of interpretations and the acceptance of more than one valid interpretation of the text. The philosophical foundations for this period have been developing throughout the twentieth century, but the breakdown of the legitimizing narrative of Western philosophy did not come until the decade following the Second World War. Writing today, within planning projection of the end of the twentieth century and the millennium, we can assess the fall-out of the debates of the immediate past. The fact that multiple answers are entertained as valid meanings of the same phenomenon does not condemn our thinking to unrestricted relativism or irrationalism. By having a clearer sense of how we interpret texts and human action, in general, we have become both more modest in our claims and more daring in our critique. Rational proof has been given its primary function of being one tool among others in the explanatory dialectic with understanding.

Note

Umberto Eco quite correctly observes that the mirror does not reverse or invert the images it reflects: "It is the observer (so ingenuous even when he is a scientist) who by self-identification imagines he is the man inside the mirror and, looking at himself, realizes he is wearing his watch on his right wrist. But it would be so only if he, the observer I mean, were the one who is inside the mirror (*Je est un autre!*). On the contrary, those who avoid behaving as Alice, and getting into the mirror, do not so deceive themselves. [...] So we use the mirror image correctly, but speak of it wrongly, as if it did what we ourselves are doing with it (that is, reversing it)" (205-206).

References

Eco, Umberto. 1986. *Semiotics and the Philosophy of Language*. Bloomington: Indiana University Press.
Eibl, Karl. 1976. *Kritisch-rationale Literaturwissenschaft: Grundlagen zur erklärenden Literaturgeschichte*. Munich: Fink.
Feynman, Richard P. 1967. *The Character of Physical Law*. Cambridge: MIT Press.
Fokkema, Douwe W. 1987. "Concluding Observations: Is There a Future for Research on Postmodernism?" In Matei Calinescu and Douwe W. Fokkema (eds), *Exploring Postmodernism*. Amsterdam / Philadelphia: Benjamins, 233-41.
Horgan, John. 1993. "The Death of Proof." *Scientific American* October: 92-103.
Hutcheon, Linda. 1989. *The Politics of Postmodernism*. New York: Routledge.
Kuntz, Paul G. (ed). 1968. *The Concept of Order*. Seattle: University of Washington Press.
Ricoeur, Paul. 1984-88. *Time and Narrative*. Trans. Kathleen Blamey and David Pellauer. 3 vols. Chicago: University of Chicago Press.
Schmidt, Siegfried J. 1985. "Vom Text zum Literatursystem: Skizze einer konstruktivistischen (empirischen) Literaturwissenschaft." *Einführung in den Konstruktivismus*, 117-33.
Stevens, Wallace. 1982. *The Collected Poems*. New York: Vintage.
Valdés, Mario J. 1985. "Concepts of Fixed and Variable Identity." In Mario J. Valdes and Owen Miller (eds), *Identity of the Literary Text*. Toronto: University of Toronto Press, 297-311.
Weiss, Paul. 1968. "Some Paradoxes Relating to Order." Kuntz 14-20.
Wittgenstein, Ludwig. 1953. *Philosophical Investigations*. Trans. G.E.M. Anscombe. Oxford: Blackwell.

Yardstick or Straight Jacket?

Notes on the Process of Canonization

Hennie P. van Coller
University of the Orange Free State

A *canon* is a collection of texts that are regarded by a specific society at a specific moment in time as valuable and worth preserving. These texts also function as points of reference for literary utterances, judgments and the study of literature (cf. Fokkema and Ibsch 1992, and Mooij 1985). This view of the canon as yardstick is in conflict with the opposing 'straight-jacket' view of Culler (1989) who describes the canon as "a sinister creature of consumer capitalism."

The whole process of canonization should, however, be viewed in relation to the process of *standardization* which is itself imbued with an inherent dichotomy: being democratic in one aspect and — in stark contrast — discriminatory (autocratic) in another. To really understand the tensions involved, one has to view literature as a systemic process with a multitude of relations, not only between texts, but between everything that stands in relation to production and consumption (Even-Zohar 1990).

Within a specific literary system, literature as a socio-political activity must be maintained. According to Even-Zohar (1990: 37) publishers, magazines, writer groups, educational institutions, mass media and critics play a central role in this regard. There is no harmony between these concurrent and irreconcilable elements, but in reality a contest for supremacy (cf. Van Coller 1992: 167). Naturally, all these participants play a role in the process of canonization, especially the *rewriters* (translators, compilers of anthologies, critics and literary historians) who in actual fact dictate the reception of literature within a community (cf. Lefevere 1992 and Ohlhoff 1993). These rewriters or "taste makers" (Van Coller 1992: 8) are mediators between earlier texts (and their reception at the time of production) and contemporary reception. In this way texts are adapted for contemporary use (cf. Ohlhoff 1993: 20).

It is clear that the majority of people are merely participants in a few canonization processes. It is mainly the creative person who is the ideal canonizer, especially when he is not only a writer but also a rewriter. The Afrikaans poet, N.P. van Wyk Louw, himself a prolific canonizer, provides reasons for this. What he himself practises is, according to Louw, rather a form of intuitive and personal criticism "that weighs each word, sometimes in a flash, that can follow rhythm in its finest folds and can absorb and judge the whole structure of a work" (Louw 1986: 305). Louw himself alludes to the reverse side of the picture: the author-critic can quite easily be prone to bias because he will have a natural affinity for work that is akin to his own (Louw 1986: 307).

In Mouton and Marais (1989: 139) a clear distinction is made between a *typology* and a *model*. A typology is a conceptual framework which entails a process of abstraction with generalization as its aim. Because abstraction presupposes selection, the relation between the typology as construct and the phenomenon it proposes to map out, is a relation of approximation. The criteria for the construction of a typology are exhaustiveness and mutual exclusiveness. The object of the typology for canonization I propose below is to serve as frame of reference for observation and the collection of data. In a later stage it may acquire a heuristic function and may even lead to the formulation of new hypotheses. To be concrete: my typology is derived from a specific 'phenomenon' — Afrikaans literature — and focusses on one author (the poet and former professor at Amsterdam, N.P. van Wyk Louw). My typology, as a frameword for analysis, should eventually be put to the test within the confines of another literary system, for instance, Dutch literature.

A typology of canonization

I distinguish the following aspects: canon linking; canon entrenchment; canon renewal: assessment, purging, and extension; canon protection; canon preparation canon popularization; and canon manipulation.

Canon linking
This is the deliberate linking of texts with other literature or literary systems, 'classical' texts, the literary tradition, etc. in a 'negative' or 'positive' way. Within the positive paradigm, linking is used to sanction a work. Although not exclusively, this method is often used by creative writers to canonize their own work. The complementary 'negative' modus operandi occurs when the deviation of a work from a norm (even for example from the literary tradition) is claimed as a reason for canonization.

Canon entrenchment
Both *canon linking* and *canon entrenchment* imply a historical attitude and perception. In the first instance the historical dimension (for instance, tradition) provides legitimacy and resonance for the text that is to be canonized. The focus thus lies in the present. In the case of *canon entrenchment* the aim is to entrench certain 'classical' texts or authors in the canon. The focus thus lies in the past. Motivation for the latter process need not, however, stem from the past. Canonization often professes the aim of creating one common cultural frame of reference, a treasure chamber which is accessible to everybody on an equitable basis and should therefore — in theory — be cherished by all and sundry. The motivation for canon entrenchment hence often stems from such an ideological stance with its focus on the present.

Canon renewal
1. *Assessment.* For any intellectual, like Louw, a constant assizement of norms and values is a sine qua non. It follows therefore that, as far as literary values are concerned, the canon as 'store-house' of value judgments (and reputations) should constantly be revalued. Such an outlook necessarily produces the realization of the relativity of one's own judgments (Louw 1986: 323), because the intellectual revaluation of authors, texts, critics and rewritings is not an activity with a focus on the past, but a prerequisite for constant renewal.
2. *Purging.* Assessment implies an uncompromizing scrutiny of authors, texts and critics. Whereas assizement therefore presupposes a critical stance, purgation is the ruthless expunging of authors and books from the canon and therefore assizement's pragmatic counterpart. Canon purgation is both diachronic and synchronic in the sense that neither the diachronic

nor the synchronic canons are sacrosanct. The rewriter's primary task is to read contemporary literary texts in a critical fashion in order to bar the inclusion of inferior texts in the synchronical canon.

The diachronical canon is the more 'stable' canon, often referred to as embodying the 'classical' texts. It is prudent to remember that these texts are not endowed with this status spontaneously: they usually share a common esthetics, cultural field of reference and historical past.

3. *Extension*. Canon extension almost inevitably implies canon renewal. Any rewriting that gives rise to the (re)inclusion of an author or texts in the diachronic or synchronic canon is a case in point. A few obvious instances of such rewriting are translation, criticism, and the compilation of anthologies.

Canon protection
Canon protection is only ostensibly akin to canon entrenchment. The first activity has to do with extra-literary threats that must be dealt with; in the South African context the constant threat of literary censorship posed by successive governments has been noteworthy. Louw's well known article "Censorship or pornography?" (Louw 1986: 400-408) is typical of a *theoretical* reflection on the dangers of censorship for the development of Afrikaans literature. His recurrent protests in the form of letters to the press, are an illustration of the *practice* of canon protection.

Canon preparation
Canon preparation is nowadays a marketing strategy of literary publishers that entails the promoting of an author, book or even topic *before* publication. As the strategy of a new movement it is often linked to a vehement attack on literary predecessors, as was the case with the School of the thirties in Afrikaans literature, and the 'Vijftigers' (Poets of the fifties) in Dutch literature.

Canon popularization
When the impact of rewriters is assessed, one tends to forget that many of them were successful and influential due to the fact that they had a large audience. Rewriters who stick to scientific journals seldom will have any noticeable impact. Louw, for example, made abundant use of so-called mass media and did not shun even magazines and encyclopaedias aimed at young children.

Canon manipulation
Manipulation of the canon is in a sense not a separate category, but the Mr Hyde lurking in the shadows in all the above categories. Manipulation takes place when objectivity and honesty have gone astray. It is especially rewriters that must be constantly aware of the dangers of manipulation: they must at all costs avoid using a crooked yardstick. Obviously so in the case of underestimation, it is even more dangerous in the case of wilful overvaluation. And here we can prudently end with Louw's warning: "Praise and popularity is always dangerous for the famous, but for the little ones it is the quenching of the small flame that they possess" (1986: 93).

References

Culler, J. 1989. As quoted in *The Times Literary Supplement* November 24:30.
Even-Zohar, Itamar. 1990. "Polysystem Studies." *Poetics Today* 11(1).
Fokkema, Douwe W., and Elrud Ibsch. 1992. *Literatuurwetenschap en Cultuuroverdracht.* Muiderberg: Coutinho.
Lefevere, André. 1992. *Translation, Rewriting and the Manipulation of Literary Fame.* London: Routledge.
Louw, N.P. van Wyk. 1986. *Versamelde prosa I.* Kaapstad: Tafelberg.
Mooij, J.J.A. 1985. "Noodzaak en mogelijkheden van canonvorming." *Spektator* 15: 23-31.
Mouton, J., and H.C. Marais. 1989. *Basic Concepts in the Methodology of the Social Sciences.* Pretoria: Human Sciences Research Council.
Ohloff, H. 1993. "Kanon en instansies — 'n Afrikaanse perspektief." *SAVAL-kongresreferate 12: Waardes in die letterkunde.* SAVAL: Potchefstroom.
Van Coller, H.P. 1992. "Die Afrikaanse letterkunde en taalvaardigheid binne die konteks van kommunikasie." *Tydskrif vir Geesteswetenskappe* 32(3): 165-177.

The Ambiguity of Canon Issues in Modernism

A Praxiological Approach

Raymond Vervliet
University of Ghent

The difficulty in defining the period of Modernism lies in the fact that, as a literary movement, it did not form a clearly outlined school, i.e., sociologically speaking it did not form a separate group with its own spiritual leaders, magazines and manifestoes. Sometimes there were contacts between individual and at times very individualistic writers like Marcel Proust, James Joyce, Italo Svevo, Virginia Woolf, Thomas Mann, Robert Musil, T.S. Eliot, Martinus Nijhoff, André Gide, Valery Larbaud, Carry Van Bruggen, Menno ter Braak, and Edgar du Perron. Nevertheless, it is their typological cohesion that has to be analyzed by reconstructing the syntactic and semantic components of the literary code considered to be typical of Modernism. Moreover, Modernism has also been located within the framework of the West-European avant-garde, thereby further increasing the degrees of difference in attitude of its practitioners towards the spirit of avant-garde.

Arnold Hauser has already pointed to these internal differences (1975: 628-630) and has also attempted to categorize their fundamental disunity. Like Jean Paulhan and Friedrich Gundolf before him, he has divided Modernism into two main movements. Firstly, we have a movement that wished to destroy language and form, and therefore banned the use of conventional forms and clichés and sought salvation in pure original inspiration. In their literature, they declared war on all attempts at conserving and fossilizing the living, flowing, intimate life of the spirit, on all forms of exteriorization and institutionalization; in short, on the whole of traditional culture. Characteristic of this movement was its effort, under the influence of intuitivism and Bergson's "élan vital," to safeguard the immediateness and the originality of psychic content. This form of literature tended towards Expressionism and Surrealism in the way it took "Urerlebnis" as its point of departure and in the way in which it dealt with the immediate facts of life and the problems of being. Secondly, we have the formally austere movement of those 'rhetoricians' who sought inspiration in historical culture, spiritual tradition and in the treasures of form and ideas in literature. Their literature was based on "Bildungserlebnis," i.e., on the experiencing of culture, and their point of departure was always a certain notion or idea or a particular issue. Despite being related to the Surrealists, these writers tended towards Symbolism and Formalism. They were representatives of a highly formalized and stylized art form; they believed in 'the magic of the word' and based their writings on the spirit of language, literature and tradition. According to Hauser, Joyce's *Ulysses* and T.S. Eliot's *The Waste Land*, both of which appeared in 1922, sounded the two basic keynotes of Modernist literature.

We can thank Hauser for having seen, at an early stage, that this literary movement along with the strongly intellectual disposition shared by its members did not consist of a clearly sealed-off homogenous unit, but, to the contrary, was characterized by a bipolar field of force. There is a danger, however, in seeing this dichotomy as an expression of opposition in poetics, for then the categories of "Urerlebnis" and "Bildungserlebnis" would neutralize the ambiguity and complexity that is so characteristic of Modernism. Allow me to explain in a little more detail by commenting on the authors presented by Hauser as being prototypical of the movement. Joyce, whom he places in the first movement, was also a highly cultured and erudite writer and his *Ulysses* can be read as an attempt at concentrating the history of culture into one highly reduced narrative pattern, i.e., a day in the life of Leopold Bloom in Dublin. On the other hand, Eliot, who belongs to the second movement, can be considered a writer who, for poetical reasons, rejected all attempts at forming a canon (Gorak 1991: 75ff.). Moreover, some researchers (Douglass 1986; Burwick and Douglass 1992) link Eliot explicitly to Bergon's vitalism and therefore to the category of "Urerlebnis." As a result, this rigid dichotomic framework has been abandoned in more recent research, but researchers continue to refer to the fundamental disunity between the "abgelehnte und wiedergefundene Tradition" (Motekat 1962: 17-19). And the bipolar framework is still considered as being inherent to Modernism (Lethen 1986: 236).

As we have already pointed out, this bipolar scheme does not point to an opposition of styles but to an opposition of institutionalized patterns of action, or, to use the terminology of Pierre Bourdieu, an opposition of dispositions regarding issues of canon. If we analyze the Modernists' notion of tradition in terms of strategies of cultural action, then this notion of tradition becomes an instrument in a symbolic battle for cultural dominance and symbolic power.

About 1920, two predispositions became noticeable within the field of literature, one of which could be termed "early Modernist," and the other "high Modernist." The early Modernist disposition is clearly visible in all forms of avant-garde art, but is also found in Modernist works in the strictest sense (see Butler 1994). Those who took the dialogue with the immediately existential and the social context as their point of departure are dominant here. The disposition that lies at the basis of this dialogue grew out of a climate in which respect for traditional cultural capital, i.e, the literary canon, was minimal. Linguistic and formal skills were put into question along with the idea of cultural baggage. The main issue then was how to reconcile art and life. This attitude stemmed from a sort of anti-professionalism. High Modernist authors, on the other hand, were characterized by an attitude that foregrounded the dialogue with the literary field. Within this field intertextual relationships with the literary canon became thematic. The disposition upon which these intentions were based stemmed from a process of education and training that did not put the acquisition of cultural baggage into question (Bourdieu 1966: 900; Guillory 1993: IX). Given this attitude, it is easy to understand why the Modernist code is characterized as being typically intellectualist (Levin 1966: 297; Fokkema 1984: 29). Here linguistic, formal and cultural skills seem to be a *conditio sine qua non* for artistic production. This pointedly intellectual outlook can be explained as being the result of a growing sense of professionalism. Here Strychacz introduces the notion of "professional ethos" in typifying the dominant disposition in high Modernism: "If a body of formal knowledge underpins a professional's power within a mass society, then the idiom of Modernist writing — arcane allusion, juxtaposition, opaque writing, indeterminacy, and so on — performs precisely the same function within mass culture" (Strychacz 1993: 27).

In order to position Modernism in the field of literature between the two world wars, it is not only necessary to examine it in relationship to the forms of avant-garde literature of the time, it should also be seen in relation to the mass culture and literature of the day. The esoteric writing strategies of Modernism functioned as a means of obtaining symbolic power within the institutions of literature, in its battle against the increasingly assertive power of mass literature that borrowed its writing procedures from traditional literature.

The hypothetical dichotomy mentioned above in no way implies that we can place each Modernist author in one of the two categories. The dispositions that lie at the basis of the activities and representations of early Modernist authors can also be found among writers from outside the movements of the Historical Avant-garde. Many are early and high Modernists at the same time, although certain dispositions will dominate from one author to the next. It also explains their ambiguous attitude towards the literary canon. This attitude can in fact be considered as a symptom of institutionalization. Has Bourdieu not already stated that "l'espace des possibles" is the main indicator of disposition? This "space of possibilities" can be defined as a set of "potentialités objectives, des choses 'à faire,' 'mouvements' à lancer, revues à créer, adversaires à combattre, prises de positions à 'dépasser'" [potential goals, things 'to do,' 'movements' to be launched, journals to be created, adversaries to be fought, standpoints to be 'gone beyond'] (Bourdieu 1992: 326). The last mentioned phenomenon is in fact the literary canon. The attitude that one adopts towards it is determined both by the dispositions one has acquired during the process of one's cultural education and by one's position in the literary field.

From a praxiological point of view, two attitudes can be discerned within Modernism. The first attitude, which is based on "Bildungserlebnis," is characterized by its tendency towards professionalism. The desire here is to create innovative literature by deeply reflecting on literary tradition. The vision on literary history held by authors possessing this disposition is explicit: one had to confront the 'great authors' of the past, thence their clear preference for intertextual quotations taken from their work. This type of writing was institutionalized by university critics, particularly by the adherents of New Criticism. Another attitude to emerge at the time was that of absolute skepticism. Writers became more critical in their attitudes and kept outside tradition. Their literary historical vision is not in fact determined by intertextual motifs but more by the way in which they sought for affinities with their own critical points of view.

This explains their openness to the Nietzschean skepticism about language and to the cult of Bergsonian vitalism. Furthermore, their attitude led to the ironic de-mythifying of the canon and even to the setting up of an anti-canon. The Modernist attitude towards the canon is, in short, highly ambiguous therefore. Not only do we find tendencies towards an anti-canon, at the same time we notice attempts at setting up a — usually highly individualistic — canon.

Seen within this praxiological frame of reference, the foremost problem we are faced with regarding these issues in the Modernist canon is how its literary history is written. This problem is two-fold in nature. In the first place, we have to examine how particular writers approach this history and then we must compile a history of the various views held by these writers of literary history. A qualified literary history of Modernism must therefore be, at the same time, a history of its meta-literature. Then this will allow us to understand the ambiguity we find in Modernism as stemming the simultaneous presence of early and high Modernist visions on literary history which were also determined both by their positions in relation to the avant-garde and to mass culture. This sort of research is also necessary as a basis for analyzing the specific nature of Postmodernism.

References

Bourdieu, Pierre. 1966. "Champ intellectuel et projet créateur." *Les Temps Modernes* 2: 865-906.
— . 1992. *Les règles de l'art: Genèse et structure du champ littéraire*. Paris: Seuil.
Burwick, Frederick, and Paul Douglass. 1992. *The Crisis in Modernism: Bergson and the Vitalist Controversy*. Cambridge: Cambridge University Press.
Butler, Christopher. 1994. *Early Modernism: Literature, Music, and Painting in Europe, 1900-1916*. Oxford: Clarendon Press.
Douglass, Paul. 1986. *Bergson, Eliot, and American Literature*. Lexington: University Press of Kentucky.
Fokkema, Douwe W., and Elrud Ibsch. 1984. *Het Modernisme in de Europese letterkunde*. Amsterdam: De Arbeiderspers.
Gorak, Jan. 1991. *The Making of the Modern Canon: Genesis and Crisis of a Literary Idea*. London and Atlantic Highlands, NJ: Athlone.
Guillory, John. 1993. *Cultural Capital: The Problem of Literary Canon Formation*. Chicago and London: University of Chicago Press.
Hauser, Arnold. 1975 [1951]. *Sociale geschiedenis van de kunst*. Nijmegen: SUN.
Lethen, Helmut. 1986. "Modernism Cut in Half: The Exclusion of the Avant-garde and the Debate on Postmodernism." In Douwe W. Fokkema and Hans Bertens (eds), *Approaching Postmodernism*. Amsterdam / Philadelphia: Benjamins, 233-238.

Levin, Harry. 1966. "What was Modernism?" *Refractions: Essays in Comparative Literature*. New York: Oxford University Press, 271-295.
Motekat, Helmut. 1962. *Experiment und Tradition. Vom Wesen der Dichtkunst im 20. Jahrhundert*. Frankfurt am Main / Bonn: Athenäum Verlag.
Strychacz, Thomas. 1993. *Modernism, Mass Culture, and Professionalism*. Cambridge: Cambridge University Press.

Once Upon a Time There Was a Researcher ...

A 'Historical' Approach to the State of Art of German Literary Studies at the End of the Second Millenium

Reinhold Viehoff
Martin Luther University of Halle — Wittenberg

After a discovery in an archive, the author can report the following: Once upon a time there was a researcher who set himself the goal[1] of questioning contemporary literary scholars at the end of the second millenium about what one should know and do in order to carry out and teach literary studies with a certain extent of awareness and a certain extent of legitimacy.

The researcher went and submitted this question to a hundred different literary scholars and asked them for a written statement. He eventually received very many, almost a hundred different answers, partly because he had asked literary scholars from all German-speaking countries. Despite all professional "idiosyncracy," a thorough analysis showed some common ground between all those asked. The researcher distinguished between three groups:

1. The majority of those, who apparently had answered from a more or less secure conscience of tradition, argued: Firstly, as a literary scholar one should know the canonized literature and the history of literature, i.e., the most important books of one's own language as well as of kindred tongues. One should be versed in the themes and motives of such books and their historical development, the genres and forms in which texts were/are written. Literary scholars should know how and with which motivations readers read and understood these books at different times. In short, the researcher learned from these answers that contemporary literary scholars should know about certain literary texts and about the historical and contemporary contexts assigned to these and considered as relevant by a more or less specified group of experts. Secondly, this position frequently occurred in unison with some other — necessarily subordinate conditions: A literary scholar should know how to treat such important literary texts appropriately, first as a historic source, secondly, as an objective of critical editorial interests and particularly as a piece of art, which should be — *qua profession* — understood, interpreted and classified both in its historical and its actual context. Thirdly, literary scholars should have systematic and complete knowledge of the tradition of the original texts as well as of the tradition of secondary texts (that is the academic statements on the original texts) as well as knowledge about how to obtain this skill via applying the relevant bibliographical rules.

From all these statements the researcher crystallized a certain essence for this group: From then on he referred to them as the *habitually theological-oriented literary studies*, because it appeared to him as self-evident that all the dominant features of knowledge in this group were based on a presupposed, sometimes ontologized self-esteem which a 'proper' literary scholar should take up towards literary studies. Furthermore, it seemed to him that in the dominant fields of knowledge of this discipline there was a concentration on the interpretation and explanation of the valuable texts and the reinsurance of the tradition. In his opinion, both points were also used for the description and characterization of the archetype of European text analysis, that is, the theological exegesis of the Bible.

The researcher did not pay any more attention to this group, particularly because he got the impression that the scholars in this group tended to regard their specialized knowledge as a kind of secret knowledge. He was led to this assumption by the numerous metaphorical, rather vague paraphrases used by the members of this group when trying to answer his questions in a more detailed way.

2. At the time when the researcher distributed his question among the literary scholars, a small fraction of the first group had split from the onto-theological tradition — although this group still seemed to agree with the dominant fields of knowledge of the first group. They assigned outstanding

approval to the notion of text (and to all its compounds). The second group differed from the first one because they had a particularly low opinion of some fields of knowledge, for instance, knowledge about methods or knowledge about the logic of conclusions. The observer came across statements saying that one should be aware of empty peripheries in which the non-existing center of reference of an infinitely undifferentiated textuality deconstructed itself from an indeterminable 'out there.' Anyway, the researcher got the impression that the answers of this group stood out by a wild, self-generating vocabulary whose communicative function seemed to consist in the creation of a ground without a figure.

Once again, the researcher did not know what to do with this group, as their answers seemed to indicate an awkward dilemma. Obviously, it was their academic intention to write about philosophy in a non-philosophical way, about literature in a non-literary way and about academia in a non-academic way. At the same time they wanted to be regarded as post-philosophical, post-literate and post-academic thinkers, poets and essayists. With this group there seemed to be an even more striking lack of academic earnestness and responsibility than with the first one. In order to validate his impression he analyzed the statements of the two groups once again. The results confirmed his own negative assessments: He found out that both groups said hardly anything or nothing at all about *useful external knowledge.*

3. Finally, the researcher managed to make out one more big group among the remaining answers. This group differed in most aspects from the first two. Almost all statements mentioned both academic as well as social pressure for modernization which literary studies could only compensate for with modified theories and new ways of research. Frequently, as a late contribution to the secularization of literary studies, members of this group requested again and again that a theory of literary studies should detach itself from the concentration on the text, which had been prevalent with the onto-theological and the anti-onto-theological approach, and should instead investigate actions.

The members of this group expected that a literary scholar should have a high consciousness for methodology, revealing itself in ideals such as precision, testability and completeness. They also asked for — as a disposition so to speak — an epistemological optimism which should go hand in hand with strong theoretical efforts to justify, to rule and to make learnable one's own doing and to offer it in such a way that it could be discussed and used by other disciplines. The analyst considered it quite remarkable that they hardly spoke of texts in an honorific sense. The answers of this group seemed to imply that a literary scholar should be an erudite and well-read social scientist, in short, a new type of cultural scholar. Among all the letters he found there was one remark which he liked very much: The new type of literary scholar should be somebody who has thrown off the egg-shells of Snow's "two-culture-culture" and who embodies a new form of social, methodological and multicultural competence.

There were some fields of knowledge — which had been mentioned only by a few members of the first group — which seemed to be very significant here.[2] It was particularly striking that the third group made use of terminology such as media, medium, new media, technology, innovation and so on. The researcher found out that media was — next to cognition, communication and culture — a key term for this approach. Apparently this group was motivated by a strong interest in (a) how and (b) with which functions (c) for a culture (d) in a society (e) under the conditions of rapid changes in the means of communication (f) because of technical innovations of the media (of communication) (g) certain aesthetic forms of communicative acts could survive.

Quite interestingly, the members of this group frequently seemed to consider the question of basic knowledge as fundamental because longer passages of their answers dealt with that aspect exclusively. The researcher got the impression that these considerations were of a heuristic nature rather than the result of a long experience in teaching and research. Nevertheless, he regarded it as stimulating to follow the sign-posts that were included in these answers.

4. Thus, the researcher analyzed the data with regard to (1) the necessary components of a basic knowledge of this new concept, (2) the most relevant fields of research and (3) what a curriculum for this approach should look like.

Concerning the question of the basic knowledge of media cultural studies he could not easily relate the answers to a coherent and uniform picture. Some scholars preferred to enumerate the deficiencies of the predecessor literary studies as a humanity. Enumerating these deficiencies was considered as one of the main tasks of this new discipline. This frequently led to a not necessarily systematic list of tasks for media cultural studies. Other answers revealed that the interviewees oriented themselves towards certain leading disciplines. Psychology, sociology, communication studies, linguistics, history or philosophy were the subjects mentioned most frequently. However, even more dominant seemed the idea that it would be important to develop a kind of interdisciplinary knowledge. Only if they succeeded in such a way that both the interest of academia as well as their "environment" would be secured, would the new concept have a chance to establish its own ethic and to prove itself as "conscience of practice."

First, the researcher formed relatively general categories of knowledge in order to allow a systematic analysis. He found statements from the following five fields of knowledge which he filled with keyterms from the answers:

Epistemology and analytic philosophy:
Analytic theory, pure research, acting, cognition, communication, culture, reflection, sense, subject, integration of theory.

Theoretical knowledge of the discipline
Assumptions, aesthetics, strategies for research, processes of action, roles of action, systems of action, interdisciplinarity, constructivity, models, transdisciplinarity.

Pragmatic knowledge
Curriculum, types of discourse, empirical methods and techniques for research, terminology, genres, competence for acting, hermeneutic research methods and techniques, genesis of canons, teaching, media offers, media-actions, media technology, text structures, competence for comprehension.

Applied knowledge
Professions, practical fields, facts, participation, instructions, rhetoric, treatments, intercultural aspects, project management.

Knowledge for legitimacy
Alternative research, consequences, function, cultural memory, achievements, relation to practice.

The researcher compared these statements with the data of the two other groups and thought that the media-cultural variant was a considerable step forward in comparison with traditional literary studies: both regarding the subject matter and the terminology employed, applied knowledge or legitimized knowledge did not appear, just as little as numerous of the methodical and social-scientific terms did not in the other two groups.[3]

A clear shift of interest regarding the objects of study could be observed. The theological variants focussed on the reconstruction of the meaning of a text and its historical embedding. The fields of research of media cultural studies, however, were much wider, related to the present and covered the whole field or system of media-related and media-conditioned acting in the social structure of modern digitalized societies. The scholars stressed the cultural significance of the media for the dynamics of social developments and emphasized the correlations between human beings and the media as dominant aims of research. Also, they intented to investigate how this correlation changes people's ways of thinking, acting and feeling in their social context.

Unfortunately, there have been no documents that could clarify whether the researcher managed to establish this concept of media cultural studies at a university, and if so, how successful he became. One will see whether this concept will have left any traces.

In the report at hand it has not been the author's aim to give a fair and final answer to the initial question of the researcher. However, he tried to give a precise account on what he found in the documents. In his opinion, it would make sense to conduct such a survey in our times.

Notes

1. The researcher did not make his goals explicit in his survey — partly for methodical reasons but also because it appeared to him as self-evident that a science should permanently reflect itself and its state.

2. According to their hand-writing and diction, these might belong to the older generation of literary scholars.

3. It is probably no exaggeration to regard this deficit of the first two groups as one of the reasons for the fact that today these two theological literary variants have sunk into the insignificance of sectarian circles.

Literature in the Mass Media

The Challenge of Changing Enunciative and Receptive Modalities

Joris Vlasselaers
Catholic University of Leuven

The introduction of literature into the modern mass media is linked to the evolution of printing technology, editing methods and publishing policies in the second half of the nineteenth century. The massive increase at the time of printed matters of all kinds provoked a far-reaching change in the patterns of discursive economy and circulation. Journalistic discourse penetrated more and more into public speech and fundamental changes in the composition of the reading public took place. The presentation and the use of literary texts in the press (daily and weekly newspapers, reviews of general interest and boulevard magazines as well) caused a change in the traditional location and functioning of literary discourse in the contemporaneous cultural field and thus modified to a considerable extent the perception of literary texts and literary topicality by the readers of these mass media products (Angenot 1986).

In the second half of the twentieth century the cultural field has been invaded by high tech audiovisual media which nowadays increasingly dominate networks of mass communication. The impact of these new types of cultural production, distribution and communication confronts the literary scholar with questions that fundamentally touch upon traditional views and methodologies used in the study of the literary production and the literary system as a whole.

In confining my analysis to the media of television and CD-i I shall focus on two major shifts: (1) The problematizing of the Modernist axioms of *singularity* and *selfpurposiveness* as necessary conditions to qualify a text as a literary work of art and the correlated axioms of *seriality* and *commodification* as inherent features of mass cultural texts. (2) The decentering of the contemporary cultural, respectively literary fields with regard to the mediating institutions, the generic specificity and definitions, the scattering and redistribution of cultural, respectively literary competence and authority.

Much research has up to now been spent on the alleged loss of verbal culture resulting from the dominance of the image, especially the moving image, as a primordial component of contemporary culture and mass communication. In my opinion, this view is rather reductionist. The crucial issue for the literary scholar in this respect lies in the investigation of how mass media impose new codifications, procedures and norms upon literary culture in our society, i.e., the combination or even substitution of specifically literary-aesthetic codes and criteria by categories and strategies inherent to the new mediated context. The challenge for literary studies consists in designing a more 'holistic' approach: to point out how the new media bring about reallocations in the mediating structures of the literary system itself on the levels of production, distribution, reception, communication, and processing.

First, we have to face the abandonment of the absolute methodological rule that postulates the prevalence of *the text* in favor of the priority of the *reading* of the text. In the context of mass media texts more than ever function as "appareil rhéthorique" within the communicational paradigm of supply and demand as dictated by mass media requirements. The perception of the text by the viewers (the new readership?) is thoroughly modified. Literature is presented and functions as an item that is highly similar to the other items in the programming and has undoubtedly lost much of the privileged status it enjoyed in the traditional humanistic education of the intellectual. Thus the literary text is partially robbed of its autonomy and is forced to enter into and to adapt itself to the encompassing structures, norms and idiomatic specificities of the new medium. The literary text in the mass media becomes a *hybrid*. The new media submit the literary text to their own syntagmatic rules through specific techniques of montage and découpage so that they guarantee a 'new' reading of the text. Moreover, the literary text is almost never presented as such in its written or printed formality, but is transmitted by means of techniques and treatments that constitute the expressive instrumentarium of the medium, for instance, the text is read or recited by well known actors or speakers, introduced and/or commented by literary 'experts,' surrounded by musical or visual backing, etc.

The dominant audio-visual components of the mass media communication tend to turn the literary text into a *spectacle*, to make it an integrated and constitutive part of an overall audio-visual performance. Dutch literature in the Netherlands and Flanders, for instance, has a lot of experience with TV-programs featuring typically literary entertainers such as Jules Deelder or Tom Lanoye (*Circus of Bad Taste*), or specific theater shows casting an ensemble of authors, musicians, comedians (for instance, the *Behoud de Begeerte* tours with the participation this year of two presumed Nobel Prize nominees, Hugo Claus and Harry Mulisch). Not to forget the professionally staged and mediatized AKO-awards ceremonies framed in the highly rated Sonja Barend talk show.

The practice of visualizing literature also includes a certain *referential fetishism* responding to the axiom of easy and total recognition, a basic requirement of every solid marketing strategy. The display of the literary possible world in the mediatized version, its 'visibility,' tends to a perception of quasi 'physical' presence of the author, the characters and the setting as belonging to a cloned virtual reality and creating a simulacrum of absolute simultaneity. The possible world of literature tends to be absorbed in the global presentation of the world by the medium.

The literary text and the reader-viewer meet in a process of *creative appropriation* and *competitive codification* that results in a displacement and blending of generic specificity. The literary text is confronted and finally adapted to the media idioms and categories. In its mediatized presentation the text ought to be treated as a translation and consequently be analyzed in accordance with the theory and methodology of *descriptive translation studies*.

In the domain of aesthetics the issues of *repetition* and *novelty* deserve special attention as to their specific use in the literary and the media contexts. According to information theory recognition and familiarity are necessary conditions for efficient communication. Television narrative strategy does not rely on informative shocks or breaks, nor on teleological closure. The medium prefers repetition and iteration to accomplish digressive openness that lets the viewer discover what s/he expects to happen and what gives him/her the recurrent pleasure of recognition. The dialectic between novelty and repetition, crucial in Modernist aesthetics, seems to be revisited in the use of all kinds of intertextual references and quotations or interdiscursive allusions and referrals (Eco 1985). The literary scholar should not disregard the impact of these mass media aesthetics of repetition and the strategies of seriality and retake on the contemporary new public when accounting for Postmodern poetics and text production, for instance. One should not ignore that nowadays a considerable amount of even experienced readers of literary texts become acquainted with the mediatized form of a work before they even cast their eyes upon the text itself.

The presence of literary artifacts as constitutive elements of mass media cultural production has also renewed the discussion concerning the traditional opposition between 'high' and 'low' culture. The concept of art as a unified domain the way it was conceived in the eighteenth century resulted in a highly problematic monolithic view of which the structural binaries 'high/low' could not account for the discursive flexibility and permeability on both sides. In our maximally mediatized era it is evident that the contemporary cultural systems have multiple centers of norm setting and diversified value scales and that such distinction made on allegedly categorical and objective grounds is unacceptable. This dispersal is mainly due to the mediation of two major cultural institutions in our society. First, there is the modern education system which no longer exclusively deals with the products and practices of so-called 'high' culture (for instance, the influence of Cultural Studies Programs on university curricula and research). And secondly, there are the mass media, which aim at the construction of heterogeneous and massive audiences often on a global scale. The new configuration of mass audiences and consumer elites, to a very large extent created by TV, have bridged the gap between high and popular cultural production since the altered means and ways of appropriating cultural goods established divergent views upon the work of art.

The issue of *cultural value* is intrinsic to the distinction between professed high and cultural production. It cannot exclusively be treated as a problem of aesthetics and artistic practice applying the qualities of singularity and selfpurposiveness as distinctive features for acknowledged high cultural production. In the contemporary cultural field allegedly high culture itself is part of the market of symbolic goods. It constitutes a special segment, a particular niche, but complying all the same with the rules and patterns of marketing strategies and with economic mechanisms.

Commodification is no longer stigmatized as cultural inferiority of popular art forms and practices. But nor can we hold on to the linear correlation of culture and class. High culture is no more to be understood as the dominant culture of a socially or economically ruling class. The process of streamlining evolves following the rules of communication theory and practice on one hand, and obeying the imperatives of professionalization that govern mass media cultural production on the other.

The emergence of a new type of readership created by the mass media compels literary studies to reconsider some fundamental elements of *reception theory*. How are the concepts of reception and consumption, reader and viewer to be defined within the new context? The reader-viewer meets the literary text framed into a simultaneously homogenized and multi-layered semiotic system and cultural field. 'Mediatized reading' is a particular kind of strongly institutionalized, although creative text processing, a discursive mix which certainly assails the sacrality of literary culture.

Finally, the issue of the use of literary material and literary life in the mass media of TV and CD-i also constitutes an interesting topic for literary historiography. Texts are to be considered as active elements of a continuous sign production of which the historical relevance is primordially retrieved in the field of pragmatics. Literary texts, like all texts, function within the networks of the media systems of a defined society at a specific moment. The reciprocity of media and mentalities necessitates the study of the communication forms, communication media and modalities as an essential component of a literary history (Gumbrecht 1985: 226-227). In this perspective the analysis of the location and circulation of discourses is of great significance. Discourses are never merely juxtaposed within a society's discursive landscape. Being signifying practices they are marked by their location, their potential of semiotic energy (intelligibility as co-intelligibility) and the institutional dynamics they exert. The discursive tissue of a society is built on a high degree of mobility and permeability, hidden traffic and overt transfers of discourses and shows the different patterns and trajectories of discourse migration, i.e., the continuous process of intertextual rewriting and reinscription across the various media (Vlasselaers 1993-1994).

Historiography during the last decades has been strongly centered upon the notion of text: the hermeneutic practice ('the world is a readable text') and likewise the narrativistic type ('the world is a scriptible text': history as textual representation and narrativism). A historiography of literature processed within the mass mediatized contexts of TV and CD-i, should also account for the referential imperatives I mentioned above and which have to compete with the truth — and reality claims of the news reports and documentary programs. This approach fits into a renewed empiricism we ascertain in some present-day historiographical projects that claim to revalorize what Johan Huizinga has termed "historical sensation" (Tollebeek 1993: 196-98). Through the experience of immediate presence and contact with the past (cf. the 'visibility' of mediatized literary texts, for instance, the impression of would-be physical presence of authors, characters, settings and of the pluriform material and intellectual contexts) a sense of actuality and authentic experience is supposed to be effected through the strategies of presentation used in the media. The panoramic literary histories edited by Denis Hollier (1989) and M.A. Schenkeveld (1993) already indicate in which direction this 'aesthetics of history' might evolve.

References

Angenot, Marc. 1986. "Ceci tuera cela, ou: la chose imprimée contre le livre." *Romantisme* 44: 83-103.
Eco, Umberto. 1985. "Innovation and Repetition: Between Modern and Post-Modern Aesthetics." *Daedalus Journal of the American Academy of Arts and Sciences* 114(4): 161-84.
Gumbrecht, Hans Ulrich. 1985. "The Body versus the Printing Press: Media in the Early Modern Period, Mentalities in the Reign of Castille, and another History of Literary Forms." *Poetics* 14: 209-27.
Hollier, Denis (ed). 1989. *A New History of French Literature*. Cambridge and London: Harvard University Press.
Schenkeveld-van der Dussen, M.A. (ed). 1993. *Nederlandse Literatuur, een geschiedenis*. Groningen: Nijhoff.
Tollebeek, Jo. 1993. "'Het boek der geschiedenis': over een versleten metafoor." *Forum der Letteren* 34(3): 184-200.
Vlasselaers, Joris. 1993-1994. "Discursive Migrations in the Literary Field." *Dedalus, Revista Portuguesa de Literatura Comparada* 3/4: 39-49.

Cultural Relativism and the Future of Comparative Literature

An Oriental Perspective

Wang Ning
Peking University

In introducing the concept of cultural relativism in the field of comparative literature and giving it new significance, Douwe Fokkema has no doubt made vital contributions, especially in many of his publications in the West and his speeches delivered in China.[1] According to one of his recent reconsiderations of cultural relativism from the perspective of international comparative literature studies, "Cultural relativism is not a method of research, even less a theory: it refers to a moral stance which may influence the scholar in his selection of research methods and theoretical positions" (1987: 1). History has proved that cultural relativism is no longer the one characterized by Eurocentrism as it used to be, nor is it a kind of West-centrism. Since misreading could produce some new significance in a different context, I would like to offer my own understanding of cultural relativism re-described by Fokkema.[2] Since it has generated some new significance in the current world, it actually offers us a new perspective from which we could observe some assumed absolutely correct things in history or in our field of study. For instance, in the past decades, it is characterized, among others, by "tolerance of other, equally valid patterns of life" (ibid.). If we apply it to the broader sense of East-West comparative literature studies, we should say, it has helped us to break through the old 'Eurocentric' mode of thinking by viewing something other than the West. This is perhaps one of the reasons why the Orient and Oriental culture have attracted the attention of international scholarship. In this respect, Edward Said's construction of Orientalism has indeed contributed a great deal to the debate on Postcolonialism, although it cannot avoid having neglected the potential power of the Orient and the latent value of Oriental culture and its inevitable role played in the new framework of comparative literature and international cultural studies.[3]

Obviously, cultural relativism could inspire us to reconsider the originally 'marginalized' or even 'colonized' Oriental culture, making it of new significance to our comparative studies of literature and culture. Starting from cultural relativism, everything exists in relation to something else, in the eyes of Western people, the Orient has indeed been both mysterious and poor and backward as compared to the advanced European civilizations. But this false image has actually become more and more problematic along with the decolonizing process in the Oriental and Third World countries, especially with the rapid progress made in China since its openness to the outside world and economic reform in the late 1970s. Just as Said has correctly pointed out, "The Orient was almost a European invention, and had been since Antiquity a place of romance, exotic beings, haunting memories and landscapes, remarkable experiences. Now it was disappearing; in a sense it had happened, its time was over" (1979:1). Here, according to Said, the Orient is nothing but an indeterminate existence in the eyes of Western people without whose observation and construction, it seems not to exist on Earth. This constructed 'Orient' in essence has nothing to do with the real state of the Orient. On the one hand, from the perspective of what cultural relativism means to us, Said has thrown light on the false image of the Orient in the eyes of Western people, but on the other hand, even he himself does not grasp the genuine spirit of Oriental culture, nor does he understand the valued notion of the Orient as he has always been staying in the center of the West, the United States. Thus, his construction of the Orient and Orientalism is still more or less problematic (Wang 1995) and has little to do with cultural relativism.

The essence of cultural relativism, to my mind, lies in the fact that it has told us that in the current world, there is no such thing as a culture being naturally superior or inferior. All cultures or civilizations, be it Oriental or Occidental, are of equal value with both strong points and shortcomings. No culture can always play a dominant role in the world, for its prime of life can never last for too long. Every culture only exists in relation to other ones, just like the case of the Orient in the eyes of Western people. The same is true of the

Occident or Occidentalism in the eyes of Eastern people. For instance, in some Oriental and Third World countries, there has appeared a sort of Occidentalism of the Occident. It is still a constructed one in the eyes of non-Western people, so it also provides a false image from the angle of the 'other.' It has different forms in different places and during different periods (ibid.). But on the whole, Eastern people, especially Chinese people, usually know much more about Western culture than Western people know about Eastern culture. That is why more research achievements have been made about the Western influence on Chinese literature than the topic on Chinese studies abroad. But in current China, the Postmodern and Postcolonial studies, together with the post-Chinese studies, are viewed by certain scholars as a kind of cultural conservatism, for these three forces, according to the critics of them, have offered Western people the image of the 'other' which is just in accordance with what Western people expect to see (Zhao 1995: 13). I think it is a sort of reaction to the haunting Occidentalism in many Chinese people's mind. Just as Said has shown that the answer to Orientalism is not Occidentalism, the once "all-round Westernization" (*quanpan xi hua*) should not be replaced by a sort of opposition to the West. In this way, to give full play to cultural relativism and maintain a tolerant attitude toward the 'other', be it Oriental or Occidental, is of certain relevance at the moment.

Now I will limit my scope to literary studies. I will argue that in view of what has been achieved in some Oriental countries, especially in China in the field of comparative literature studies, the established framework of the 'three forces (schools) dominating' over international comparative literature studies, namely, the French School, the American School and the former Soviet School, can no longer exist along with the two facts: the dissolution of the former Soviet Union and the rise of Oriental countries, such as China, India and Japan. The recovery and the subsequent flourish of comparative literature in China has attracted the attention of international scholarship, which has realized its splendid cultural heritage and literary achievements. India, with its richness in classical aesthetics and long cultural tradition and literary heritage, has become more and more important in international cultural studies, especially in the recent prevalence of the Postcolonial debate which ruthlessly undermines the authority of Western imperialist power and its discourse, paving the way for a real pluralistic orientation of literature and culture. Japan, as one of the most modern developed countries in the world, always attaches great importance to re-establishing its cultural image. We still remember the superb organization of the ICLA Congress in 1991 in Tokyo which has inspired Indian and Chinese colleagues to submit a proposal to host one of the ICLA triennial congresses at the turn of the century. Thus I will, from the Oriental perspective of cultural relativism and inspired by it, re-orient the framework of international comparative literature studies as the European force with France as its center which is characterized by the empirical study of literature and reception studies, the North American force with the United States as its center which is characterized by theoretic interpretations and interdisciplinary studies between different cultures and fields of learning, and the Oriental force with China, India and Japan as its joint center which is characterized by cross-cultural, cross-linguistic and cross-traditional studies between the East and the West. Only the achievements made by these three forces can reflect the state of the art of international comparative literature studies. And only through the cooperation between the Eastern and Western scholars can comparative literature have a bright future. That is what I have understood by the significance of cultural relativism.

The other significance of cultural relativism to me is how to confront the strong lash of current cultural studies. As for this, many Western scholars are very much worried about the future of comparative literature, for cultural studies has actually broken through the myth of 'the literary canon' and expanded the scope of literature. The same is true of the Chinese critical circles, although their attitude is somewhat different.[4] Undoubtedly, in the latter part of the 1980s and the beginning of the 1990s, especially after the international Postmodernism debate, cultural studies has gradually become a major interest of academic studies. It is regarded as one of the major challenging forces against current comparative literature studies, for it has undermined within Western culture the power of literary discourse and broken the once charming charisma of canonical literature, deconstructing the artificial demarcation between elitist culture and popular culture, that between the 'pure' literary genre and the sub-literary genre, that between literature and culture, especially the mass media, and most important to us, the demarcation between Oriental literature and Occidental literature. No doubt the traditional domain of literature is largely expanded. Thus even Harold Bloom, who was once involved in the Deconstructive attempt to undermine Western critical discourse in the 1970s, rises up to defend the legitimation of the Western canon in answer to the challenge of cultural studies. He shows his discontent in his recent book *The Western Canon*:

> Cultural criticism is another dismal social science, but literary criticism, as an art, always was and always will be an elitist phenomenon. It was a mistake to believe that literary criticism could become a basis for democratic education or for societal improvement. When our English and other literature departments shrink to the dimensions of our current Classics departments, ceding their grosser functions to the legions of Cultural Studies, we will perhaps be able to return to the study of the inescapable, to Shakespeare and his few peers, who after all, invented all of us. (1994: 17)

He is correct in protecting the literary canon from being affected by the lash of cultural studies, but he is not so tolerant to the existence of the discourse beyond the literary canon, which is dangerous to the future of literary criticism and literary studies. Then can we think of letting the two forces co-exist and complement each other? To my mind, it is unnecessary to be afraid of the strong impact of cultural studies, for if we think of our 'literary canon' beyond the limited scope of the 'West' and if we always deal with literature in a comparative way, not just within the Western context, or if we consider the relative power of cultural studies and the relative legitimation of canonical literature, we can certainly see a bright future for comparative literature in the new turn of the century. As for this, I am always optimistic.[5]

Notes

1. As Douwe Fokkema is a frequent visitor of China and gives lectures in some leading universities and research institutes, such as Peking University, Nanjing University and the Chinese Academy of Social Sciences, he is chiefly known as a scholar of literary studies, especially in Postmodern studies rather than contributing to the rethinking of cultural relativism. This is partly because of translation, but still, within the field of Chinese comparative literature circles, he is known for his reconsideration of cultural relativism, especially for his friendly attitude towards China.

2. It should be pointed out that some Chinese scholars misunderstand Fokkema's attitude towards cultural relativism. In their view, he is a scholar characterized by a Eurocentric mode of thinking. They have actually ignored his sympathetic attitude towards and firm support to Chinese comparative literature studies.

3. As for the detailed description of the new framework of international comparative literature, see my relevant publications both in English and in Chinese. Here I will not go into detail.

4. Interestingly enough, those Chinese intellectuals who once strongly advocated socialist market economy are now very much worried about the loss of the so-called 'humanistic spirit' (*renwen jingshen*) which is both problematic and indeterminate although it is rather attractive to the critical circles at the moment.

5. In this aspect, some of my Western colleagues in the field of literary studies, such as Terry Eagleton and Ralph Cohen, share my view. They did express their sympathetic attitude towards cultural studies at the International Conference on Cultural Studies: China and the West (August 1995, Dalian, China), which to my mind has paved the way for a real equal academic dialogue between Chinese and Western literary scholarship.

References

Bloom, Harold. 1994. *The Western Canon: The Books and Schools of the Ages*. New York: Harcourt, Brace and Company.
Chen Xiaomei. 1994. "Occidentalism as a Counter-Discourse." Paper delivered at the 14th ICLA Congress, Edmonton.
Fokkema, Douwe W. 1987. *Issues in General and Comparative Literature*. Calcutta: Papyrus.
Huntington, Samuel. 1993. "The Clash of Civilizations?" *Foreign Affairs* 72(3), In *A Foreign Affairs Reader*, 22-49.
Inglis, Fred. 1993. *Cultural Studies*. Oxford and Cambridge: Blackwell.
Moser, Walter. 1994. "Etudes littéraires et études culturelles: Repositionnements." A plenary paper delivered at the 14th ICLA Congress, Edmonton.
Said, Edward. 1979. *Orientalism*. New York: Vintage Books.
—. 1993. *Culture and Imperialism*. London: Vintage Books.
Wang Ning. 1995. "Wenhua xiangduizhuyi, wenhua duoyuanzhuyi he bijiaowenxue dongfang xuepai de jueqi." ("Cultural Relativism, Cultural Pluralism and the Rise of the Oriental School of Comparative Literature.") *Beijing daxue xeubao (Journal of Peking University)* 5: 64-68.
—. 1996. "Toward a New Framework of Comparative Literature." *Canadian Review of Comparative Literature* 23(1). (Forthcoming.)
Zhao, Yiheng. 1995. "'Houxue' yu Zhongguo xin baoshouzhuyi." ("'Postism' and Chinese Neo-Conservatism.") *Ershi yi shiji (Twenty-First Century)* 27: 4-15.

Should Literary Studies Be Unreadable?

Jean Weisgerber
University of Brussels

vous nous assommez avec vos grands mots. Ne paraissez point si savant, de grâce. Humanisez votre discours, et parlez pour être entendu.

La Critique de l'Ecole des Femmes, scene 7

Some contemporary literary criticism undoubtedly smacks of sleeping draughts. No matter how interested you may be in the problems discussed, you soon grow drowsy — as though "of hemlock you had drunk." Not unlike the celebrated Victorian Nanny, the author insidiously lulls you to sleep, but instead of music you are treated to a cacophony of neologisms and erudite tonguetwisters. A nap in this case is a healthy reaction; it brings relief and eventually saves the day.

In my view, the best examples of arcane contemporary critical jargon are to be found in France and North America, two areas where the disease has reached epidemic levels, spreading contagiously to other countries. A brief survey of some patently pathological cases will enable me, I hope, to trace the phenomenon back to its source; however, as usual in all medical case studies, I shall leave the names of the patients unmentioned.

In all likelihood, poetry may be held responsible for the proliferation of methaphors and puns in critical prose. Based on word associations and as such closely connected with Freud's theories about the unconscious, jokes not only please the reader, but also lift inhibitions. It is therefore difficult to estimate the respective influences of literature and psychoanalysis on this device. The use of metaphors and a disrupted syntax can be ascribed to a blending of genres which goes back a very long time. With his *Crise de Vers*, representative of the trend, Mallarmé already set an example of affectation, mannerism and abstruseness the Avant-garde and the postwar neo-Avant-garde were only too glad to follow. Who would not be nonplussed by the following commentary on a painter?

> Ceci aussi, du reste, sera resté sans exemple — du tout. Un(e) oevre déjà, détachement, coupure décisoire, d'une décision cependant flottante, non pas du nouveau, ceci ne se *voudrait* ni Art, ni non-art, surtout pas peinture-peinture ou dessin-dessin — à quoi ceci sera re-semblant — théorie de tautologies ou autres opposition — ne se voudrait pas. L'inédit de ce ductus, etc.

What does this actually mean except that the artist in question stands out, alone of his kind? This could be said in six words. Heidegger and Lacan, in particular, once two of the great gurus of the Humanities, were fond of such gibberish which has repeatedly and successfully been parodied:
Cygnifiant?

> L'ayatollah Can dit de l'Ecole freudienne de Paris: "dis/soute"? En la canbale maison freudienne, bris sûr, donc. Par quoi ces affres affreuses? Par oxysme peut-être. Ou par isianisme (ex acerbé par qui?). Sauf à inférer qu'en l'anneau tors de l'intoxygence magistrale, ce chant-geant mouvement re-tors cygnifie. Mais, tue jusqu'à l'heure (pas l'heur) de la lettre envolée de Guitrancourt, sourd-elle en fin l'invective parricide: "Va donc, eh, tors dû"? (Michel Kajman, *Le Monde*, Jan. 11, 1980)

Critics, like poets, resort to numerous images. Scientific lingo, an inexhaustible source of metaphors, fulfils several functions. As the branch of knowledge referred to is usually in fashion, the borrowing is a badge of modernity; on the other hand, it suggests that criticism is a science, thus reviving the old dream of *Literaturwissenschaft*; last but not least, it testifies to the same abhorrence of the everyday language of common sense as the avant-garde: in its own way, it, too, declares war on the bourgeois. It thus appears that literary studies simultaneously compete with poetry and science: traditional barriers between the genres are pulled down. Two centuries ago, in Voltaire's time, history and criticism were still part and parcel of literature; nowadays many of us take the opposite view (in the name of progress?) and try to reduce them to specialized technologies. The result is splendid isolation.

Terms may be borrowed from philosophy, from the numerous varieties of Marxism (less popular, however, since the fall of communism) or from the vocabulary of feminism with due regard to the taboos of sexual harassment and political correctness. A smattering of semiotics may also come in handy. But all this cannot compare with the boom of linguistics and psychoanalysis. Witness this purple patch:

> en tenant compte de la dichotomie des pulsions, on s'explique aisément la constitution des oppositions phonologiques dès les premiers morphèmes prononcés par l'enfant: *mama* et *papa*, /m/ labial, nasal, liquide, et /p/ labial, explosif, traduisent par des moyens articulatoires la succion et l'explosion, le 'da' et le 'fort' freudiens, l'oralité incorporante et l'analité destructrice. On retiendra la pulsion orale des liquides (l'), (r'), (m) et des voyelles antérieurs fermées; la pulsion anale des voyelles postérieures ouvertes; la pulsion urétrale des constrictives non-voisées (f), (s), (S) et éventuellement la tendance à la phallissisation de cette pulsion dans les constrictives voisées (v), (z), (ʒ); la pulsion agressive, de rejet, dans les explosives sourdes (p), (t), (k) ou voisées (b), (d), (g); la pulsion érectile-phallique du (r) apical.

The underlying obsession, of course, is about defecation, a concept which easily leads from Freud to phonetics, more especially such consonants as liquids and explosives. Unfortunately, this analysis sheds a most unexpected light on a widespread pronunciation — for instance in Scotland or in Spain. For it is hard to believe that the millions of men, let alone women, who roll their r's all over the world are feeling at the same time a 'pulsion érectile-phallique.' Wishful thinking? Anyway, if this were true, they would be an awkward predicament in most circumstances, if not in bed. Whether in *Academe* or Hollywood, sex is in. It has become a cliché in most of our films while in criticism erotic connotations and associations spread like weeds. Some are downright comical, at times without the author's being aware, as in the preceding example. In the long run, however, they become as tedious as the continual sermonizing of Victorian novelists. As expected, polysemy makes the translation of puns a very difficult affair so that the translator can feel obliged to repeat the original text between brackets to avoid misunderstanding (!):

> What gives you a rise (*vous fait bander*), theoreticians, and throws you into our band (*bande*), is the coldness of the clear and distinct; (Note: The text plays here on the various meanings of the French 'bander': 'to bind' and 'to blindfold', as well as [colloquially] 'to have an erection'; ed. and trans.) in fact only of the distinct, which is the *opposable*, for the clear is nothing but a suspect redundancy of the distinct, translated into a philosophy of the subject. Arrest the bar, you say: get out of pathos — here is *your* pathos. Beautiful and stupefying (*médusante*), in effect, is the severe disjunction which suspends.

Eventually proving too vague and ambiguous, language is discarded altogether and a graph or formula is used as a substitute. Here is a fine example which

Should Literary Studies Be Unreadable?

refers to the way a story is told:

(a) état premier (latent) du système

(b) état second du système
    (intervention de l'événement)

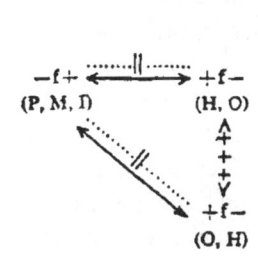

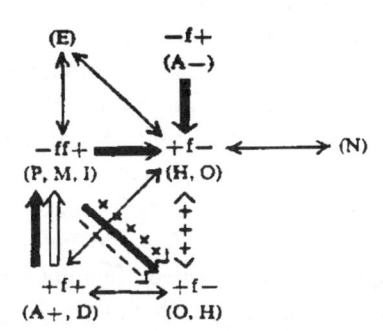

Who would be able to recognize in this shape the poetic grace of *The Golden Bowl* or *To the Lighthouse*? Ridicule never killed anyone, judging by those who dream of summing up, say, the *Ode to a Nightingale* in an equation.

It could be argued that like 'metalanguage' these devices serve to explain, simplify and illuminate. No doubt they sometimes do, but do they really work here, even if the reader knows what the symbols are all about? A rewarding experiment consists in trying to render critical jargon into everyday language: nine times out of ten, the oracle of the Pythia boils down to a concatenation of dismaying commonplaces. Another argument for justifying hermeticism is more ingenuous: paradoxically, it regards unreadability as a source of pleasure. Yours is indeed the pleasure to decode — provided the message is worth the time and effort involved. However, as we have just seen, this often does not apply. The time you do not grudge spending with Yeats and Eliot would be wasted on Lacan's disciples.

The simultaneous attraction of poetry and science in literary studies somehow reminds us of those rival brothers in the twenties: Surrealism and Constructivism. According to the tenets Marinetti introduced into literary practice — his 1909 Manifestoe is as much of a prose poem as the platform for a movement — theoreticians and critics increasingly masquerade as poets, scientists, and philosophers instead of performing their duty. This also means that they misjudge their own capacities. Critics should not further their own interests in the first place (this is a kind of hubris) but mainly those of the people about whom and for whom they write, that is, authors and readers. They do not perform the ceremony; they just act as servers.

It must be granted that the development of 'metalanguage' stems from a commendable ambition, namely to bring literary studies closer to science. However, there are limits to compromises and concessions. As little logical and rational in essence as the people who produce it, literature appeals to an independent artistic feeling. Since it grows every day, its precise outlines cannot be traced as the recent row about 'littérarité' has shown. Literary facts are not always easy to verify, nor are they as predictable as the effects of gravity; and most of them do not lend themselves to experiments. As a consequence, the study of literature has little in common with the exact sciences, an ambiguity which should be recognized as an asset but turns out to be a stumbling block. Ironically, the most resolute adversaries of jargon are Positivists and rationalists, that is, people who are the traditional defenders of science. This paper, however, does not question whether it is advisable to reject science and reason, on the contrary. Let us rather put it another way. Is it necessary to isolate literary science from the general public, that is, to reserve it for insiders? It goes without saying that we cannot manage without a minimum of technical terms, provided we define them carefully. But there is no point in indulging in them. We are not supposed to show off, but to clear up. Intelligence, subtlety, and profundity are not tantamount to obscurity, as such distinquished scholars as Huizinga, Wellek, Levin, Schama, and Douwe Fokkema have shown. It is a pleasure to read them; they practise a *fröhliche Wissenschaft* in the literal sense of the phrase.

Such scholars perform the social task that pertains to scholarship. Unintelligible to outsiders, jargon is the privileged language of a caste: the initiates. In fact, it acts as a card denoting membership of an exclusive set, admitting you to the Ivory Tower, far from the ignorance and vulgarity of the masses. Ultimately, it demonstrates a refusal or an incapacity to communicate, a specific disease of modern society. It is high time we eradicate it.

Holier Than Thou

Literature, Science and the Empirical Turn

Lies Wesseling
University of Limburg

Ever since its inception in the school of Russian Formalism, the new-fangled discipline of general and comparative literature has aspired towards a scientific status. Together with the urge to transcend national boundaries, this ambition has strongly compelled students of literature to formulate universal definitions of literature. The provocative essays of the Russian Formalists aimed primarily at grasping the elusive phenomenon of 'literariness.' This intellectual endeavor has proved to be a powerful legacy which has been handed on to new generations of scholars up to this very day, albeit that it has changed considerably along the way.

The notion that new disciplines should legitimate themselves by circumscribing their own object of inquiry is not exclusive to the study of literature, of course. This mode of legitimation ultimately boils down to the idea that the boundaries of scientific disciplines should correspond with divisions that inhere in reality itself. In other words, disciplines should found themselves on natural kinds. However, everybody agrees nowadays that literature is not a natural kind, if such a thing exists at all. The search for literariness has been exciting and fruitful, but not because it has produced the intended result. Instead of revealing universal literary features, the efforts to fixate the boundaries of literature have made us keenly aware of its social and historical variability. Nevertheless, the evaporation of literariness has not deterred literary scholars from aspiring towards a scientific status, nor has it weakened their interest in specifically literary properties.

It did effect a salient shift of research focus, however. Rather than studying texts which have been inserted into the category of literature for whatever reason, literary scholars now investigate the ways in which different social and historical groups define and deal with the literary. The study of literature has undergone an empirical turn through this change of emphasis from stylistic analysis and interpretation towards sociologically and psychologically informed inquiries into literary group behavior. A strict separation of the object- and meta-level of inquiry rather than a universally valid definition of literature serves to bolster up claims to scientific prestige nowadays.

The ascent of literary studies towards the honorific title of science both corresponds with and diverges from developments in the theory, sociology and history of science in a confusing sort of way. It is not just *literaturnost* which has proved to be a chimera. The whole notion that the boundaries of scientific disciplines should correspond with natural kinds has become highly controversial, to put it mildly. Most theoreticians and historians of science are extremely skeptical about the idea that the discovery of new domains of reality gives rise to new disciplines. One generally prefers to attribute an inherent drive to automatically generate new disciplines to science, which is concomittant with its tendency towards specialization. The subsequent distribution of tasks (and funds) over ever changing networks of disciplines is decided by academic politics rather than the nature of reality, as Bruno Latour has pointed out. While literary scholars undauntingly persevere in their efforts to acquire a scientific status, the theory of science has moved in the opposite direction. In the wake of Thomas Kuhn, it tends towards relativizing rather than underlining criteria for demarcating science.

To complicate matters further, the philosophy of science has also undergone an empirical turn, but the connotations of this development differ from its literary pendant. Where the philosophy of science is concerned, it means that its proponents exchange their normative role for a descriptive stance, which produces an ever increasing awareness of the historical and social variability of the institution of science. In the case of general and comparative literature, on the contrary, the empirical turn comes down to a last ditch attempt to found and legitimate literary studies as a science. True enough, proponents of the empirical study of literature carefully avoid the propagation of simplistic, positivistic scientific norms, opting for a more sophisticated, Constructivist epistemology instead, but this merely reproduces the same incongruity.

Whereas Constructivism in the philosophy and history of science blurs the boundaries of science, literary scholars use it as a fund of arguments for boosting their scientific prestige. Thus, one strives to be holier than Thou.

The intricate pattern of parallels and divergences between the study of literature and the philosophy of science invites alternative reactions to the failed pursuit of literariness. In view of the contemporary relativization of science, it does not make much sense to invest so much time and energy in reflections upon one's own status as an academic discipline. Considering the historical variability of both science and literature, efforts at delimiting and defining the boundaries of a discipline and its object in general terms cease to be compelling. In my view, however, we can make a virtue out of necessity, but this requires that we redirect our attention from the meta-level to the object-level of inquiry.

Because literature addresses a wider audience and therefore fulfills a more important cultural function than the study of literature, questions concerning the intellectual status of literature are more relevant than the rather self-centered issues surrounding the scientific aspects of literary scholarship. It seems to me that historians of literature could make a valid contribution to the brand of intellectual history which describes and explains changes in networks of academic disciplines, by demanding attention for the place of fiction within this differing distribution of intellectual tasks.

Admittedly, such a project requires that we come up with a working-definition of 'literature,' but the old traps and pitfalls can be avoided if we content ourselves with a negative definition. For our purposes, John Limon's pithy formula in *The Place of Fiction in the Time of Science: A Disciplinary History of American Writing* (1990) will do. Limon defines literature as "the undisciplined discipline," which emphasizes the fact that literature is the only remaining amateur discipline with an intellectual aura within contemporary culture. This situation contrasts starkly with the state of affairs surrounding the turn of the previous century, when science at large was an amateur affair. In the course of the nineteenth century, however, the natural sciences developed into professional disciplines, which systematically selected and trained people for the vocation of science. Various traditional humanities, as well as a number of new social sciences, followed in their wake. Disciplines which develop into closely knit professional communities are able to stake out and defend their own field of inquiry, and to ensure a certain uniformity in the ways in which the object is approached. After these preliminary operations have been carried out, a certain amount of local progress or historical linearity becomes possible for that particular discipline.

Not so literature. Physicists may decide to write a novel in their spare time at any moment, but it is not that easy for a writer to become a physicist. People are not really trained for authorship. Furthermore, the audiences for literature and science also differ. Scientists write for a small, well-defined audience of peers. Writers, on the contrary, address a wide and rather diffuse audience. All this goes to explain why the borders of literature are highly violable, as students of literature know very well. Literature does not only lack a set of universally definable formal features by means of which literary language may distinguish itself from ordinary language, but also a problematic of its own. Its themes may overlap with issues in the sciences, humanities, politics or religion. However, this violability of literary boundaries should not be considered as a weakness, but as a strength. The polyphonic intertextuality of literature as described by Mikhail Bakhtin, Salman Rushdie and Carlos Fuentes enables writers to fullfill an instrumental role in the give-and-take between science and culture. Let me explain.

Contemporary historians of science concentrate their attention on those moments at which rival solutions to a scientific problem vie with each other, and take an interest in analyzing and explaining the subsequent victory of one option over the others. However, the history of science has largely ignored the question of what happens to the discarded options. According to Wolf Lepenies, the disqualified theoretical alternatives do not disappear from the cultural scene altogether. They may live on in the underground regions of literature. Literature is able to incorporate and preserve 'falsified' or 'outmoded' points of view because it is free from the historical linearity which is cultivated by science. As T.S. Eliot and Thomas Kuhn have argued independently from each other, science kills its own past, contrary to literature, which continually revitalizes its own tradition as something valuable in and for itself. The development of new modes of writing does not necessarily require that older modes are condemned to oblivion. This does hold true for science, however, because scientific problems are thought to have only one correct solution. As T.S. Eliot's contribution to the revival of the Metaphysical poets demonstrates, writers are always "undead." There are no principal obstacles to the reappearance of past poets on the cultural scene. This does not apply to scientists, who are far more easily subjected to the *damnatio memoriae*.

It would be a mistake, however, to conceive of literature as the wastebasket of science. Literature never merely preserves insights from science, for as soon as literature incorporates scientific ideas, these are necessarily contaminated by the viewpoints of the "undead" who may live on indefinitely within the synchronous, monumental order of literature. When progressive science is absorbed by the intertextual network of literature it acquires richer and older cultural connotations than it could possibly have within the context of a well-circumscribed discipline. Thus, literature both preserves and transforms scientific points of view. The latter aspect is important, for it explains why interactions between literature and science need not boil down to a one-way affair. Wolf Lepenies has given various examples from the history of science to illustrate this point. Eighteenth- and early nineteenth-century psychology, for instance, concerned itself with the development of the individual, as well as with the subconscious and deviant, pathological behavior. When psychology developed into a professional scientific discipline it discarded these topics in favor of preoccupations with the conscious thought of 'normal' adults. This does not mean that previous topics and insights disappeared entirely. They were taken up and transformed by the Romantics, which eventually enabled them to make a comeback in the shape of Freudian psychoanalysis. Thus, we should not take the historical linearity which forms such an important part of the self-image of practising scientists too literally. Discarded scientific ideas may also make a comeback, provided that they are not easily recognizable as such.

Worries about a gap between the two cultures have largely abated in the Anglo-Saxon world. An interesting field of inquiry has sprung up in its place instead, which may pride itself on such distinguished representatives as N. Katherine Hayles, Gillian Beer, George Levine and George Rousseau. It seems to me that the comparative historiography of literature and science implies a worthy research programme for coming generations of literary scholars, who will have to sacrifice the reassurance of a clearcut disciplinary identity to greater intellectual relevance. Instead of then taking the empirical turn for the royal road towards scientific prestige, they could carry out historical case-studies of concrete interactions between science and history, thereby striving to be *plus royaliste que le roi* and holier than Douwe.

Something New From the Old Alphabet

A Match for Giono, Borges and Calvino?

Sytze Wiersma
Utrecht University

> The smile of daybreak was just beginning to brighten the sky, the sunlight to catch the hilltops, when a group of men in brigand gear peered over the mountain that overlooks the place where the Nile flows into the sea at the mouth that men call the Heracleotic. They stood there for a moment, scanning the expanse of sea beneath them: first they gazed out over the ocean, but as there was nothing sailing there that held out hope of spoil and plunder, their eyes were drawn to the beach nearby. This is what they saw: a merchant ship was riding there, moored by her stern, empty of crew but laden with freight. This much could be surmised even from a distance, for the weight of her cargo forced the water up to the third line of boards on the ship's side. But the beach! — a mass of newly slain bodies, some of them quite dead, others half-alive and still twitching, testimony that the fighting had only just ended. To judge by the signs this had been no proper battle.

So begins a famous fictitious prose narrative, set in a scene of fight, villainy and adventure. The band of brigands, amazed as they are, inevitably infect us with their curiosity and wonder. Through their eyes we see remnants of festivities, tables set with food, men battered to death. With them we stay initially "on the mountainside like the audience in a theater, unable to comprehend the scene." Some lines later we set off down the hillside, instinctively dissociating ourselves from piracy and focusing on a small area of the beach. Zooming into close-up we spot a girl of indescribable beauty. Armed with bow and arrows, she sits on a rock and gazes steadily and with affection at a wounded young man lying at her feet. Despite her great distress at her plight, she has "an air of courage and nobility," and we are too glad to listen to the words with which she tries to cheer and hearten her miserable love. She fails for the time being, but their little moving dialogue starts the action of a long story that keeps us captivated until its unexpected dénouement.

In this narrative, intricate events are elegantly dealt with on the basis of a solid literary framework. The *in medias res* opening and its sequel have been integrated through a variety of flash-backs and anticipations. Past, present and future are intertwined into a sparkling game of fictional and narrative time. We eagerly learn the young couple's identity, guided as we are by some effectual system of embedded narration within a main third-person narrative. At the heart of this frame story we unfold, together with one of the narrators, a precious ornament, a fabric embroidered in some magic script and telling us that the girl we met in misery is the daughter of an Ethiopian queen. While conceiving her child, that was borne white-skinned, this black queen, we read, had kept her eyes turned on the painting of a white goddess. This sounds rather insubstantial but over long stretches of text, plot and subplot slowly mesh together to create a compelling world of encirclement and, more specifically, of reflection. The whole story, after a pattern of multiple reflection, mirrors love, reality, other texts and itself. It does exemplify indeed a narrative technique that matches the subtle reflectiveness of a Borges, Giono or Calvino. Actually the story was written in the third century. It has come down to us under the title *The Ethiopian Story of Theagenes and Charikleia*. Its author, a certain Heliodorus of Emesa who wrote splendid Greek, made his work a very literary piece of writing, larded with allusions to earlier literature, in particular the Homeric epics and Euripidean tragedy. Most allusions are specific. By the end of his book, for instance, when the princess has been recognized by her father and her mother (who, "unable to control herself for joy, set up a sort of animal howling"), the author treats his educated readership to a literary variation on the *Odyssey* (19.209ff.), where Odysseus' heart is said to be wrung by his wife's distress as she mourns him: "but his eyes, as if they were made of horn or steel, never wavered under their lids." Heliodorus' king is just as deeply touched by his wife's emotions: "his heart was moved to compassion, but he stood with his eyes fixed as unblinkingly on the scene before him as if they had been of horn or steel, fighting back the welling tears" (all passages from Heliodorus are given in a translation by J.R. Morgan, published in Reardon 1989). Such salient imitations reminded the ancient readers of their Homer and of other writers, long since canonized. In its own time and, again during the Renaissance, Heliodorus' *Ethiopian Story* ranked with the classics. Alonso López Pinciano, the leading literary theorist of the Spanish Golden Age, pleaded for a position alongside or even superior to the epics of Homer and Virgil. In his *Poetics* of 1596 Heliodorus' book is the ideal work of classical (Aristotelian) literary art, with its *in medias res* beginning, its *peripeteia* (dramatic turning point) in the middle and recognition scene at the end. It was much read and greatly appreciated in Spain, Italy, France and England during the sixteenth and seventeenth centuries. Shakespeare, somewhere in his *Twelfth Night*, specifically alludes to it (Reardon 1989: 377). Authors like Tasso, Calderón, Lope de Vega, Cervantes, Racine and Sidney were influenced in various ways by Heliodorus' *Ethiopian Story*, and also by some other stories passed down from late Greek and Latin Antiquity (Hägg 1983: 1).

As a literary form all these narratives are highly eclectic and imitative. The way they mingle pathos with adventure reminds us of the *Odyssey*, Homer's romantic epic. Besides, they are characterized by the sentimental element Euripides introduced in tragedy, and by the combination of imagination and fact we know, for instance, from Herodotus and from Xenophon's *Cyropaedia*. Theophrastus' method of character drawing, the narrative and rhetorical techniques of New Comedy, Ovid and the Alexandrian elegists, the idyllic sceneries of pastoral poetry, all these (and other classical) elements return in the dozen of works that remain from a literary genre that flourished in the Roman imperial period. Some of the remaining specimens are clearly influenced by the Greek cultural revival of the imperial age known as the 'Second Sophistic.' The genre has thus been drawn into the predominant literary trend of the time. This has left its mark on both form and content (Hägg 1983: 34ff.). Longus' *Daphnis and Chloe* and Achilles Tatius' *Leucippe and Clitophon* are no less sophisticated than Heliodorus' *Ethiopian Story* in their plot construction, digressions and play with narrative perspectives. In Longus' charming pastoral romance narrative of adventure organically gives place to description of scenery and sentiment. Achilles Tatius chiselled his digressions with meticulous accuracy: short, asyndetic units for the description of people alternate with a more fluent style for the surroundings (Hägg 1983: 45). Here we find all rhetorical devices which the Second Sophistic gave access to: graphic quality, richness of detail, rhythm, assonance, etc. In *Leucippe and Clitophon* the latter is his own narrator, who keeps up suspense and illusion with a subtle alternation technique that blurs the distinction between first-person and third-person narrative. From a restricted ego-perspective which discomfits the reader in the beginning, finally he happily arrives at omniscience (Reardon 1994). One of the major surviving works of Latin fiction, Apuleius' *The Golden Ass*, has plausibly been interpreted as an "open-ended problem text that the reader must supplement" (Winkler 1985: 241). In this ego-narrative with many interpolated or embedded stories the real subject is the act of narrating itself.

There is no reason to infer (as has been done) that this type of literature, with its immensely rich literary inheritance, was considered second-rate in Antiquity. Apparently it attracted writers of talent and imagination who with wit and virtuosity dealt with the traditional theme of love and adventure. What is more, during the sixteenth and seventeenth centuries their works were famous models to be adapted, imitated or dramatized. To mention only a few books, modelled on (Goethe's favorite story) *Daphnis and Chloe*: Sannazaro's *Arcadia* (1504), *Diana* (1559) by Jorge de Montemayor and Honoré d'Urfé's *L'Astrée* (1607) ran into several internationally well-known editions.

In the eighteenth century, however, these ancient prose narratives fell victim to bourgeois enlightenment and were dismissed in criticism as amusing, but inconsequential, adventure stories. Their readership, concentrating on the somewhat trite and commonplace content, gradually lost touch with their artful and self-conscious literariness. In short, ancient fiction vanished from the literary canon, to which it obviously had belonged since late Antiquity, and remained beyond the mental horizon of most modern literary historians.

One need not applaud John Winkler's provocative claim "Borges and Nabokov have nothing on Apuleius" (Winkler 1985: VII) to acknowledge the artistic and technical resemblances between ancient and modern prose fiction. A vast amount of recent classical scholarship (about 200 books and articles since 1980) makes clear that much ancient fiction is at least a match for Borges and Nabokov. Its narrative reflectiveness, intricacies of plot construction and portrayal of characters and actions representative of real life (Reardon 1989: 350-351) compel us to reconsider the exclusive attribution of the rise of the novel to bourgeois culture of early modern Europe. Could modern fiction only develop because the classical canon, with its universal rules and traditional prohibitions, had lost ground (Fokkema and Ibsch 1992: 55-56)? Did not in ancient times, within a highly traditional literary climate, still dominated by the poetry of Homer and Euripides, bloom a genre of considerable similarity? And should we not apply to it the same generic category we use for the great variety of writings that constitute our modern fiction? Comparative study of the novel in the Graeco-Roman world would furnish fiction studies with their proper historical basis. Moreover, it would cast new light on the question, provoked by the experiments of a Borges or Calvino, what we are doing when we call a text a novel.

References

Fokkema, Douwe W., and Elrud Ibsch. 1992. *Literatuurwetenschap en cultuuroverdracht*. Muiderberg: Coutinho.
Hägg, T. 1983. *The Novel in Antiquity*. Oxford: Basil Blackwell.
Reardon, B.P. (ed). 1989. *Collected Ancient Greek Novels*. Berkeley, CA: University of California Press.
Reardon, B.P. 1994. "Achilles Tatius and Ego-narrative." In J.R. Morgan and Richard Stoneman (eds), *Greek Fiction: The Greek Novel in Context*. London and New York: Routledge, 80-96.
Winkler, John J. 1985. *Auctor and Actor: A Narratological Reading of Apuleius's* Golden Ass. Berkeley, CA: University of California Press.

From Cultural Relativism to Cultural Respect

Yuan Heh-Hsiang
The Chinese University of Hong Kong

Culture reveals its character in many ways. Its growth and decline are synonymous with the rise and fall of a civilization, and also signify the continuation of a great tradition or its degeneration. Anthropologists study the culinary habit of different tribes to distinguish the civilized from the savage. Comparative educators study the educational systems of the ancient Greeks and the early Chinese to find both nations devoting great efforts to inculcate a national character of *areté* or *chün-tze* in their citizens. Students in religion find in their study of religious ritual various versions of belief in the creation and preservation of life, and they also find in them the given value which causes rivalry and division, and accommodation and reconciliation. Human history is an open book showing us a fluctuating development of such processes. The study of culture is not simply 'a trip to the museum' to see the past as a fossilized existence, incomprehensible and sometimes dead and meaningless; it is rather a learning process from which we draw an enlivening inspiration to search for the true meaning of the present so that we can understand, with greater tolerance, the diverse cultures which form the living reality of our present. The study of comparative literature is a starting point for such an endeavor.

The purposes of comparative literature study are varied. They can be looking for common ground underlying the study of 'branch cultures or literatures' within a main source culture, probing into the interrelationship among the many arts to show the relatedness of all cultural activities, or searching for an unbiased understanding of the relationship between the influencing and the influenced culture without unduly emphasizing the importance of one and neglecting the significance of the other. Among all, none is more important than a respectful recognition of a culture for the value of its own existence. However, such recognition does not come easily. Looking back into the history of our search, we see stages of development from Said's *Orientalism* to the advocacy of cultural relativism (among whose advocates Douwe Fokkema certainly ranks foremost in literary studies), showing diverse perspectives leading to a conclusion that the ultimate state of the discipline is one that neither voices Eurocentrism or imperialism, nor advocates anti-imperialism or oriental supremacy. The intention is to avoid perpetuating a certain political perspective which may lead to any prejudicial conclusion.

Glancing through the 'established' ideas of culture, two examples can be found in the Greek and the Chinese concepts of the civilized and the barbarian, to cite from the ancient civilizations to give historical backing to the argument. In the *Odyssey*, when Odysseus talked about the Cyclopes, he considered them "barbarous," meaning that they spoke a different language and had a different political system from the Greeks. The old Chinese idea of the 'central kingdom' suggested a categorization of nations into the central, presumably important or significant for its cultural and social achievements, and the peripheral, those comparatively less important and less influential because of their lack of such achievements.

For the ancient Greeks the achievement of their civilized state was the discovery of a cultural-political system which included the diffusion of the art of writing, the invention of coinage that led to trade and colonization, the opening of the whole Mediterranean world to commerce, and, perhaps most important of all, the political recognition of the rights of communities. And the center was always Greece, with her ways of thinking (philosophy), of governing (politics), and of creating (arts). Thus we see the diffusion of the Greek culture throughout the Western world in the early days of Western civilization until later when other cultures and civilizations merged with it to form the cultural tradition of the Western hemisphere.

China had a similar experience in her early days of culture formation. The initiating position was definitely Sino-centric; the very word *chung*, the middle or the center, posits a mental attitude of being in the center culturally and in every other sense. Thus for the early Chinese, *man-yi* (the barbarous and alien) became a synonym for 'foreign' or 'foreigner,' anything or anyone that was not Chinese. The concept implies an idea very much the same as that of the early Greeks, though lacking the Greek sense of ontology and teleology and differing from it in including a moral principle which emphasizes self-cultivation as the ultimate aim of human existence. Thus for the early Chinese, politically and philosophically, the intention was never conquest but instead the cultivation or emulation of a behavior based on the abstraction of the ideal *homme*. This is why we detect the strong cultural influence of China in most of the Asian countries, barring those under the colonial rule of Western powers in the eighteenth and nineteenth centuries. India has had its own glorious cultural history, yet Indian Buddhism also strongly influenced Chinese philosophical and religious ideas through assimilation.

The two examples cited suggest a view of relativeness regarding different cultures. Relativism itself does not mean much until it is related to a specific concept. Cultural relativism in a commonly understood context means that different cultures have different beliefs, moral, philosophical, or what not, and that they are often incompatible as such beliefs are only relative to a particular culture; therefore, there is no sense in asserting one as more valid or valuable than the other. The practices of polyandry in pre-revolution Tibet and polygamy in China till the twentieth-century communist revolution are social phenomena belonging to a cultural condition and should be viewed as such by social anthropologists. When ethics or moral concerns are not the issue, cultural relativism provides an explanation. In the same manner we can look into the practices of dressing in the red or white for weddings in China and the West, or wearing white or black for funerals. Applying this to the study of comparative literature, one sees perhaps more clearly that it is also a matter of relativeness. In comparative literature, the view of relativism has contributed considerably to a better understanding of the 'non-mainstream' literatures, meaning African and Third World literature. The early practice of comparative literature studies, being Eurocentric, only points out the 'incompleteness' of the field. When the idea of *Weltliteratur*, stretching Goethe's idea a bit, is brought up in an attempt to broaden the field, we can easily accept it as to mean two things: (1) that there is "an honorable role" reserved for "us" (any one nation), (2) that all national literatures are to be included within the embrace of comparative literature studies.

But this also should mean that the study of comparative literature, now having advanced from a narrower confine to a broader one, should not stay in a condition of 'political fermentation,' agitating for a stance of anti-colonialism, anti-this or anti-that. The advocacy of relativism, I presume, has done away with that 'mental attitude.' The political struggle should be over now among the group of internationally minded comparativists (which, of course, does not mean the 'struggle' was not a hard one). It is now time to advance to another even more laborious task, to truly look into our subject with a committed sense of reverence, based on cultural relativism.

The Medieval map drawer usually placed the less known and the unknown at the bottom of his map beyond the land of the known, so the further "one moves away from the center-point of Jerusalem, the more deformed and alien things become" (Camille 1992: 1). This is a cultural habit. Relativism has changed that; the marginal becomes just as important as the central. But, in order to make it so, a proper sense of respect for the marginal must be cultivated and affirmed. What comparatists are doing now is to rewrite Pliny's *Natural History,* to make "the blemyae, cynocephali, giants, pygmies, and many others all human," metaphorically speaking. Here, respect for a different culture is the starting point.

Cultural respect pushes cultural relativism one more step, but it is based on cultural relativism. As Fokkema suggests, cultural relativism "is not a method of research, even less a theory" (Fokkema 1984: 225, 239); it is a mental attitude which emphasizes tolerance toward "other patterns of culture," suggests Fokkema. That, however, still implies "looking" at other patterns of culture from "the position" of "this pattern." There is still a center. Tolerance in this sense simply means 'being sympathetic.' More is still needed to turn this sympathy into a mental habit that embraces different cultures on equal footing. In a sense, cultural respect implies just this by keeping a distance from one's own culture in order to give oneself a 'negative capability' so that one may 'correlate' all cultures. The American 'salad bowl' concept is a good demonstration of this, despite the fact that in reality it nearly breaks the nation. The fact that different ethnic groups of writers in the US claiming themselves as Afro-Americans or Asian-Americans or Spanish-Americans illustrates well their understanding of the problem. Under the umbrella of 'one nation' diversity is permitted to accommodate different cultural expressions without losing either harmony of the whole nor individuality of the 'parts.' Such a prototype society can perhaps serve as our model for the 'comparative literature community.'

Cultural relativism and cultural respect are not theories; they are attitudes which influence out thinking habits. In comparative literature study, they also constitute a possible guiding principle through which we hope to realize the idea of *Weltliteratur.*

References

Camille, Michael. 1992. *Image on the Edge: The Margins of Medieval Art*. Cambridge, MA: Harvard University Press.

Fokkema, Douwe W. 1984. "Cultural Relativism Reconsidered: Comparative Literature and Intercultural Relations." *Douze cas d'interaction culturelle dans l'Europe ancienne et l'Orient proche ou lointain*. Paris: UNESCO, 239-225.

Western Literary Theory in China 1985–1995

Yue Daiyun
Peking University

Since the policies of reform and openness were initiated in the 1980s, Western literary theories have flooded into China. These theories, however, have not been randomly imported without relation to local context. On the contrary, the successful introduction of any theory has been dependent on a process of sifting, transforming and selection based on Chinese social reality and cultural context. Looking back on all the Western theories that have been introduced into China in the past decade or so, some general characteristics are notable.

First, in a spirit of reaction to Soviet literary theories that stressed only social environment and social effect, advocates of American New Criticism have attracted wide interest through their concepts of the "affective fallacy" and the "intentional fallacy," which sever the relationship between the original text and society. This approach deliberately omits consideration of the effect on the reader and the intentions of the author, and focusses on the text alone. By opposing the approaches that had been standard in China for a long time — based on such things as a fixed historical background, differences of classes, stereotypes of characters — the interpretive close reading approach of New Criticism has provided a new route to understand literary works.

Second, Marxist literary theory, which can be traced back to the turn of this century in China, and which still has considerable influence in its Soviet-style, has seen a rebirth among critics who are exploring both the development of Marxism in the West over the past few decades and the possibility of a Marxist renewal in China. The works of Walter Benjamin, Theodor Adorno, and Jürgen Habermas were of particular interest to young Chinese scholars.

Third, there are some new Western concepts that had not existed in China before, and that seemed barely applicable in the Chinese literary tradition. One outstanding example is Freud's theory of psychoanalysis, arguably the most translated, published, and popular theoretical topic in the field of literature during the eighties. Chinese traditional literary theory seldom touched on psychological analysis, and analysis related to sex and the subconscious was unheard of (although there are a lot of books how to interpret a dream). Freud's theory did have some impact on literary creation after it was first introduced in China in the 1930s — for example in the novels of the Neo-sensualists (Xin Ganjue Pai). However, because of the war and for ideological reasons, its influence soon disappeared. Yet Freud's theory again strongly influenced literary creation and literary analysis during the 1980s.

Fourth, other Western theories attracted attention in China because they shared common ground with certain traditional Chinese literary concepts. These theories quickly gained broad understanding and sympathy. Hermeneutics is one example. Since ancient times in China, much attention had been devoted to the commentaries and annotations of its classics. Even Confucius did not claim to have contributed anything new, but only to have recounted and annotated the learning of those who had come before him ("I am," he said, "an interpreter, not a creator." (述而不作) As Chinese culture developed over thousands of years, it has comprised two traditions: 'I interpret the Six Classics,' and 'I use the Six Classics to interpret my thought.' (我注六经与六经注我) The former aims at explicating the meaning of the classic works, while the latter uses the classic works to support one's own point of view, and to document its correctness. There have also long been expressions in Chinese learning such as 'infer the fundamentals through the investigation of particulars' (推末以至本), which means from the understanding the specific to understand the general); and 'explore the fundamentals to obtain the particular' (探本以穷末), which means from understanding the situation as a whole to understand the details. It is relatively easy to link these arguments with concepts such as the 'hermeneutic circle' in Western hermeneutics.

There is also common ground shared by Western reception aesthetics and traditional Chinese aesthetics, in that both emphasize the relativity and multiple perspectives of aesthetic appreciation, and the subjective understanding of the reader based on personal experience. There is a Chinese expression,

'The difference between a mountain peak and a mountain range is in the perspective of the viewer.' (横看成岭侧成峰,上下高低各不同) A famous expression from the *Poetic Talk from the jiang Studio* (姜斋诗话) says that "an author writes with one meaning, while each reader understands it in his own way." (作者用一致之思,读者各以其情而自得) Both these sayings share a basic point of view with Western reception aesthetics. Because of these shared features, Western hermeneutics and reception aesthetics have rarely been opposed or resisted in China.

A final important phenomenon in the field of literary research during the 1980s has been the rapid rise of comparative literature. Because of the more open intellectual environment, theorists have been anxious to assess Chinese literature in an international context. The relationship between Chinese and foreign literature very soon became a topic with which many scholars were concerned. At the same time, the introduction of Western theories made it possible, by referring to different theoretical systems, to understand the characteristics of Chinese literary theories more deeply. These references should not be used to put an occidental frame over Chinese literature, but to understand Chinese literature in the context of world literature, and to find a mirror ('the other') to observe the self.

For obvious reasons, an important turning point came in 1989. Because of political reasons, many publishing houses were shut down, or their leadership was replaced. Lively discussions were stopped abruptly, and the idea of rewriting literary history was criticized and suppressed as a conspiracy to subvert the forty years' history of literature led by the Communist Party (though, in fact, few took an active interest in the process of criticism).

In the 1990s, the most influential Western trends are Deconstruction, New Historicism, and Postcolonialism. The concept of Deconstruction began to gain ground, especially among those who grew up during the Cultural Revolution. This is a generation that went 'from genuinely believing everything to genuinely dis-believing everything.' The spirit of Deconstruction suited them quite well: to go from determinism to indeterminism, from a method of one-track reasoning, characterized by unitary authorities, to a multi-perspective mode of thinking, characterized by plurality, decentralization, and variety. Some principles that had never been doubted were now questioned and challenged, such as the contradiction and coherence of the dichotomies of *appearance-essence, inevitable-accidental, liberty-necessity, signifier-signified...* It is not exaggerated to say that Deconstruction had brought to Chinese intellectual circles a liberation of thinking.

After the works of Douwe Fokkema, Ihab Hassan, and Jean François Lyotard were translated, Postmodernism not only became a hot topic of literary criticism, but also had a response in the field of literary creation, resulting in the emergence of a group of avant-garde writers such as Yu-Hua, Ge-Fei, and Su-Tong. When the concept of Postmodernism was first proposed, it led to debates and attacks from different people. Some of them insisted that China is only at the first stage of its modernization, and therefore it is too early to talk about Postmodernism. But many others believed that Postmodernism is not to indicate a certain period, but a flexible approach to explain the chaotic reality, a point of view to observe reality in a multi-perspective way. They maintained that it is natural to pick up such a way to view the disintegration and chaos of ideology in China during the past few decades and especially after the absurdity of the Cultural Revolution. Moreover, the argument that the superstructure of a certain era is solely determined by its own economic base can no longer be defended, because culture, mentality, morality, all the spiritual elements have an impact on the superstructure. In addition, the above-mentioned theories are not that strange to Chinese culture. They easily bring to mind the ancient Daoism of Laozi and Zhuangzi, with its idea of relativity, skepticism, transcendence, detachment and playfulness.

It is interesting to see that another indigenous trend, that of 'seeking native culture' or 'seeking the roots,' soon joined forces with the Western New Historicism. According to New Historicism, there are two kinds of history: history of events and history of narrative. What we usually talk about is history of narrative, which is a text inevitably restricted by the perspective of the narrator, the understanding of the reader, and the social background of a different time. Therefore, the 'root,' the indigenous culture they are looking for, cannot possibly have a unitary logic; it is rather a constant change of things becoming subject to a multiplicity of new narratives and interpretations. Thus, in the end, the search for an indigenous culture is a reconstruction of the native culture by contemporary people from a contemporary perspective.

Postcolonialism stresses that each culture possesses its own rationality and legitimacy. The cultural clusters founded on the basis of race, common language, and shared history, possess a special cultural cohesive force and a cultural identity. Edward Said proposed in *Orientalism* that under the conditions of colonization, cultural identity based on cultural conventions was distorted by Eurocentrism. Lacking power, the colonized also lack their own narrative and mode of discourse, and so they can only be interpreted by others — often the colonizers. In this situation, the colonized have no choice but to establish their cultural identity in terms of the discourse and culture of their colonizers.

Obviously, Postcolonialism goes along with the political needs of the Government. To prevent the so-called 'peaceful evolution' (from socialism to capitalism) and 'spiritual pollution' of foreign imperialism, Postcolonialism provides evidence that most Western concepts and ideas, including freedom, democracy, and human rights are all part of a Western ideological frame forced on Chinese reality. On the other hand, the proponents of Postcolonialism advocate that in order to revive Chinese culture, it will be necessary to expel all Western terminology, concepts, and modes of thinking, because these are expressions of Western discourse and thus are spiritual fetters imposed on the Third World by colonizers. It is not hard to find a latent 'Great China complex' in their thinking. According to them, Chinese culture is better than all others. Therefore, after displacing Eurocentrism, a Chinacentrism may seem inevitable. I do not mean to play down the significance and active meaning of Postcolonialism in China. It opened up a wide field to race, gender, class and ethnology studies, which are very much fruitful. What makes me feel worried is that the emergence of these two trends mentioned above may be a dangerous sign to lead to a new form of isolation, even to a new cultural subjugation.

In conclusion, whether it be in the area of Humanism or Deconstructionism, the impact of Western literary theories on China is obvious. These two trends of thought also continue the debate in Chinese literature over 'art for art's sake' versus 'art for people's sake,' which had been going on since the beginning of this century. On an even deeper level, these two trends are a manifestation of the divergent approaches of the Confucian and Daoist schools. The former advocates *maximizing its utility to society* (经世致用), while the latter advocates *detachment of natural spontaneity*. (逍遥于自然)

How Empirical Is the Empirical Study of Literature?

Rolf A. Zwaan
Florida State University

Meanings are still wonderful after we have traced out the cognitive processes that underlie them. Science adds to the wonders of appearance the wonders of explanation. It follows the path from wonder to resonance, and then back to a deeper wonder.

Herbert A. Simon (1994)

The claim I wish to defend here is that the answer to the question posed in the title should be: "Not nearly enough." In addition, I would like to defend the claim that two steps are necessary in order for the empirical study of literature to become a viable research area. First, proponents of the empirical study of literature should take the word 'empirical' more seriously. Since the concept of an 'empirical study of literature' (ESL) was launched, few reliable and convincing empirical studies have actually been published and most of them were by cognitive psychologists. Many literary scholars sympathetic to the ESL seem to live under the impression that 'empirical' is a synonym for hollow rhetoric and/or inventing a new jargon for existing concepts and ideas. The results of this are detrimental to the field in several ways. For example, it alienates the researchers who are actually doing the empirical research.

The second step that is necessary for the ESL to become a viable research area is an emphasis on the continuity in literary research from the Formalists, Structuralists, and reading-response theories to the ESL. Douwe Fokkema is one of the very few theorists who have recognized the importance of continuity and have provided thoughtful analyses demonstrating the relevance of Formalism and Structuralism to the ESL. Emphasizing discontinuity by dismissing all previous research as irrelevant and/or flawed does nothing but alienate the mainstream literary scholars.

In the remainder of this article, I will argue these points in more detail, starting with the second one. I should point out up front that I am writing from the perspective of a literary-scholar-turned-cognitive-psychologist. My research interests have gravitated towards more fundamental issues in cognitive psychology than the study of literary comprehension processes and I feel that my current perspective is that of a relative outsider. The downside of this is that I may not be up to date on the recent developments in the ESL. So if recent developments prove me wrong, then I apologize. The advantage of a position on the sideline is usually that one can analyze the situation in a dispassionate way. However, this turns into somewhat of a disadvantage when one is asked by editors to write a polemic chapter, as is the case here. In an attempt to overcome these disadvantages I have attempted to use my own experiences to (1) elucidate my position and (2) fuel my polemics.

Continuity in research

The Empirical Study of Literature was launched as a new paradigm in the study of literature in the early 1980s. According to the new view, literature was no longer to be viewed as a corpus of texts but as a social system of interactions. This also meant that the privileged method of investigation was no longer interpretation but a range of empirical methods that were developed in psychology and sociology.

When Douwe Fokkema first exposed me to these ideas — in a course on the empirical study of literature — they sounded very exciting to me. I had always experienced a conflict between the inherent subjectivity in literary interpretation and my desire to be a scientist and it seemed as if the Empirical Study of Literature (ESL) was offering a resolution of this conflict. I therefore embraced the ESL in my Masters thesis, a version of which was later published as Zwaan 1987.

However, I soon grew skeptical about the viability of an ESL. Douwe indicated in his typical subtle way that we should not throw out the baby with the bath water by dismissing all pre-ESL literary research. Particularly, Douwe thought that Russian Formalism and Prague Structuralism might have a great deal to offer with respect to hypotheses about literary comprehension, a sentiment that was shared by Will van Peer who had recently joined the

Department of Literature at Utrecht University. I gradually became convinced that the ESL position was, indeed, too radical. Not only was it unwise to dismiss decades of serious research, it did not go over well with mainstream literary scholars either.

Thus, I set out in my dissertation research to test several hypotheses about literariness that were derived from the works of Russian Formalists and Prague Structuralists, employing cognitive-psychological research methods, such as reading-time measurements and recall and recognition tasks. I obtained empirical evidence for a literary mode of text comprehension. The same texts were read and remembered differently when they were presented as literary stories than when they were presented as news stories (Zwaan 1993). The texts were read more slowly when presented as literary texts than when presented as news stories. This is consistent with the Formalists' notion of defamiliarization, which impedes perception. Furthermore, subjects showed better memory for the actual wording of the texts but worse memory for the state of affairs reported in the texts when these texts were presented as literary stories compared to when they were presented as news stories. This is consistent with Jakobson's notion of the dominance of the poetic function in literature and the secondary role of the referential function.

In Zwaan 1994, which was published in a leading cognitive psychological journal, I replicated and extended these findings. One important extension of my previous research was a detailed analysis of sentence-reading times (Experiment 2) which demonstrated that not only were the reading times longer when the texts were presented as literary stories but the pattern was also different, suggesting that the subjects were focusing on different information when they thought the text was a literary rather than a news story text. Specifically, these analyses revealed that the subjects allocated more resources to surface information and fewer resources to referential information during literary comprehension. These results were highly consistent with the recognition data. Moreover, they demonstrated that the difference between literary and news comprehension is qualitative rather than quantitative. I have attempted to demonstrate how these results can be theoretically and computationally modeled in the framework of an influential and well-specified cognitive-psychological model of text comprehension, Kintsch's (1988) construction-integration model (see Zwaan 1993: ch. 6, and Zwaan 1995).

Recently, other researchers, such as David Miall and Don Kuiken in Canada and David Hanauer in Israel have tested other Formalist and Structuralist hypotheses using reading-time and recall or recognition paradigms. It seems to me that this is a fruitful line of research. It extends earlier research in literary studies in ways that are (or should be) informative to both literary scholars and cognitive psychologists. In order for the ESL to become a viable field, this type of research should be encouraged and be conducted on a larger scale, ideally as a collaborative effort of literary scholars and cognitive psychologists. My experiences have taught me that many cognitive psychologists are open to this kind of research, provided it meets certain methodological standards.

Focus on empirical research

As I mentioned earlier, when I began work on my dissertation, I had grown skeptical about the ESL. Although a great deal of lip service was being paid to empirical research many scholars seemed to prefer metatheoretical debates over actual empirical research. I became increasingly concerned about this. Dietrich Meutsch and I voiced this concern in our introduction to a special issue of *Poetics*: "contemplating what constitutes empirical research and what does not is rather vacuous if actual empirical research is never carried out" (Meutsch and Zwaan 1990: 5).

During the work on my Masters thesis I had become interested in empirical research on text comprehension. I considered this work to be highly relevant to the ESL. Thus, I proposed to use cognitive psychological methods to study the comprehension of literary texts, such as the measurement of reading times, at the Second IGEL conference in Amsterdam in 1989. However, this proposal met with some hostility on the part of several proponents of the ESL. Frankly, I was somewhat surprised and annoyed by this, as were several cognitive psychologists attending the conference who seemed more receptive to my proposal.

It was then that I began to realize that IGEL was home to two very different groups of researchers. On the one side there were the individuals who were genuinely committed to the advancement of empirical research on literature. Literary theorists such as Douwe Fokkema, who regarded the ESL as a natural next step in the study of literature and cognitive psychologists such as Art Graesser, who regarded the study of literary comprehension processes as an enrichment of the psychology of language. On the other side, there were the individuals who liked to use the epithet empirical (particularly when applied to themselves) but were in reality not committed to advancing an empirical study of literature. It was and is unclear to me why this attitude exists.

The dichotomy in ESL became even more manifest at the Third IGEL conference in Memphis (1992), which was organized by Art Graesser. Graesser had invited a large number of leading North-American cognitive psychologists who were interested in literary text comprehension. My impression was that many cognitive psychologists were somewhat perplexed by the more radical Constructivist contributions to the conference. To the extent that these contributions could be considered constructive, they seemed to offer nothing more than a new jargon for well-known concepts in cognitive psychology. To the extent that they were radical they seemed no more relevant to empirical research than Poststructuralist thinking or any other current mode of thinking in literary studies. The radical Constructivists, on the other hand, seemed to think that the cognitive psychological research was in large part 'atheoretical,' which was, ironically, the exact same, and totally misguided, criticism mainstream literary researchers had always voiced concerning the ESL. Empirical research often looks trivial to those who are uninformed about the theoretical background of the research. However, one would expect those individuals who like to print the word empirical in capital letters to be well-informed about theoretical, methodological, and empirical issues involving research on text comprehension. In his introduction to a collection of empirical studies from the conference, Art Graesser described the situation from a cognitive psychological point of view: "Literary critics [Graesser rightly seems to include various ESL members here] have furnished a pretheoretical sketch of some of the components and properties of a literary communication system that may be relevant to psychological theories of aesthetic comprehension. Empirical research must be conducted in order to determine which of these components and properties have an impact on the reader" (Graesser 1993: 2). I happen to agree with this position.

So where does the ESL go from here?

I offer a two-pronged answer to this question. What I think we need is (1) a stronger focus on rigorous empirical studies of literary processes (for instance, in comprehension, production, reviewing, dissemination, and so on) and (2) more efforts to theoretically demonstrate the continuity in literary research from Formalism and Structuralism to empirical research. A critical mass of convincing empirical results, for example with respect to the role of literature in cultural education and cognitive aging, should eventually appeal to everyone in and outside of literary studies who is not completely irrational. Douwe Fokkema has made a similar argument many times and I sincerely hope that he will continue to be a thoughtful and eloquent advocate of these viewpoints.

References

Graesser, A.C. 1993. "Introduction." *Poetics* 22: 1-3.
Kintsch, W. 1988. "The Role of Knowledge in Discourse Comprehension: A Construction-integration Model." *Psychological Review* 95: 163-182.
Meutsch, D. and Zwaan, R.A. 1990. "On the Role of Computer Models and Technology in Literary and Media Research." *Poetics* 19: 1-12.
Simon, H.A. 1994. "Bridging the Gap." *Stanford Electronic Humanities Review* [On-line] 4. (Available: http://shr.stanford.edu/shreview/.)
Zwaan, R.A. 1987. "The Computer in Perspective: Towards a Relevant Use of the Computer in Literary Studies." *Poetics* 16: 553-568.
—. 1993. *Aspects of Literary Comprehension: A Cognitive Approach*. Amsterdam / Philadelphia: Benjamins.
—. 1994. "Effect of Genre Expectations on Text Comprehension." *Journal of Experimental Psychology: Learning, Memory, and Cognition* 20: 920-933.
—. 1995. "Towards a Model of Literary Comprehension." In B.K. Britton and A.C. Graesser (eds), *Models of Understanding Text*. Hilllsdale, NJ: Erlbaum, 241-254.